Translating Rimbaud's *Illuminations*

This book is a sequel to Clive Scott's *Translating Baudelaire* (UEP, 2000), and a further development of its translational techniques. It argues for the intimate connections between literary translation and experimental writing, using a selection of Rimbaud's *Illuminations* to explore the different ways in which the translator can re-imagine and re-project source texts.

Clive Scott offers translations of a selection of Rimbaud's prose poems—setting out to invest the poems with expanded potential by reshaping them and by inserting them into new expressive environments. At the same time, he proposes a re-definition of the relationship between literary translation and creative writing. He suggests that the translator's imagination can operate more effectively if it fully exploits the space of the page, if it adopts tabular rather than linear ways of thinking.

Clive Scott, a Fellow of the British Academy, is Professor of European Literature in the Faculty of Arts and Humanities at the University of East Anglia. He has published in the areas of French and comparative versification, translation, and photography, and is currently working on the relation between translation and experimental writing.

Translating Rimbaud's

Illuminations

Clive Scott

UNIVERSITY
of
EXETER
PRESS

First published in 2006 by
University of Exeter Press
Reed Hall, Streatham Drive
Exeter EX4 4QR
UK
www.exeterpress.co.uk

© Clive Scott 2006

The right of Clive Scott to be identified as author
of this work has been asserted by him in accordance
with the Copyright, Designs and Patents Act 1988.

British Library Cataloguing in Publication Data
A catalogue record for this book is available
from the British Library.

Paperback ISBN 0 85989 769 9
Hardback ISBN 0 85989 770 2

Typeset in 10.5/13pt Plantin Light
by XL Publishing Services, Tiverton

Printed in Great Britain by Antony Rowe Ltd, Chippenham

Contents

Acknowledgements

An earlier version of part of Chapter 6 appeared in *Centre for Translation and Intercultural Studies Occasional Papers* (vol.2, 2002, 45–57). I would like to thank *The Sun* (© NI Syndication, London) for permission to reproduce page 23 of its 23 July 2001 issue (see Appendix III (c)), and the *Daily Mail* for permission to reproduce page 4 of its 23 July 2001 issue (see Appendix III (d)). I owe important debts of gratitude to Derek Cullen, whose copy-editing was as encouraging as it was rigorous; to Anna Henderson, who saw the book through the press with such resourceful energy and vigilance; and to Simon Baker, for his consistent and much-valued support.

Introduction

The impulse to write this book came from five directions. In *Translating Baudelaire* (2000), I had brought myself to the persuasion that free verse was a 'proper' translational response to regular verse, partly because the lineation of free verse increases expressive resource without entailing lexical licences, partly because free verse *compels* readerly/writerly idiosyncrasy, and partly because contemporary translation has an obligation to its own characteristic forms. It seemed logical, therefore, to ask how other, more extreme modernist and contemporary forms might be harnessed to the business of translation. Free verse stands at a cross-over point, because it is at once a practice of free textuality (lineation, margins, de-metrification and localised re-metrifications), the image of an improvised text, an open text, and at the same time a characterisation of the space on which it is inscribed, the score for a voice which it has somehow activated. In pushing beyond the limits of free verse, I shall inevitably be emphasising the latter dimensions of free verse and pushing into those areas of poetic output—words in freedom, concrete poetry, calligrams, *poésie sonore*—which lie just beyond free verse. We should remember that Marinetti had already (1913) taxed free verse with continuing artificially to channel 'the flow of lyric emotion between the high walls of syntax and the weirs of grammar' (Apollonio 1973: 99) and that Apollinaire had confidently predicted free verse's imminent demise in a letter to André Billy of July 29 1918:

> Quant aux *Calligrammes*, ils sont une idéalisation de la poésie vers-libriste et une précision typographique à l'époque où la typographie termine brillamment sa carrière, à l'aurore des moyens nouveaux de reproduction que sont le cinéma et le phonographe.

1

[As for the *Calligrams*, they are an idealisation of free-verse poetry and a specific application of typography at a time when typography is coming to the end of its brilliant career, at the dawn of new means of reproduction, like the cinema and the gramophone.]

Secondly, and in closely related fashion, I had increasingly felt that, in the translation of poetry, we need better to understand the space of the page as the translator's mental landscape, or imaginative territory: that is to say that the notion of 'style' might be relocated from language itself to the space which language was called upon to inhabit or map out; that is further to say that just as the page awaits its poem, so the spatial style of the translator awaits its source text (ST). This textuality-space is the imagination of the translator, first and foremost perhaps a mental space, a receptive and activating chamber. But it is also the potential space of other spaces: social spaces, geometries Euclidian and non-Euclidian, cosmic spaces, graphic and painterly spaces, reading spaces. Much has been made of the space of the page, and also, incredibly little. This space is frequently referred to as blank space, empty space, the silence of the white sheet. That is to say that the white of the page is thought of as something featureless, where interpretation, association, mental elaboration, of the written text, can take place unhindered, where no trains pass and where one has no fear of the imminent intrusion of a meteorite or a drum majorette. No benefit is to be gained, apparently, from thinking of this space as three-dimensional, already occupied, busy with its own activity, yet alone as n-dimensional. Of course, any spatial configuration also has temporal implications, and, as I have argued elsewhere (1998: 97–101), our grasp of the many possible interactions of the text's several layers of temporality is in its infancy. The translator who undertakes to release the potential spaces within the text, and the perceptual modes that go with them, or the potential environments in which the text might take place, must also think of the ways in which the temporal dimensions of textuality generate, or need, space to express themselves.[1]

Two obvious and related clarifications are needed here. In printed verse, the poem is the whole *page* rather than the printed text alone. It is not just that the poem relies on spacing to define its lineation and its stanzaic configuration. This is dangerously to reduce page-space to gaps which act simply to circumscribe and demarcate what is printed. The space of the page is what the poem is projected into, and the question for us is what that space represents, what its coordinates are, what kind of resonating chamber it is. Furthermore, when one speaks about blank space in verse, one should speak about it less as blank space, existing as it were outside the perimeter of the verse, and more as *ajours*, in the way that this word is used by the contemporary French poet André Du Bouchet, that is to say as space in an architectural design or in lace-work, which is fully integrated into the structure of the work, as part of its being and effect.

What I am trying to do through the performance of text in the space of the page is to suggest to the reader a certain *mode d'emploi*, instructions for use. It should be a familiar contention that translation does not indicate to its reader how it should be read. Reception theories are able to develop because they can exploit reliably supposable contracts between the text and the reader. But what contract does a translation presuppose? About this, translation theory, focused as it so often is on the process of translation itself, is amazingly reticent. On the one hand, we have the critical reading of translation which concentrates on the validity of the translation to the exclusion of the uses to which a particular translation might be put. On the other hand, we have the ignorant reader who is presumably consuming the translation with no questions asked and no specific demands being made. The translator's principal concern, it seems to me, should be less about *what* is read than about *how* it should be read; the former flows from the latter. And the mode of reading should, where at all possible, be integrated into the translation. The activation of the space of the page is the activation of a mode of reading and the promotion of perceptual mechanisms suggestive of the ways in which a text might map out its future. It is also an invitation to readers to read this space to their own psychic tunes, to mould space to their own perceptual imperatives. It is for this reason that, having developed a linguistic version of a text, I rarely change it; my various page-designs are ways of re-circulating the language of the texts.

Third, I wanted to confront the prose poem as a translational problem. I shall have more to say in Chapter 2 about the name and nature of the prose poem, but I should emphasise from the outset that, for me, the prose poem is a virtual genre producing virtual texts, both potentially pre-metrical and post-metrical, both potentially a memory of verse-lyricism and a projection of other, 'prosaic' kinds of expressivity. For many, the prose poem is a counter-discourse (Terdiman 1985), a discourse of oppositionality (Stephens 1999) by very virtue of its generic hybridity, its refusal to normalise the distinction between poetry and prose; but, for a variety of reasons, this revolutionary subversiveness has never allowed the prose poem to move from the literary margins, however much may have been made of certain individuals who practised it. One might attribute this relative political ineffectiveness to the self-contradictions with which the genre is ripe; one might equally attribute it to the prose poem's refusal to declare its hand. Baudelaire's celebrated prefatory letter to Arsène Houssaye is an argument for the prose poem's inclusiveness, its adaptability, its formal nonchalance:

> Nous pouvons couper où nous voulons, moi ma rêverie, vous le manuscrit, le lecteur sa lecture; car je ne suspends pas la volonté rétive de celui-ci au fil interminable d'une intrigue superfine. Enlevez une vertèbre, et les deux morceaux de cette tortueuse fantaisie se rejoindront sans peine.
>
> (Baudelaire 1975: 275).
>
> [We can cut wherever we like, I my reverie, you the manuscript, the reader his reading; because I am not attaching the rebellious will of the reader to the unending thread of an intricate plot. Remove a vertebra, and the two pieces of this tortuous fantasy will have no difficulty in joining together again.]

Baudelaire seems anxious to give his restive reader plenty of rein. The prose poem is not, *as it is*, a discourse of taboo-breaking; it creates the space for taboos to be broken and only the reader, or translator, can embody or configure the act. My translations attempt to lead the prose poem out of its equivocations, to explore some of its virtualities, because one of my premises is that translation should not translate a text (in its inertial state) but a reading process, a reading process which challenges readers of the translation to read their own way back into the source text. In this sense, meaning, for the reader, remains a latency; it rises to the surface but is never extracted. On the contrary, it is allowed to sink back, to recover its embryonic quality and its availability to intuition. I am not trying to convey a false impression of what the prose poem is: we already know what the prose poem is, we can consult the ST, and there are a sufficient number of 'straight' translations of Rimbaldian poems in this book to remind us of the textual origins of more experimental versions. I am trying to relocate the business of translation so that it is no longer in the text, but in the spaces of a psycho-physiological encounter with the text. In order to establish an existential relation with the text, upon which meaning might be predicated, I must re-enter the dynamic of my own reading by re-entering the pulsions of my own voice, the hesitations and momentums, all of which is, for me, to re-enter my own duration.

Further justifications for this approach are to be found in Rimbaud's own apparent inability to settle into a particular model of the prose poem and to make any definitive peace between the contrary urgings of poetry and prose. If some have argued that it is possible to draw clear lines of demarcation between Rimbaud's verse-practise and his prose—in the formal compulsions at work in 'Marine' and 'Mouvement', for example (see Guyaux 1991: 165–78; Murat 2000)—and that the discovery of units of verse within the *Illuminations* à la Fongaro (1993) is a dangerous delusion, the best advised position still seems to me to lie in making the most of Rimbaud's very unsteadiness, to lie in the kinds of view expressed by Guyaux in 1985: in remarks on Rimbaud's uses of line-initial upper and lower case in 'Marine' and 'Mémoire', Guyaux speaks of his 'idée d'un mimétisme réciproque de la prose et du vers' (1985a: 157), and in arguing for a Rimbaldian poetics of the line—but 'ligne' rather than 'vers'— Guyaux describes this unit as 'une phrase ou un vers en puissance, comme elle peut ne pas l'être' (159). In taxing Baudelaire for resorting to a form that is 'mesquine', Rimbaud adds 'les inventions d'inconnu réclament des formes nouvelles' (letter to Paul Demeny, 15 May 1871). Historically, it may be more appropriate to apply this last remark to Rimbaud's so-called *Derniers Vers*, but it anticipates that formal open-mindedness that seems to characterise the prose poems, from their paragraphing to their punctuation.

Underlying this general view of text, of a spatial disposition and supplementation which foregrounds the reading of text, both as visual and vocal performance, is the assumption that, in poetry, *parole* exceeds *langue*, cannot conveniently be seen as a generative transformation of *langue* and cannot be recovered by *langue*. The principal reason for this separation of *parole* from *langue*, of *parole*'s discovery of an autonomous existence, is poetry's maximisation of the materiality of language, of a materiality which must exist at the expense of conventional discourse-creating syntax and which is almost bound to operate anarchically. The practice of interpretation, against which I shall take up the cudgels, is the reduction of the poetic *parole* to *langue*, with the materiality of language in the role of submissive adjuvant. Translation also, too often perhaps, threatens to reduce the poetic *parole* to a *langue* of what the poet 'really wants to say'. Quite clearly, what I would want to propose is that this scheme be reversed: that translation perform the *langue* of the ST as a *parole* which is irreducible to a *langue*, but which demonstrates what capacities for *parole* lie within the ST.

My fourth concern relates to the translation of the Rimbaldian text in particular. Having read a variety of translations of the *Illuminations*, I found myself coming to the conclusion that linguistic choice of itself could not make the difference, in two senses: (a) it could not establish a way of making difference of choice count; (b) nor could it *translate* Rimbaud, that is, release the energies of the Rimbaldian text in such a way that we, as modern readers, catch their fire. Under (a) I certainly do not wish to disparage the achievements of Rimbaud's translators[2] or to suggest that they are turning in diminishing circles: I am exaggerating a predicament for polemical purposes. But I do believe that predicament to be real. Where Bernard (1962: 244), for instance, gives us 'Whistlings of death and circles of faint music' as a translation of 'Des sifflements de mort et des cercles de musique sourde' ('Being Beauteous'), Treharne offers 'Deathly hissing sounds and circles of muffled music' (1998: 73) and Sorrell 'Hisses of death and circles of muted music' (2001: 267). And certainly we can argue meaningfully about the range of 'siffler' and about the character of 'sourde' (distance? obstruction? pianissimo?); and we can ask about the intended atmosphere (light-hearted? aggressive? celebratory?) and the likely agents of these sounds; and we can enjoy the different phrasal musics of these translations: /xx/—x/x...x/(x)/x (with silent offbeat attached to 'faint'?); /x/x/—x/x...x/x/x; /xx/—x/x...x/x/x. But while I can discern and describe these differences and their effects, I cannot see, textually, what makes them count, because I cannot relate the text to a theatre of operation. Meaning and interpretation are less at stake than, as Rimbaud puts it here, 'la Vision, sur le chantier' [the Vision, in the process of construction], with its accompanying 'frissons' [shudders] and 'la saveur forcenée de ces effets' [the frenzied flavour of these effects]. What, it seems to me, would make difference count is the textual *projection* of the lexical constituents.

My fifth motive is the belief that translation must see itself principally as experimental writing, for reasons which I explore in Chapter 1. The exploration of the literariness of translation is by its nature bound to entail experimental writing, to make the writing of avant-gardes—Cubist, Futurist, concrete, Lettrist—of particular interest to translation. These avant-gardes are not movements which are historically played out, but styles of literary production as relevant as ever they were. Translation must be prepared to share with avant-gardism its struggle against a certain marginality, a certain shady lack of credibility. Literary translation thus inevitably entails multiple translations. A work has never done with re-imagining itself. There is, unfortunately, in translation a teleological heritage which is to do with translation's educational embedding and the concomitant pursuit of the optimal *corrigé*; but translation will only have *exemplary* value if being an authority for the ignorant is what is at stake. If such a situation does *not* obtain, if translation is a kind of literary production for those who know both the source and target languages, then translation, acting within assumptions of knowledge, will be able to operate with more point as an extension of a field of perception, or the gamble of an expressive possibility. There is no point in telling someone something they already know.

We have mentioned that literary translation inevitably entails multiple translations. To the reason already adduced, we might add the following uses of a multitranslational practice:

1. If we assume that translation is an effort not to fix a relatively definitive interpretation of a text, but to embody an ongoing relationship with it (which may include interpretation, but is more to with the reading experience itself, the fluctuations of association, intertextual memory, modality, function, context), then multitranslation is a way to capture the *autobiography* of this relationship.

2. If we assume that an ST is one realisation of a set of expressive potentialities which *predate* the ST and consist of the suggestivity of forms and rhythms, different collocational energies, different nuances of tone and register, etc., if, that is, we look upon translation as the exploration of the ST's putative creative provenance rather than as a communication of its message, then translation must be multiple. This is a view of translation which closely corresponds to that of Walter Benjamin, outlined in 'The Task of the Translator' (Schulte and Biguenet 1992: 71–82).

3. If we feel bound as translators to trace, in translation itself, the associative network that an ST has traversed as it comes towards us across time and/or space and to register past texts that may be audible within it, then this itinerary from an antecedent past to the translator's present must constantly be re-traced, since the itinerary is full of detours and digressions and chance encounters. I tried to begin a task like this in my montage translation of Baudelaire's 'Le Voyage' (Scott 2000: 218–46).

4. I have elsewhere (2000: 71–93) suggested that, in the translation of poetry, the translator should find ways of standing off from the ST, the better to find his/her own voice among the voices of translation and thus the better to know how the target text (TT) might want to approach the ST. The method I proposed was intralingual multitranslation, translations of other translations. Multitranslation is as indispensable to translational process as it is to translational product; indeed, one might argue that one of the important functions of multitranslation is to erase the distinction between process and product, to remind us that translation takes place in Bergsonian duration, is an existential and psychological situation as much as it is a cultural one.

I can confidently expect this book to be read with a degree, or moments, of irritated scepticism or exasperated disbelief. It may seem that I am attempting to turn translation into a conceptual art, and, indeed, it would be true to say that this is part of my purpose. But, more fundamentally, I am trying to explore the limits of translational activity, to open up those dimensions of text and textual response which translation easily overlooks, to develop translational means sensitive to the variety of Rimbaud's own attitudes and textual practices, and, most particularly, to take translation off the page and into the reader's head. I am trying to imagine what might be meant not by 'translating a text' but by 'translating the being-in-consciousness of a text'.

What is recorded in the following pages is not just a desire to drink translation to the dregs, but—and this is also of crucial importance—a desire to pace round and round Rimbaud, to do justice to a readerly experience which will not hold still, which will never have had enough of re-conceiving his texts, of trying to be equal to his challenges. Rimbaud has been read to countless tunes, none of which can muster a final chord. And in the space of this nervous restiveness, all is still to be reinvented; this restiveness itself deserves its diary of searching, essaying. My translations do not have the ambition of exemplarity; they are intended as exemplars of different kinds of translational conduct, for which I hope the reader will envisage improvements and alternatives. If, from time to time, I fall off the edge of the translator's still square world, then a log of the unsuccessful voyage of discovery may still have value for 'd'autres horribles travailleurs' who 'commenceront par les horizons où l'autre s'est affaissé!' (letter to Paul Demeny, 15 May 1871) [other horrible workers (who) will begin from the horizons where the other finally collapsed].

The crude graphic means I have used in these versions may be the source of some mirth or disbelief. I would beg the reader to think beyond these means, towards what might be achieved, or at least to consider these means cumulatively, in the hope that the whole is something more than a sum of the parts. I entertained the idea of consulting a professional typographical designer, if only to relocate what might be meant by 'collaborative translation'. I considered exploiting computerised enhancement to its limits, but was afraid of falling into what is meretricious or predictable about these resources. I have much faith in what hypertextuality and multi-media flexibility might contribute to translation, but for the purposes of the present venture, I felt happier working within limitations—A4, black and white, my own collages, my own simple graphics—simply to maintain the sense of handwork and to keep the project within one translatorial predicament. Many of these devices, by their shortcomings, require much imaginative sympathy from the reader;

but, as we have said, part of translation's present problem is precisely how it can and should engage the reader in the translational enterprise. Besides, reading, and reading Rimbaud more particularly, is quite properly a process of 'reaching for', not for understanding so much as for a way of inhabiting the poet's psycho-perceptual world. And another concern remains of grave importance: that readers of translation, however extensive or not their grasp of the source language, should, by very virtue of their reading of a particular translation, wish to become translators themselves. If translation can become a properly creative undertaking, it will do so by its very contagiousness.

If I have justified fears that my translations may cause some embarrassment in the reader, I also hope that these general points will be conceded: (i) that translation, whether intratextual or intertextual, is an inevitable doodling in any reading, is the natural means by which reading is registered as a creative act or impulse; (ii) that DIY translation not only encourages all readers to become translators, but, more specifically, it gives readers the opportunity to express not merely what the ST has triggered, but what they have brought to reading in the way of mindsets, professional knowledge and cultural baggage.

In the chapters that follow, argument periodically turns to painting, to cinema, to photography as well as to different modes of literary critical analysis, in an attempt both to do justice to the multifariousness of the Rimbaldian text and to shed light on the translation process itself. There are many who are deeply suspicious of the pressing of metaphor into the service of definition. Lori Chamberlain's (1992) exploration of the semi-covert sexism to be found at the root of standard translational metaphors is not the only reason to beware figurative descriptions of linguistic processes; Eliot Weinberger finds that the habit of analogy masks the uniqueness of translation:

> I have always maintained—and for some reason this is considered controversial—that the purpose of a poetry translation into English is to create an excellent translation in English. That is, a text that will be read and judged *like* a poem, but not *as* a poem. Translation is an utterly unique genre, and all the traditional analogies for it—a musical or theatrical performance, a metaphor, a reading, an act of criticism—are inadequate. In fact, translation is such a familiar and intrinsic part of any culture that one wonders why there is this perennial need to explain it by analogy: we do not say that baking is like playing the violin.
>
> (1999: 243)

But this sounds to me like obscurantism trading under the flag of plain-dealing. To compare baking with violin-playing would be second nature to, say, Proust, and it would be precisely because baking is both unique and familiar, unique, and thus only to be approached through a network of kinships, and familiar, so that we could renew our perception of it only by adopting different spectacles.

Our proposition is that what makes translation unique is its needing constantly to be *re-imagined* as a mode of writing; it cannot usefully be *defined*. Translation is an activity for which it is possible to have creative ambitions. It is a fluid and unresolved practice; or at least it is only resolved in those contexts in which it is designed to provide a particular service, and I will argue that to treat translation as a service for those ignorant of the source language is to do the literature of translation no service. Each time the translator engages with a text, he needs to think his way towards the relation that the translation will express, the creative posture it will be informed by. This thinking one's way creatively into the translational is an essential part of translation's literariness: there is no privileged version of translation, there are no sine qua nons, no best practice. And in order to locate oneself in this shape-shifting world of possibility, it is inevitable, desirable, that one should describe it, not in and for itself, but relative to other creative activities with which it might share certain isomorphisms.

Additionally, recourse to metaphor as a way of describing practice is an integral part of the argument for translation as a form of spiritual autobiography, of life-writing. Translation has been much exercised by the invisibility of the translator, since Lawrence Venuti's groundbreaking book (1995); the visibility of the translator is certainly a question of proper acknowledgement, critical credit, legal rights. But, more especially, it is the translator's taking literary possession of the process of translation, which in turn entails the making visible of the currents of association, investigation, aspiration, that intersect in the translator's mind. This autobiography, an autobiography of reading and writing, is about the ST both as subject and as an instrument by which the translator explores his own voice and creative proclivities. But in saying this we must not forget that the ST is also the instrument by which the translator explores the expressive potentialities of different poetic forms, and the relationship between forms as repositories of generic and ideological prejudice or possibility. And underlying all these preoccupations is the core concern: how translation can constitute its own literature, that is both a literature specific to translation and a literary language adequate to the needs of translation.

The book's opening chapter is a set of reflections about translation, about translation's relationship with creative writing and with interpretation, and about what might constitute a literature of translation. It does not attempt to develop a theory of literary translation, so much as to establish founding propositions and lay out speculative objectives. It is not primarily concerned with Rimbaud—although it begins to prepare itself for that encounter—and, indeed, several of its pages are devoted to an analysis of François-René Daillie's translation of Wordsworth's 'The Daffodils'. But moves like this are necessary to the elaboration of possible models of literary translation. Although the space of the page is the book's abiding preoccupation, Chapter 2 offers translations of 'Après le Déluge', 'Aube' and 'Jeunesse: Sonnet' as a means of confronting the complex world of Rimbaldian temporality, caught between the cyclical and the linear, between explicit temporal indication and modality, between the indexical and the non-referential; it also investigates the ways in which translation can capture these temporal collisions in the unfolding of rhythmic texture. Since one of the book's principal concerns is the rendering of the materiality of language, Chapter 3 addresses the problems associated with the translation of the acoustics of voice into the text. There are senses in which any written text is no longer spoken (however speakable), no longer has an originating voice, so that the translator has to develop strategies by which this voice might be imagined and the text made vocally accessible. This chapter focuses on a translation of 'Enfance I', setting the translational process within a much broader consideration of voice quality and its communicability. Chapter 4 continues to preoccupy itself with the voice, not so much as a presence within the text, as an animating force moving through the text, as the agent of metamorphosis; in this guise, the voice undoes the recuperative mechanisms of interpretation which draw so heavily on the principle of juxtaposition. This chapter continues to explore the 'Enfance' cycle, offering translations of 'Enfance III' and 'Enfance IV', before turning to 'Ornières'. Inevitably it re-engages with questions of textual temporality and rhythm. Three translations—of 'Parade', 'Fairy' and 'Vagabonds'—again make up the argument of Chapter 5, marking out the stages of an enquiry into how translation might make visible the silences behind or within words, the silences between words or phrases, and the silence of a whole text. By this last is meant a translation which is as if already in another dimension, a text which the ST has made possible, which was a virtuality of the ST, but bears no apparent resemblance to it. Chapter 6 is a chapter of transition, in the sense that concern with silence as the 'site' of the 'elsewhere' of a text and its language, and with the temporality of the reading experience, when texts lose their linearity, shifts over to the broaching of questions about translation's involvement with space and with the arts of noise. This transition is mapped out in the shift from a concrete translation of 'Départ' to a Futurist one, and is followed by rendering of 'A une Raison' which looks to blend the concrete, the Futurist and the Lettrist, and to trace the ways in which noises, working with rhyme, repetition and rhythm, can sculpt the spaces of a text. Chapter 7 examines translational space from a point of view which reformulates and extends the foreignisation/domestication controversy. The translation of 'Fête d'hiver' is approached through questions about 'Chineseness' and 'Chinoiserie', about perspectival and planar space, about the ekphrasis of reproduction and the ekphrasis of fictionalisation, all within the broad context of the rococo. The reciprocal interferences of colonist and colonised, space and place, are pursued, in more detail, in a rendering of 'Démocratie', and the chapter closes with an account of 'Royauté' which considers it both as a power-struggle between narrator and protagonists, and as a *fait divers* negotiating its position in a tabloid newspaper. It is through treatments of the 'Ville(s)' poems that Chapter 8 principally addresses Rimbaud's visions of cities and their spaces. The structure of the sonnet, the vehicle for the translation of 'Ville', is explored as a collision of street-maps, and parallels between the signifying modes of poems and cities are investigated through the proper noun. This leads into an assessment of montage as the aptest 'medium' for urban translation, in versions of both 'Ville' and 'Villes I'. The chapter ends with an attempt to convey the vertigo of urban perception in a chronophotographic/photodynamic version of 'Les Ponts'. Chapter 9 is devoted to an enquiry into the spaces of reading. Through translations of 'Mystique', it pursues ways of representing the 'rumeur' of the Rimbaldian text, and of communicating optic and haptic perceptions of text, and considers textual space in relation to the convex and concave. This produces a Cubist model of Rimbaldian reading space which is explored through renderings of 'Antique', the last of which, a version à la Gertrude Stein, provokes a brief discussion of translation as pastiche. The Conclusion looks back reflectively over travelled roads.

1

Translation and Creativity
Reflections on a Relationship

This book is interested in 'traductologie', as defined by Antoine Berman: 'La traductologie: la réflexion de la traduction sur elle-même à partir de sa nature d'expérience' (1999: 17) [Traductology: translation's reflection on itself, based on its nature as practice]. Although reflections such as these are theorisations of translation practice, they have no theory in view; and they have no theory in view partly because they share Berman's belief that a general theory of translation cannot exist, 'puisque l'espace de la traduction est babélien, c'est-à-dire récuse toute totalisation' (1999: 20) [since the space of translation is Babelian, that is, resists any totalisation], but more especially because translation is about relationships with texts, changing, multiform and heterogeneous relationships, which concern the psychological and existential situation/predicament of the translator more than they concern the linguistic proximities and distances between two texts. Quite simply, translation is first and foremost an act of writing; the ST is not so much to be translated as to become an episode in a writer's life and perhaps a crucial instrument in a writer's apprenticeship. By virtue of its linguistic incompleteness ('Les langues imparfaites en cela que plusieurs' (Mallarmé 2003: 208) [Languages being imperfect in that there are several of them]), the ST forces TTs into existence and, in so doing, forces the translator to define himself as a re-writer of the ST. Translation is never less than a reflection about language; but most especially, it is a reflection about language as a potentiality of expression for a particular translator-writer.

It is not difficult to bestow on translation the status of a creative act, particularly when we can view translation as an integral part of the writing activity of any creative writer. Robert Lowell tells us that translation was for him a way of negotiating the creative doldrums, of, we may assume, finding a new creative wind; of *Imitations*, he writes: 'This book was written from time to time when I was unable to do anything of my own' (1971: xii). Emily Salines (1999: 19–30) shows how different kinds and degrees of translational activity nourished Baudelaire's 'original' output. And Michael Alexander (1997: 28) reminds us that 'There is for Pound no distinction between his own work and his translations'. But while the evidence of practice makes creativity unproblematic when we consider the author-translator, we are confronted by a tangle of controversy when it comes to identifying and locating creativity in the conduct of the translator-translator.

We might identify four inbuilt transformational dangers in translation which militate against its literarisation. First, the TT (target text) tends to make the ST (source text) more intelligible.[1] Myriam Diaz-Diocaretz is surely right to point out that, in 'standard' assumptions about translation, the target text (TT) will be more communicative than the source text (ST) simply because it must, in order to be clear, derive from specific interpretative moves:

> Communication, a property not predominantly present in the poetic language of the ST may take over the primary function of an aesthetic work in translation, because a literary work exists, obvious as it seems it must be mentioned, only for those who can understand its language (linguistic code). When translating a poetic work, one of the primary purposes is that it must be done in such a way that the text is made accessible and intelligible—on the level of competence—to the receptors.
>
> (1985: 10)

However, Diaz-Diocaretz is also prepared to envisage a TT which diverges significantly in its meanings and effects from the ST:

> While the readings of the source-text engender interpretative operations, the translator produces an equivalent text in the receptor-culture which will, in turn, furnish a new chain of significations that perhaps did not belong to the original response.
>
> (1985: 2)

This begs questions about 'equivalent text' and does not sit entirely comfortably with Diaz-Diocaretz's identification of the translator as an 'omniscient reader' (1985: 16). It seems, with its 'perhaps', to allow for an element of the aleatory and to accept as inevitable that the TT will activate 'a new chain of significations' (thanks to the interferences of the translator's subjectivity). In the end, it may seem that Diaz-Diocaretz is rather evasive or equivocal about the relationship between the translator as omniscient reader and the translator as 'acting writer', who co-produces an already existent 'text' and in so doing gives it a new identity. One might equally find a rather awkward discrepancy between Diaz-Docaretz's espousal of a Jakobsonian view of the 'poetic' as self-reflexive, or self-regarding, at the same time as she pursues a pragmatics-based agenda ('[The translator] seeks to understand the orientational features of language which relate to the situation of utterance' (1985: 25)). I take these contradictions, or positional uncertainties, to be symptomatic of an approach to translation which wishes to marry the taxonomic, the linguistic and the literary, rigour and thoroughness with an acknowledgement of creative caprice.

If translation seeks to increase textual accessibility, then its manner of achieving this is crucial. The second transformational danger of translation is the conversion of the linguistic/textual into the metalinguistic/metatextual. Translation is an interpretation of, and response to, a given linguistic configuration, not to a set of putative pretextual phenomena. The creativity of translation all too easily becomes assimilated to this hand-to-hand struggle with grammatical and syntactical resistances, connotations, tonal ambiguities, in the ST. In such instances, the ST is a given—i.e. it is assumed to have achieved its expressive ambitions, to say what it wants to say—and the translator's art is all in the consolidation and communication of that given. But we have no reason for making these suppositions, other than that there is no reason to make the contrary supposition. I am trying to promote a creativity which relates to text rather than to language, to whole-text rather than to localised problems within it, which is unpredictable in its operations but explicable in its effects, which is not constituted by sets of responses so much as by an overriding textual perception or enterprise.

The third transformational danger concerns the relation of form and content: translation, inevitably, tends to spring them apart, for reasons outlined by Yves Bonnefoy:

> We must understand that writing, the act of writing, is in itself an unbreakable unity whose formal operations are conceived and executed in constant interaction with, for example, the invention of the images and the elaboration of meaning. [. . .] But this necessary freedom is not, unfortunately, within reach of the translator. In his case, meaning, the whole meaning of the poem, is already determined; he cannot invent anything about it without betraying

the intent of the author. Consequently, were he to decide to adopt the alexandrine or the pentameter, this regular pattern would be for him nothing but a frame to which the meaning would have to adjust itself, obliging him to pure virtuosity.

(1979: 377)

This is perhaps to underline the need for the translator to reimagine the ST as a total creative enterprise, and is one of the reasons why, in the wake of Bonnefoy, I have promoted free verse as the ideal translational medium: quite apart from the arguments about free verse's *inevitable* organicity (is this battle too easily won?), free verse constantly confronts the translator with formal decisions (about degrees of metrico-rhythmicity, lineation, lay-out, rhyme) which ensure that no frame becomes a justification for certain linguistic collocations, and that each structural configuration is sense-giving. In the present work, I have, if anything, attempted to take a further step towards the indissolubility of form and content, in opting for versions that, in one way and another, abut concrete poetry.

The fourth transformational danger relates to the proposition that poetry is designed to maximise the materiality of language. At the moment, the materiality of a text is what is seen as constituting its untranslatability. Robert Frost famously declared that: 'Poetry is what is lost in translation'. But his immediately following remark is not so frequently cited: 'It [poetry] is also what is lost in interpretation' (Untermeyer 1964: 18). Denied access to the materiality of the ST, translators cut their losses, concentrate on the translation of meaning, by interpretation; the materiality of the ST is 'retrieved' by means of salvage operations: equivalence, compensation.

But we should remind ourselves that linguistic materiality is not itself a stable value, but is subject to constant historical re-negotiation. If we looked to the eighteenth century, we might argue that linguistic materiality related to aesthetic decoration and to rhetorical ingratiation, to the auditory fluency of text (euphony); in the nineteenth century, to subliminal pantheistic kinships, to verbal instrumentation ('correspondances'), to alternative syntaxes, to the projection of the paradigmatic on to the syntagmatic. Today, we are perhaps more persuaded that linguistic materiality makes manifest the anarchy and uncontrollability of the human organism, in eruptions of -lalias (echolalia, coprolalia, glossolalia), in Tourette's syndrome, in the pulsional upbubblings of the semiotic, in all kinds of psychosomatic revelation. This materiality is a vital channel of the reader's engagement with the text, of a psychphysiological engagement which makes reading an inevitable rebellion against interpretation, with its sanitising, ordering and cerebrating conduct. This book seeks to pursue translational strategies which have linguistic materiality as their constant focus. Interpretation cannot, should not, be dispensed with: it is the means whereby works are made public and susceptible of collective debate. But we should recognise that interpretation is, in many senses, a failure of reading, a loss of psychophysiological contact with the text.

Interpretation has been attacked from several quarters (for example, Sontag 1994[1964]; Culler 1981; Meschonnic 1999). Susan Sontag's first move, for example, is to distinguish between the *experience* of art and its *theory*, suggesting that theory has overly concerned itself with questions of (detachable) value, with the way a work of art can justify itself, and more especially with the way it can justify itself by what it *says* (1994: 3–4). Sontag's references to the codedness of interpretation and her call for an erotics, rather than a hermeneutics, of art (1994: 14) slips us easily across to Barthes. We might want to locate his objections to interpretation in his attitudes to the *lisible* and we would be right to do so inasmuch as the activity we imagine as the contrary of interpretation, reading, is an activity designed to recover the *scriptible* of a text. Translation is often a performance of the *lisible* in that it is designed to *promote* not just the ST, but a certain critical vision of the ST.

But the particular Barthesian assault on interpretation that I wish to summon is that enshrined in the *punctum/studium* duality (1980) (if we are allowed to transfer this from photography to literature). *Studium* is that corporate and culturally average relationship with the object (photograph), an interpretative relationship designed to make the object instructive, and to draw on a common, already acquired body of cultural expectation. With *studium*, interpretations are already predicted by the corpus of knowledge from which they emerge. *Punctum* installs a confrontational relationship with the image, where the confrontation itself cannot be defused or solved by interpretation, although it may involve recognition. It is unpredictable, it lacerates, pricks, is visceral, and has no outlet in discourse; it belongs to the dark of the individual, to involuntary memory, to desire, to the singular, to the non-cultural and non-coded; it fractures the 'unariness' of the object. *Punctum* cannot be planted in a work; it is what the spectator/reader adds, but is already there.

Sontag's 'Against Interpretation' suggests other ways of outwitting interpretation. One of the solutions lies in the cinematic, in the production of images whose speed, fluency, metamorphic relationship and directness of sensory address, prevents the engagement of any interpretative mechanism:

> Ideally, it is possible to elude the interpreters in another way, by

making works of art whose surface is so unified and clean, whose momentum is so rapid, whose address is so direct that the work can be. . . just what it is. Is this possible now? It does happen in films, I believe.

(1994: 11)

The possibility of translating Rimbaud cinematically, and the interpretative implications of such a move, are explored in Chapter 4.

Closely related is the solution through the senses: 'What is important now is to recover our senses. We must learn to *see* more, to *hear* more, to *feel* more' (1994: 14). Sensory involvement with the text releases us, as film does, from the 'itch to interpret'. And if anything in Rimbaud's own writing might warn us against jumping too quickly into the interpretative free-for-all that his poems have generated, then it would precisely be: 'Cette langue sera de l'âme pour l'âme, résumant tout, parfums, sons, couleurs, de la pensée accrochant la pensée et tirant' (letter to Paul Demeny, 15 May 1871) [This language will be of the soul and for the soul, synthesising everything, perfumes, sounds, colours, thought catching hold of thought and pulling].

Ironically, Rimbaud's wild, subversive, scandalous writing finds itself enmeshed in, incapacitated by, the web of concessive interpretation. Interpretation, foxed, finds its way into polysemy (x could be a, or b, or m, or y), only to discover polysemy as a founding literary virtue. This self-multiplying analysis is, in many senses, a product of silent reading in that it does not involve the body and does not have, or want, to make up its mind. Ultimately we may feel that interpretation in Rimbaud's work has become self-defeating; accounts are multiplied and either leave the reader bemused by the prospect of paying his money and taking his pick, or require some generalising superordinate synthesis, beyond the individual text, which will reveal an underlying Rimbaldian stylistic policy,[2] or a network of generical subsets.[3] These latter strategies belong to what Todorov would call 'la critique paradigmatique' (1978: 243–4) [paradigmatic criticism], but they have their staunch defenders.[4]

At all events, the great 'advantage' of translation is that it has no generalising refuges, and certainly does not seek to generate an increasing critical distance from the individual text, a distance itself generated by the proliferation of alternative readings. Instead, it seeks to take the reader back to the text qua text, that is to say as something prior to interpretation, where potentiality does not mean itemisable alternative readings, but a maximised capacity to mean. Translation is not what tells us what Rimbaud is all about; translation is what suggests to us ways in which we might most profitably read Rimbaud, and in such a way that the space/time between ST and TT is fully taken into account, made evident, made visibly active in the TT. If we are to make Rimbaud more intelligible, it will not be by straightening his 'crooked' texts, but by articulating the sense he makes for our own time, and thus the sense we make of ourselves.[5] Peculiarly, interpretation only takes that *décalage* into account implicitly; 'Rimbaud' slips effortlessly back into Rimbaud.

On the basis of these transformational dangers, and in the light of certain goals which, I believe, translation should set itself and which this book sets out to pursue, I would lay out the following founding propositions.

1. Founding propositions

1. That the primary purpose of literary translation is not to mediate between readers and texts in languages they do not know. While translation in this guise might be a subordinate element in the network of translational functions, it should not, as largely at present, act as the superordinate function. The superordinate function of literary translation is to promote translation as literature, or the literature of translation. In this sense, the translator has more important obligations to translation itself than to the source text (ST); the habit of conceiving of the ST as the locus of translation's moral debates with itself has diverted translators' attention from their 'obligations' to their medium and its development. Assumptions are made that literary translation simply exists and that our first task is to understand its relations, hierarchical and cultural, with 'first-degree' literature (polysystem theory, and so forth; see, for example, Lambert 1998: 130–3); in fact, the literature of translation has to be made with each translation.

Part of my objection to the paramountness accorded to translating foreign texts for the ignorant reader lies in the unacceptable 'system of exchange' that it entails: it involves too much authority being given to the producer of a text, which is inevitably unreliable, by a reader who is necessarily unable to judge either the degree of reliability or the quality of what he/she is reading. Another part of my objection is that where a version or versions of a translated text already exist, further translations destined for the ignorant reader tend to justify themselves by linguistic variation, by playing through remaining alternatives, if only to avoid 'plagiarism'. These variations may well produce real expressive and semantic differences, but they have the curious effect of seeming to exhaust the ST, to bleed it dry of potentiality; after all, it is not the connoted meanings of a word that we are trying to translate, but the connotative power of the word itself.

At the same time, these lexical/linguistic variations remind us that choice is being made among a selection of alternatives *that is already available* (in the dictionary or thesaurus), that is *universally* available. And the criticism of such translations is usually, precisely, a review of available choices, where the critic evaluates whether option X is, or is not, better than option Y. But these are choices that *anyone could make*, supplied with the requisite information. The advantage of the 'qualified' translator is that he/she can make these choices more efficiently; but they are still the same choices. Consequently, every translation turns out to be a curate's egg, and the kind of choice which should be peculiar to a *literature* of translation, a creative, existential choice, not so much available as inevitable, the choice that nobody else could make, the choice that expresses a relationship with, and a vision for, the ST, the choice which does not simply set out to display the ST's meaning (possible meanings), but reinvents the ST in order to re-embody its expressive energies, this choice is reserved for translational heretics, self-translators, and writers creative in their own right (!?). My second proposition is closely related, namely:

2. That the literary purpose of translation is to ensure that the ST *makes progress*. I have argued elsewhere (2000: 47–70) that a certain kind of translation has the effect of turning the SL (source language) into a dead language, the ST into a dead-language text.[6] My comments above, on the way that 'linguistic-variation' translation may seem to exhaust the ST is a similar anxiety about the 'fossilising' or 'immobilising' effect of translation on the ST. If a text is to have an after-life, is to survive in translation, then the literature of translation must ensure that the continuing life of the ST is not merely a back-reflection of the TT, but is something that the TT acts to create, the translator as if entering into a partnership with the author, a collaboration which, to use Tony Harrison's term (1976: vi), 're-energizes' the ST, re-configures the expressive potentialities of the ST. My position is thus diametrically opposed to the situation outlined by Anthony Pym whereby 'translation is defined by a relation of equivalence which denies the very possibility of any such value added, since the output is supposed to be directly exchangeable for the input' (1992: 52); this is a recipe for premature fossilisation if ever there was one. *Literary* translation does not interpret the ST, or transcribe its meaning, but re-embodies the ST, re-articulates its literariness; if the TT can be said to be performance of the ST, then it is not the recital of an ST which already possesses itself, its completeness, but the acting out of implications that the ST cannot have foreseen, the acting out of a literary selfhood diversely, repeatedly and unpredictably coming to itself afresh.

But what we also mean by the ST's making progress through translation, is its continual drawing closer to us, or even outpacing us, across space and time. Translation is not a commemorative process, a way of remembering the ST and updating that memory; to use these notions is to look too exclusively from the point of view of the TT. The ST is being encouraged to traverse a space and/or time which it does not yet know. As it traverses this space/time, so it encounters the poetries that postdate it, poetries which are part of the translator's consciousness and through which the world has been variously re-imagined. We might express this difference—between translation as (a) commemoration and (b) as progress of the ST—diagrammatically, thus:

(a)   ST ← TT (ST + 5yrs)
                 ← ← TT (ST + 10 yrs)
                 ← ← ← TT (ST + 15yrs)
(b) ST → ST (TT at 5 yrs) → ST (TT at 10 yrs) → ST (TT at 15yrs)

In (a), while successive TTs make progress, the ST remains marooned in its own origins. In (b), as the ST passes along the corridor of posthumousness, through successive TTs, so it is invited at every turn to rethink its literary choreography, to restage its semantic dramas, to reproject itself as literary experience. In other words, the translator becomes the representative of the ST in its after-life by acting as the representative of that after-life; what translation translates is the ST's perpetual discrepancy with itself, not the discrepancy between two languages.

So the translator takes upon himself the task of extending the expressive relevance of the ST, of exploring the ST's potential to be other, to operate in other creative contexts and to animate other ways of thinking about its subject. This is to assume not only that any text is, in some sense, unfinished—it can never grasp how it might be imagined, it cannot control what might be intuited in it, it cannot predict the uses to which it might be put—but also that every text desires to be other. Translation is an eroticisation of the ST; it allows the ST's desire to express itself and, at the same time, re-projects that desire into the blind field of a future; translation works to turn the pleasure of the ST into Barthesian *jouissance*. But if we are shifting the emphasis from linguistic variation to textual re-projection, or, expressed in other terms, from translation conceived of as the solution of *problems* of linguistic transfer, to translation conceived of as a response to textual *opportunities*, those opportunities being principally provided by the space/time that lies between the ST and the translator,

21

then we must know what we mean by text, and that leads to my third proposition, namely:

3. That the text of the ST is, by definition, an expanded and expanding text. There are three senses in which this is so, and it is the third sense that principally concerns me in this book. Genette potentially did translation studies a great service by including translation within the much broader purview of transtextuality (1982): this move quite simply shifts translational consciousness out of preoccupations with the feasibility of linguistic (cultural) transfer into a sense of how open, and naturally assimilative of each other, texts are, and how much translation is itself more a weave of quotation, pastiche, imitation, allusion than a self-defining and separate activity. And I would emphasise the notion of 'weave'. I have no objection to typologies of translation; they enlarge our awareness of the range of possible translational moves (see, for example, Eco 2001: 99–130). But they tend implicitly to promote the ideal of unmixed, non-hybrid products, products which can be clearly identified (so is this, once and for all, a translation or a paraphrase?), when, on the contrary, we may aspire to versions whose means cannot quite be brought into focus, which change kaleidoscopically, which are intended to be experienced as fluid.

The life of a text is a process of accretion, accumulating to itself, and discarding, meanings, intertexts, varying functions and roles within the (cultural) landscape:

> Si le traducteur ne restitue ni ne copie un original, c'est que celui-ci survit et se transforme. La traduction sera en vérité un moment de sa propre croissance, il s'y complètera *en* s'agrandissant. [. . .] Et si l'original appelle un complément, c'est qu'à l'origine il n'était pas là sans faute, plein, complet, total, identique à soi.
>
> (Derrida 1985: 232)
>
> [If the translator neither restitutes nor copies an original, it is because the original lives and transforms itself. The translation will truly be a moment in the growth of the original, which will complete itself *in* enlarging itself. [. . .] And if the the original calls for a complement, it is because at the origin it was not there without fault, full, complete, total, identical to itself (trans. Graham 1985: 188).]

But if I have bracketed 'cultural', it is because the translator is both a public representative and a private poet, so that he operates both with a structuralist version of intertextuality, an intertextuality of shared cultural reference, operating in accordance with a nameable set of categories (quotation, allusion, parody, travesty, forgery), and a post-structuralist version, where intertextuality is the instigator of textual anarchy, textual chaos, depriving the author of rights to, and control of, his own language, and inviting the reader to let intertextual fantasy have its way, as that which defines the permutative vagaries, the inexhaustibility, of the reading experience.

At all events, we might begin by saying that the ST in the TT is an expanded and expanding text by virtue of its intertextual existence, its borrowings and lendings, its metatextual and architextual baggage, the associations it generates in the reader; some of these I tried to incorporate into my translation of Baudelaire's 'Le Voyage' (2000: 218–46). Secondly and relatedly, there are the paratextual features (blurbs, publicity, prefaces, footnotes—see Genette 1987) which constitute the readerly contexts of both the ST and the TT, an important part of the conditioning of readerly response. This leaves open an important question: how far should it be a distinguishing feature of the literature of translation that the textual actively incorporates the paratextual/contextual within its borders, so that the text is supported, made to radiate, associatively unpacked, in a variety of ways? Such a move might be a way of further implicating the reader in the text, of maintaining an awareness that the text is a translation, and of installing a different rhythm of textual assimilation, a rhythm which might, again, be a distinctive characteristic of the literature of translation.

Finally, there is the textual space itself, in the strictly physical sense. This space, the space of the page, of the double page, of the unfolding book, this is, as it were, the consciousness of the translator, into which the translated ST comes to bed itself, which distributes the text according to the way that the text is imagined in the translator's mind. Thus the text is certainly not just the words; it is the text and its *Lebensraum*, the text and its space, or rather its place, where that place is defined by the translator, by the translator's inhabitation. The space of the page is not what is left by the text, but what makes the text, as *ajours* [openwork] make lace or architectural tracery. Space is at once the translator's imaginative field and the text's own consciousness of itself.

Translation is principally about putting a text into a new expressive environment. This is what I understand translation as recontextualisation to mean: not putting a text into a new context of reception, but into a new context of projection. Correspondingly, the space of the page should suggest to the reader a certain *mode d'emploi* [instructions for use]. Translation studies, focussed as it so often is on the translation process itself, has done very little to develop a reader-response theory. Given the general absence of translator/reader contracts, and the general passivity of readers of translation—particularly ignorant readers—it is vital that modes of reading are, where at all possible, integrated into the translation. The activation of the space of the page is the activation of a mode of reading, the promotion of perceptual mechanisms suggestive of the ways in which a text might come home to itself.

In Barthesian terms, and as already intimated, the object of translation is clear: to translate a Work into a Text, to translate the *lisible* [readerly] into the *scriptible* [writerly], to translate the culturally institutionalized into the culturally undefined, re-inventable, open-ended. It is this process, these notions, which make multi-translation inevitable, not because of the ST, but because of the different ontological status of the TT. The ST is substance, while the TT is methodology, to be experienced *only in an activity of production*. The TT seconds the ST in the deferral of signification; the TT does not arrive at an interpretation but at a dissemination; the TT is a plurality (by connections, overlappings, variety of perspectives) (Barthes: 1984).

2. Four models of literary translation

On the basis of the founding propositions above, I would like to propose four models of literary translation.

The first kind is what one might describe as a re-definition, or relocation, of textuality. Textuality is, in the written text, a set of verbal relationships, partly prescribed by complex formal and syntactic conventions, partly free. But what is principally important is that the isolatedness, or circumscribedness, or system-potential, of this textuality draws the text into modes of meaning which are not *quite* covered by other known verbal organisations. This is inevitably a theoretical supposition which it would be extremely difficult to demonstrate in any conclusive way. But it is sufficient that it allows us to imagine the senses in which the 'known language' is insufficient to account for and cope with the textuality of text and that, therefore, for reader and translator alike, each text, to a greater or lesser degree, requires a re-imagining of language. But for the translator this re-imagining, which is already necessitated by writing in a 'foreign' language, produces a consequent requirement to re-imagine a textuality which is equal to it. I prefer the phrase 'equal to' to 'equivalent to', because equivalence always implies the already existent.

At the centre of textuality, then, lies a paradox: the more one advances into a text, the more one experiences its compulsions, its determination to multiply its interwovenness. But the more, concomitantly, one loses one's grasp and control of its multiplicity. And this loss of control is exacerbated by the unpredictability of what strikes us as readers, the irregular patterns of readerly attention. It is these factors which help to generate the Barthesian *scriptible*, the plural text:

> Dans ce texte idéal, les réseaux sont multiples et jouent entre eux, sans qu'aucun puisse coiffer les autres; ce texte est une galaxie de signifiants, non une structure de signifiés; il n'a pas de commencement; il est réversible; on y accède par plusieurs entrées dont aucune ne peut être à coup sûr déclarée principale; les codes qu'il mobilise se profilent *à perte de vue*, ils sont indécidables (le sens n'y est jamais soumis à un principe de décision, sinon par coup de dés); de ce texte absolument pluriel, les systèmes de sens peuvent s'emparer, mais leur nombre n'est jamais clos, ayant pour mesure l'infini du langage.
>
> (Barthes 1970 : 12)
>
> [In this ideal text, the networks are multiple and interact with each other, without any single one being able to control the others; this text is a galaxy of signifiers, not a structure of signifieds; it has no beginning; it is reversible; there are several points of entry none of which can be declared, with any certainty, to be the principal one; the codes activated by it stretch away *as far as the eye can see*, they are undecidable (their meaning is never subject to a principle of decision, apart from a throw of the dice); systems of meaning can take possession of this absolutely plural text, but their number is never finite, since the unit of measurement is the infinity of language.]

In creating an alternative ST in the textuality of the TT, we want to ensure that difficulties are treated as opportunities, that impossibilities generate licences. We need to create a TT which produces its own unfulfillable demands, in which any choices made become the property of the text, in which each move releases new expressive possibilities which must, in their turn, be responded to. The TT must generate its own kinds of formal knowledge, its own web of expectations, associations, surprises.

To illustrate this proposition, I would like to look briefly at François-René Daillie's translation of Wordsworth's 'Daffodils' (see Appendix I for full texts). Daillie's version makes its first constitutive decision in its choice of verse-line: the decasyllable, but not the classical 4//6 model, rather the nineteenth-century 'Romantic' 5//5 variety. This choice already sets certain architextual coordinates and calls forth an available readerly context: we shall find this 5//5 decasyllable exceptionally in the work of Marceline Desbordes-Valmore ('La Rose flamande'), for example, very

25

occasionally in Musset, more frequently in Leconte de Lisle, Cros, Corbière, Verlaine; we expect it to provide a tetrametric shape (such as 2 + 3 + 3 + 2), closer to the Wordsworthian iambic tetrameter than either the 4//6 decasyllable—usually trimetric—or the octosyllable—usually dimetric or trimetric—would get. So Daillie seems to be making an accentual rather than a syllabic choice. But the phrasal nature of French accentuation means that either or both of the decasyllable's hemistichs might be a single pentasyllabic rhythmic span, as here in:

l. 4		//	une légion
l. 9	Elles s'étendaient	//	sans un intervalle
l. 14		//	plus allégrement
l. 16		//	par leur enjouement
l. 19	Car si je repose	//	
l. 20		//	ô béatitude
l. 22		//	de la solitude
l. 24		//	avec les jonquilles (perhaps (2+3))

Not surprisingly, these instances gravitate predominantly towards the second hemistich, as the line's initial impetus radiates out, spends itself, in feelings of spiritual lightness or transfiguration. This sense of radiation is more physical—numbers, spatial extent—in ll. 4 and 9. And it is fitting that the pentasyllabic measure with which the poem closes should be the daffodils themselves, the source of both animated multitude and spiritual replenishment. It is the pentasyllable that allows, encourages perhaps, the expansive but interruptive stillness of the apostrophe of l. 20, itself adumbrated by the apostrophe of line 3:

Quand soudain je vis en foule—ô mirage !—

Apostrophe is not a feature of the ST, but for Daillie the fixedness of the decasyllable's caesura creates those tensions in syntax and word-projection for which apostrophe can act as a timely release.

The animated variety of the daffodils is embodied in the odd number of syllables in the hemistich, since this most frequently produces a segmentation—3+2 or 2+3—in which a one-syllable difference makes outlines vacillate and prevents the establishment of any sense of regularity or equilibrium. Daillie makes no use of the 4+1 combination, but on three occasions resorts to 1+4, to wit:

l. 13   Les vagues dansaient, pleines d'étincelles   2+3+1+4
l. 21   Vient illuminer l'œil intérieur   1+4+1+4

In each of these instances, the monosyllabic measure fixes points of light, glints—the words that Wordsworth himself uses to describe the light given off by the daffodils are 'twinkle' (like stars), 'sparkling' (like waves) and 'flash'. And l. 21 perfectly captures, in its twofold insistence on this sudden moment of focus followed by a tetrasyllabic movement of suffusion, a process that Pound tries to capture in 'In a Station of the Metro': 'In a poem of this sort one is trying to record the precise instant when a thing outward and objective transforms itself, or darts into a thing inward and subjective' (quoted in Ruthven 1969: 153).

In comparison, Wordsworth's own metric may begin to look rather too homogeneous and insensitive. One might justifiably bewail the English ear's unresponsiveness to syllabic values and its reliance on the reassuring regularity of beat. To identify the metre of 'The Daffodils' as iambic tetrameter is to commit oneself to a through-read, non-phrasal treatment of the line, which masks the variety of segmentations, in favour of an unproblematic affirmation of the metre. But even if one uncovers the phrasal complexity in, say, the second stanza—

3' or 4' / 3 / 2
3' / 5
2 / 6
5' / 3
3' / 2 / 3
4 / 4

[note: the apostrophes indicate segments which end with an unstressed syllable]

—one realises that the English ear is more likely to identify a sequence of punctuations, of pauses of varying length, than a sequence of rhythmic segments redistributing iambic tetrameter in a range of re-configurations.

One might argue a similar French advantage in rhyme. The rhymes of 'The Daffodils' are exceedingly dull: from a semantic point of view, one might single out the fitting antonyms 'cloud/crowd', and the equally fitting kinships of 'trees/breeze', 'glee/company', 'mood/solitude', 'fills/daffodils'. But one feels no concertedness in these conjunctions, just as one feels no orchestration of, say, open and closed syllables in the rhyme position. The semantic suggestiveness of the French rhymes seems to me altogether greater, and we must remember that rhyme is one of those devices which is not merely a device, but a language likely to relocate or redistribute the patterns of association, either intertextually—Daillie rhymes 'étoiles' with 'intervalle', while I am reminded of connections with 'toiles' and 'voiles', those alternatives to which rhyme *inevitably* alludes—or by the new connotations of the combination—'monts' rhyming with 'une légion' takes us to Roman, or indeed Punic, armies crossing the Alps, opening up a martial dimension in these daffodils which 'host' might, but only just, conjure up; 'grises/brise' sets up a rather more melancholy and Verlainian atmosphere, against which the daffodils rebel.

'Grises/brise' and 'béatitude/solitude' are the only rich rhymes in Daillie's version: he does not seem to have sought to exploit French's discrimination between degrees of rhyme, and is satisfied to operate, untendentiously, with a mixture of *rime pauvres* and *rimes suffisantes*. But in other areas of French rhyming, Daillie has taken greater liberties: I refer here to the rules that govern permissible pairings and the alternation of masculine and feminine rhymes.

And this leads on to a second species of literary translation, namely a translation which gives a special place to, and whose literariness is characterised by, kinds of licence or formal reinvention which non-translation writing might find alien or unacceptable. Translation should not be afraid to develop its own panoply of forms and styles, which would lie closely alongside those of non-translation literature. I have elsewhere suggested that the rhymeless sonnet might be such a form, but only on condition that rhymelessness itself be re-theorised. At the moment, unrhymed translations tend to be so because the translator cannot manage the rhyming of the ST. This is a rhymelessness by default, rhymelessness as a counsel of despair, a familiar sacrifice of language's materiality in the interests of salvaging sense. The first step in such a re-theorisation would be to return to Abernathy's distinction (1967) between the rhymeless and the anti-rhymed, where rhymeless verse is verse to which no rhyme-canon is systematically relevant and where the anti-rhymed is characterised by negative constraints, that is, it presupposes the existence of a rhyme-canon (in the SL/ST) which, in the name of its own difference, it systematically avoids or refuses. Anti-rhyme is, therefore, on the face of it, more significant than rhymelessness, or entails, at least, an account of rhymelessness which makes it more significant.

Anti-rhyming might then also be reckoned to have cultural-historical implications. Rhymelessness suggests a more inchoate existence, where decisions about verbal relationships have still to be made, where acousticity has yet to be harnessed as a structural and expressive resource, a form of pre-rhyming. Correspondingly, anti-rhyming would represent post-rhyming, a growth beyond acoustic mechanisms which instantiate anticipation and memory. Alternatively, one might think of anti-rhyming as a rhyming fit for a new age, for readers sensitive not to the similarities of sounds, but to their differences, a rhyming of the rhymeless or the acoustically unlike; or at least a rhyming practice involved in the kinds of almost ultra-aural or infra-aural rhyming, suggested by Jules Romains and Georges Chennevière (1923) and by Jean Hytier (1923), where acoustic similarities exist at the very limits of perceptibility. For his part, Daillie brings a liberated rhyming practice to bear on Wordsworth, in which he allows himself to rhyme singulars with plurals, feminines with masculines, and to disregard alternating gender or alternating patterns of consonant + vowel and vowel + consonant. This means that he can make his own map of the femininity of the daffodils ('jonquilles') as it interacts with the vestigial masculinity of the poet. The first stanza, among other things, sets an androgynous cloud ('nuage', masculine noun, feminine rhyme) against an equally androgynous (but in reverse) host ('légion', feminine noun, masculine rhyme), but with the adumbration that rhyme gender, the gender dictated by lyric imperative rather than grammatical rule, will decide which principle—solitude/singleness/meditation or multiplicity/gregariousness/sensory involvement—predominates. Not surprisingly, the rhymes of the second stanza are exclusively feminine, so completely do the daffodils occupy the stanza's space. The third stanza engineers a perfect balance between feminine and masculine, to the extent that the final rhyme 'guère/offert' is shared between them, as a compromise, and fittingly so since the poetic mind does not interrupt the vision ('je ne songeais guère'), at the same time as the daffodils do their utmost to share themselves with the spectator ('qui m'était offert'). In the final stanza, it is still the poet's inwardness that generates masculinity ('songeur/œil intérieur'); but the experience of that inwardness depends on the invasion, the darting in, of the remembered daffodils; only thus can 'béatitude' and 'le bonheur de la solitude' be produced.

Daillie presents us with the lure of reinvented 'rules', rules more attuned to the unfolding drama of his own particular reading of Wordsworth, and more attuned to the need to maintain a linguistic materiality which is in no sense a diluted copy (or even equivalent) of the original, but rather an inscription into the poetic structure of expressive resources peculiar to his own language. But it is not just a new language of rhyme and rhymeless-ness/anti-rhyming which might constitute a distinctive literature of translation. I have elsewhere suggested (2002a: 78–9) that punctuation, too, might have a special part to play in literary translation, particularly as a device which might 'make visible' the ST's subtextual agenda and bring to the textual surface specific perceptions of temporality and vocal rhythm.

Punctuation is an indispensable instrument for dramatising meaning, for psychologising speakers, for indicating the logical and affective relationships between utterances. The resources of typography and layout equally might be put to special translational uses, for much the same purposes as punctuation.

I have also wanted to suggest that our understanding of prose as a translational medium needs urgently to be reassessed, in terms of its rhythmic and dispositional resourcefulness. Our sensitivity to prose as a translational reformulation of the ST has been much blunted by our attitudes to so-called 'plain prose' translation. What might we make of a French prose version of 'The Daffodils', but laid out as decasyllabic lines, or gradually metamorphosing into decasyllables? Equally, I would want to argue that free verse has a special significance as a translational medium, not only because it activates the page as an expressive arena, so that the page becomes a stage on which translation can perform itself, can become performance, and a musical score, a record of the vocal traces that the translation has inserted into the ST, but also because it provides the translator with a way of introducing himself into the ST, of intervening in the ST, without its necessarily entailing a revision of the linguistic material itself. Additionally, free verse is sufficiently open-structured for the translator to be able to inject supplementary material, an accompaniment which can explore associative reverberations.

This latter observation brings me to a third kind of literary translation, namely a translation designed to trace in its writing the geographical and temporal distances the ST has travelled in order to be in the here and now. The translator simultaneously acts as a translator of a text and as a historian of the text, tracking the text's varied life in an intervening posthumous space in which it has been adapted, adopted, imitated, quoted from, alluded to, has been the subject of numerous associations in a multitude of reading minds. This history of the ST's life between its first place and time and the here and now can, of course, never be comprehensive or final (official); it is bound to reflect or embody the translator's autobiography as reader and member of a culture. And it is a history which might as much involve the ST's pre-natal as its post-natal life: the ST is as much made of a past as it generates a future; and that past, too, is a mobile and unfixable mix of potential influences, models, presences. The model of literary translation offered here is one which leaves the ST 'intact', but interleaves it with other literary materials, created for the occasion by the translator, or quoted from other sources (in translation or not). What underlies this particular version of literary translation is the presence of a textual accompaniment which might be a commentary on the ST, an extension of the ST, a tracing of the resonances of the ST in other texts. In short, this kind of montage translation is designed to insert paratextual materials (prefatory matter, annotations, commentary) into the space of the text, while maintaining the 'integrity' of the original. This is a model which accepts that the TT must be an expansion of the ST, if it is to capture something of the ST's inevitably proliferating after-life.

My final version of literary translation is the one which is most significant for the present Rimbaldian enterprise. Like the third option, this final model conceives of translation as the vehicle by which the ST makes progress through the time and space it did not yet know at its birth. But whereas the third option leaves the translator as the reader and observer of the ST and its aftermath, the fourth option engages the translator as the maker of the ST's new being, as the one who adapts the ST to new creative and perceptual environments. I have already indicated, perhaps, what this might mean at the level of the page and the page's space: the page's space is precisely what can ensure the making visible of those energies within the ST which, in a new age, have conjured up new structures to embody them. Whereas, therefore, the third model imagines the ST proceeding by a process of accretion and self-enlargement, barnacles on the boat, the fourth model imagines that the ST is only the beginning of an infinite sequence of makeovers which would not only remove the artificial and unfruitful distinction which is customarily made between translation, on the one hand, and imitation, adaptation and so on, on the other; but would also allow the translator more fully to make the kinds of choice we have called existential and irreversible, rather than find himself obliged to make choices which are made meaningless by their activation of universal opinion and their consequently provisional nature.

It is not intended that any of the models of literary translation mentioned above should make so-called 'straight' translation redundant. But we should recognise that straight translations serve a different ethic of translation, and from our point of view, their value resides in their allowing the reader to assess what the *literary* translator has done with the raw material, i.e. the straight translator empowers the reader to judge the literary translation and to understand what position it has travelled from. The straight translation still remains an unreliable text and should not be endowed with undue authority. But it does help to indicate not so much what the ST means as where it was as a text, what its expressive position was, when it was published.

I certainly do not think that these four models can or should be maintained in watertight compartments: literary translation is an inclusive and unbounded activity which may wish to shift its ground within the space of a single work (there is no innate virtue in consistency). And it may be that certain approaches to literary translation are difficult to classify in relation to the models presented here: I cannot tell whether my transformations of Baudelaire—sonnet > villanelle > free-verse villanelle; inverted sonnet > rondeau; pantoum > terza rima (2000: 94–119)— belong to model I or model IV: they are at once formal choices which entail a set of obligations not derived from the ST (model I); and at the same time, the pushing forward of Baudelairean formal choices towards the revival of other Romance fixed forms characteristic of the late nineteenth century, with the consequent redistribution of the ST's expressive orientation (model IV).

It should be the effort of translation to turn the TT into a signifier, as a total text. Too frequently, we examine the TT only as an exercise in linguistic equivalence—has it managed to do justice to the ST?—and fail to see it as an independent but multiple form of parasitical writing. Let us propose, then, that the TT is a translated *quotation* of the ST, in its entirety as it happens, though a fragment would be sufficient. By virtue of this entirety, quotation slips into plagiarism legitimised only by the technical expedient of acknowledging the ST's author. This leads translation into the literary strategies of Oulipo, based on the example of Lautréamont: 'Le plagiat est nécessaire. Le progrès l'implique. Il serre de près la phrase d'un auteur, se sert de ses expressions, efface une idée fausse, la remplace par l'idée juste' [Plagiarism is necessary. Progress entails it. It sticks very close to an author's formulations, uses his expressions, erases any false ideas, replaces them by true ones]; the translator becomes a fully paid-up member of the 'Institut de Prothèse Littéraire' [Institute of Literary Prosthesis]. But plagiarism need not necessarily act in one direction only— the good plagiarist will make the ST look like 'plagiat par anticipation' [pre-emptive plagiarism]. The world of Oulipo is a fair-minded one: 'Ainsi justice est rendue et chacun reçoit-il selon ses mérites' [Thus justice is rendered and each receives according to his merits] (Oulipo 1973: 23). At the same time, this reconstitution of the text inevitably raises questions about imitation and parody, about the ways in which imitation compensates for its imperfections by self-promotion, and parody excuses its failures through self-parody.

One begins to see that the failure of translation lies as much in the invisibility of translation as in that of the translator. By the 'invisibility' of the translation I mean its inability to affirm itself as a particular kind of writing and as a particular kind of complex and problematic relationship with the ST or hypotext. Hitherto this complexity has been locked into the linguistics of translation and not into its ontology. Translators might benefit from an Oulipian view of literature more generally, namely that literature is something infinitely to be put to new uses, to be made utilisable, or is something constantly to be created, without inhibitions about competence, qualifications or inspiration.

If Oulipo can afford to be so cavalier about literary creation, it is because Oulipians are ready to exploit the innate imagination of structure itself and of language. Immediately the TT changes the words and the order of words of the ST, the translator shifts into a combinatory or factorial or permutative poetry, which suggests indefinite continuation. It is the release of this inbuilt permutative potentiality by the very act of translation which permits translation to adopt a different posture from that of the ST. Oulipo is 'littérature potentielle' [potential literature] because its poems are *examples* of structures which can be put to other, multiple uses. The translations of Rimbaud's *Illuminations* which follow here are similarly exemplary, are similarly invitations to the reader to permutate their ingredients and structural possibilities.

If I make this point about Oulipo, it is not only because it is an experimental writing which an experimental translation ought to be cognizant of. It is also to underline a regret that translation (studies) is not more constantly turned towards the contexts of its own modernity. Translation too often seems to want to bury its consciousness of the literary world it inhabits, in order to occupy only the world projected by the ST, yet without pursuing a policy of thoroughgoing historicism. Translators may properly complain about the invisibility of translators; but it is perhaps to a degree true that, in terms of the manifold currents of contemporary writing, they have had their heads in the sand.

For the translator wishing to promote 'experimental translation' as an independent and self-justifying translational mode, two strategies seem to present themselves. Either he argues that experimental translation occupies a particular place in the overall translated life of an ST, a particular place which can only comfortably come into existence if the ST has already been treated to conventional translation processes, so that the 'ignorant' reader has some meaningful point of comparison or departure. Alternatively—and particularly if the translator rejects the assumption that his work is designed for the ignorant reader, but, on the contrary, believes that his work is primarily designed for the a reader familiar with the SL and the ST—then experimental translation might be proposed as the only worthwhile response to any ST (if you can read Baudelaire in the original, why bother to translate him 'conventionally', unless to exercise your English?).

But experimental translation is only made meaningful by the

presentness in the reader's mind of Rimbaud's ST (or indeed its 'plain prose' translation). This is for me an important thing to say because from it devolve two significant claims:

(a) Translations which may seem to flaunt their ludic, disrespectful self-conceit are intended as respectful and appropriately complex meditations on how an ST might renew itself in its posthumousness, how it might keep abreast of itself in changing times. As already mentioned, translations are about measuring distances, and not so much about measuring the distances between two cultures/languages—these measurements will always tend to come to the same conclusions—as about measuring the distance the ST has covered in order to become its translation.

(b) In 'standard' translations for ignorant readers, the ST is inevitably sacrificed. Its very absence presupposes an obligation to be faithful and reliable (whatever these terms might mean); and conversely, faithfulness/reliability, as a translational practice, almost entail the absence of the ST (even in a bilingual edition). A 'deviant' translation *necessitates* the ST, does not draw closer to it, but draws it closer. In other words, experimental translation affirms a kinship, and this parental model gives a truer impression than any talk of re-interpretation. All in all, one might argue that all conventional translations relate to the ST as cribs, as substitute texts in times of need, while with experimental translations, no gesture of substitution is made: the TT depends, for the fullness of its existence, on the fullness of existence of the ST.

But these moves might equally attract to themselves a searching question. If you are acquainted with the SL and the ST, why does your experimental translation have to be interlingual rather than intralingual? Even though any act of translation is justified (by what right do we seek to suppress any act of self-expression?), the question is worth answering, if only to make a point:

1. Every language contains another. The very materiality of language creates estrangements in the reader, which in their turn generate re-configurations of letters, phonemes, morphemes, which echo with other languages. There is a big danger that if one attempts an intralingual translation of Rimbaud, one betrays his own ambitions for a 'langue universelle', for a panglottism, for a reversal of the curse of Babel.[7] One betrays, too, perhaps, the fact that any language is

already an amalgamation of languages, through borrowing, occupation, colonisation, word derivation, word assimilation. To produce an intralingual translation of Rimbaud would be to insert his own language back into itself as something more constrained, more subject to its own identity, a subordinate form of the superordinate enterprise that the *Illuminations* are. Rimbaud's writing emerges from a polyphonic source which includes 'la littérature démodée, latin d'église, livres érotiques sans orthographe, romans de nos aïeules, contes de fees, petits livres de l'enfance, opéras vieux, refrains niais, rhythms naïfs' ('Délires II: Alchimie du verbe', *Une saison en enfer*) [unfashionable literature, Church Latin, hardly literate pornographic books, novels read by our grandmothers, fairy tales, children's books, old operas, nonsense refrains, simple rhythms].

2. The translator has by definition a 'bilingual' consciousness of texts and that bilinguality, that double perspective, is the identifying characteristic of the literature of translation.

3. The ST is certainly modifiable, in the sense that any commentator may ask us, for example, to re-imagine its disposition. But in the act of translation, the ST *must* be modified. The translator has this licence, this warrant, built into the very act he is undertaking. Many would argue that this licence should be minimised, that translation should seek to mask the process of modification as much as it can. Others are of the opposite persuasion: that modification, inevitable as it is, should be freely confessed, indeed should be amplified, so that what was a licence becomes a creative obligation. But we should beware of thinking of this creative obligation as freedom. Freedom suggests, on the contrary, a lack of obligation, cavalier attitudes, the translator's pleasing himself.

4. The making progress argument. Translation is Bergsonian in that the ST is already in the TT, not as a past looked back to, but as an integral part of the present, constantly available to the present. If we were to adapt Klee's adage, we would say that it is not the purpose of translation to reproduce the ST so much as to make the ST visible, to liberate its subtexts and those versions of itself it was unable to see simply because of its position in space (another language) and time.

What is difficult for us is the implicitly dual nature of language itself: language is both the capturing of *Erlebnis* (unmediated, unsifted, unselected immediacy) and its transformation into *Erfahrung* (knowledge, assimilation). In some senses, language protects us against the very thing that it delivers us to, and in the same process. Literary movements will attempt to favour one side of this equation against the other (inasmuch as syntax is a metabolising agent, we might say, for example, that Futurism's words in liberty, its holophrastic leanings, are an attempt to install a verbal experience which is able to vacillate between epiphany and trauma). One might also argue that the 'conflict' between rhythm and metre is a conflict between the desire to register unprocessed impressions/impressionability and the social need to ensure corporate metabolisation.

One might go on to argue that translation is, in the normal way, a process of further metabolisation, a form of delivery of the ST which is a protection against it. There is a sense in which the decision to translate is a decision to make an ST part of cultural knowledge—to turn the ST from a potential *punctum*-giver into a *studium*-provider. The desire, in this book, to establish the translator as explorer of the ST and, at the same time, as self-explorer, rather than as servant of the community, is an attempt to reverse this trend. Our most pressing question is how to get back to a Rimbaud whose texts really do threaten 'madness' (Todorov 1978: 253), from a Rimbaud whose texts are trumpeted abroad as 'maddening' and then quietly brought to their senses by a course of interpretation at the critical group practice.

2

The Rimbaldian Prose Poem
Questions of Time and Rhythm

It was probably in 1874 that Rimbaud collected together and transcribed the poems of *Illuminations*. Most of them were to appear in the Symbolist journal *La Vogue* (edited by Gustave Kahn) in May and June 1886, and a small *plaquette* edition (edited by Félix Fénéon) was published by the journal in the same year. But it was only in 1895 that a complete edition became available (including the hitherto unpublished 'Fairy', 'Guerre', 'Génie', 'Jeunesse' and 'Solde'), published by Léon Vanier. Two of the prose poems—'Dévotion' and 'Démocratie'—have no manuscript versions. The dating of the poems, their 'correct' order—if ever they were designed to have one—must remain matters of conjecture, although scholars have engaged in fascinating speculations of varying degrees of persuasiveness (for a critical edition of the manuscripts, see Murphy 2002; for a discussion of possible architectural principles at work in the *Illuminations*, see Murat 2002: 229–98).

These texts are therefore of a highly unsteady kind. The first text that we will address, 'Après le Déluge', has, for example, in its BN manuscript, 'après' written above the first line, between 'Aussitôt' and 'que', but crossed out in pencil—Eigeldinger's concordance edition (1986), however, begins 'Aussitôt après que', as does Steinmetz's 1989 edition; 'fut' appears with a circumflex; there *may* be an exclamation mark after the first 'oh', indicated by a faint mark; 'tira' *might* have originally been in the present tense; the 'maison de vitres' was originally a 'maison en vitres', etc. There is an inevitable danger that what evidence there is becomes conclusive evidence, when, in truth, these texts must be regarded as still being in the process of composition, or at least as textually unresolved. This does not give the translator extra licences; but it does encourage a certain attitude towards these texts: they are unquiet, still bubbling with their own possibilities, snatched untimely out of creative flux, indeed, still enacting that creative flux.

These caveats and qualifications should colour translational responses to Rimbaud's typographical details more generally. Capitals, it seems, are always ready to burst out of lower case in acts of assertive self-identification, as if Rimbaud found it necessary to flirt with modes of allegory and parable, if only to withdraw from them. In 'Fête d'hiver', 'Méandre', to judge by the manuscript, may have a capital *or* lower case initial (although it is usually resolved as a capital), while the 'c' of 'Chinoises' has been amended from lower case to upper. The capital of 'Elle' in 'Angoisse' was originally in lower case, as was the capital of 'Démon'.

And even though a distinctive punctuation system is a vital part of Rimbaud's creative language, it, too, should perhaps be treated with some flexibility by the translator: if only because these punctuation marks are as much elements in a suprasegmental expressive prosody as they are signals of particular syntactic configurations (see Murat 2002: 333–60). Rimbaud's use of the dash, as we have mentioned, has received consistent critical attention, such as Murat 2002: 343–65; Macklin 1990; and earlier Lapeyre 1981: 448–50: 'le système du "tiret combiné" isole des plans psychiques, taille des facettes dans le phrase, assurant à la poésie rimbaldienne cette allure de kaléidoscope' (449) [the system of the 'combined dash' isolates different psychic levels, carves facets into the sentence, endowing Rimbaldian poetry with this kaleidoscopic movement]. And at the time of the first publication of the *Illuminations*, we discover in *La Vogue* itself (4 April 1886) a more general interest in the psychophysical properties of punctuation marks and accents: under the rubric 'Curiosités', an article cited from a provincial newspaper expresses the following view: 'Le tiret ne trace-t-il pas matériellement le passage à un autre ordre d'idées? Il est horizontal, il conduit l'oeil sans lui permettre de s'écarter de la ligne: il fait transition' [Does not the dash materially trace the shift to another order of ideas? It is horizontal, it conducts the eye without allowing it to diverge from the line: it engineers transition].[1] The *tiret* picks up the voice when it threatens to slacken, throwing it forward into new realms of perception; it expresses those mental leaps, those urgent ellipses of thought, those foreshortenings of imaginative activity, with which Rimbaud's poems abound. The *tiret* is one of the instruments with which Rimbaud designates and develops not just a specific utterance, but the mentality of the whole text.

We are also inclined to forget, in our need to see the nineteenth-century prose poem with some generical clarity, the complexity of the part prose has played in the transmission of subjective experience. Prose has as much provided an alternative vehicle for standard lyric modes (hymn, elegy, ode, idyll) as it has for ill-defined and cross-bred genres: the recounting of dreams (Rimbaud's own untitled piece of 1864–65 and his 'Les Déserts de l'Amour' of 1872 (?)), meditations, reveries, promenades, the intimate journal (Rimbaud's 'Un cœur sous une soutane', 1870), the free-standing descriptive piece, rhapsody, fantasy, biblical paraphrases (parodies) (Rimbaud's 'Proses évangéliques', 1873). I would still want to put the question I put in 1990:

> What if it is in the nature of the prose poem to have no status, to be
> a real hybrid with ever-shifting parameters, precisely because it is a
> site of exchange and intersection (110).

Leroy (2001: 9) also reminds us that: 'il est clair, en effet, que la poésie en prose classique a longtemps eu pour horizon le vers, qu'à la rime et à l'inversion près, elle a cherché à reproduire' [It is clear, in fact, that classical prose poetry has had verse as its horizon, and it is verse that, apart from rhyme and inversion, it has sought to reproduce]. The persuasions of the prose poem in the nineteenth century may have been diametrically opposed to such a dependency, and we have no reason to suppose that Rimbaud wished in any way to hark back to this tradition of 'vers affleurant sous la prose' [verse surfacing from within prose]; but we might reckon that Rimbaud was well aware of critical and readerly anxieties about the aesthetics of prose, and that, accordingly, he had some interest in the 'vers blanc' as a textual mirage, as the expression of a deep psycho-aesthetic uneasiness, and that he was happy to exploit it as parodic allusion or as a sop to expectation. Antoine Fongaro's listing of 'segments métriques' in the *Illuminations* (1993) has called forth responses of deep scepticism (Cornulier 1994; Murat 2000), which are in many respects justified; but these pseudo-lines deserve to be thought about differently, in ways more in tune with prose's equivocating malleability.[2]

The more recent history of the prose poem teaches us how much it wishes to exist alongside free verse, the one a psychoperceptual modulation of the other (e.g. Reverdy, Éluard, Char, Bonnefoy, Deguy, Réda). It is for this reason, if for no other, that we should beware of insisting that, within *Illuminations*, the rubbing shoulders of prose and 'free' verse (not merely 'Marine' and 'Mouvement', but 'paradigmes syntaxiques' within the paragraph, verset, 'couplet', 'alinéa') lays upon us the obligation to distinguish strenuously between them. We should, in this respect, take the part of Rilkean angels. What does matter, as always, is the accentual flexibility of French, and thus the inevitable imbrication of reminiscences of regular verse-lines, and sentences, clauses, phrases that fall out, 'accidentally', as decasyllables or dodecasyllables. The prose poem does not *justify itself* by such reminiscences; it has no need of them. But, equally, part of its point is memory and its transcendence. The reader must be allowed to remember, even as he/she is swept along by the inadequacy of memory, by the sense that it cannot be a convenient refuge, that it cannot be permitted to inhibit the experimental nature of reading. The discovery of, say, octosyllabic sequences in Rimbaud is not a point of destination, but a point of departure, which asks us to remember that what we recognise may depend on the *degree* to which we accentuate (where 'degree' refers to frequency and/or intensity), and that the prose poem is a space in which all degrees may have their hour. Mallarmé certainly knew what he was talking about, when, in reply to Jules Huret's literary 'enquête', he affirmed:

> Le vers est partout dans la langue où il y a rythme [. . .]. Dans le genre appelé prose, il y a des vers, quelquefois admirables, de tous rythmes. Mais, en vérité, il n'y a pas de prose: il y a l'alphabet et puis des vers plus ou moins diffus. Toutes les fois qu'il y a effort au style, il y a versification (2003: 698).
>
> [Verse exists wherever in language there is rhythm (. . .). In the genre called prose, there are lines of verse, sometimes admirable ones, of all rhythms. But, the truth is, there is no prose: there is the alphabet and then lines of verse dispersed to a greater or lesser degree. Whenever there is a pursuit of style, there is versification].

He was merely pointing out that the fact of accentuability allows different accentual pressures to be applied to any syntagm, and the more pressure, the more 'versification'. This question of variable degree of accentuation has not been sufficiently investigated in French analyses of the rhythmicity of prose sequences, partly because of an unwillingness to admit paralinguistic input (pausing, loudness, tempo, tone, and so forth).

Different scholars have also brought different attitudes to the status of the texts, in terms of their textual autonomy. André Guyaux, the indispensable guide to the establishment and history of the texts, and to their critical discussion, is of the view that:

> Pourtant chaque fragment est envisagé en lui-même et pour lui-même. J'ai pratiquement écarté tout point de vue comparatif, sauf parfois pour faire une liaison. Le premier impératif m'a paru être celui qui respecte l'autarcie des fragments, leur particularité, l'idée

qu'ils gouvernent eux-mêmes leur propre sens. Le principe du fragment est qu'il casse le fil qui le relie, hypothétiquement, à une totalité.

(1985b: 14)

[And yet every fragment is envisaged in and for itself. I have put to one side any comparative perspective, except, from time to time, to make a connection. The primary imperative seemed to me to be the one that respects the autonomy of the fragments, their particularity, the idea that they themselves dictate their own meaning. The principle of the fragment is that it breaks the thread which binds it, hypothetically, to a whole.]

Such an approach—and we need to acknowledge, if not accept, Guyaux's distinction between the prose poem and the Rimbaldian 'fragment'—has the virtue of discouraging those kinds of criticism which Todorov (1978) categorises as aetiological, esoteric and paradigmatic, none of which face up to the central question: whether the principal message of the *Illuminations*, rather than lying in some content established by thematic or semic decomposition, does not lie in the *way* that the sense appears, or, perhaps, disappears. But there is a danger that the proof of the aesthetic integrity of the prose poem will be seen to lie in, among other things, its semantic autonomy. More recent commentators have wanted to suggest the opposite, that it is within the disruptive and interrogative function of the prose poem to have no aesthetic integrity, that the prose poem is a peculiarly ragged, open and dialogic form, which manhandles texts, which may have lyric, self-reflexive ambitions, back towards the referential. Those critics who have favoured a Communard version of Rimbaud's poetic project (for example, Denis 1968; Ross 1988) are more than others anxious to demonstrate the continuities to be established between text and contextual actuality.

On questions like these it would be unwise for the translator to adopt attitudes which might prematurely constrain translational decisions. The translator is someone who is translating his way into the texts, who wants to find a critical version of Rimbaud which coincides with his own translational intuitions. This may well involve the translator in self-contradiction, but then it may well be that, as readers of Rimbaud, we find it easier to live with contradiction, or with a dialectical dynamic, than critics for whom a convincing interpretation is a professional credential. And as I have already insisted, translation is not a way of communicating an interpreted text, but rather of conveying the experience of reading, an experience which is always developing and which can never, therefore, wholly sacrifice other 'texts' to the self-sufficiency of the one at any particular moment in question. The writer's identity derives from the privileging of a certain language, a certain intertextuality; the writer's lack of identity derives from the ultimate unpossessability of language and the indiscriminate ubiquity of intertextuality. The translator's identity derives partly from an adaptation of the writer's identity, partly from the way in which he colonises the writer's lack of identity.

Thus, first and foremost perhaps, reading the *Illuminations* is reading the drama of their restive form, the prose poem (see Murat 2002: 299–333, for remarks on the range of forms in the *Illuminations*); the problem for the translator, after all, is as much how to translate the prose poem in order to reveal and maintain its literary vitality, as how to translate Rimbaldian lexis and syntax. In describing what takes place when a verse-poem becomes a prose poem, it is usual to propose that (a) rhyme and (b) 'mesure' are removed (where 'mesure' refers to those rhythmic measures whose constitution and combinations are more or less predicted by a presiding isosyllabic principle). For Roger Little (1995: 13), the disappearance of rhyme has to do with the shift from oral/aural to visual transmission, while rhythm is already less central to French verse than to English. With both these views we shall have cause to disagree.

(a) The removal of rhyme reminds us that the prose poem has little interest in mnemonicity: it may remember but does not ask to be remembered. Those gestures of effacement that we encounter in the Rimbaldian prose poem, Fargue's suspension points, or other kinds of dispersive closure (dissonance, irony, metalinguistic turns) are all perhaps expressions of this characteristic. Mnemonicity is ultimately about textual survival, that is, the survival of a text in its non-interpreted, or pre-interpreted, integrity. This is perhaps to argue that the prose poem is under greater readerly pressure than the verse-poem, the pressure of comprehension, of consumption, the pressure to be entirely coincident with itself in the moment of reading; this may be why the Rimbaldian prose poem generates a disproportionate degree of frustrated puzzlement. And this, in turn, entails the reader's attempting to confine, to close down, the prose poem's ontological flexibility, which its elusive rhythmicity is there to protect. Rhythm's presence as metre in the verse-poem is pre-interpretative; it preserves the existence of the verse-poem and at the same time maps out/stakes out/measures out its textuality; the verse-poem demands to be remembered by those very devices by which it does its own remembering. Rhythm in the prose poem does not map out textual space, cannot work as a textual cadaster, but instead constantly questions itself, improvises itself, interrupts its own continuities. If regular verse preserves a seamless continuity between textual organisation and memory, if it promises the recurrences of cyclical time, if rhyme identifies the present as the meeting place between past and future, the prose poem launches us into the unprotected presentness of linear time, where no recurrence is predicted and where no continuity between textual structure and memorial activity exists.

The prose poem, like Western man perhaps, has opted out of the seasonal, out of cyclical and recurrent time ('Barbare': 'Bien après les jours et les saisons' [Long after the days and the seasons]; 'Adieu': 'Mais pourquoi regretter un éternel soleil, si nous sommes engagés à la découverte de la clarté divine,—loin des gens qui meurent sur les saisons' [But why regret an eternal sun, if we are committed to the discovery of divine light,—far from those who die by the pattern of seasons]). Instead it has put its money on linear time—with its allied notions of progress and history—which has located it in the no man's land between memory and anticipation. It thus finds itself less bedded in time than the animal and mineral world, less reassured, less certain of the benefits of waiting. But it does make it possible for the prose poem to go out and meet its destiny, pre-emptively; as Rimbaud himself puts it: 'La Poésie ne rhythmera plus l'action; elle *sera en avant*' (letter to Paul Demeny, 15 May 1871) [Poetry will no longer rhythmically inform action; *it will be ahead of it*]. More detached from time, more driven by temporality as teleology, it invents its own motivations, objectives, futures, but with a peculiar impatience, a peculiarly urgent insistence. It makes no sense for the prose poem to consent to time; in the end, it must chase, or be chased by, it. Otherwise it would drift, pointlessly; rhythm would unravel itself in a play of unending and insignificant variation. In linear time, there is always the dice throw of the once-and-for-all, but also the promise of originating something, something which must be launched into an infinity. The brevity of the prose poem is perhaps the mirage it wishes to create for itself, of mid-term destinations which can survive long-term. In cyclical time, possibility is always reborn—one only has to wait for the next coming—but it is only the possibility of re-entering the same in a different configuration; here, what seem like founding acts only re-establish the pattern. What we want to create in our reading of Rimbaud, is a translational practice inhabited by linear time: as we have already argued the ST does not come back in the TT, it moves forward through it. Translation launches the ST, and does so by casting the dice which can only ever have a future orientation.

But we also need to suggest that linear time is relentlessly raw. It is a time which cannot see itself as necessarily adding up, so that it cannot come round again, nor can it properly sediment itself, minutes into hours, hours into days, days into weeks, weeks into seasons. . . If there is no temporal embedding beyond the moment, then the moment, in its passage, is all that there will be, and that moment will gradually gravitate towards the instant. By this I mean that while the moment allows different kinds of metaphoric and metonymic relation with other moments, and thus seems expandable, while it is charged with a sense of subjective presence, of inhabitability, with the will to signify and persist, the instant is seized only in itself, as a slice of time so thin that it tends to exclude us, to evict us from ongoing process, to deprive us of things, to let them fall away behind us, rendered insignificant by a once-only-ness. Does this suppose that one must pitch one's tent at the very intersection of these two temporalities?

This differentiation between temporalities might be expressed by the difference between the apostrophe (moment) and the exclamation (instant). We shall have more to say about Rimbaud's use of these figures in Chapter 6. Suffice it to say for the moment, that Rimbaud's texts witness, it seems to me, the gradual theft of apostrophe, its gradual absorption into exclamation. Apostrophe remains in the soft, elasticised and habit-generated temporality of the child. Adolescence entails the shift from the cyclical to the linear. The prose poem is about this transition, with the dice loaded towards the linear.

In translating 'Après le Déluge', therefore, I am trying to translate two imbricated things: the experience of the prose poem as a linear time which bears the traces—sometimes wanted, sometimes unwanted—of a cyclical time it cannot recover; and, thus, the experience of the prose poem itself as the embodied experience of 'Après le Déluge':

After the Flood

As soon as the 'Flood' had subsided,
A hare
      pulled up—stock still
              in the CLOVERS   the swaying
BlueBELLs
                        and
                        and   said its prayers
to
the
rainbow   through   the WEB
                                  of the spider

Oh, the precious stones, going into hiding,

— the flowers already looking about them

In the filthy high street, the stalls went up, and the boats were
hauled towards the sea, layered, see, high up, as in old prints.

  The blood flowed, at Bluebeard's—in the slaughterhouses—in
the circuses, where God's seal made the windows blench. Blood
and milk flowed.

The beavers built. The mazagrans steamed in the estaminets.

In the large glass-paned house,
          still streaming with water,
          the children in mourning
pored over the breathtaking pictures.

A door slammed, and,
on the village square,   the child whirled his arms,
                    and was understood
                    by the WEATHERVANES
                    and the STEEPLECOCKS
                         all around,   under the cloudburst.

Madame X set up a piano in the Alps. The mass and the first
          communions were celebrated at the hundred thousand
          altars in the cathedral.

The caravans left. And the Hotel SPLENDIDE was built in the
chaos of ice and polar night.

From that moment, the Moon could hear the jackals howling across
the deserts of thyme—and clog-hopping eclogues grunting in the
orchards. Then,
in the violet,
budding
copse,
Eucharis
                    told me it was
                    spring.

Well up, pond;—   Foam

> Swamp the bridge and
> Inundate the
> Woods;

and black drapes and organs
                                        — lightning flashes and thunder
Well up and surge forward; Waters and sorrows, well up and
make the Floodwaters
                                                                swell again.

For, ever since they dispersed—oh! the precious stones burrowing
down, and the flowers, open!—everything's foundered! and the
Queen, the Witch who lights her embers in the earthen pot, will
never care to reveal what she knows and we don't.

For me, whatever else 'l'idée du Déluge' may indicate, the phrase
acknowledges the inevitable process of conceptualisation/representation
which accompanies any designated phenomenon. Language itself is
representation unless it finds a new life for itself. The hare's prayer is
already *mediated* by the spider's web. This 'Flood', then, might well be that
image by which the imagination is not so much released as transfixed,[3] and
whose memory cannot be erased—not itself a revolution,[4] but an
opportunity for revolution, with, unfortunately, already built into it, an
indoctrination confirmed by God's rainbow seal. This is the rainbow by
which, elsewhere, the poet feels himself to be damned ('J'avais été damné
par l'arc-en-ciel' [I had been damned by the rainbow]—'Alchimie du
verbe'), since the covenant's effectiveness is founded on the *representation*
(interpretation) both of the Flood and its aftermath; even the children are
inhibited by the sense of loss ('in mourning') and by the framed iconicity
of the 'breathtaking pictures'.[5] The moment of promise is the single child
who, breaking out of the glass-panelled house, this building still in the grip
of the Flood ('still streaming with water'), becomes the generator of a new
weather, on the human scale. The poet's opportunity lies in the 'après',
and perhaps in the immediately after ('Aussitôt que'); the opportunity
disappears in the 'depuis' and 'depuis que'; it is the 'Aussitôt' which
conjures up, immediately, an indefinite article ('Un lièvre'), the article of
the first-time, the inhabitual, the exhilaratingly random, the beginning of
all possible narratives, the wilful, the unaccounted-for. But the spider's
web (for Denis 1968: 1262: 'la voie hiérarchique des Pouvoirs civils et
religieux' [the right channels of the civil and religious Powers-that-be]) is
already there. Here lies the paradox of the literary text: it attempts to make

new a language which is already there; the very 'recurrentness' of language hobbles its capacity to take flight (in both senses of the word). The emergence of the child from the house of glass reasserts the indefinite article ('Une porte claqua'), and although, again, it is immediately absorbed into a weave of definite articles, it is the signal not of separate, if concerted, activities, but of secret understandings, in the world of *le temps*. Even Madame X's piano, far from embodying the further relentless colonisation of Nature's furthest outposts by bourgeois conventionality (piano = salon and salon music) still seems to me, thanks to her pioneering singleness, to relate to the child, to promise new harmonies, to relate to that fertile conjunction of the feminine voice and the arctic grottoes and volcanoes at the end of 'Barbare' (though a piano in the Alps may be a parodic equivalent). At all events, once we have crossed the line between 'Après/Aussitôt' and 'Depuis', the indefinite article has a sorry companion in 'ennui'; here the indefinite provides 'ennui' not with a heady liberty and randomness, but instead an enveloping pervasiveness which prevents its being set at a distance sufficient to enable its definition. This shift in temporal perspective, from after to since, also enacts a shift from protagonism to narration: so that, what looks like a directly performed invocation of the waters begins to take on the complexion of *reported* direct speech.

The Flood then has a truly paradoxical force: on the one hand, it represents representation, that which needs to be transcended; on the other hand, it is precisely the opportunity for transcendence and therefore must be summoned forth ever again. It is at one and the same time the memory that must be discarded, if new energies are to be released; and it is the memory that must be remembered if we are to supply ourselves with new trajectories. And on the face of it, as I have translated this poem, it is a text in which linear time (the instant, the indexical [but not necessarily the referential]) cannot shake off the clinging remnants of the cyclical and in which the cyclical cannot persuade the linear to take it back.[6] Childhood may have desirable freshnesses of vision, but it is threatened by habit and self-circumscription.

How does Rimbaud counter the inevitabilities of comfortable cyclical time? By a double method: by bringing perception into a raw, unprocessed proximity to the spectator/reader (my use of capitals embodies this impulse); or by bringing the spectator/reader close to what may still be iconic rather than indexical (deictics, modality of tense, definite articles). Both of these modes assume the installation in the reading process of real time: capitalisation is designed to introduce that element of unexpectedness, defamiliarisation, visible insistence which will make the difference; I have tried to bring out the immediacy, the implied copresence of addresser and addressee in the same instant, to be found in 'là-haut' (rather than 'en haut'), by insisting on deixis ('see'); the past historic acts not so much to situate events in time as to express an attitude towards, or desire for, those events: the past historic makes them perceptually peremptory, irrevocable, sudden, explosive, and the ubiquity of the definite article is designed not so much to convince us of our familiarity with these things or of their genericity, but again to have deictic value, precisely as if one were referring to the constituents of a *present* painting, engraving, image transposed to the past by narrative (the possibility of 'tira' being 'tire'; the sudden shift to the present of the imperatives; the cross-over between present and past historic in -ir and -ire verbs: 'dit' (bis), 'blêmit' and 'établit'; the present of deixis ['là-haut']).

These temporal crossovers, the reference to a language which is potentially new but already there, and to an indexicality which is non-referential, will perhaps bring to mind again Barthes' notion of *punctum*: 'Dernière chose sur le *punctum*: qu'il soit cerné ou non, c'est un supplément: c'est ce que j'ajoute à la photo et *qui cependant y est déjà*' (1980: 89) [Last point about the *punctum*: whether or not it is perceived, it is a supplement: it is what I add to the photo and *yet what is already there*]. Like the experience of *punctum*, the Rimbaldian word is supercharged with deixis and modality; it is intensely 'perceived' and yet has no reference, nowhere that we can locate it. Its power to lacerate, therefore, relates to what Barthes will say about *punctum* further on, that it is the experience of Time ("*ça-a-été*" [*that-has-been*]); it is the thing which, in being there for the first time, has already been. In some senses, the past historic is this noeme of photography, this tense-modality in which the acuteness of temporality, the imperiousness of temporality is proportional to the acuteness, the imperiousness, of perception. Photography belongs to the linear time of the irretrievable and that is why its referentiality is always slipping away from it, even while its indexicality clings on. What does something that you see now refer to, if it is a 'this was'? Is its indexicality present and its referentiality past? The Rimbaldian word/image, like the photograph, is caught between the desire to be a contact with reality and the inescapability of representation. And indexicality shares with deixis the principle of copresence: if both instal the *hic et nunc*, both, too, are inhabited by the relativity of the shifter (see Collot 1980: 65). We shall return to deixis in Chapter 4.

But there is another sense in which the Rimbaldian/*punctum* image does not refer. Its indexicality lacerates you with something already there but which *demands to be*, even if a memory, a memory more reinvented than remembered. In linear time, just as one can create oneself forwards, one can equally create oneself backwards. So we fall into a kind of verbal ecmnesia, where evidence from the past constitutes an exclamatory present.[7] Prose, like *punctum*, has the capacity to place us in an uncoded world in which the processes of socio-symbolic metabolisation do not operate, and we are left, unequipped, with the task of assimilating raw phenomena.

I have also aimed, therefore, to produce a text which seems to be finding its way back to verse and to be finding its way forward to prose, without being able to make up its mind. We should remind ourselves that, in some senses, the prose poem is already a translation, a metatext that has become textual by virtue of the loss of the verse original (see below). Part of the prose poem's restlessness is no doubt owed to this ambiguity of its textual status. Equally, the prose poem, by virtue of its very rhythmic inchoateness, is both non-metrical and potentially metrical. Accordingly, the clinging memory of cyclical time, the memory of an *Urtext* of which the ST is a translation, the memory of a kind of regular verse which haunts, and which one tries to undo, creates sharply conflicting tugs in the verbal texture, even where, and particularly where, perhaps, a way into the forward impetuses of linear time seems to have been found. My translation tries to capture some of these tensions not only by alluding variously to the verset, the 'couplet', the paragraph, but also by entertaining moments of recovered metricality, often where one least expects them:

still streaming with water	× / × × / ×
the children in mourning	× / × × / ×
and was understood	× × / × /
by the WEATHERVANES	× × / × /
and the STEEPLECOCKS	× × / × /
told me it was	/ × / ×
spring	/
. . . . . .	
Swamp the bridge and	/ × / ×
Inundate the	/ × / ×
Woods;	/

Additionally, I have tried to emphasise those moments when prose syntax itself, the 'paradigmes syntaxiques' [syntactical paradigms], create a chorus of rhythmic variations and leitmotivic repetitions, as if both wishing to achieve and wishing to avoid some complex orchestration; this occurs particularly in the paratactic activities of the Flood's aftermath, such as:

In the filthy high street	× × / × / ×
the stalls went up	× / × /
and the boats were hauled	× × / × /
as in old prints	× × / /
The blood flowed	× / /
in the slaughterhouses	× × / × / ×
in the circuses	× × / × ×
made the windows blench	× × / × /
The beavers built	× / × /
The mazagrans steamed	× / × × /
still streaming with water	× / × × / ×
the children in mourning	× / × × / ×
A door slammed	× / /
on the village square	× × / × /
The caravans left	× / × × /

These rhythmic interweavings consolidate no measure. Variation is the principle that sustains a certain freedom of decision, a freedom of phrasal shaping, which neither impedes continuity nor urges repetition. The octosyllable is not a variation of, say the hexasyllable; each, to be themselves, must enjoy the monopoly, and slip into the cyclical; the linear moves forward through its metamorphoses which, indeed, may echo what has gone before, but by imagining it in other company, as part of another configuration.

As we move to our consideration of the absence of (b) 'mesure' in the prose poem, we need to note that rhythmic presence in the prose poem, as we have been describing it, constantly allows the linguistic to be appropriated by the performative. We might argue that in verse, the function of metre is to confirm the 'linguisticity', the text-determined nature, of rhythm. In English verse, this happens by processes of stress-promotion and stress-demotion. In French, similar processes occur, with the difference that they have profound consequences for syntactic segmentation, for the way in which elements within the syntactic chain relate to each other. While we might look upon English as an accentuated language, in which certain syllables have a certain accentual flexibility (weak and strong forms), French is an accentuable one, that is, a language in which accents are latent and can be activated, or not, under a whole set of different conditions and reading styles. What is often noticeable in the scansion of prose poems is the desire of analysts to provide them with rhythmic credentials, and thus linguisticity/textuality, by re-installing the notion of 'mesure', not in a strict sense, as a certain regime of length and combination of rhythmic measure, but as an organisational principle which guides the writing process and is 'owned' by the text itself, as part of the text's being. Thus Marcel Cressot (1974: 287–96), while maintaining that prose has a rhythmic system of its own, allows for the presence of *vers blancs* within it (when emotion demands) and adopts the scansional methods of Maurice Grammont, whereby the number of rhythmic groups in the syntactic protasis are measured against the number of rhythmic groups in the apodosis. Henri Morier (1975: 852–72), for his part, proposes a prose rhythm based not on number of groups per unit (accentual reading), but on the syllabic constitution of consecutive groups, meticulously characterised by his own notation; for Morier, the prose poem is to be distinguished from poetic prose by its greater degree of musicality and rhythmic organisation. And we have already had cause to mention Fongaro's listings of the 'segments métriques' [metrical segments] to be found in the *Illuminations* (1993).

These strategies have a verse perspective in the sense that the rhythm of a passage is treated as the single linguistic matrix of all possible scansions (i.e. what is said precedes the saying of it); the prose version of this relationship should rather be that the rhythm of a passage is the polymorphous sum of all possible scansions (i.e. what is said coincides with the saying of it) (see Meschonnic 1982: 275). We might suppose that each genre of written language defines, to a degree, in a distinctive way, the status of the speaking/reading voice, and solicits the voice in a distinctive way. Genres are different kinds of theatricalisation of the voice. We acknowledge that verse partly disembodies the voice, makes it abstract; this is the diction of verse, this helps us to see that rhythm in verse is established elsewhere, is generated by what is to be said. Rhythm is both part of the poem as shared experience, its trans-subjectivity, and part of its memorability. Verse's dictional stability relates directly to its codedness; a particular voice can read an alexandrine as though it were only ten syllables, but it is powerless to usurp the twelve syllables of the alexandrine, their metrical necessity, their metrical equality (not isochronicity).

The prose poem, on the other hand, is highly uncoded (hence our difficulty in defining it) and has no syllabic stability. Without the need to keep open trans-subjective channels, the rhythmic world of the prose poem allows the vocal solipsisms of the *flâneur*, while the crowd of other voices, other rhythmic versions, mill around. But this solipsistic solitude cannot maintain itself, however much it may protect itself with paralinguistic differentia and complexity; other voices, vocal multitudes, intervene. The reader-*flâneur*, having momentarily perhaps found his natural voice, envisages others, slips into others, enters the theatre of available dictions, where his own voice must now, too, be acted. And, in the end perhaps, critics' construction of a rigorous poetics for the prose poem is motivated by a desire to escape from the chaos of the paralinguistic, of the paralinguistic multitude, into the linguistic, from the rhythms of idiolectic saying into the rhythms of the said, the voice of the written.

As already anticipated, we do not need to rehearse the prose poem's formal debt to, and continuing kinship with, translation. A consequence of the prose poem's translational nature is its generation of a metatextual blind field, of a sense that it is reaching towards another (verse) text which we may think of as originary, as lost, and which we need to reconstruct.[8] This might lead us to suppose that, whatever critics may say about its autonomy, or 'gratuité', the prose poem is an open and unstable form. Prosaic rhythm only serves to endorse this supposition.

The first and most obvious concern that is likely to beset the translator of prose, therefore, is the arbitrariness of choice. Every choice can of course be justified in one way or another, but there are many instances in which one choice and its justification is no better than another choice and *its* justification. In my translation of 'Aube' (see below), one phrase began to focus my attention on the issues mentioned: 'et les ailes se levèrent sans bruit'. One might easily identify this as a decasyllable (as Fongaro does (1993: 340)), but that would entail counting the e mutes, and would still leave one with problems of shape. Does one simply read it as:

> et les ai/les se levè/rent sans bruit $3 + 4 + 3$

Or does one introduce a *coupe lyrique* as a way of generating an atmospheric envelope, a sense of the uncanny, and thus of achieving a classical caesural division (by a device that no classicizing poet would entertain):

> et les ailes/ se levè/rent sans bruit $4' + 3 + 3$

Or it might be read less eventfully, more prosaically, with an extended closing measure:

> et les ai/les se levèrent sans bruit $3 + 7$

Or, perhaps, after all, it is an octosyllable:

et les ail(es) se levèr(ent) sans bruit   3 + 3 + 2

At all events, I translated it, with little forethought, as 'and the wings that there were noiselessly took to the air'. Later, I checked my rendering against Varèse's ('and wings rose without a sound', 1957: 81), Bernard's ('and wings rose without a sound', 1962: 268), Fowlie's ('and wings rose up silently', 1966: 215), Schmidt's ('and wings rose soundlessly', 1976: 163), Sloate's ('and wings soared soundlessly', 1990: 79), Treharne's ('the wings rose noiselessly', 1998: 111), and Sorrell's 'and the wings lifted without a sound' (2001: 287). This array just looks like a determined effort to ring *all* the changes. Of course, there are differences: 'soared' presupposes something about the size of the wings; the translation of the definite article has modal and deictic implications, to which we have already adverted; 'noiselessly' or 'soundlessly' describe, to my ear, the absence of sounds which might otherwise have been expected, while 'silently' generates no such expectation; 'silently' and 'without a sound' imply, again to my ear, a greater intentionality than either 'noiselessly' or 'soundlessly'; 'without a sound' asks to be placed after the verb, rather than before it; a noise is cruder, less aurally assimilated, more random, than a sound. But these considerations aside, these versions might be thought to be pretty much of a muchness. Faced with this corrosive intrusion of the arbitrary, I realised that what mattered to me was not so much the words I had chosen, 'in themselves', but what they were able to project, or rather, how they themselves might be projected. What I mean by this is quite simple. Presented thus:

$$\times \times \quad / \quad \times \quad \times \quad / \quad / \quad \times \times \quad / \quad \times \quad \times \quad /$$
and the wings that there were noiselessly took to the air

the line consists of two anapaests followed by two dactyls and a final stressed syllable, articulated around a fulcrum of juxtaposed stresses: '. . . were/noise(lessly)'. These contiguous stresses create that syncopation, that buffering silent off-beat in the throat between them, which is the moment of sudden animation, release, coming to life. I can maintain this generative reversal of anapaest into dactyl in an alternative lineation:

and the wings that there were
                    noiselessly
                    took to the air

But here there are two further adjustments: by its isolation, 'noiselessly' not only becomes more challenging, alien, mysterious, but it also gathers intention; and 'took to the air' breaks out of the dactylic mode, to establish itself as an independent choriamb (/xx/), swinging from stress to stress. This variation leads me directly into another:

and the wings that there were
noiselessly took
to the air

where the swinging choriamb occurs a line earlier, allowing the final line both to resume the anapaestic pattern of the first line and to situate itself further from the ground—'the air' is here free space, uninhabited and expanding ether. This then suggests one further re-disposition:

and the wings that there were
noiselessly
took to
the air

In this final version, I am playing with back-and-forth rhythmic reversals: two anapaests reverse into a dactyl, which, shortened to a trochee ('noiselessly' > 'took to' = /xx > /x), reverses again into an iamb ('the air'); or, expressed in other traditional metrical terms, a rising rhythm shifts to falling, only to rise again in the final line. By disposing the words in this way, too, I derive some added semantic benefit: 'took to' having recovered some room of its own, can gravitate towards its other meaning, 'took a spontaneous liking to'. One might argue that 'the air', similarly, gains access to its musical potentiality. But there is no inherent virtue in polysemy.

The prose poem folds all these possible segmentations into itself. Is it then to betray the genre to draw them out, by typographic means, or at least to make this buried treasure visible? In the strictest sense, I am sure that it is. But if we have lost the art of reading prose, of knowing how to find its treasures; and if we remind ourselves that the translation is a provisional outfolding of textual possibility which should be folded back into the 'straight' text after use, then there is ample justification. Writers like Terdiman (1985), Monroe (1987) and Murphy (1992) have been at pains, and quite rightly so, to alert us to all that is subversive and interrogative in the prose poem. I would also want to suggest that Rimbaud's *Illuminations* are a dramatisation of a predicament embodied in the prose poem. 'Aube' also clearly allegorises this condition; as Guyaux puts it:

Se dérobant au jour et aux ténèbres, moment insaisissable de transition, elle constitue la naissance du jour sans pouvoir se constituer elle-même. On ne la voit guère, on ne la saisit pas. Elle passe entre les yeux. Elle est la fin de quelque chose et le commencement du contraire.

(1985b: 153)

[Giving both daylight and darkness the slip, this elusive moment of transition constitutes the birth of the day without being able to constitute itself. It is hardly visible, it cannot be grasped. It passes subliminally. It is the end of something and the beginning of its opposite.]

The prose poem is that chthonic material in which precious stones are buried and from which they may emerge, and from which wings may take flight. I have previously asked (1990: 110): 'Is the prose poem [. . .] a kind of proto-*vers libre*, a passage of prose in which one or more free-verse poems are buried, in a palimpsestic state, masked by the soil of prose, but awaiting their disinterment?' What is masking in prose are its equivocations about syllabification (the counting (or not) of the *e atone*, synaeresis or diaeresis) and segmentation (the varied possibilities of phrasing, complicated by potential pressures of lineation). The prose poem is the medium of all possibilities, and reading/translating is to some extent the thrusting of possibility into linear time; even Fongaro's discovered 'reminiscences' of verse-lines undergo this transformation: Benjaminian fragments of history which must make history, not as mirages of revival—it would require a context of other, isosyllabic lines to warrant that scenario—but as relics that can only survive by making new lives for themselves, not as memories but as opportunities. Of course, when critics write about Rimbaud's poetic ambitions they are usually, but not surprisingly, writing about the ambitions *they* have for Rimbaud's poetry. It is no different with translators.

Already we are embroiled in that web of contradictory impulses which make it difficult to keep a steady eye on objectives. We imagine a Rimbaud both writing, and writing about, a half-glimpsed linguistic utopia; in 'Aube',[9] he is both the narrator (perfect tense) and the protagonist (preterite and imperfect tense). But how confidently can we tell one from the other? Is it really all over before we begin? We imagine a translational enterprise which enjoins upon us not a task of interpretation, but the devising of ways to project Rimbaldian language so that it has a different *being* (rather than different meanings); but we constantly fall back from this vision of new linguistic being to familiar strategies of allegory and metaphor. There is perhaps nothing to be done: perhaps reading Rimbaud is to make inevitable this falling between two stools. What losses of faith are we, as readers, subject to?

My translation of 'Aube' is, then, a limited archaeology. It is a 'frayed' text, a text beginning to liberate itself in a dishevelment: the 'wasserfall blond qui s'échevela à travers les sapins':

Dawn

I've held
the summer dawn
         tight in my arms
         a minute long

Nothing yet was stirring on the palace façades. The water lay dead still. The shadows stayed bivouacked up by the wooded road. **I walked along**, nudging breaths awake, moistly warm and life-filled, and the precious stones looked about them,
   and the wings that there were
                noiselessly took
                to the air

The first venture? A flower told me its name, in the pathway already glinting with pale, fresh reflections.

I laughed at the wasserfall, its fair hair unravelling through the pines: at the silver-lit summit I recognised the goddess.

Then, one by one, I lifted her veils. In the avenue, waving my arms. Across the plain, where **I betrayed her** to the cock. In the city, she made off among the belfries and domes, and scampering,
         like a beggar,
              I chased her
                    along the marbled
                    quais

At the top of the road, near a laurel wood, **I put my arms round her**
                        in her massed veils
                        and **felt**
                        something

>   of her
>   immeasurable body.
>   Dawn and the child fell together at the foot of the wood
>
>   It was noon
>   when I
>   finally
>   opened my eyes

One of the implicit arguments of this book is that the prose poem helped to foster certain fundamental shifts in our perception of verse-textural mechanisms, the shift from rhetoricity to performativity, from the determination of accent by syllabic structure to the determination of accent by improvised phrasing, and the shift from exostructure to endotexture. Crudely put, we shift from a text whose coherence derives from the combination of constituent parts, designed to be immediately recognizable to the reader, and with an inbuilt rhetorical or rhythmic pedigree, so that they already make sense of the matter they carry, to a text whose coherence derives not from the sum of the parts but from the set of interactions that they release at a textural level, at the level of the half-heard and the associatively aleatory. The Rimbaldian text does not make sense of itself, by virtue of structural indices; it has to be made sense of by the active inhabitation of its acoustic networks, its rhythmic imbrications, and the connotative affinities within it. Commentaries (see, for example, Kloepfer and Oomen 1970; Guyaux 1985b) have drawn out the undeniable exostructural patterning to be found in these poems; but these are not so much goals of aesthetic achievement as beginnings, triggers of transphrastic promiscuity, measures of modulation, platforms of interaction.

The child (reader) embraces the veiled Dawn and feels something of her immeasurable body. What one feels as one vocally palpates this translation is, I hope, the play of x x (in anapaest, dactyl, choriamb, second and third paeon), because this double-weak configuration conveys Rimbaud's Cubist prepositionality ('in my', 'on the', 'at the', 'near a', 'to the', 'in her', etc.); the poet is both travelling protagonist and the disembodied eye of the camera; one-point perspective yields to planar jumps, so that the very movement of time destabilises space, destroys its continuity.

I have, in broad terms, tried to exploit rhythmic diversity in two ways. First, I have engineered sequences of progressive variation, for example:

>   and scampering,   × / × ×

> like a beggar,   × × / ×
>
>> I chased her   × / ×
>>
>>> along the marbled   × / × /
>>>
>>>> quais   /

(i.e. 2nd paeon > 3rd paeon > amphibrach (remove weak head-syllable) > iambic (alternation initiated by amphibrach).

Or:

> in her massed veils   × × / /
> and felt   × /
> something   / ×
> of her   × ×
> immeasurable body   × / × × / ×

(i.e. ionic > iamb (heart of ionic) > trochee (syncopated reversal) > pyrrhic (the tune) > 'flanked' choriamb (the measures of the three previous lines combined).

Secondly, I have created echoes of identical or closely related rhythmic phrases, probably operating at a half-heard level, e.g. choriamb and variation: 'tight in my arms', 'on the palace façades', 'and the wings that there were', 'noiselessly took', 'told me its name', 'glinting with pale', 'I laughed at the wasserfall', 'I lifted her veils', 'waving my arms', 'belfries and domes', 'immeasurable body', 'Dawn and the child', 'opened my eyes'; 2nd and 3rd paeon: 'the water lay', 'in the pathway', 'unravelling', 'I recognized', 'In the avenue', 'In the city', 'and scampering', 'near a laurel', 'my arms round her'.

Clearly, these two categories of rhythmic phrasing interfere with each other, and often the distinction between them depends entirely on choices of segmentation. Otherwise, there are resurgences of the iambic sequence with which the translation begins; but the blunt matter-of-factness of iambic is always likely to be undermined by the swinging cadences of the rest of the adventure, such as

> Across the plain where I betrayed her to the cock

where × / × / × / × / × / × / easily slips into × / × / - × × × / × - × × /.

One of those linguistic elements whose being Rimbaud changes is tense. For him, in tenses, modality all but replaces temporality; from his verbs we derive a stronger sense of how things happen and of attitudes to events, than of when they happen. If it is important to translate Rimbaud's opening *passé composé* with an English perfect, it is not only to indicate that the action has persisting consequences, but also to mark the assumption of a responsibility by the agent, to increase the challenging self-assertiveness of the declaration. The *passé composé* is part of the confessional mode of *Une saison en enfer* ('Je me suis séché à l'air du crime'; 'J'ai reçu au cœur le coup de grâce'; 'J'ai avalé une fameuse gorgée de poison'), but here, as there, the tone—insolent? self-indicting? regretful? ironically grandiose?—all but escapes us. And it is worth insisting: the *passé composé* invites tonal speculation in a way that the more 'innocent' past historic and imperfect do not. Not surprisingly, all instances of the *passé composé* in 'Aube' occur with the first-person singular, and only one, the inaugural first, can be comfortably translated as a perfect. I have resorted therefore to the simplest and least intrusive way of indicating the instances of the *passé composé*, namely a bold typeface.

As noted by Guyaux, 'l'imparfait des trois premières phrases désigne tout ce qui est préalable à l'éveil' (1985b: 149) [the imperfect tense of the first three sentences designates all that is prior to the awakening]. This would seem to be the tense of inertial resistance, but since two of the instances are negative, and one governed by 'encore', we can feel pressure already being applied to them. The second brief appearance of the imperfect ('fuyait', 'chassais'), also introduced by a *passé composé* ('je l'ai dénoncé au coq') has a very different character. The moment of the flight and the pursuit has, built into its imperfectivity, a certain longing for perpetuation, for a goal-oriented and linear dynamic that would not disappoint.

It is as if the *passé composé* were the agent of tense modulation, the magician who produces changes of atmospheric pressure, changes in the possible futures of a world. The past historics which are conjured by 'J'ai marché' certainly have an exhilarating peremptoriness, unexpectedness, and, like all past historics, they open up for us something anarchic, something absolutely assertive: *libre arbitre*. But, by the same token, they generate no connections; they are explosions of instants that create no history and potentially leave no traces; they suddenly remove, supersede, what they just as suddenly granted. These verbs relate to each other only by the accident of sequence, of consecutiveness. Otherwise, they isolate themselves in spaces of their own. The poet here does what he can to make a narrative, to imply causality, to endow sequence with consequence But the resources called upon are hardly equal to the task: coordinating conjunctions, relative clauses, coordinating punctuation (colon), adjectival and adverbial indications ('La première entreprise fut . . .'; 'Alors. . .'). These devices are as disjunctive as they are conjunctive: 'et' is purely aggregational, the relatives, which need to be restrictive, drift into the non-restrictive, the colon problematises relationship as much as confirms it (what does it mean?), and the adjectival/adverbial inserts stand out too insistently from a tense which has a high degree of unselfconscious spontaneity in it.

One way of sharpening our sense of the modalisation of tense is to build into our apprehension of text a sense of the music of *désinences* and their assimilation into contextual acousticity. Guyaux (1985b: 150) most pertinently brings to our attention the dissemination of the /ɛ/ of the third-person plural of the past historic into the immediate textual environment:

> Le son *è*, caractérisant la désinence du passé simple à la troisième personne du pluriel, se propage alors dans la phrase pour signifier par de multiples échos que l'instant est privilégié: (. . .) *les haleines vives et tièdes, et les pierreries regardèrent, et les ailes se levèrent* (. . .).
> [The /ɛ/ sound, characteristic of the ending of the past historic in the third-person plural, thus spreads through the sentence to signify, by its multiple echoes, that this is a privileged moment: (. . .) *les haleines vives et tièdes, et les pierreries regardèrent, les ailes se levèrent* (. . .)].

English verb forms do not have the endings which can act as the distributors of acousticity in the same way. But I have tried to use verb-roots, personal pronouns and adverbs to similar purpose. It is the pronoun 'I' (in 'I've held') which attracts 'tight' and 'my'; 'walked' has an adumbration in 'water' and an after-echo in 'warm', consolidated by the alliterating w's (see also 'wooded', 'awake', 'wings'); the word-initial schwa of 'along' is picked up by 'awake' and 'about'; the /eɪ/ of 'betrayed' seems to generate the following verbs 'made off', 'chased' and closes in 'quais' (pronounced /ke/ or /keɪz/); finally, 'put' and 'felt' produce 'fell' and 'foot', to complete the chiastic pattern, with 'wood' as an after-echo. It is not, therefore, quite possible for this translation to claim that tense (ending) has enacted its modality in the acoustic associations it activates; but at least verb-forms themselves seem, perhaps, to propel linear time towards a consummation, expressed in the temporary suspension of chiasmus, before time again intervenes. Acoustic instants, flickering across the text, become a moment.

Dawn and the child, text and reader, fall together at the foot of the wood. It is already too late at the awakening. I certainly would not wish to push this convenient parallel too far. But there is a sense in which, during the sleep of childhood/dawn, Rimbaud suggests, faculties of intuition and sensory cross-connection, sensitivity to rhythmic or phonemic invitation, the ability to thrive on the unresolved, on the spaces of intersection and transition, are all active, potent. Childhood is both the risk and the freedom of parataxis, the risk and explosiveness of the past historic. When one awakens, perhaps, modality becomes tense, the tense of dragging time.

To finish this chapter, I would like to offer a version of the second of the 'Jeunesse' cycle, 'Sonnet', partly because this poem confirms how improvised Rimbaud's practice is, partly because it allows me to take journeys in temporality that I believe Rimbaud has taken.

It is reliably assumed that 'Sonnet' received its title as an afterthought, when Rimbaud realised that his text covered fourteen lines, thanks to the size of the paper on which it was written:[11]

> Le titre de *Sonnet* procède d'une (re)lecture parodique après transcription—peut-être indice d'une allusion à ou d'une collusion avec Verlaine: elle est induite par la disposition du manuscrit (un papier plus large ou plus étroit aurait tout changé).
>
> (Murat 2000: 261)
>
> [The title, 'Sonnet', derives from a parodic (re)reading after transcription—perhaps indicative of an allusion to, or collusion with, Verlaine: it is brought about by the layout of the manuscript (a broader or narrower type of paper would have changed everything)]

The speculation about Verlaine here is based on the similarity between the concerns of the opening lines ('chair/ ô aimer') and the subject (and expression) of Verlaine's sonnet 'Invocation' (sent to Lepelletier 16 May 1873), which, after significant revisions, became 'Luxures' in *Jadis et naguère* (1883). This in turn has led to the attribution of certain of the terms: 'calculs' (= Verlaine, stratagems employed to keep Rimbaud), 'impatiences' (= Rimbaud, see 'Vagabonds'), 'danse' (= Rimbaud, see 'Phrases'), 'voix' (= Verlaine, so frequent a feature in his verse). Alternatively, the dualities are ascribed to the founding duality ('Chair/Amour') of Verlaine's poem (Raybaud 1989: 176–86). Rimbaud will also have noticed that the layout in the manuscript creates *rimes embrassées* in the first four lines ('chair/ verger; - ô/ prodiguer; - ô/ terre') and that 'Mais à présent' creates a convenient *volta* or turn, even if it does occur a line too early. But it only goes to bear out his own impatience.

But even if it only occurred to Rimbaud by chance to capitalise on the layout of his poem in its title and thus add parodic zest to his dialogue with Verlaine about the flesh and love, about pastoral prodigality and georgic labour, the prose poem is no stranger to the sonnet. There are other *Illuminations* in which one feels the urgings of sonnet structure (for example, 'Fairy', 'Mystique', 'Ville'); Baudelaire's 'Le Désespoir de la vieille' looks like an enclosed sonnet in the manner of his 'L'Avertisseur'; Mallarmé's prose translations from Poe include a 'Sonnet à la Science'; one might be excused for thinking that Pierre Louÿs's *Chansons de Bilitis* (1894) are a prose sonnet-sequence, a formal 'modernisation' of what purport to be translations of elegies, idylls and epigrams; more recently, one thinks of Jouve's translations of Shakespeare's sonnets (1969). And if, as we have already pointed out, the prose poem frequently wishes to be seen as the translation of a verse original, then I have tried to take the journey back to origins:

> *Man* of common constitution, was not your
> Flesh a fruit hanging in the orchard;—o
> Childhood days! The body a treasure to expend;—o
> Loving, Psyche imperilled, or
>
> Psyche's strength? The earth had inclines thick with princes
> And artists, and race and progeny
> Urged you to crimes and mournings: your destiny
> And risk, the world. But that labour long since
>
> Fulfilled,—you, your calculations,—you, your bouts
> Of impatience—are no more than your dance
> And voice, unfixed, unforced, although a reason
>
> For a double happening of invention and advance
> —in human brotherhood and discretion throughout
> the image-empty universe—the present season
>
> Only now esteems the dance and voice
> Reflected both in justice and in force.

Rimbaud saw a piece of prose on the page and fell to thinking it might be a sonnet. The translator wrote a sonnet only to find that the material fitted the page but not the form. There were two options: to translate a prose sonnet into a 'tailed' verse sonnet, as here; or to translate the prose sonnet so that it fitted the page as no more than a piece of prose. This latter solution (see Appendix II (i) for text) allows the performance of a symbolic act.

In leading the wayward sonnet back to prose, one is asking prose to re-embed the sonnet in its own undifferentiatedness, so that prosodic structures are free to re-imagine themselves and so that particular elements cease to be bound by pre-ordained roles (rhyme-words, line-initial words, markers of caesuras). What we begin to understand is that, as the nineteenth century progressed, the prose poem shifted its position in relation to verse. Under the Romantic dispensation, the prose poem promoted its guarded, or muted lyricism, by advertising itself as the imperfect shadow of a lost poetic origin; the reader was invited to imagine the intense lyric springs that lay behind the prosaic garrulousness; the prose poem was a straining back towards form, towards the clouded Idea. As, with Symbolism, verse and prose began to converge, so prose itself became the origin, the primordial mud from which any number of flowers might spring. The prose poem is the medium to which verse returns to replenish itself and from which new segmentations, new acoustic arrangements, constantly emerge: 'Oh les pierres précieuses qui se cachaient,—les fleurs qui regardaient déjà' [Oh the precious stones that hid themselves,—the flowers which already looked about them].[10] But in Rimbaud's world, the mineral of the past can find new life as the vegetable of the present: 'et les pierreries regardèrent' [and the precious stones looked about them]; and, in Rimbaud's world things buried in the earth do not require a strenuous archaeology: they de-sediment themselves: 'bijoux debout sur le sol gras des bosquets et des jardinets dégelés' [jewels standing on the muddy soil of the groves and of the little gardens in the thaw] ('Enfance I').

Memory, then, should not belong to the cyclical and recurrent, nor to the excavated; memory, too, naturally de-sediments itself as part of linear progression, of the creative drive: 'Ta mémoire et tes sens ne seront que la nourriture de ton impulsion créatrice' [Your memory and your senses will only serve to feed your creative impulse] ('Jeunesse IV'). In transposing 'Sonnet' into a 'purer' prose, we are merely confirming what the poem already speaks of: the transition from a past balanced precariously between 'péril' on the one hand, and 'force' and 'fortune' on the other, a world rich in myth (Psyche), nobility (princes) and art, but which for that very reason preconditions one to anti-social acts (crimes) and the habit of regretting loss (mournings). Through the work of the poetic 'travailleur' one enters a present in which the arts of ongoing temporality, of linear time (voice and dance) are the very models of justice and force, a present which motivates a new fraternalism and altruistic self-effacement (discretion). This is a world in which static representation, images, have no place, are superseded by the lived dynamics of voice and dance, the principle of metamorphosis. About this latter principle we shall have more to say in Chapter 4; but we should at least immediately insist that the thrusting of this 'sonnet' further towards linear time is also the means whereby its particular set of concepts (force, fortune, peril, and so forth) can begin to shake off any obligation to a stable set of values/meanings, and, like Rimbaud and Verlaine in dialogue, can continually adjust relationship, and take up new colourings and functions. The telegraphic syntax, the impatiences of the dash and its abrupt cross-cuttings, produce a dance of sense which it would be unwise to try to systematise (mea culpa). This is the space of the unfixed and the unforced. The specificities of 'toi' and 'toi' are absorbed in the multiform 'votre', which is itself further de-identified by the adoption of the definite article. And by disenfranchising one particular acoustic system, a system enjoying something of a repressive monopoly, namely rhyme, we release other sounds, and the rhyme-words themselves, to animate the hubbub of the text.

The prose poem thus abandons the otherworldly 'studio'-time of regular verse and opts for lived time, but a lived time constantly intersected by other temporalities. It would be convenient if we could identify the prose poem with Bergsonian *durée*, but its linear time is leaner, more driven by external pressure. In fact, the Rimbaldian prose poem makes it difficult to distinguish between inner and outer, I and other, the representative and the indexical. But this ambiguity means that we must always read tense for aspect and modality as much as for tense, and we must always find the time buried in non-temporal words: if Rimbaud's combinations of abstract and concrete nouns disorientate the reader, it is partly because they belong to different temporalities; abstractions are syntheses of experience which presuppose a past, a period during which they have been tried out, nourished and have achieved a currency, while concrete nouns are subject to the existential vicissitudes of their referents, even in the world of hallucination. Our investigations into Rimbaldian time will be resumed in Chapter 4.

3

The Voice in Translation I
Translating Subdiscursive Sound

A speaker, a heavy smoker of about 65, overweight, sceptical but generous, reads a sonnet by Shakespeare. In this act, a voice, which in its normal communicative functions is not listened to as a voice, designates itself. The voice as voice makes itself audible, Shakespeare's words sculpt this voice, rather than the reverse; Shakespeare makes it desirable to hear this voice. Shakespeare becomes this voice's temperament at the time; a text by Byron or Ted Hughes would produce other inflexions and colourings. We are inclined to think that speakers are only incidents in the life of a text. But the contrary is true: texts are parts of our physiology, absorbed into our vocal cords. So, a task: to imagine a translation which is not only a text, but a textualised vocality through which a voice could embody itself. I prefer 'vocality' to 'voice' here, because what I envisage in a text is something rather more generalised, not a voice but the quality of voice, available to be actualised by *a* voice. But the voice is not quite as unified as that indefinite article would wish: our encounter with our voice, as heard by others, outside, is as traumatic as our encounter with the mirror; the voice inside our heads is only ever heard by us, will never be heard by anyone else.

Any propositions made about the presence of voice in poetry should be qualified by an awareness of what we lack (Meschonnic 1982: 277–96): any anthropological history of the voice; a proper understanding of the relation between the natural (inherited) voice and its cultural manifestations,[1] between the voice and its dictions; a comparative history of the voice/poetry connection: perhaps, in translating Rimbaud into greater vocality, I am pursuing a peculiarly national proclivity:

De Wordsworth à Hopkins, à Pound et à Eliot, la nouveauté

poétique s'est toujours faite en anglais dans un rapport nouveau au parlé, jusqu'aux beatniks et à Charles Olson. La voix y est nécessairement située par le primat, ou l'histoire, de l'oralité. [. . .] Les traditions poétiques qui régissent la modernité en français, toutes diverses qu'elles sont, convergent toutes vers une censure de l'oralité, et de la voix.

(Meschonnic 1982: 290).

[From Wordsworth to Hopkins, Pound and Eliot, poetic renewal has always been produced in English by a new relationship with the spoken, up to and including the beatniks and Charles Olson. The voice necessarily finds its place there through the pre-eminence, or history, of orality. (. . .) The poetic traditions which govern modernity in French, diverse as they are, all converge on a censoring of orality and of the voice.]

One of the observations that might emerge from an anthropological history of the voice would concern the attitudes towards the voice shared by the speech-trainers of professional actors. Here, the voice carries the metaphysical burden of whole-person identity, of self-centering, and becomes a magnetic point of convergence for a bundle of self-projective impulses.[2] The voice is the way we resist the insidious inroads of non-vocal or non-identity speech: jargons, cybernetic modes, text-messaging. Speech training seems to wish to maximise self-expression and communication as two aspects of the same operation, two complementary and reciprocally enhancing initiatives:

Your voice is the means by which you convey your inner self and your inner thoughts and feelings in an immediate way to other people—the outside world. It is the outward expression of your inner self, a sort of channel from inside to outside, and is therefore a very particular expression of you and your personality.

(Berry 2000: 6)

The development of voice control involves self-discipline and the vigilant anticipation of any backsliding which signals the deactivation of will and choice, or surrender to 'spontaneity':

If, on the other hand, by spontaneity you mean that state where our unconscious motivations take control and we are being run by our habitual responses—who needs it?

(McCallion 1998: 25)

But Robert Bresson sees the training of the voice as entailing its detachment from the body: under the heading '*Voix naturelle, voix travaillée*' [*Natural voice, trained voice*], he writes: 'La voix: âme faite chair. Travaillée comme chez X, elle n'est plus ni âme ni chair. Instrument de précision, mais instrument à part' (1988: 67) [The voice: soul made flesh. Trained as in the case of X, it is neither soul nor flesh any more. A precision instrument, but an instrument separated from us].[3] Clearly, some distinction should be made between uses of the voice in 'institutionalised' or 'perennialised' environments (acting, recitation, lecturing, political speechifying) and the spoken which 'néglige tout cadre et toute finalité institutionnelle, pour "coller" à l'élan de la parole et un dynamisme de la pulsion' (Collomb 1997: 20) [disregards any framework, any institutionalised purpose, to 'cling' to vocal impulse and a pulsional dynamic]. And clearly, while metrical verse may be seen as institutionalising the voice (or, rather, transcendentalising it), the prose poem opens up a space in which the voice can recover some of its lost 'pulsionality', can range widely across its own diversity, its responses to contradictory beckonings, to changing tonal possibility, to tensions between the holophrastic and the hypotactic.

It seems logically impossible, with a language communally shared, for each of us to affirm his/her own unique perception of reality. Ironically, communication and self-expression seem often to be at loggerheads. As Paul Valéry puts it: 'Le langage constitue un autre en toi' [Language constitutes an other in you] (quoted by Stimpson 1995: 23). This sense of language-use as a process of dispossession—language dispossesses us of our world, we are dispossessed of language—is a founding conviction of post-Cratylic, and especially Saussurean, thinking, and vocal training can only allow us to master language as an available instrument of communication; it cannot lead us back to the integrity of the linguistic body ('Tout le corps humain présent *sous la voix*' (Valéry 1960: 549) [The whole human body present *within the voice*]). I find it curious, in these circumstances, that more has not been made of the singularities and inimitabilities, of the human voice. No doubt part of the reason for this absence of attention to individual vocal characteristics is a corresponding emphasis upon the shared systems of voice-use which are subsumed within paralinguistics. In *some* senses, the voice is overlooked by that very discipline, linguistics, which seems most to affirm its presence.

When linguistics *has* turned to voice quality, as most comprehensively perhaps in John Laver's *The Phonetic Description of Voice Quality* (1980), it has had to acknowledge the limits of its knowledge:

In his *Institutes of Oratory*, Quintilian wrote that 'The voice of a person is as easily distinguished by the ear as the face by the eye' (c. III, Book XI). The importance of an individual speaker's voice in everyday social interaction, as an audible index of his identity, personality and mood, could hardly be overstated. Yet we know now only a little more about the factors that give rise to different qualities of voice than Quintilian did.

(1980: 1)

Laver chooses, for his investigation, a broad view of what constitutes voice quality ('a cumulative abstraction over a period of time of a speaker-characterizing quality, which is gathered from the momentary and spasmodic fluctuations of short-term articulation used by the speaker for linguistic and paralinguistic communication', 1980, 1) and looks to do justice to this broader view by concentrating his attention on 'settings' (the 'background, auditory "colouring" running through sequences of shorter-term segmental articulations' (1980: 2)), rather than on segments (single sounds). But ultimately Laver admits that he must largely leave aside the 'idiosyncrasies' of voice quality, those features which relate to the purely organic, the accidents of an individual's vocal apparatus; his principal preoccupation is with the uses to which voice-settings are put, as signals of group membership and instances of social codes. If anything, the study of phonetics, in linguistics, has been peculiarly aphonic, in the sense that voice-sounds are devocalised, isolated, purified, made almost abstract as IPA notations, and thus exist in a milieu without an acoustic, without resonance and without the body. And the literary analysts, for their part ('myself among them, booming with the worst') convert the unavailability of the voice in the text into the notion of 'verbal music', as if language without voice had a describable acousticity; but only the voice can make language sound.

We might present the situation described in the previous paragraphs in the following manner:

Pronunciation	Articulation
(voice quality, timbre[4])	(expressivity, training)

<<<<<speed>>>>>
<<<<<pausing>>>>>
<<<<<tone>>>>>
<<<<<loudness>>>>>
<<<<<intonation>>>>>
<<<<<degree of stress>>>>>

semiotic	symbolic

68

My present argument is a simple one: the paralinguistic features listed (speed, pausing, and so forth) have two faces, one turned towards the innate physiology of the voice, its timbre, the other towards expressive resourcefulness, towards strategic uses of paralanguage; in criticism, we have ceased to acknowledge the existence of the former (left-hand column); put another way, the right-hand column exists at the expense of the left-hand column; put another way, voice is superseded by its own expressivity.

The sense of the collision of two principles at the heart of language is a vivid one, and is often expressed, although in contradictory ways, as the collision between vowels and consonants. Lecourt (1999: 16) argues that vowels belong to sound or the voice, are emitted, and are a resource we share with animals; consonants, on the other hand, belong to articulation, are indeed articulated, and are a resource peculiar to humans; consonants order and give shape to vowels, transform vowels into language. In the light of proposals like this, one might care to revisit the comparative significance of open and closed syllables, and, in French, to masculine (most frequently open) and feminine (most frequently closed) rhymes. On the other hand, consonants, produced by stopping or impeding the airstream, are non-harmonic noises, while vowels, produced with the airstream unobstructed, are harmonic (musical) sounds.

These two principles might equally be related to Kristeva's psycholinguistic distinction between the geno-text, that pre-systemic process which includes psychic drives finding their way to articulacy, and the pheno-text, the text which has achieved system, which obeys the rules of communication, which presupposes a subject of enunciation and an addressee (1974: 83–6). And if the geno-text is the semiotic in the symbolic, then we might ascribe to the voice the power to activate or dredge up those semiotic presences: 'Si on peut l'imaginer dans le cri, les vocalises ou les gestes de l'enfant, le sémiotique fonctionne en fait dans le discours adulte comme rythme, prosodie, jeu de mots, non-sens du sens, rire' (1977: 14) [If one can imagine it in the cry, in vocalises, or the vocal gestures of children, the semiotic in fact functions in adult speech as rhythm, prosody, word-play, the non-sense of sense, laughter].

Kristeva's geno/pheno distinction is borrowed by Barthes as 'géno-chant' and 'phéno-chant' in his differentiation of the voices of Charles Panzéra and Dietrich Fischer-Dieskau in his 1972 essay 'Le Grain de la voix' and its 1977 sequel 'La Musique, la voix, la langue'. Panzéra's cultivation of the 'grain de la voix' means that his voice emerges directly from his body, 'du fond des cavernes, des muscles, des muqueuses, des cartilages' (1982a: 238) [from deep in the cavities, the muscles, the mucous membranes, the cartilages], is principally located in the throat and is concerned with the diction, the pronunciation, of his language. Pronunciation is about the phonetic production of language, about acoustic quality in the voice. Barthes sums up: 'Le "grain", ce serait cela: la matérialité du corps parlant sa langue maternelle : peut-être la lettre; presque sûrement la signifiance' (1982a: 238) [The 'grain' is that: the physicality of the body speaking its mother tongue: perhaps the letter; almost certainly its *signifiance*]. Fischer-Dieskau's singing on the other hand, concentrates on expressivity, subjectivity; it privileges the lungs, breathing, and is concerned with articulation, that is to say, with the clarity of projected meaning, with the coded ways of communicating feeling, with a rhetoric of the voice. The 'grain de la voix' is geno-textual in the sense that it is where the pulsional life of the speaker's/singer's body, and the pulsional life of language in its materiality, conjoin; the geno-text is a play of signifiers where meaning is always in the process of being made, unmade, re-made; it is 'un jeu signifiant' [a signifying play]—of ever-emergent, but no more than emergent, articulacy—'étranger à la communication, à la représentation (des sentiments), à l'expression' (1982a: 239) [nothing to do with communication, representation (of feelings), expression]. The expressive voice, on the other hand, is pheno-textual inasmuch as it is achieved signification, can represent a signified, and inasmuch as its resources and effects have been systematised, made as fully articulate as possible, in the service of communicative and expressive efficiency. But Fischer-Dieskau's accomplishment as a singer involves the sacrifice of the uniqueness of German in the interests of 'une culture *moyenne*' (1982a: 241) [an *average* culture], a clear translingual perception of what is expressively possible; whereas Panzéra's singing realizes the body of the French language in the body of his own voice; he gives the Frenchness of French in the particularities of a pronunciation which has not generalised itself into an articulation. Panzéra, unlike Fischer-Dieskau, does not sacrifice being to function.

But it has been no easier for writers to separate out the various components of voice. In Chapter 10 of *Nana* (1880), Zola describes the qualities of Daguenet's voice which ensure his success with the ladies and their immediate effect on Nana herself:

> Les grands succès de Daguenet auprès des dames étaient dus à la douceur de sa voix, une voix d'une pureté et d'une souplesse musicales, qui l'avait fait surnommer chez les filles Bouche-de-Velours. Toutes cédaient, dans la caresse sonore dont il les enveloppait. Il connaissait cette force, il l'endormit d'un bercement

sans fin de paroles, lui contant des histoires imbéciles. Quand ils quittèrent la table d'hôte, elle était toute rose, vibrante à son bras, reconquise. Comme il faisait très beau, elle renvoya sa voiture, l'accompagna à pied jusque chez lui, puis monta naturellement. Deux heures plus tard, elle dit, en se rhabillant: 'Alors, Mimi, tu y tiens, à ce mariage ?'

(Zola 1968: 313)

[Daguenet's successes with the ladies were owed to the softness of his voice, a voice of musical purity and suppleness, which had earned him the nickname 'Velvet-Mouth' among the good-time girls. All women surrendered to the sonorous caress which enveloped them. He knew the power of his voice, he lulled her [Nana] to sleep with an endless lullaby of words, recounting ridiculous stories. When they left the *table d'hôte*, she was all flushed, quivering on his arm, reconquered. As it was a fine evening, she sent her carriage home, accompanied him on foot to his lodgings, and went upstairs without ado. Two hours later, she said, as she dressed: 'So, Mimi, you're still set on it then, this marriage ?']

It is not difficult to reconstruct some of the features of this irresistible voice, simply because Zola seems to have described it by listening to it in the text, by making it audible to himself (and to the reader). The first string that strikes us is probably /da/ (Daguenet) > /da/ (dames) > /dy/ (dus) > /dusœR/ (douceur) > /vwa/ (voix), which tells us of a voice voicing on initial consonants, gradually establishing a vibrato which ends by communicating itself to Nana ('vibrante à son bras') and which still rings in her order to her coachman ('renvoya sa voiture'). In fact, this latter clause is informed by voice (/vwa/: 'renvoya', 'voiture') ostensibly Nana's, but, one feels, itself permeated by Daguenetian inflexions. The vocalic run that we encounter here takes us from low, unrounded (/a/), through high, rounded (/y/, /u/), back to low, unrounded (/a/), in what already feels like a gesture of flirtation; but it is in the dark warmth of /u/ that this voice is most at home ('souplesse', 'Bouche', 'Velours'), a /u/ which apparently plays on, plays against, its high, front, but still rounded partner /y/ ('pureté', 'musicales', 'surnommer'). It is also apparent that while Daguenet may score with the throaty vibrations of /d/, /v/ and /b/, he also manipulates the suggestive whispers and tendernesses of unvoiced alveolar /s/ ('douceur', 'sa', 'souplesse', 'surnommer', 'cédaient', 'caresse sonore'), unvoiced bilabial /p/ ('pureté', 'souplesse', 'enveloppait', 'paroles') and unvoiced labiodental /f/ ('fait', 'filles', 'force', 'fin'). There is also much to be made of the lateral alveolar /l/.

But is this an itemisation of particular phonemes that Daguenet exploits, manipulates, in order to achieve this copulation through the ear, which translates itself, almost immediately, into 'real' intercourse (i.e. right-hand column of paralanguage)? Or is this an attempt on Zola's part to use a set of phonemes to capture the timbre of Daguenet's voice whatever he is saying (i.e. left-hand column of paralanguage)? Or a mixture of both? We cannot really tell. But it is another feature of voice I want to isolate at this point: the way in which voice subverts and redistributes language, undoes its etymological differentiations by pressing the suit of homophony. As we have mentioned, 'voix' is to be heard in both 'renvoya' and 'voiture', but the etymological origins of each 'voix' are different: the '-voy-' of 'renvoya' derives from 'via', while the 'voit-' of 'voiture' derives from 'vectura' ('action de transporter') and thus from 'vehere'. The voice quite literally scumbles etymology and encourages the fantasy of false etymology. And this tendency may result in powerful, surreptitious affects. /ã/, as a prefix, is an important player in this passage— 'enveloppait', 'endormit', 'renvoya'—but it has two contradictory meaning-clusters: (a) within, and gradual process to an end point ('encercler', 'encadrer', 'endormir', 'envelopper', 'embrasser'); (b) motion away, point of departure ('emmener', 'envoyer', 'enlever'). In this passage, one might argue, the latter cluster is ousted by the former, so that 'renvoya' *sounds like* a re-encompassment, a re-envelopment, by voice: Nana's instruction to her coachman is like an imitation of Daguenet's effect on her. Rimbaud's own vocal characteristics might seem to encourage similar kinds of auditory 'misunderstanding' and mistaken assumption.

We know quite a lot, from scattered fragments, about Rimbaud's accent/pronunciation, but little about the physiological variables of his voice. Verlaine remembers the adolescent 'de qui la voix très accentuée en ardennais, presque patoisante, avait ces hauts et ces bas de la mue' (quoted in Steinmetz 1999: 102) [whose voice, with its strong Ardennes accent, almost *patois*-speaking, had the high and low pitches of puberty]. Robb's reading of the evidence suggests an equally self-affirming vocal presence: 'Rimbaud's own accent was thick and distinctive, with emphatic working-class vowels' (2000: 57). But this socio-regional 'loyalty' also seems to have been impressionable: 'To Verlaine's dismay, Rimbaud even managed to lose his provincial accent, which suggests a serious concession to the prestige of Paris' (Robb 2000: 139). Delahaye speaks of the displacement of the 'bel accent ardennais' [attractive Ardennes accent] by 'l'accent *faubourien*' [the accent *of the suburbs*] (quoted in Chambon 1983: 7), and tells us that, as an epigraph to 'Vieux Coppées VII', Verlaine noted: 'L'accent parisiano-ardennais *desideratur*' (Verlaine 1962: 1142).

Linguists have indicated to us what Rimbaud's accent is likely to have entailed (see, for example, Chambon 1983 and Steinmetz 1999: 102, footnote: 'tendance à la vélarisation du [a] antérieur, désorganisation des é fermés et des é ouverts, confusion des glides [w] et [y] (« huit » est prononcé « oui » et inversement « oui » devient « ui »), éventuellement difficulté à discriminer [ã] et [õ] dans des mots comme « blanc », « blond », etc.') [tendency to velarisation of the front /a/, confusion of closed /e/ and open /ɛ/, confusion of glides /w/ and /ɥ/ ('huit' is pronounced 'oui' and conversely 'oui' becomes 'ui'), possibly a difficulty in differentiating /ã/ and /õ/ in words like 'blanc', 'blond', and so forth], and we have Verlaine's 'Vieux Coppées IV—IX' as an indication of what regular verse might sound like if modelled on a Rimbaldian delivery. A further speculative insertion of the Rimbaldian voice into his own texts is suggested by Robb:

> In fact, the poem thought to be Rimbaud's wildest display of prosodic irregularity—'Bonne pensée du matin'—has a regular rhythm if the voice is allowed to recite it instead of counting its syllables, while some of his 'incorrect' rhymes are perfectly harmonious when pronounced with what Verlaine called Rimbaud's '*parisiano-ardennais*' accent.
>
> (2000: 162)

And the critical apparatus of Albert Py's 1967 edition of the *Illuminations* lists apparent instances, in the manuscripts, of the 'désorganisation des é fermés et des é ouverts': for example, 'Dèluges' (4), 'près' for 'prés' (27, 42), 'dèvorante' (60), 'Pèlopponèse' (63), 'dèfense'(63), 'Mètamorphoses' (69). These kinds of acoustic 'slippage' seem to parallel those grammatical and formal slippages to which we have already referred.

But it is not a Rimbaldian voice that we would wish to reconstitute in the text; simply a vocality, a voice quality which would reconnect the materiality of the text with the materiality of the body.[5] And beyond that we wish to restore orality to the text, too, to produce a translation which, although written, re-installs the conditions of the oral tradition.

We are accustomed to making distinctions between the oral and the written, as distinct uses of language, with different forms and different communicative intentions/assumptions. And it is usually assumed that when a written text is read, it does not yield up its writtenness, since that writtenness is indelibly inscribed in its lexicon and its syntactic structures— the voice performs or recites the written text as *énoncé*; the voice is the *énonciation* of an *énoncé*, the saying of the already said. What would happen, however, if, through strategies of layout and presentation, the written text would allow the voice to transform it into the oral? The difficulty is that writtenness loads the dice in favour of right-hand paralinguisticity. Too easily the written text becomes a passive, available scenario designed for displays of articulacy. Valéry describes the change from oral to written as involving the transformation 'du rythmé et enchaîné à l'instantané—de ce que supporte et exige un auditoire à ce que supporte et emporte un œil rapide, libre sur une page' (1960: 549) [of the rhythmic and sequential to the instantaneous—of what an audience accepts and demands to what a rapid eye, moving freely across the page, accepts and carries off]. There are senses in which the next chapter will encourage us to agree with this opinion, but for the moment I would want to suggest that the difference between the written and the oral is a language-perceptual equivalent of that developed by Norman Bryson (1983: 87–131), in a pictorial context, between the gaze and the glance: while the gaze (the written) is optic (i.e. scanning of outlines, spatial relationships), governed by perspectival space, disengaged, contemplative, interpretative (about the subject), paternal, omniscient, the glance (the oral) is haptic (i.e. interest in surfaces, textures, tactility), governed by planar space, furtive, oblique, experiential (about perceiving the subject), maternal, imperfect, self-correcting, self-distracting. But our business is not to destroy this tension, by subduing the gaze, but to equalise it, to draw the gaze back towards the glance and vice versa, to build a translation on the interplay. Maintaining certain ambiguities between the written and the oral is important if one is to write a poetry in which new musics become possible, and if one is to try to establish the continuities, rather than the ruptures, between the written and the spoken. And the text we produce in our translation of 'Enfance I' must move in such a way that expressive, ventriloquial paralinguistics (right-hand column) can get no lasting purchase on it; in other words, we must avoid phrasal cohesion and thwart the articulative impulse. This is not to say that expressivity should be entirely banished; our task is to restore a balance of fruitful conflict in which one side is heard against, and complicated by, the other. It seems peculiarly apt that the landscapes of 'Enfance I' are all, characteristically, set on borders and dividing lines: 'sur des plages'; 'À la lisière de la forêt'; 'sur les terrasses voisines de la mer'.

We are also tacitly assuming that the recovery of voice, of a text-immanent voice, is intimately related to the convergence of a literary-ideological development and a form. Jean-Pierre Bobillot suggests that Rimbaud had reached a limit of tolerance as far as institutionalised verse-speech was concerned—

C'est, n'en doutons pas, que pour l'auteur du *Bateau ivre*, au point

où il en était arrivé, alors, de son évolution poétique et de sa
réflexion, il fallait de toute urgence en finir avec ce qu'il y avait de
faux, d'arrogant et de dérisoire, dans la manière dont on pouvait
alors dire—et écrire—les vers.

(2002: 244)

[Let us have no doubt about it, for the author of *Le Bateau ivre*, given
the point he had then reached in his poetic evolution and thinking,
it was necessary, as a matter of urgency, to have done with what was
false, arrogant, derisory, in the manner in which it was, at that time,
possible to speak—and write—verse].

—and that across his work we discover 'ces mêmes engrappements de
phonèmes, indéfiniment repris, recomposés, comme anamorphosés, qui
pourraient au bout du compte désigner une manière de *signifiant
primordial*' (2002: 249) [these same clusterings of phonemes, indefinitely
re-used, recomposed, as if anamorphosed, which might well, in the end,
point to a kind of *primordial signifier*] (this takes us back to creative activity
as 'bricolage'). We might then suppose that Rimbaud turned to the prose
poem/poetic prose as to a genre/medium which lets the voice sink back
into itself, which, because not sustained by regularities of various kinds,
recovers all its paralinguistic diversity. A string of twelve syllables in a prose
poem may be a reminiscence of an alexandrine, but it is not an alexandrine
largely because, as we have said, it belongs to real time and does not fulfil
anything, any expected configuration; the voice negotiates it from scratch,
without guarantees or directions, which is why, in return, it negotiates the
voice.

We say of non-metrical verse that it recovers a locus of enunciation, or
at least the possibility of a locus of enunciation, and with that it potentially
recovers a pragmatics, an illocutionary force, and 'illocutionary force
individuates sentences as utterances' (Griffiths 1989: 41). In fact, the
notion of a located speaker is complicated by three factors in the translation
we have before us:

(a) By speaking this text, I make it mine, but I make it mine at a level
which denies my voice an *expressive* coherence; in some senses, the
text is mine despite me; it is the instrument by which my voice is
revealed, in its physicality, just as, conversely, my voice reveals what
is purely material in language. I speak language's being rather than
its concertedness, its phonetics just prior to its taking up a place in
a phonological system:

L'écriture à haute voix, elle, n'est pas expressive; elle laisse l'expression au phéno-texte, au code régulier de la communication; pour sa part elle appartient au géno-texte, à la signifiance; elle est portée, non par les inflexions dramatiques, les intonations malignes, les accents complaisants, mais par le *grain* de la voix [. . .]. Eu égard aux sons de la langue, *l'écriture à haute voix* n'est pas phonologique, mais phonétique; son objectif n'est pas la clarté des messages, le théâtre des émotions; ce qu'elle cherche (dans une perspective de jouissance), ce sont les incidents pulsionnels, c'est le langage tapissé de peau, un texte où l'on puisse entendre le grain du gosier, la patine des consonnes, la volupté des voyelles, toute une stéréophonie de la chair profonde: l'articulation du corps, de la langue, non celle du sens, du langage. (Barthes 1973: 88–9)

[*Writing aloud* is not expressive; it leaves expression to the pheno-text, to the regular code of communication; it belongs, for its part, to the geno-text, to *signifiance*; it is carried not by dramatic inflections, clever intonations, self-regarding accents, but by the *grain* of the voice (. . .). In consideration of the sounds of the language, *writing aloud* is not phonological, but phonetic; its aim is not the clarity of messages, the theatre of emotions; what it seeks (in a perspective of bliss) are the pulsional incidents, language lined with flesh, a text in which one can hear the grain of the throat, the patina of consonants, the voluptuousness of vowels, a whole stereophonic account of the deep flesh: the articulation of the body, and of the tongue, not of meaning, or of language.]

(b) But my voice also releases the autonomy of language, its associative inventiveness, its capriciousness, decorative and insightful, gratuitous and revelatory. Sounds are surprised to find themselves words and vice versa, just as the universal language of pure phonemes is surprised to find itself adopting national identities and eccentricities of idiolect. My voice generates, but cannot process, this wandering in the multicursal acoustic labyrinth.

(c) And at the same time, knowledges (intertextual, etymological, morphological) are tacitly outstripping pure acoustic productivity, uncovering motive, justifying and rationalising, seeming to free the text from the voice. But these knowledges, coming from everywhere, need not substitute interpretation for vocality. Interpretation dispenses with the voice, returns to linguistics, and in so doing promotes text at the expense of body; the voice merely becomes a way of displaying writtenness. But we can imagine an intertextuality in which intertexts are not so much identified and lifted out of text, restored to their autonomy, as assimilated into a weave of phonetic, rhythmic and intonational activity. Intertexts relate to Rimbaldian memory in the sense that they are the past given back to the present in new forms; but they are also, like any piece of language, the raw materials of enunciation.

Voice guarantees in the text a suffusive transphrasal presence. In this sense, it escapes the localising effects of expressivity. In his essay on another singer, Gérard Souzay, entitled 'L'Art vocal bourgeois', Barthes taxes Souzay with conceiving of art as 'une addition de détails réunis' [an aggregate of combined details], or a 'perfection pointilliste', and adds: 'Cet art analytique est voué à l'échec surtout en musique, dont la vérité ne peut être jamais que d'ordre respiratoire, prosodique et non phonétique' (1957: 170) [This analytical art is doomed to failure, in music above all, whose truth can only ever be of a respiratory order, prosodic and not phonetic].[6] If we turn the transphrasality of sound into verbal music, it becomes the orchestration of meaning, linking words in ways alternative to syntax. It turns syntagmatic progression into constellational arrangements of phonemic stars. But in doing this, we dangerously suppress modality, the posture/position of the speaker. The transphrasality of phonemes is the sense-giving of the speaking subject and a releasing of the text's invisibility, those elements which it could not contain as writing, that borderline between the verbal and the pre- and post-verbal. Reading verse aloud is not an act of interpretation but of restoration. Texts are the instruments whereby voices come into their own. It might then become one of the tasks of the translator actively to elicit, solicit, this voice, not to leave the voice implicit as it was in the ST, but already to anticipate its wayward movement across and through the words. We thus find ourselves in an *énoncé* inhabited by, often threatened by, often overridden by, an *énonciation*. These recurrent sounds look to bend sentences in directions they had not imagined.

The proposition that Rimbaud developed towards a freeing of voice from institution or habit is borne out by the lexis of voice in the *Illuminations*. I do not wish to itemise the variety of noises and vocalisations with which the *Illuminations* are liberally scattered.[7] But I do want to recall those uncanny continuities between the human voice and the voice of the world. If one looks into the lexis of *Illuminations* for evidence of unmistakably human word-production, one may be surprised by their scarcity: there are no instances of 'mot(s)', nor of 'parole(s)'; apart from the poem-title, 'phrase(s)' is used only in connection with music ('Guerre'). There is one instance of 'parler': the king-consort of 'Royauté' 'parlait aux amis de révélation, d'épreuve terminée'; and those who speak through 'dire' are a flower ('Aube'), a hare ('Après le Déluge') and the nymph Eucharis ('Après le Déluge'). These trends are reinforced in 'Enfance I' by the fact that shipless waves do the naming. And if we investigated 'cri(s)'and 'crier', we would find human agents ('Royauté', 'Fairy' (?)), but also 'La calèche du cousin crie sur le sable' ('Enfance II') and 'La chasse des carillons crie dans les gorges' ('Villes II'); 'chant', 'chanson' and 'chanter' produce an equally diverse set of vocal origins: a bird, new misfortunes, blood, groups of belfries, companies, as well as children, the young 'Entertainers' (from 'Parade'), a couple. 'Voix' itself (singular and plural) seems to score relatively highly (nine instances), but three of these belong to 'Jeunesse' ('Sonnet' (2), 'Vingt ans' (1)), two to 'Solde' and two to 'Phrases'; the other, single occurrences are to be found in 'Parade' and 'Barbare'. About the voices of 'Jeunesse' we shall have more to say below. About the other instances, one might just point out that the 'feminine' voice at the end of 'Barbare', using volcanoes and arctic grottoes as resonating cavities, seems to be the force which both re-centers the earth's body and harmonises, gives expression to, its varied features ('les formes, les sueurs, les chevelures et les yeux, [. . .]. Et les larmes blanches' [the shapes, the sweats, the heads of hair and the eyes (. . .). And the white tears]). And in 'Solde' (see Appendix II (ii) for translation), among the items for sale, we find: 'Les Voix reconstituées; l'éveil fraternel de toutes les énergies chorales et orchestrales et leurs applications instantanées; l'occasion, unique, de dégager nos sens !'; this voice is, among other things, the voice of /e/, the /e/ of élan, lifting away from inertial states, setting loose, and the past participial /e/ of summarily achieved goals, haunted perhaps by brevity ('instantané' is not, of course, a 'genuine' past participle, but an adjective modelled on 'momentané'; here, however, the structural parallelism between the first two phrases, with considerable amplification in the second, encourages us to pair 'instantanées' with 'reconstituées').

My own re-wedding of translation with an oral tradition has the following agenda:

> 1. The ST is rewritten in such a way that it continually emerges from and returns to, a 'flux phonatoire' [phonatory flux]. This helps to guarantee *signifiance* against signification: the sense-making/sense-losing of a dynamic and unfinished relationship

replaces the semantic stasis of a text corralled for interpretation by being read *through* as it were *equidistantly*. And sense distinguishes itself from meaning by being (a) infused with a subjectivity and (b), relatedly, constructed from an unfixed experiential totality rather than from visible linguistic evidence alone. One binding element of this experiential totality is rhythm, with its flexible variability.

2.   Sense-making is auditory/oral vision, the unknown, because it is always crossing boundaries or going beyond horizons, losing articulacy by virtue of inadequacy or excess. But 'perdre l'intelligence de ses visions' [losing the understanding of his visions] (to Paul Demeny, 15 May 1871) is a guarantee of having seen/heard/said them; seeing/hearing/saying prevents them from taking refuge in the hearsay of meaning, in its reductions and extrapolations. The very presence of voice, as rudely disruptive or musically irresistible, will de-semanticise verbal constructs.

3.   The voice is its own 'noise', its own interferences; it cannot disengage its message from itself, it clings parasitically to itself and obscures its own clarity. This 'noise' may be a kind of phonic matrix out of which all visions are woven, which ensures that all phrases, sentences, reach beyond themselves, in uncontrollable ways, fray at the edges, which makes every future available in the 'signifiant primordial', that this infinitely permutatable constellation of sounds is. But it also means impaired hearing, the inability to repeat, the inevitability of Chinese whispers, an imperfection which is a liberation, the process on which translation itself depends. Imperfections of audibility are like the practical causes or consequences of imperfections of memory.

4. The voice projects words at things, other people, whereas written language often persuades us that words *belong* to things. Written language repeats what is already there (in the dictionary) and endows it with absolute visibility; speech recreates what we can never be absolutely sure of. But spoken words are actions that require response; we can pass the written by (see Ong's 'Agonistically toned' category, 1982: 43–5).

5.   The voice wants to go forward; what it leaves behind is not the reconstructible whole but something imperfectly remembered (see Ong's 'Additive rather than subordinative' category (1982: 37–8)).

But this forwardness gives phonic material a more clearly projective, generative function, as much to instal buccal expectation as to recuperate hidden networks. One might argue that the prose poem is a way of capitalising upon the projective nature of French accentuation; end-rhyme in regular verse not only isolates and guarantees the isosyllabic, it arrests and reverses the projective impulse.

But because of its singularity, there are certain features of the psychodynamics of orality that the writing aloud of the Rimbaldian prose poem eschews. It does not favour aggregative formulation (cumulative, formulaic word-clusters, 'épithètes de nature'); it does not consolidate itself with redundancy; it is not by nature conservative or traditionalist. These factors may alert us to the nature of Rimbaud's oral predicament, as we arrive, finally, at our translation of 'Enfance I':

Childhood [I]

"Nou bwouè djé?"
-Nihaé bwoué djé

This	idol	Pa[o]nzéro
	isles	
	I'll (aspirate)	
black-eyed	and	yellyell o! (ho[a]rse)haired,

unsired and
   without

       saliss en la sa ontouraj,

nobl -er -ure -air (*accelerando* re mi) than   fabula

Mexhican & phlegmish   mexindian und Flamcan: demesne?

azure UPstart INsolent verdure, runs along beaches dubbed burbled

blurbed by nonshippt (*sempre scherzando*) waves with ,,,,,,,,,,,,,,,,;
          names

The Voice in Translation I: Translating Subdiscursive Sound

(*feroce*) gREEKK, SLLAv, celTICC

On the forest's edge _—_ -
_—_ _ _ ★★
the dream flowers
ting, tink, ting, tink, glow, glint. . . . .
gleaming
the GIrl
with lips
of orinj
/dɔRãʒ/

knees crossed in the crissTALclear
fludde that wells, wells UP
ourdo*ME*lizana*OUR*
ourdo*ME*lizana*OUR*
gola*DO*manaxi*TURE*
from the *ME*/*ME*// /fields,

NAKedness
shaded
striated
and clothED

by rainbows,
                    flora,
            and—aura -
the sea

*Ladies*pirouswirlandpivotingONTHETERRACES. . . . . overlooking

            the sea; giRLs and giant S's, proud blacklackackckk women
    in thee
    verdigris   MOSS ; jules eric'd on m'luddies'

SOIL (in the thawed groves and gardenettes) (ohyankee) [o sesame]

_____ [vocalise] _____

young mothers and big sisters (refrain, refrain) their eyes full of

        pilgrimimages, sultan(a)(ah)(ha)s, prince S's with imper(v)ious
DEPORTURE
and
        [white]   overbaring apparel (refrain: mé viré la ribur: the
feathered fan), GIRLS

from ELSWEAR (hellsinawe)
  and the sh !sh ! quietplease suffering.

What a let-down, the time of the "mmmmdearbody" and the
"mmmdearheart".

            Madel mo'baral q'ancheba
            Latcharetch lamakh vakhana
            Don naq'a kas-kast'e-n tivboch
            Soda hhetj'ouch hhal-'ap'ana.

How good it would be
             in old age
To journey up, high, into the mountains
To spend time
            on a horse's back
The pleasure of seeing it all again

In 'Enfance I', the final line rejects a certain kind of orality, precisely an orality built on the aggregative; this is the language of the *culture* of caress, of lullaby, of an eroticism that has become sentimentalised. We may hear in these phrases reminiscences of Baudelaire's 'Le Balcon':

Ailleurs qu'en ton cher corps et qu'en ton cœur si doux ?

and 'Femmes damnées: Delphine et Hippolyte':

« Hippolyte, cher cœur, que dis-tu de ces choses ? »;

we may even hear kinships with the similarly damning close of Rimbaud's own 'Ouvriers' ('Je veux que ce bras durci ne traîne plus *une chère image*') or of 'L'Éclair' (*Une saison en enfer*) ('Alors,—oh !—chère pauvre âme, l'éternité serait-elle pas perdue pour nous !'). But this may only go to show that literature, too, is subject to the debilitating effects of encultured vocality, that intertexts are memories that sap and seduce, that create lineages and dependences. Even the poet himself is vulnerable to cross-textual repetitions which are like a deeply negative version of 'On me pense' [I am thought] (to Georges Izambard, 13 May 1871).[8]

Ong describes oral cultures as 'empathetic and participatory' (1982: 45–6) and the inverted commas of this last line tell of an empathy that is non-reciprocal, in which a 'degraded', enervating orality precisely uses the formulaic as a trace of the lost, a quotation, a mnemonic for something now only in the body's memory. Quite clearly Rimbaud is looking for a world not of the vocative but of the accusative. The second-person is 'vieillerie poétique' [poetic old hat], to be washed away in the third-person of the prose poem. Those apostrophes which continue to appear, are either moments of unreflective lyricism, or are thrust away towards the third person by a demonstrative adjective or a definite article ('O cette . . .', 'O le . . .'), or gravitate towards exclamation (as in 'Jeunesse: Sonnet').

Rimbaud is out to establish a new kind of orality which we might argue is referred to in 'des plages nommées, par des vagues sans vaisseaux, de noms férocement grecs, slaves, celtiques'; here speech is seen to emerge from pre-colonised ('sans vaisseaux') natural encounters (between waves and shore) whose strange musics coincide with the still inarticulate/unformed ('férocement') languages of [pre-Christian] proto-civilisations ('grecs, slaves, celtiques'). In other words, our orality (phonology) is potentially a storehouse of natural imprints, of onomatopoeia—not in the sense of the *representation* of natural sounds quickly conventionalised as part of its assimilation into 'official' language, but in the sense of the natural world speaking directly through language. The music of language, whatever else it might do, gives us back to, and gives back to us, the natural environment.

This transference of nature's music to the music of language is to be found in Rimbaud's poem devoted to his forebear in 'voyance', Ophelia. She, too, is driven to inarticulacy by vision—'Tes grandes visions étranglaient ta parole' [Your grand visions strangled your words]—but, the poem implies, the thwarting of human articulacy allows the voice of nature to speak, to inhabit the human ear and thence language itself, as a kind of shadow or sprinkling of sounds:

- C'est que les vents tombant des grands monts de Norwège

$$4+2+3+3$$

T'avaient parlé tout bas de l'âpre liberté $\qquad$ $4+2+2+4$

[It is that the winds, coming down from the great mountains of
Norway had spoken to you, under their breath, of harsh freedom]

After the chiastic configuration of the nasals /5/ and /ã/ ('tombant des
grands monts') in the first line, instigated by the 'vents' and pivoting
around the caesura, the play between the voiceless and voiced pair /p/ and
/b/, supported by /t/ and /l/, holds us as if poised between the subdiscursive
and the discursive; and the crucial contacts, again around the caesura,
between the low, back, unrounded /ɑ/'s of 'bas' and 'âpre', and between
the high-mid, front, unrounded /e/, provide the interchange between
'natural' speech and human meanings, whose reflective reciprocity is
driven home by the chiastic structure of the line's rhythm 4+2+2+4. And
/ɛ/ endorses the connection between the landscape ('Norwège') and its
concept ('liberté').

Ophelia is an important presence in my translation. She is one of the
'petites étrangères', whose 'elsewhere' is an anarchic geography of demotic
and courtly, demonic and saintly.[9] But she is also, in my mind at least, the
figure of the second paragraph. This section I have cast as lyric utterance,
invested by verbal madness, finally becoming song (see below for further
comment). Ophelia's songs, Dunn tells us (1994: 62), 'are like an inversion
of patriarchal speech, a release of repressed psychic energies and unmet
emotional needs'. And song itself exaggerates and intensifies vocalization;
in song, 'the voice seems to have a less mediated relationship to the body,
perhaps because there is literally more body in the voice—more breath,
more diaphragm muscles, a more open mouth' (Dunn 1994: 52–3).

Intruding into this primordial dialogue, human language—'cher corps',
'cher coeur'—is a screen which intervenes, cuts us off from the other
orality. Clearly, this new orality, this speaking the world, this music of
being, is a fragile creation which constantly succumbs to meaning, to the
too-knowing manipulations and expectations of these 'innocent' acoustic
materials. On the other hand, this new orality is not bound to the memory
of a primordial status quo: Rimbaud's 'future Vigueur' grows out of a
vision of:

(. . .) des archipels sidéraux! Et des îles
Dont les cieux délirants sont ouverts au vogueur:
- Est-ce en ces nuits sans fonds que tu dors et t'exiles,
Million d'oiseaux d'or, ô future Vigueur?—

[starry archipelagos ! and islands whose delirious skies welcome
the wandering sailor:—Is it in these bottomless nights that you sleep
and live out your exile, you countless golden birds, o future Vigour ?]

and entails endless proliferation, through the rigorous engineering of the wildest fictions.

Ong, basing himself on the work of Goody and Watt (1968), also identifies the homeostatic as a defining characteristic of oral communities: 'That is to say, oral societies live very much in a present which keeps itself in equilibrium or homeostasis by sloughing off memories which no longer have present relevance' (1982: 46). Uninhibited by the etymological and semantic sedimentation preserved in dictionaries, oral communities constantly update the meanings of words in response to the changing environment of their production, casting off any unwanted connotations of previous use. This feature does not seem appropriate for a writer as mired in memory as Rimbaud. But we might well argue that Rimbaldian homeostasis is merely a more complex version of the one we have described, precisely because it is an orality *disengaging itself* from the written.

One can begin to see what advantages a translation practice orientated towards oral values might have. But more generally, the sloughing off of memories, or at least of accurate memories, opens language up again to the fruitful illusions of false etymology, mistaken morphology and the persistences of the misheard and the misread. Rimbaud's commitments to the past are to a past re-surfacing in the present, to a past not so much recurring as pushing forward. Past languages, past times, past texts are not to be unearthed from their deep stratum, enriched by sedimentation, but to be released as things which sedimentation has for too long constrained, restrained, suppressed.

I wanted to begin this poem with a language as good as lost, partly because this is what childhood may be, but more importantly because this particular language, nonuya, is an oral language whose writability depends on transcription. I have adopted two kinds of speech-mark for this pair of lines, first 'ancient' and then modern, in order, punctuationally, to enact a stepping forward, a de-historicisation, whereby the extinct and defunct throws off factuality to become fiction, a memory which becomes an invented memory, a regret which generates a desire, a memory which resurrects a project. The past is both tragically lost and becomes a potentiality.[10]

In this instance, I am using a French transcription to which no English transcription corresponds (unreliability begins with the failure to use an unwritten written language, IPA). It is a written through which I must recover an oral, as best I can, an oral to which no written can do justice, an oral which is produced by an ethnic voice, and the individual voices of all its speakers. French language would hear it one way, English another, like the quacking of a duck. These lines that I have written are not French, but nor are they nonuya.

Nonuya is all that has been left by the *seringueiros*, the harvesters of rubber ('relatives', perhaps, both of Rimbaud's colonists and of his *comprachicos*), who decimated this Amazonian language by rape, castration, slavery, murder. (This is the conduct of translators who go to a language for its meaning). How many are left and what do they know of the language of their ancestors? This language has certain particularities: it has a large botanical and zoological lexicon (a large vocabulary for species of ants) and it is extremely rich in pronouns which register the shape and tactile qualities of objects (long, short, flat, spherical, conical, and so forth). But it is a language which is no longer spoken; its existence, its spokenness, is an idea, to be reconstructed in the imagination. All written texts are no longer spoken; they are texts without an originating voice, to which readers can, temporarily, only *lend* their voices; but what is produced is the voice of language/text rather than the language/text that has issued from a voice; and the voice of language is the voice of the right-hand column, rather than of the left.

If you were a speaker of nonuya, on the edge of its extinction, how would you want to speak it? You would, I imagine, want to speak it in such a way as to establish it, as to affirm its phonological system, its rhythms and intonational curves. One would not want to exercise its right-hand paralinguisticity. One would want to speak it in such a way that nonuya was everywhere and in all its manifestations simply present to itself. Just as subjectivity is transferable and individuality is not, so articulation is transferable and pronunciation is not, so expressivity is transferable and voice quality is not. Nonuya then stands at the threshold of this translation as an exemplary instance, as a language which asks us searching questions about vocality and orality and suggests to us what our aims should be.

We tend to think of poetry as an art in which expressivity is paramount. But poetry, like transcribed nonuya, is repeatedly re-establishing itself as another language, a language we do not quite speak, which the voice merely visits. The voice of regular verse is an unsituated voice, without a textual locus of enunciation. Perhaps then we should translate a language we do not speak into a language we do not, cannot, write. Then voice would be the poem's blind field, the only thing that would make sense of the nonsense. Perhaps we should translate a text in such a way that the voice is both there and not there, so that the text though technically written is not really written, so that the 'written' is not a language, but a language heard and misheard. Language is a mirage, a delusionary medium, where, the written and the spoken have peculiar ways of crossing their wires: when Viv from Peter Reading's 'Ukelele Music' says/'writes':

> *this is called 'Narrow' which plays on a fiddle, all the time Roam burnd*
> *but why it Brakes is because. my man has FIXED it last week*

we cannot tell whether she is guilty of mis-spelling or of mis-hearing. Transcription is tantamount to creative mishearing, creative inasmuch as it makes us wonder what is being spelt out; translation is tantamount to creative misunderstanding, since the points of contact between languages are always, potentially, points of disproportionate divergence. If, in the last sentence of Rimbaud's 'Les Ponts'—'Un rayon blanc, tombant du haut du ciel, anéantit cette comédie'—I translate 'un rayon blanc' as 'a beam of white light', it will be assumed that 'beam' means a ray of light and is not trying to insinuate a broad smile, or long thick bar of wood or metal, or gymnastic apparatus, or indeed a pair of hips. It begins to look as if translation requires language to act self-devaluatively, precisely in order to be (more) intelligible. Put another way, one might argue that the ST constantly works to suppress the TT, to confine its effects, to distract the reader from its spontaneous richnesses. And yet also, while the notion of 'broad grin' can be mediated by the translation 'beam', as an *implicit* constituent, to translate 'rayon blanc' by a 'broad white/bright grin' would be to invite the charge of unjustified liberty; and yet such a translation is *unjustified* as a liberty only because it has complicated the thought processes necessary to retrieve it, and in so doing has offended against principles of relevance. One might argue that the converse is also true, that the various possibilities that exist in 'rayon' (for example, 'envergure', 'domaine', 'gaufre', 'degré', 'étagère') are effectively stifled by the translator's choice. But then the ST does not exist only in the TT, whereas the TT finds it difficult to convince the reader that it has a right to crawl out from under the ST.

One way of representing the relationship between nonuya, transcription and translation might be as follows:

[Voice of nonuya] → Transcription (French, misheard) = homophonic 'translation' (what does it sound like?—voice maintained)

   → Transcription (English, misheard) = homophonic 'translation' of French (what does it sound like?—voice maintained)

→ Translation of the transcription(s) (what does it mean?—
voice disappears)

While the transcriptions point us back to a voice which cannot be
recuperated, and which can never write itself, translation wants to release
written meaning from voice, in order that meaning can be revoiced, by a
voice which does not need to correspond with the original utterance. What
I want to create is a translation on the cusp between transcription and
translation, where transcription is tantamount to mishearing, and
translation enacts similar processes of slippage, so that experiences of
double-take (anamorphosis) occur not only within transcription and
translation, but also between them.

In answer to the opening in nonuya, my translation ends with some
lines of tsova-tush, a dying language of the Caucasus. Only forty languages
are now spoken in the area; sixty have disappeared. Tsova-tush looks as if
it will be the next casualty. The people who speak it (between 1,500 and
4,000, all over the age of fifty) live in Georgia, but linguistically and
ethnically they are more closely related to neighbouring Chechens and
Ingush. Tsova-tush is another non-written language, spoken by a
mountain people, sheep-raisers and horse-lovers, with the remnants of an
animistic religion among them; the language is rich in locatives, reflecting
their free and vivid relationship with space and movement. But here, in
Rimbaldian fashion perhaps, I have betrayed my own trust and provided
a translation. Just as Rimbaud comes back to the 'ennui' of 'translated'
terms of endearment (where translation is a making acceptable, for general
consumption), so, too, I withdraw from my own text, assuming the guise
of the parent who translates his/her child for the benefit of a neighbour
unattuned to the child's dialect. Writtenness comes to cover over and wipe
away the traces of the oral; translation apologises for the quaint
gratuitousness of transcription.

There are five lines in the translation which are quotations from Lettrist
poems:[11] 'saliss en la sa' and 'mé viré la ribur' are taken from Patrick
Poulain's 'Trois morceaux en forme d'espoir', and the three-line sequence
beginning 'ourdo*ME*lizana*OUR*' from Jean-Paul Curtay's 'Ville éternelle'.
I chose 'mé viré la ribur' because I was looking for a language which might
evoke Gauguin's Polynesian paintings and in particular the bare-breasted
Woman with a Fan (1902), the 'translation' of a photograph of his cook's
wife, Tohotaua (1901), into the image of a princess (?). This image wears
a white wrap, a colour carrying connotations of power and death for
Marquesan culture, but representing virginal purity for the western viewer
(Brettell 1988: 490); like the panglottal language, colour has endless

anamorphic possibilities.

More generally, the insertion of these Lettrist lines is designed to activate principles implicit in Lettrism, in particular: (a) Lettrism as '*art de la foule*' [*art of the crowd*] (Curtay 1974: 37) as opposed to 'une consommation pour une élite' [a consumable commodity for an elite]; (b) Lettrism's pre-verbality, its sources in the cry, in pre-articulate vocal dynamics; (c) Lettrism's refusal to be confined by a vocabulary, and its concomitantly infinite capacity for elaboration; in Lettrism words are never formed; (d) Lettrism's cultivation of non-expressivity, in the service of the intuitable sense of the whole; (e) Lettrism's embodiment in language of muscular impulses; for example, letters which solidify, or rigidify (k, d, b, g, c), and letters which relax, or give (f, l, h); (f) Lettrism's attempt to create a language inhabited by virtuality, by the infrasonic and the ultrasonic; 'sons' are 'sens', and sense thus lies always beyond the poem (the poem's temporal frame is always 'supertemporel' or 'hyper-chroniste'); (g) Lettrism's espousal of infinite acoustic transformability as the creative motor. These principles, it seems to me, are deeply in tune with Rimbaud's own enterprise; and they also constitute a set of guidelines for a translation which seeks to tackle the ST in its origins, in its pre-textual or proto-textual being.

In many senses, the failure of Lettrism is also instructive. The Rimbaldian enterprise has failure built into it, the acknowledgement of its necessary compromises and backsliding. But the nature of its failure may be the true measure of its aspirations. Enterprises like these do not find their readers. How would we characterise Lettrism's failure?

(i)   It develops alphabets and/or numbers with inbuilt equivalences to physiological sources (conventional and supplied as a key).
(ii) It gravitates towards 'wordism'.
(iii) It gravitates towards poetic forms/formations with an inbuilt recognisability.

But Lettrism has transcription at its heart, in two senses. First, it practised the 'disfigured' transcription of other texts, particularly in its formative years;[12] secondly, any Lettrist poem will present itself as being a potentially imitative construction, imitative, that is, either of a language we do not know or of noises yet to be identified. And if I have used onomatopoeia for the music of the flowers, it is because of its natural affinities with Lettrism, because it, too, is a transcriptional language, and as such has the following characteristics:

(i) The direct acoustic transcription ('ting tink') removes the grammaticality that the word has in the ST ('tintent'); accordingly these sounds are as if their own agents and will not subject themselves to any hierarchy of syntax. In any syntactic chain, direct onomatopoeic transcription can be inserted at any point, as an interruption.

(ii) These words then 'contaminate' words in their vicinity. Perhaps 'glow' and 'glint' are not verbs or nouns, but similar acoustic notations, in which case the experience becomes synaesthetic: through these words we see how light manifests its various intensities in a range of sounds.

(iii) Onomatopoeic words reflect fruitfully on the extracts from Lettrist texts, dragging elements we want to identify as part of the known language system into a world of sounds we do not know. Is 'our' a possessive adjective or a sound we have not yet heard, or cannot put a name to? Is it, perhaps, the sound made by a swing-door? Or the yaw of a loose cart-wheel?

(iv) Finally, we should remember that onomatopoeic words such as these are like any direct vocalisations of a human utterer: 'g-r-r-r-r', 'yuck', 'blaat'. Indeed, they are, to all intents and purposes, eruptions of speech in the natural world. And like vocalisations, they have access to real time: without the narrative frame of reported direct speech, these words might burst into the very present of their speaking.

Among other translational decisions and associative networks that perhaps deserve comment are:

(a) 'idol' produces 'isles' partly because idol > idle triggers 'Une île paresseuse où la nature donne' [a lazing island where nature begets] (Baudelaire's 'Parfum exotique'), partly because 'isles' conceals 'I'll' as 'idol' conceals 'I'd'; 'I'll' then emerges into the open, while 'I'd' remains in hiding ('[black]-eyed'). This plays out the tension between future and conditional, in their abbreviated, colloquial forms: the future which is openly asserted and confidently predicted is accompanied, in the verbal shadows, by a more tentative, less ambitious, equivocation.

(b) 'Pa[o]nzéro' refers to the clash between the voices of Panzéra and Fischer-Dieskau, the voices of pronunciation and articulation, with which this chapter began. It makes the point (paon [peacock] + zero) that, in the pronouncing voice, there is no self-display, and further implies (Pan + zero) not only that the classical golden age as envisaged in 'Antique' is out of reach, but also that the feminine world of 'Enfance I' has no place for the satyr, whether male or androgynous. Here we can see how writing often analyses and disaggregates what is fused in sound. Sometimes it is able itself to combine what speech would have to separate, to make phonetic discriminations (e.g. hoarse, hoarse).

(c) My musical markings, in the first paragraph, have two functions: to remind us that the voice in *Illuminations* is, among other things, the passage to music, to new musics ('Barbare', 'Parade'); and to refer to 'Jeunesse III' ('Vingt ans'), where the music is, by contrast, downbeat and elegiac: '—Adagio—Ah! l'égoïsme infini de l'adolescence, l'optimisme studieux: que le monde était plein de fleurs cet été! Les airs et les formes mourant. . . .' [—Adagio—Ah! The infinite selfishness of adolescence, the studious optimism: how full of flowers the world was that summer! Melodies and forms dying. . .]. Here the poet is separated from the voices of his earlier visionary instruction ('Les voix instructives exilées. . . .'), and in his impotence he calls up a vocal music ('choeur') as soothing balm, made of glasses and nocturnal melodies. As Guyaux points out (1985b: 113), there are potential 'glissements' here: 'clamer' > 'calmer'; 'cœur' > 'chœur'. At all events, the robust, synthesising, singular voice and dance of the preceding 'Sonnet' seem beyond recall.

(d) At the close of the first two paragraphs, with their evocations of singular feminine figures ('cette idole', 'la fille à lèvre d'orange'), mythicising and then more intimately lyrical, I wanted to push the lyricism of the latter to a culmination, and register the pressure towards obsessive or delirious pattern in the French (the repeated triads, first of verbs and finally of nouns) (see remarks on Ophelia above). I have not produced triads, but two quatrains, each with alternating syllabic quantities 3-2-3-2. Rather in the manner of Paul-Jean Toulet's *Les Contrerimes* (8-6-8-6), the alternation is counterpointed by the '*rimes embrassées*': the inner lines rhyme, while the outer lines, unrhyming, point up a paradox, or help convey the unrestrictedness of space.

(e) 'Blacklackackckk' is an attempt to *say* the mesmerising intensity of the blackness of these women (a reason for 'superbes') and its multiple nuances.

(f) 'jules eric'd' is clearly a homophonic transcription of 'jewels erect', designed to make the most of sexual innuendo ('eric'd' = an interesting variation on 'roger'd'). In one sense, this is a debased currency; it has nothing to do with the preservation of an oral language under threat of extinction, but is a reductive process which repeatedly brings language back to genitalian functions. On the other hand, it achieves a fusion of transcription and (intralingual) translation and produces one of those anamorphic experiences Bobillot referred to. This kind of linguistic double-take reveals other languages in language, acts as an acoustic equivalent of Saussurean anagrams. Besides, the connections between jewels and erotic fantasy are well attested (e.g. Diderot's *Les Bijoux indiscrets* and Baudelaire's 'Les Bijoux').

(g) '(ohyankee)', quite apart from the action it suggests, is triggered by the 'jardinets', a seeming anticipation of Laforgue's lines from 'L'Hiver qui vient' (a seasonal reversal of Rimbaud's thawing Spring):

> Et le vent, cette nuit, il en a fait de belles !
> O dégâts, ô nids, ô modestes jardinets !
> [And the wind tonight, a fine mess it's made of things! O havoc, o nests, o modest little gardens!]

'(ohyankee)' thus becomes Laforgue's reaction to the 'corrupting' presence of Baudelaire ('Les Bijoux') in the little gardens—Laforgue identified a 'yankee' strain in Baudelaire's writing.[13] Laforgue, with his cultivation of a Hamlet persona, also helps to herald the arrival of Ophelia at the end of the paragraph.

(h) '[o sesame]' is a response to '(ohyankee)': the lyric apostrophe answers the vulgar exclamation, and the word that takes us back to Ali Baba and the *Thousand and One Nights*, the magic formula which gives access and opens all doors, answers brash modernity and racy familiarity. The square brackets leave unresolved whether 'sesame' will indeed throw open confinement, or whether it has lost its magical potency.

It might be said that all I have achieved in this translation of 'Enfance

I' is to provide my text with notations of ambiguities of sound which, paradoxically can only be visually retrieved; that, ironically, my plea for the restoration of voice to text has produced an affirmation, a consolidation, of the rich resources of the written, of the multiplicity of signals it can give to the eye; that this poetry cannot be spoken. But this is precisely the kind of poetry which, by making the voice impossible, *because it is impossible* (all texts are no longer spoken), makes it possible as the absent agent. Conversely, the poetry which apparently makes the voice possible, in fact makes it possible only as a temporary visitation, because the voice of the text has become a featureless and universal availability of the text to voice.

Expressed another way, by writing a poetry which is slung between polarised visuality and vocality, the visual makes the vocal a real possibility. The enjoyments of the visual are constantly interrupted by the pull of inchoate, unrealisable vocality. And its very unrealisability exerts a huge pressure of failure, of desiring the voice and its reassuring at-homeness, and which can only be a language we do not know. And because we do not know it, it must exist whole, undivided, unfragmented, somewhere. We are vouchsafed glimpses.

We say that language is both in the semiotic of maternal non-differentiatedness (this its pure acoustic materiality, its rhythmics and phonetics, its respiration, pronunciation and reading/speaking) and the symbolic of paternal separation (its metrics and phonology, its syntax, articulation and interpretation). The voice is caught between the twin appeals of Panzéra and Fischer-Dieskau, between a voice which simply comes from the body and the voice which is ventriloquial, transferable, able to express any self or any otherness, between a voice which inhabits words and a voice which delivers them, between the voice as eros, carnal, and the voice as agape, sublimated.

Paralinguisticity itself totters between not exceeding the text, between simply affirming the presence of the semiotic (the left-hand column), and outdoing the text, amplifying the symbolic (the right-hand column). And the dice are loaded against the left-hand column simply because this never-ending dispute takes place in a written medium, the medium of the paternal gaze rather than the maternal glance, the medium which looks to transcend dialogue, to haul the dark subterranean world of the '-lalian' and organic to a surface where it becomes visible only as lexicon and syntax. Can the translator do anything to make the playing field leveller?

4

The Voice in Translation II
Moving Images

In the previous chapter, voice had two principal significances: as performed linguistic materiality, it registered expulsions from the body, and linked the sounds of the body with the sounds of the world; additionally, it was something whose intelligibility was jeopardised by its own noise, a condition which was seen as an agent in the voice's creativity. In this chapter, I want to turn to voice as that which removes meaning, in the sense that the unfolding of the voice in time turns series into serial, juxtaposition into metamorphosis.[1] Metamorphosis is a notion conjured with by many Rimbaldian critics,[2] but little attention is paid to what it might entail for readerly consciousness, and it often refers to A becoming B by a process of change which happens *between* A and B, rather than existing *within them*. Our initial subjects in this chapter are the third and fourth poems of the 'Enfance' cycle, about which, it seems to me, Berranger (1993: 255) strikes just the right note, as a prelude to our enquiry:

> Les cinq parties du texte forment des mémoires imaginaires, virtuelles: il serait absurde d'y chercher terme à terme des souvenirs autobiographiques à replacer morceaux par morceaux dans l'ordre chronologique comme un puzzle. Ce sont plutôt des images chatoyantes qui se forment et se déforment en passant sous nos yeux, ou des vues de lanterne magique, plaques colorées que le lecteur va mettre en mouvement.
>
> [The five parts of the text form imaginary, potential memories: it would be absurd to look, formulation by formulation, for autobiographical reminiscences to put back in place, piece by piece, in chronological order, as in a jigsaw. These are, rather, shimmering images which take shape and lose shape as they pass before our eyes,

or slides from a magic lantern, coloured plates that the reader sets in motion].

There is a great danger that the pursuit of the autonomy of the prose poem, as that which necessitates its relative brevity and warrants our treating it as self-reflexive, will conceal from us the novel experience generated by its images, by virtue of the prose poem's being a frayed and self-dispersive form: in fact the prose poem, and the Rimbaldian prose poem in particular, is an ensemble destroyed by the passage of time. This often happens quite literally, as the close of poems such as 'Aube' or 'Royauté' or 'Les Ponts' makes clear. Expressed in another way, the written text is destroyed by the passage of the voice. In 'vocalising' the ST, the translator disseminates it, frays it, mortalizes it, dissolves it. The voice ruptures a condition, a condition of permanence, availability, reversibility, beyond-the-speakable.

What makes it particularly difficult to think moving images is that there is no *gap* (a notion belonging to spatialisation) within which to create a tendentiousness, a tension, a constructive space. One might argue that film-editing—as the introduction of cuts—and the concomitant art of montage is an attempt to recover juxtaposition from metamorphosis, simply because the language of juxtaposition is so much easier to motivate and to manipulate. In similar fashion, the voice is never uninterrupted movement through time; syntax will not allow it to be so, nor will the physical limitations of respiration; patterns of segmentation, pausing, the shaping features of intonation, all seem designed to make 'text' recuperable, to frame elements of the sequence and endow them with arrestedness. We might also suggest that deixis (the demonstrative, the definite article, the formulae of location in time and space) acts to immobilise, to isolate, to frame. Despite Bergson, the credo of imagery in the twentieth century is related to the instant (single frame) (Imagism, Futurism, all the arts of simultaneity) and to (spatial) distances between (static) phenomena (the policy of 'long-range' metaphor as developed, for instance, by Marinetti, Reverdy, Breton). But these compromises or resistances do not invalidate the drift of the argument: Bergson himself would agree that such isolations are necessary to our ability to identify, categorise, understand. But it is peculiarly within the power of the translator to minimise these agents of immobilisation, simply by undermining their conventional operation, by thwarting the voice's attempt to satisfy its own convenience, or by frustrating its capacity to contain what it triggers, to prevent the escape into all kinds of collusion and conspiracy of the elements it thought to put in order. I am imagining that interpretation is a process whereby the spatialisation of text and a structure of montage are retrieved from a reading experience which denies them. As we have indicated before, to read a text with interpretation in view, is to read *through* that text, in order to emerge on the other side of that text, in order to escape from the temporality/immediate historicity of reading into the dead textuality and temporal shapelessness of critical autopsy. I want to make the image an experience within *durée*, not an object of contemplation.

The voice must understand itself in order to speak, but need not in order to read; reading may precede understanding, as a run-through, a rehearsal:

> . . . lire à haute voix figure, quant à la parole [. . .] cette éventualité que les lèvres sont premières à appréhender, que l'esprit sur l'instant n'appréhende pas du tout. . . l'esprit sur l'instant est aveuglé. . . on a souvent beaucoup de mal à comprendre ce qu'on est en train de dire à haute voix.
>
> (Chappuis 1979: 88)
>
> [Reading aloud projects, as to language (. . .) that eventuality that the lips are first to apprehend, that the mind on the spur of the moment does not apprehend at all. . . the mind on the spur of the moment is blinded. . . one often has a great deal of difficulty in understanding what one is in the process of speaking aloud].

It is easy to believe that the written text holds its meaning, that within its frame, whether implied or suggested, all is there. And we think, because its completeness depends on its virtuality (its writtenness) that we shall never be able to get it all out, that every new voice will bring both something new and the acknowledgement of an inexhaustibility. When we watch a film, we are not in a position to say what we see; and perhaps we are never in a position, however many times we see it. The experience with a spoken text may be somewhat similar.

It is no surprise that as Bergsonian thinking made its appearance in the late 1880s, dance was re-imagining itself in the drape-dancing of Loie Fuller, who first appeared at the Folies-Bergère in 1892. In drape-dancing, the energy of dance is simply the body passing through time in such a way that it is always different from itself, and that difference is embodied in a sequence of othernesses, the coming into existence of images, or images of an image (flame, flower, cascade, vase, butterfly). There are two things that are significant for us in Fuller's dance: first, for the terms of our argument, its connection with the cinematic. The 'cinétisme' of the Fullerian dance—

Elle [Loïe Fuller] abolit la dimension narrative du spectacle en remplaçant la progression linéaire d'une histoire par le cinétisme protéiforme des ses sculptures impalpables et lumineuses. L'enchaînement du narratif laisse ainsi la place au jeu de la métaphore et de la métonymie qui sont les catégories primaires de l'inconscient se manifestant comme langage.

(Lista 1994: 26)

[She (Loïe Fuller) destroys the narrative dimension of performance, replacing the linear progression of a story with the protean kinetics of her impalpable, luminous sculptures. Narrative sequence thus makes way for the play of metaphor and metonymy, which are the primary categories of the unconscious in its linguistic manifestation.]

—found its immediate expression in early cinema, from the kineograph to the hand-coloured short (Lista 1994: 16–30), and in allied techniques (projectors of coloured light). Secondly, as it manifested itself in literary depictions of dance, Fullerian practice raised questions about the relation of her unfolding metaphors to time. Valéry's Athikté (*L'Âme et la Danse*, 1921) (Socrate: 'Ne sentez-vous pas qu'elle est l'acte pur des métamorphoses ?' (1960: 165) [Do you not feel that she is the pure act of metamorphosis]) seems to snatch from Time its continuous instantaneousness: Socrate: 'Mais qu'est-ce qu'une flamme, ô mes amis, si ce n'est *le moment même* ?', 171 [But what is a flame, my friends, if it is not *the very moment*]; Phèdre: 'Elle fait voir l'instant', 172 [She makes the instant visible]). The dance of Colette's Renée Néré (*La Vagabonde*, 1910), on the other hand, seems to belong to a world of smoother, uninterrupted transitionality:

Je danse, je danse. . . Un beau serpent s'enroule sur le tapis de Perse, une amphore d'Égypte se penche, versant un flot de cheveux parfumés, un nuage s'élève et s'envole, orageux et bleu, une bête féline s'élance, se replie, un sphinx, couleur de sable blond, allongé, s'accoude les reins creusés et les seins tendus. . . [. . .] Il n'y a de réel que rythmer sa pensée'.

(1965: 53–4)

[I dance, I dance. . . A beautiful snake coils up on the Persian carpet, an Egyptian amphora tips, pouring a torrent of perfumed hair, a cloud rises and vanishes, stormy and blue, a big cat springs forward, crouches, a sphinx, the colour of golden sand, recumbent, resting on its elbows, its back concave, its breasts thrust forward. . . (. . .)

There is no reality other than giving rhythm to one's thought.]

These are differences of perspective to which we shall shortly return, in our consideration of the translation of 'Enfance III':

Childhood III

In the wood - there is   Abird WHosE: s.o.n.g. stops you in your
/t/r/a/c/K/s and brings bLuSHes to your   CHeeKs Thereisa cLocK wh-ich
does not CHimE..... there isa; muddy poTHoLe AND in   it a nest of WHite
?creatures. there is a
sinKing caTHedraL   AND a   rising LAKE.
(There is a) *smallcarriage* abandoned, in the, THicKet or, running, down, the
path trAilingribbons. [THere] [is] a troupe of strolling: pLayers, cHiLdren, Costumed,
glimpsed//
th r ought he   wood's **Ed*ge***   going along the road.
and when you are Hungry and THirsty - a finiSHing touCH - THere............
is somEonE to   CHaseyou   awAy.

My strategy is a very simple one, although it may sound somewhat paradoxical. If the prohibition of space within the prose poetic text is likely to perpetuate habits of spatialisation; if the embryonic signs of stanzaic verse-space in the prose poem (i.e. spaces *between*, as in Bertrand's 'strophes', or as frequently in Rimbaud) has led some critics to conclude that textual spatialisation is one of the prose poem's teleological pathways, then by introducing space *within* the prose poem, I wish to drive spatialisation out, momentarily at least. The space introduced *within* the prose poetic text is the *time* of the voice, a space traversal which is as it were erased as the voice negotiates it, not left behind; this is the space of voco-psychic and voco-affective duration, assimilation, dynamics. A proposal like this would not, however, be complete if one could not as easily remove space as introduce it. One needs to be able to enact those moments of intellectual compression when the appetite for further encounters with text produces elisions or accelerations of attention.

What does this mean? It means that the text aims to generate an absolute contingency, that it is unique, irreducible to any reformulation, deep re-structuring, or founding knowledge. It is a text which is still in the territory of the ST, not linguistically, as foreignisation, so much as experientially as performance. And inasmuch as the ST is itself a performance, it is a performance of a performance. I know that here I am on tricky ground. Linguistically a performance without competence cannot be, unless one imagines a text in which meaning ever only occurs by chance. And culturally this text which we are about to tackle presupposes perhaps a 'deep knowledge' of the 'poème-inventaire' [inventory-poem] (with the 'fatrasie médiévale' [medieval miscellany] as its forebear and a subsequent genealogy in Apollinaire, Prévert, Vian), or of the submerged cathedral of Ys (> Lalo, 1888, and Debussy, 1905), or the strolling players/child-actors of Banville, Apollinaire, Picasso (Berranger 1993, 267–8). But what we can imagine is a performance in which competence does not have the status of a decoding, nor takes us out of the text we are in; competence in this world is not what makes performance possible, but contrariwise is what performance triggers, unpredictably, as a personal memory or association rather than as a prior public possession.

One of the reasons for transforming this particular poem into a moving image is the degree of transformation required, since this 'il y a' construction seems expressly designed to immobilise the image and thus to generate those instants of perception which we associate with Imagistic thinking—'an intellectual and emotional complex in an instant of time' (Pound), or 'the precise instant when a thing outward and objective transforms itself, or darts into a thing inward and subjective' (Pound). The cinematic destroys the instantaneousness of its frames in favour of a single image-stream:

> Le film (au sens matériel: la pellicule) est bien une collection d'instantanés—mais l'utilisation normale de ce film, la projection, annule tous ces instantanés, tous ces photogrammes, au profit d'une seule image, en mouvement.
>
> (Aumont 2001: 181)
>
> [The film (in the material sense: the celluloid strip) is indeed a collection of snapshots—but the normal use of this film, its projection, nullifies all these snapshots, all these photograms, in favour of a single, *moving* image.]

I have, therefore, instead of omitting it, tried to turn the repeated 'Il y a' to my advantage. Now 'Il y a' is both repeated and not; it does not stabilise or homogenise perception, but, on the contrary, unsettles it, re-orientates it, recontextualises it. Our encounter with images is governed by constant adaptations of view, and of proxemic and kinesic relationships. The 'Il y a' here is no longer a consistent point of reference, implying a perceptual and psychic equidistance from all the images, but the reverse, the very agent of adjustment, variation, mobility.

This mode of presentation is initially designed to achieve two objectives: (a) not to use typography to encrypt the meaning of the prose poem, so much as to dramatise, actualise, the passage of words through the voice-mind; (b) relatedly, not so much to claim lasting validity for its own typographic idiosyncrasy as to propose a model, adaptable, manipulable, but a model nonetheless, of a translation of the reading of 'Enfance III'. These two objectives deserve further commentary. Dramatising the passage of words through the voice-mind involves two large operations: the writing of the paralinguistic into a linguistic existence, not comprehensively, but sufficiently to give this sense of a text intimately and intensely inhabited by hesitation, pause, intonation, rhythmic impulse, stress, changes of tempo, etc.; the writing of exploration and puzzlement into the text in the form of a complex rhythm of attention, whereby potential acoustic patterns sporadically rise to consciousness, whereby words become sequences of strange morphemes, whereby partnerships and collocations are fused or sundered, whereby different linguistic phenomena operate at different levels of consciousness. These two aspects are, of course, different sides of the same coin and here, I hope, cross over into each other, through the punctuation.

The punctuation I have used is intended to both mark the syncopations, constrictions, liberations of voice and to serve mental operations. In the former of these pursuits, I have maintained clause-final full-stops and some commas (for example, 'pLayers, children, COstumed, **glimpsed**') in conventional roles, to imply/indicate a verbal surface which continues to operate, but as if at a cartographic distance from the hand-to-hand encounters of the vocal explorer. In short, this kind of punctuation takes place at 'la lisière du bois', at the extremity of a perception which remains embedded in the labyrinthine meanderings of inner assimilation. *Within* the wood, punctuation serves the glottal stops, the exhalations, the breath-drawings, of a reading mentality which experiences release (the colon), desires prolongation (suspension points), hesitates over after-image (comma), momentarily resists progression (semi-colon), amplifies and relishes (the full stops in 's.o.n.g.'), undergoes jarrings of being (slashes in 'tracks'), and sudden contractions of visual field (slashes after '**glimpsed**'). The dashes surrounding 'a finishing touch' are designed to hang ambiguously between a standard parenthetic function (as the poet withdraws, laconically, from his poem's interiority) and a pair of relationships ('Hungry and Thirsty—a finishing touch'; 'a finishing touch—there is somEonE') in which the dash functions as a gesture of exasperation, or ironic bitterness, where the 'parenthesised' phrase ('a finishing touch') does not operate metatextually, but recovers its textual immediacy, as responsiveness rather than comment.

Before we examine the implications of this transformation, let us look more closely at the presiding 'il y a', and more especially at the 'il y a + NP + relative clause', which is the informing template of utterance, even when it is concealed ('Au bois, il y a un oiseau dont le chant. . .'; 'Il y a une fondrière d'où pointe un nid. . .'). In some instances (Jammes, Apollinaire) this construction may act as a 'belle formule optimiste' (Breton), a re-gathering of the world seen in a pristine, self-presentative innocence. But its darker side, the side to be developed in Trakl's 'Psalm', is one where 'il y a' announces the apparently disordered evidence of a controlling design, of unreadable motive, the suspended state of helpless notation before a consciousness comes to possess the fruits of its planning:

> Schweigsam über der Schädelstätte öffnen sich Gottes goldene Augen.
> [Silently over the place of skulls open God's golden eyes.]

What is important in such a poem is the stalling of narrative; phenomena refuse to reveal a protagonism, to spend their withheld semantic menace in the pursuit of declared and limited objectives. Part of the poignancy of Trakl's 'Psalm' is its attempt to initiate narratives which might create the possibility of constructive participation. And in this respect, the relative clause is extremely powerful: it increases the contingency of the action, it increases the very agency of the agent (the 'qui' is the very decision to act and the sign of an unconstrained freedom to act) and the veiled intentionality of the action; and, at the same time, it as if withdraws action from the sphere of the narrator/spectator and confines it to its own immediate locale. We may feel that we have a context of action here—the wood—but none of the activities which take place within it spread into the environment, have an 'atmospheric' value. This isolation of elements from each other and the final 'enfin' create the impression of a rebus, of a language which is merely a way of concealing another language, which does not set out to establish its own presence, or any presence within it.

And yet observations like these do not, I think, justify the assertion made by Naliwajek (1982), on the back of Georges Poulet's *La Poésie éclatée: Baudelaire, Rimbaud* (1980), that 'Son existence n'est jamais une durée continue. D'où l'importance du moment présent dans l'œuvre de Rimbaud. L'immédiateté de ce qui se trouve vécu intérieurement est communiqué le plus souvent « par une parole essentiellement exclamative, souvent monosyllabique »' (126) [His existence never achieves continuous duration. Hence the importance of the present moment in Rimbaud's work. The immediacy of what is experienced internally is most frequently communicated 'by an essentially exclamatory, often monosyllabic, utterance']. Or, at least, it might mislead, for two reasons: first, there is a difference between a poetic vision which emerges from the failure of a *durée* to sustain itself and the pursuit of an essentially discontinuous and therefore infinitely repeatable present. Second, Naliwajek equally wants to affirm:

> Chez Rimbaud, on observe un effacement des choses réelles, leur disparition et leur évaporation. C'est le désir de fixer, d'arrêter les choses et les visions fuyantes qui fait énumérer au poète ce qu'*il y a*. Mais rien ne peut être fixé. Rien n'est saisi. Tout échappe, tout fuit.
>
> (1982: 139)
>
> [In Rimbaud's work, one observes an erasure of real things, their disappearance and evaporation. It is the desire to fix, to arrest objects and fleeting visions, that leads the poet to enumerate what *there is*. But nothing can be fixed. Nothing is grasped, Everything escapes, takes flight.]

The time which appears to take us continually away from ourselves, is itself potentially a *durée*, not identified, producing an existential anxiety which looks to things either to fix themselves or to repeat themselves. Involuntary memory teaches Marcel to see what is secretly benign in Time's depredations: what is apparently lost, and lost for history, is cumulatively stored in the individual's *moi profond*. 'Enfance III' looks like the product of chronometric time, a sequence of discontinuous but homogeneous instants, whose overall significance is an aggregate of perceptions/memories, whose final constituent is signalled by 'enfin', rather than the 'natural' *progression* of undifferentiated perception/memory.[3]

What my translation attempts to do, therefore, is to reveal the *durée* which lies beneath, or within, the progress of chronometric time (sentences), to uncover the ongoing, future-directed work of memory masked by the fragmentary *recollection* of memories. The process of projection in cinema transforms the sequence of temporally homogeneous still images, moving at a constant rate (24 frames per second), into an unbroken continuum in which length of shot, variation in camera movement and pace of zoom, and so forth (together with the activation of the spectator's inner time) produce qualitatively heterogeneous flow. Put another way, my translation is an attempt to replace the ekphrastic by the cinematic. What this latter entails is the shift from the framed without blind field to a framed which is always moving into a blind field, that is to say, a framed field which can be motivated by desire, fear, and so on and in which images are seen to have immediate consequences, repercussions (without these necessarily constituting a narrative). In ekphrasis, a present is ascribed to the represented elements, a present of commentary ('A knife lies on a table, whose legs are ornately carved'), but this is a present of deixis, of presence to the spectator, not a present of existence; the process of depiction itself belongs to the past. In the cinematic, on the other hand, the present is a present of existence, of unfolding event and of spectatorial experience of event. This present may be illusionistic (the action is in fact already over, in the can), but it is no less embedded in ongoing subjective experience. While, in ekphrasis, language describes the present of a relationship, in the cinematic, language describes the present of an experience; in ekphrasis, the present is a simple present (without the possibility of a future), while, in the cinematic, the present is a continuous present (demanding a future).

Of course, in describing dispositions of time, we must move with the utmost circumspection, for three principal reasons: (i) as we have already pointed out, evidence of temporality is found not only in tenses (conventionalised, chronometric time), but in the temporal modalities and motilities of all words; (ii) the perception of time, the quality of its nature and passage, is inevitably intimately bound up with the subjective reading experience; (iii) 'theories of time', accounts of temporality, are as much driven by ideology and psycho-social context as different perspectives on space—does the present exist or is it a notional point of transition between a past which is getting longer and a future which is getting shorter, or vice-versa, or both? Or does the present alone exist, a present variously inflected by pasts and futures? There is not a kind of Rimbaldian time conveniently unified and consistent with itself, according to which a Rimbaldian world, conveniently unified and consistent with itself, ticks; there are manifold temporal experiences to be had in the reading of Rimbaud, consonant with the multi-dimensionality of temporal experience itself:

> Mais quel en est le temps—présent, passé, ou futur ? Est-ce un 'il y a' qui évoque un passé, dont le souvenir seul dure encore ? Ou un 'il y a' qui situe les images dans un présent éternel, un 'il y a' qui n'est que présent et présence au moment où l'on dit le poème ? Ou est-ce, au contraire, un 'il y a' qui suggère seulement ce qui est possible, ou serait possible, quelque part, à l'avenir: ou bien, ce qui ne pourrait jamais exister, nulle part ?
>
> (Hackett 1982: 218–19)

[But what time is it set in—present, past or future? Is this an 'il y a'
which evokes a past, whose memory alone still survives? Or is it an
'il y a' which situates the images in an eternal present, an 'il y a'
which is only present and presence at the time of the poem's being
read? Or is it, on the other hand, an 'il y a' which suggests only what
is possible, or would be possible, somewhere, in the future: or
indeed, what could never exist anywhere?]

And thus an important task of the translator is a re-configuration or re-
inflection of the temporalities he perceives within a text, a re-configuration
which responds to changing ideologies or technologies of time (for
example, Bergsonism, the cinema), or registers more accurately his own
temporal experience of the ST. Of course, these elements cannot be fully
controlled by the translator any more than they could by the writer of the
ST. But the translator can at least make such temporalities available.

In fact, in translating the ekphrastic into the cinematic, we are turning
the voice as external commentary, or mediation (voice over), into voice as
projector, as a generating principle acting from within the experience it
utters. This paralleling of the voice with the projector has other suggestions
to make. In projecting the text, the voice brings the subject within the space
of the image. Sam Rohdie, viewing projected *autochrome* images, reports:
'No visual experience I had had seemed to enclose me so directly or
transport me into another universe so real-seeming and so without
substance' (2001: 51). But the *apparent* lack of substance—light is no less
material than any other aspect of matter—the purely aerial or acoustic
nature of the image, its appearing only to disappear, hides another kind of
density, a sense of the image as a layering of space/acousticity: in
advocating the glass slide as against the paper print, Frederick Evans
argues: 'Glass conveys with perfect truth the sense of depth, of aerial
image, of innumerable planes inseparably connected, which is the inborn
right, the natural character and privilege of the lens-given image' (1992:
71). Thus the screen, or page, the *énoncé* which is the trace left by the
énonciation, is not strictly speaking the image/text *itself*, is not where the
image/text *is*: the screen or page merely interrupts the projection of light
or voice in order to make it visible to us, as a cumulative, protean
continuum.

One might argue that the individual voice, in its agonism, implies the
suppression of other voices. The projected image carries its own light
within it; light from other sources would enfeeble that self-contained light;
the projector demands ambient darkness. The printed image, on the other
hand, being only a reflective surface, requires light from elsewhere, a public

light which makes the image universally available. I hope that my own treatment, as much out of graphic necessity/limitations as anything else, manages, to some degree at least, to reconcile a practice which makes translation an embodiment of the individual voice actualising an individual body, with the notion of the universal availability of text. In my imagination of things, *énonciation*/a performance of the ST leaves behind, as a trace, an *énoncé* (the printed TT) which then becomes the scenario for infinite other *énonciations* (performances). This is, as it were, a bringing to the surface, and the horizontal distribution of, a depth, and as such is a further manifestation of a pattern that seems fundamental to Rimbaud's writing.

One of the functions of capitals in this particular translation is to present, conventionally, or as a convention of text, the changing proxemics of reading, the moving camera. This can only be a coded indicator, since the visualisation of images is itself an aleatory and unspecifiable activity; but at least it is a reminder to us as readers to use our visual imaginations with a touch more inventiveness. And the capitalisation of 'AND' is to remind us that 'proxemics' relates not just to the visualisation of images but to the reading process itself—we are at any given point psychologically closer to the *énonciation* or further from it. If close-up is potentially a movement of psychological vertigo or fascination, it may equally be the eruption of pulsional secrets. How would these capitals manifest themselves in the voice—as a variation *of some kind* (loudness, enunciatory clarity, tempo).

These capitals clearly have another function, too: to establish or reinforce the suprasegmentality or trans-sententiality of voice (rhythm, tone, intonation). Here again capitalization can be no more than a conventional indication of the fact that acousticity is not so much to do with euphony or with the creation of semantic affinities as with resisting the segmentations of metre, or sense, or time. This is not to say that I have not attempted to create some significance through pattern, but I have retained an element of the aleatory and the unsystematic. But, as mentioned earlier, this translation is intended more as a permutable example than as a final version. There are principally two patterns of capitals:

1. Those letters which act as the annunciatory signs of the sudden and pivotal formation of 'LAKE' and its subsequent dispersal; 'awAy' is the final fragmentary manifestation: the sought-for image has metamorphosed into an expulsive event. We might want to associate the rising lake with 'Après le Déluge', with new floodwaters, polarised against the sinking cathedral of conventional worship ('La messe et les premières

communions se célébrèrent aux cent mille autels de la cathédrale'). Or we might explain these things as Hackett explains them: 'A-t-il simplement vu une cathédrale reflétée dans l'eau d'un lac qui semble monter pour rencontrer la cathédrale qui semble descendre ?' (1982: 221) [Did he simply see a cathedral reflected in the water of a lake, which seems to rise to meet the cathedral, which seems to sink?]. But we must not lose from sight the underlying proposition: that as we read, the (moving) image is a gathering into a knot, into a momentary recognisability, and the subsequent dispersal, of a group of acoustic particles; there are kinds of anticipation, pre-hearings, just as there are kinds of memory, echoes caught, but all from within movement itself, not from structure. It is these energised acoustic particles gathering in different combinations and configurations which allows us to see the unfolding text as metamorphosis. In my translation I have selected 'lake' as my demonstration case, but in reality all or any words, all or any images, are susceptible of the same processes of acoustic constitution and dissemination.

2. The second body of capitals concerns the CH, SH, TH WH combinations. These might be said to belong to the other pole of the image field, the 'sinking cathedral', but their principal function is to act out the shifting surface of the voice, the modulating and dispersive acousticity of language, as it traverses the unvoiced (CH, SH, TH /θ/), the voiced (TH /ð/), combinations where one phoneme silences the other (WH), words in which the combination is a trick of the light and the phonemes are pulled apart by a glottal stop ('pothole'), and single fragments of these combinations , a C, an H, performing other functions in other words. Here, then, the metamorphoses inherent in language, language itself as metamorphosis, is underlined, but in a way which also shows that our awareness of these metamorphoses is subject to the metamorphoses of our own attention—sometimes the consonant + H pairing is not picked out at all, often the single constituents of the pairings pass by unnoticed. The audibility of language is subject to the unevenness of vocal projection and auditory response, and to the voice's own noise.

But it is still difficult to understand this metamorphosis as a mode of imagining. It is true that it is largely a mechanism of continuous association: thanks to the singing bird, the clock that does not chime is time that has no music; the bird is still in the 'nest' of the white creatures, who, in their pothole, are transformed into 'communiantes' sinking with the cathedral; or the ribbons of the little carriage are part of the sartorial trappings of the child players, who share, too, something of the carriage's abandonment and precipitous flight. Phonetic connections, too, help words to melt into each other, superimpose themselves on each other: 'CHeeKs' is still audible, even if scattered and reversed, in 'cLocK which', which in turn is still audible in 'not CHimE'; 'trAiling ribbons' is still within earshot in 'pLayers, cHiLdren'. But our task as auditors of this text is not so much continually to discover links which change our interpretation of the object (that is to say, a process of repeated anamorphosis—although this is an inevitable concomitant of metamorphosis), as to occupy the flow of self-succeeding images and experience it—just to recall the terms of Frederick Evans—as 'innumerable planes inseparably connected', as the cumulative density of aerial perspective, as layers of duration collapsing into each other.

Does it help to think of this poem as cinema? Are these images the equivalent of photograms, or of still images, i.e. images which have a full future and require a future, or images which insist on their autonomy or on their own autonomous time/instant within a linear time which assigns them to the past. Either the 'il y a's' of 'Enfance III' are an imaginary museum, experiences interpretable but uninhabitable, irrecuperable or only *almost* generative of futures (child's carriage, bird, beasts), however much they are sustained by a life of their own. Alternatively, we are driven through these images not as the flotsam and jetsam of a past, but as a sequence of photograms, given a future and the continuity of dissolves, by the voice that speaks them. It is this latter perceptual posture that we have tried to use translation to install; if the poet is, at the end of the poem, excluded, it is not from the wood of childhood but from his own *durée*.

When we watch a film, we can safely identify what in the sound track lies within the world of the image (natural noises, the voices of the protagonists) and what lies in the world of the spectator (the musical score, a narrator's voice-over). The voice from the world of the spectator is essentially ekphrastic (still photo); the voice from the other side is cinematic (photogram, film). In 'Enfance III', our argument is that the act of translation has the power to transfer the voice from 'this side' of the screen to the 'other side'. In 'Enfance IV', the voice is already on the other side, but the movement is still that of framed verset by framed verset, in a stepped progression, and it is this that translation-as-'voice projector' must first undo:

Childhood IV

I am the saint, at prayer, on the terrace— as the peace-loving kine graze their way down to the sea of Palestine.
I am the scholar in his d a r k armchair. The branches and rain lash against the l i b r a r y casement.
I am the t r a v e l l e r walking the high road through the s t u n t e d woods; the d i s t a n t thunder of the s l u i c e s drowns out the sound of my steps. I spend long m i n u t e s gazing at the m e l a n c h o l y g o l d e n washing hung out by the setting sun.
I might easily be the child abandoned on the jetty pushing out into the open sea, the d i m i n u t i v e errand boy, walking along the lane whose crest touches the sky.
The paths are rough to the feet. The hillocks are covered with broom. The air becalmed. The birds and river-springs so far away! It can only be the world's end, up ahead.

Childhood IV

I am the saint, at prayer, on the terrace — as the peace-loving kine graze their way down to the sea of Palestine. I am the scholar in his dark armchair. The branches and rain lash against the library casement. I am the traveller walking the high road through the stunted woods; the distant thunder of the sluices drowns out the sound of my steps. I spend long minutes gazing at the melancholy golden washing hung out by the setting sun. I might easily be the child abandoned on the jetty pushing out into the open sea, the diminutive errand boy, walking along the lane whose crest touches the sky. The paths are rough to the feet. The hillocks are covered with broom. The air becalmed. The birds and river-springs so far away! It can only be the world's end, up ahead.

By this simple device I am trying to achieve a threefold effect: (a) I am trying to accelerate the eye's/voice's movement over the verbal material (or at least trying to create the impression of this acceleration); (b) I am trying to produce a greater disorientation in the eye/voice by making it more difficult to identify and retrieve the syntactic segmentation, and thereby to demonstrate (c) that it is only the conventionally horizontal continuity of prose which allows the reader to convert sequence into juxtaposition. It is too easy for us to assume that where a certain sequence is repeated, whatever the typographic disposition, the same linguistic structure will equally be repeated, and that this structure will yield to the same organisational imperatives or tendencies. This assumption cannot be made.

Typographic disposition is the choreography of the dance of the voice; change the choreography and the voice will dance differently. Vertical choreographies are the choreographies of free fall; there is no perceptual anchorage in a horizon, words/images are more abruptly encountered; although the eye still looks ahead, the spans are briefer and the voice more likely to stumble, less likely to shape syntactical phrasing (by intonation, significant pausing, and so forth). In short, the voice is forced back from the pole of articulation towards the pole of pronunciation. This is, as I say, a simple device. But it perhaps helps to highlight the ways in which, *without interfering with the language of the text*, translation might release new perceptual attitudes towards the text. Rimbaldian criticism itself, without recourse to translation, has laid out the multiplicity of possible responses to the semantics of the Rimbaldian text. What translation is particularly empowered to do is rethink the reading mode employed for the text, whatever the semantics. Our underlying argument all along in this chapter has been that it is not the meaning of the text which is at stake but how the meaning is read. The way in which the voice is choreographed inevitably changes the nature of our encounter with images. The voice compelled to move in a certain way deprives the reader of juxtapositional and reconstitutive options.

It is usual, when analysing 'Enfance IV', to refer to Rimbaud's observation in 'Alchimie du verbe': 'À chaque être, plusieurs *autres* vies me semblaient dues' [To each being, several *other* lives seemed to me to be due]. But what follows is usually omitted, namely: 'Ce monsieur ne sait ce qu'il fait: il est un ange. Cette famille est une nichée de chiens. Devant plusieurs hommes, je causai tout haut avec un moment d'une de leurs autres vies—Ainsi j'ai aimé un porc' [This gentleman does not know what he is doing: he is an angel. This family is a litter of puppies. In the company of several men, I chatted aloud with a moment of one of their other lives—

In this way, I loved a pig]. Whatever wry smirks may be nestling in this catalogue (Verlaine?), and however much Rimbaud may write these metamorphoses off as 'sophismes de la folie' [sophisms of madness], the real difference from 'Enfance IV' lies in the use of articles. In the 'Alchimie du verbe' passage, the indefinite article turns these into temporary and inconsequential transformations, produced as if by moments of absent-mindedness. In 'Enfance IV', the definite articles nail the poet into roles which sound like an inevitable destiny or a sacred duty.

But, here again, we must proceed carefully. One might argue that the particular modalities with which definite and indefinite articles are endowed, depend very much on the circumstantial syntax. 'Enfance III' seems diametrically opposed to 'Enfance IV' in its enumerative insistence on the indefinite article, which, in 'Après le Déluge', we associated with the liberated, wilful, future-oriented, random. But in 'Enfance III', the 'relative clauses' by which the lead-nouns are governed, are restrictive rather than non-restrictive, and thus these phenomena lose their apparent innocence and assume a mysterious sense of purpose: the 'relative clauses' tell us what they are there expressly to do. The guilelessness of the child's world is already haunted by the web of fate/social system. In 'Enfance IV', we find something of the converse: the definite article seems here to express the inclusive-generical, but this is invested with a strange contingency by the embroideries of the circumstantial, which begin to replace genericity (conceptuality) with the indexicality of a fortuitous here and now ('— comme les bêtes pacifiques [. . .]'; 'Les branches et la pluie [. . .]'; 'la rumeur des écluses [. . .]'). What then seems to happen in the final verset, just after the shift to the hypothetical ('Je serais bien [. . .]') and negative and disenfranchised (but still with its glimpses into a circumstantial beyond the role: 'partie à la haute mer'; 'dont le front touché le ciel'), is that this circumstantiality itself, now informed by a certain malice, becomes the defining agent, the poet correspondingly the patient and the previous circumstantiality no more than a regret ('Que les oiseaux et les sources sont loin!'). Our particular disposition of this poem tends to undermine any sense of hierarchy, of a lead-clause in each verset followed by a secondary 'decorative' gloss. The circumstantial has a much better chance of establishing itself on the same 'protagonistic' plane as the 'Je'. This makes the metamorphoses of patient > agent and agent > patient more mysteriously imperceptible.

In Chapter 2, we spoke of indexicality without referentiality, because of referentiality's past-orientedness—it depends on recognition, identification, knowledge. Here, in the world of vocal metamorphosis, we have to envisage the still photograph becoming photogram (film still) and referentiality itself not as lost (in the past) but as a future possibility. 'Enfance IV' seems to offer us the clearest justification for Rimbaud's acts of summary erasure in other poems, or apparent nostalgia for the cyclical (as in 'Barbare', 'Solde'): the future is not the promise of infinite metamorphosis; it comes to an end. Images have their own logics and designs which metamorphosis may give free rein to; the innocent becomes the guileful, the circumstantial the central; the road, like the voice-projector, insists that we fare forward, if only to a premature full stop.

The Rimbaldian text, as presented here, is a self-diversifying spread of self-mutiplying possibility. But this is not, apparently, a scenario that Rimbaud is able to sustain. 'Enfance IV' ends with the prospect of the (temporal/spatial) end of the world, so that however many roles the poet may envisage for himself, in a process of increasing hypothesis, the *terminus ad quem* of 'single-file' forward temporality cannot be evaded. Because of the reciprocal interferences of unending and widening meta-morphosis, and straight-line temporal linearity, the present translational enterprise is left with an undecidable question: is the principle of change in movement/duration a sequence of continuous dissolves or a sequence of plucked instants, a film projected in motion, or a pre-projected film of discontinuous, homogeneous frames, where each frame is likely to surrender its photogrammatic status and become a still photograph? My argument would be that the exhilaration of the Rimbaldian text enjoins upon us not to lose the photogrammatic from view and that translation is one way of ensuring that this happens. Unless we confront these wider implications of the Rimbaldian text, translation may not discover what its real function is. At its most basic, translation is trying to make sure that, by dispositional means, the Rimbaldian present tense is as progressive/continuous as it is punctual and iterative, that it holds this tri-dimensional value.

Up to this point, I have not concerned myself with the motor of metamorphosis, with the shaping propulsion of the voice's choreography, rhythm. We have already broached and pursued the question of prose-poetic rhythm in Chapter 2, and here I would like to return to a translation of 'Ornières', which first appeared in another context (2002a: 170–75) and in which I tried both to convey the multidimensionality of the reading experience and to show how rhythm might enact the 'jolts of Rimbaldian imagining'. In this poem, the passage of vehicles describes the perceptual shape of their becoming.

Unfolding rhythm registers the temperamental shifts, the notes of obsession, the psycho-physiological vicissitudes of the voice. Of course, regular verse itself allows some degree of improvisatory dynamic within the constraints of metre, no versification more so than French perhaps. But regular verse, by its very regularity, encourages the through-reading of lines, and a disembodied style of voice. Prose encourages the infiltrations of the paralinguistic, voice having to cope with the unpredictable, the unsupportive, the inimitable and newly discovered. Prose's appropriateness to translation derives from its insistence on the improvised, on the being-made, on the non-guaranteed and non-predictive. Prose throws questions of segmentation into the melting pot. Ultimately, neither the phrasal nor the intraphrasal segment has any necessary priority, and consequently, choices of rhythmic grouping are less constrained, more diverse. Prose rhythms are a latitude, a field of variation created by a poem. Within this field, the rhythmic measures metamorphose into each other and out of each other, create a multitude of relationships and kinds of dialogue. Part of our purpose in the translations of Chapter 2 was, precisely, to install a principle of rhythm based on variation (albeit with leitmotivic threads: one can modulate backwards as much as forwards) rather than repetition or regular recurrence.

Ruts

1.	The summer - to the right-	× / × × × / (2) (6)
2.	Dawn ROUSES the leaves AND	/ / × × / × (3) (6)
3.	mists AND noises of this	/ × / × × × (2) (6)
4	corner of the park, and -	/ × × × / × (2) (6)
5.	*to the left* - the slopes	× × / × / (2) (5)
6.	hold, neTTed in their	/ / × × × (2) (5)
7.	violet shadows the thousand	/ × × / × × / × (3) (8)
8.	by-flashing RUTS of *the wet*	/ × × / × × / (3) (7)
9.	*road.* Faëry[4] procession.	/ / × × × / × (3) (7)
10.	And so it is: waggons loaded	× / × / / × / × (4) (8)
11.	with wood-Gilt, *gilt-wooden*	× / / / / × (4) (6)
12.	animals, poles and multi-	/ × × / × / × (3) (7)
13.	many-coloured Canvases,	/ × / × / × × (3) (7)
14.	pulled at full gallop by	/ × / / × × (3) (6)
15.	20 dappled-circus horses,	/ × / × × × / × (3) (8)
16.	AND the children AND men	× × / × × / (2) (6)
17.	on beasts to make jawsdrop;	× / × × / × (2) (6)
18.	- 20 vehicles, m-bossed,	/ × / × × × / (3) (7)
19.	flag-decked, n-flowered,	/ / × / × (3) (5)
20.	like the carriages of the	× × / × × × × (1) (7)
21.	olden days, or fairy-told,	/ × / × / × / (4) (7)

22.	FILLED with kids mockered	/ × / / × (3) (5)
23.	up for a sub-urban past-	/ × × / / × / (4) (7)
24.	orale;—AND yes even coffins	× / × / / × / × (4) (8)
25.	under their nocturnal	/ × × × / × (2) (6)
26.	canopies, tossing their	/ × × / × × (2) (6)
27.	ebony-Plumes, AND slipping,	/ × × / × / × (3) (7)
28.	briskly, by, to the trot,	/ × / × × / (3) (6)
29.	of the, great blue, and	× × / / × (2) (5)
30.	*black, blue-Black*, MARES.	/ / × / (3) (4)

In this translation, as in 'Enfance IV', I have tried to re-form prose, for these are not lines of verse, even though their unjustified right margin leaves the lines with a degree of option on verse-being. Any prose with a standard format will seem to have surrendered itself to an obligation, to have agreed to a whole-page discursiveness, continuity, which removes from it a capacity for the impetuous and impatient (Baudelaire's 'prose poétique [. . .] assez heurtée pour s'adapter [. . .] aux soubresauts de la conscience' (1975: 275–6) [poetic prose (. . .) jerky enough to adapt itself (. . .) to the jolts of consciousness].

My original purpose here was not to produce an orchestration of rhythmic measures, but to create in the reader a more generalised sense of syncopation and rhythmic angularity. Given the choice of format, my version had to be less fluent than the source text, and perhaps less consistent in register and tone, more impulsive about syntax and lexicon. I have called upon visual aids in the construction of this syncopation, of these restless rhythmic re-launchings. Displacements of beat and rhythmic double-takes—and here anamorphosis (see Chapter 3, and, here, footnote 1)—are engineered by, among other things, the following means:

(i) Capitalisation. First, by this device I wanted to lift 'and' from its modality as agent of linguistic control, as continuity man, unobtrusively negotiating soothing and conciliatory liaisons (and implying pattern and teleology—as in the Bible or fairy-tales), and, instead, to give it more eruptive and interruptive energy. In this sense, I am taking my cue from Hopkins, from the tenth line of 'The Windhover':

Buckle! AND the fire that breaks from thee then, a billion

As I have remarked elsewhere (1986: 128), I do not regard this as Hopkins' way of asking us fully to stress a normally unstressed lexical item, as Charles Scott does (1974: 95, 103), although I would expect the weak /ən(d)/ to be promoted to /ænd/. Rather, I look upon it as a way of visually alerting the reader to what Holloway (1947: 43) calls 'an emotional intonation', which, as Hopkins' lecture notes explain, 'when not bound to the particular words will sometimes light up notes on unemphatic syllables and not the verbal stresses and pitches'. I have paired these moments of emotional illumination, not only for immediate rhythmic purposes, but also to underline the conjunction's power to magnetize attention and/or textual invention, to serve the imperiousness of vision.

I should add that capitalization of 'and' also allows it to participate in the sub-Joycean sexual sub-text formed by the string 'ROUSES - AND - AND - RUTS - AND - AND - FILLED - AND - AND - MARES'. This is not only to imprint the text with the 'sub-urban pastorale', but also to install a level of sensory inarticulacy in a text which is perfectly articulate, to place us in the position of not knowing how many narrators this particular vision is capable of activating, or how many levels of consciousness may be operating at the same time. The other capitalizations—of 'Dawn', 'neT Ted', 'Gilt', 'Canvases', 'Plumes' and 'Black'—are again pairings, this time of voiced/voiceless doublets, part of a design to use 'Ornières' as the consonantal equivalent of 'Voyelles', a design which also explains 'm-bossed' and 'n-flowered'; as Rimbaud himself points out: 'Je réglai la forme et le mouvement de chaque consonne' [I regulated the form and movement of each consonant] ('Délires II: Alchimie du verbe', *Une saison en enfer*).

(ii) Hyphenisation. Hyphenisation in this translation is designed, certainly, to increase the sense of impatient dynamism, verbal elements being welded together in the poet's insatiable appetite for experience. But often the hyphen seems to have mis-located itself (e.g. 'dappled-circus' rather than 'circus-horses'), or to have forced the wrong combination (e.g. 'fairy-told'), or to have raised unlooked-for linguistic dilemmas (such as 'wood-Gilt, *gilt-wooden*'), and accordingly to pose questions about the appropriate position and strength of stress.

(iii) The non-grammatical use of commas. My punctuation follows the punctuation of the Lucien-Graux (BN) manuscript pretty closely, for the most part. I have introduced parentheses for the indications of direction ('A droite', 'de gauche'), I have replaced 'et' by a comma at 'pavoisés et fleuris', and added a comma between 'des carrosses anciens' and 'ou de contes'. It is in the final section that I have taken most liberties, introducing commas here with an iconic rather than grammatical function. I have tried to imitate the interwoven trotting of several horses, since this is the music of the last lines and since there seems to be concealed in 'filant au trot de' a knowledge that the musical accompaniment is in fact an unravellable clatter of shoes: ×/×,/×,/,××/,××//,×/×/,/ ('AND slipping, briskly, by, to the

115

trot, of the great blue, and *black blue-Black*, MARES').

I have introduced some lexical coinages intended to chime with Rimbaud's own 'bossés', coinages which are not so much root-and-branch neologisms as exploited flexibilities in the language, flexibilities which are as familiar as they are strange, and the more disorientating for that: possible mis-hearing, possible errors, possibles teases, opening up routes which might take us through the looking glass. And in the same spirit, I have italicized three phrases, not because they have anything in common, but because italics may help us argue the case for 'crossing over', into another dimension of awareness or imagination. Most obviously, perhaps, *'gilt-wooden'* is meant to lead the reader back to 'guilt-ridden', and then 'ridden' as a literal possibility for these roundabout animals. And the 'g(u)ilt' that rides these wooden animals is perhaps the same that provokes Rimbaud's own much-quoted renunciation in *Une saison en enfer* ('Délires II: Alchimie du verbe'):

> J'aimais les peintures idiotes, dessus de portes, décors, toiles de saltimbanques, enseignes, enluminures populaires; la littérature démodée, latin d'église, livres érotiques sans orthographe, romans de nos aïeules, contes de fées, petits livres de l'enfance, opéras vieux, refrains niais, rythmes naïfs.
> [I loved stupid paintings, decorated lintels, stage scenery, the backcloths of street entertainers, shop-signs and inn-signs, popular illuminations; literature that was out of fashion, Church Latin, illiterate pornography, novels our grandmothers read, fairy stories, children's books, old operas, nonsense refrains, simple rhythms.]

The italicisation of 'to the left' has it in mind to open up another spatial dimension, and, at the same time, to express the desire to penetrate that dimension, to release the energies of a different typeface. One's suspicion is that the 'juments bleues et noires' have emerged from the 'ombre violette', that they are the 'ombre violette' which presides over the road and its cortèges. Finally, the italicization of 'black blue-Black' also alerts us to another dimension, not of semantics or space, but of pre- and post-intertextuality.[5]

As intimated earlier, I did not, here, wish the reader to be so aware of the rhythmic variation of individual measures/'feet', but to feel the movement, often bumpy and unquiet, of larger spans. Consequently, my tabulated scansion—rhythmic pattern + number of stresses + number of syllables—is designed not so much to show the continuities and modulations between different rhythmic phrases as between whole lines.

Metamorphosis, here, I would want to argue, is as much a matter of movement between sections as within them, and this coincides with our uncertainties about the make-up of the procession(s) itself/themselves: while the dash preceding 'Même', and its capital letter, seem to indicate a different cortège, or different part of the same cortège, one cannot as confidently say that the earlier sections, those of the 'chars' and the 'véhicules', also separated by a dash, are not different views of the same group of wagons: they share 'vingt' and other elements create parallels— 'toiles bariolées/ pavoisés'; 'chargés/ pleins'; 'bois doré/ bossé'. Perhaps the dash here is as assimilative or appositional as it was disjunctive and enumerative with 'Même'; punctuation, too, is subject to metamorphosis. Besides, if this is a 'Défilé de féeries', if the 'chars' and 'véhicules' are a product of the dawn light on the right, the mists and noises, and the funeral cortège is a configuration of the 'ombre violette' on the left, and if all are conjured into motion by the 'mille rapides ornières', then parallels and distinctions are themselves no more than a trick of the light, as the growing day choreographs and fluidly sculpts its own emergence.

At all events, the poem is a single movement which falls into four interconnected sections. Lines 1–6 supply a relatively low stress-count and a relatively stable syllable-count, as contextual elements are brushed in. Line 7 provides a transition of slack uneventfulness (three stresses in eight syllables) before the 3:7 ratio, introduced by the 'acceleration' of the ruts, climbs to 4:6 in line 11, whose chiastic arrangement enacts its pivotality. And then we slip back through 3:7 to an easing of tension in ll. 16–17, as human figures appear and the peaceable 2:6 of the opening lines is picked up again. Line 18 begins a movement which is, in some respects, the reverse of the one we have just been through: its 3:7 echoes the 3:7 of line 8 which initiates the climactic push to line 11; but in this moment of recollection, we sink to our lowest level of perceptual activity at line 20, but then re-gather momentum towards line 24. Line 24 is another line of transition, as the funeral cortège comes into view, and from this point the lines shorten, syllable-by-syllable after line 27, as if the horses were coming into sharper focus, or closer, or becoming more phantasmal. Because, on the other hand, the stress-level is maintained, we arrive at the peculiarly dense darkness of line 30, three stresses in only four syllables. So the pattern, according to this account, runs something like: 1–6 / 7 / 8–17 / 18–23 / 24 / 25–30, with a pivotal apogee at line 11, in the 8–17 section, and a pivotal nadir at line 20, in the 18–23 section. The apparent symmetry of this sequence is, of course, an illusion of spatialisation and homogeneously quantified sequence; but the reader will perhaps feel a certain shape in the unfolding groups of lines with their transitional buffers.

It is always likely to occur to the sceptical mind to put again the question we have already asked (see above, p. 34): Why is translation necessary to this operation? Why don't you just introduce your typographical quirks and punctuational interferences into the ST itself? A true, if mystificatory, answer would be: 'it is only Rimbaud in my own language which incurs, necessitates, this typographical choreography'. Translation is an act of exfoliation, which peels off the text's pre-constitutedness or its perenniality. And the insertion of another language is what achieves this exfoliation because translation is less about imitation than about interrogation. The foreign language is, in other words, less a re-coding of a message already received from the ST, than the instrument by which we read the ST, is, as it were, that which takes us back to the ST, the reader's lens which inevitably reconfigures the text and necessitates a *posture* in the reader as much, if not more so, than interpretative inventiveness. One might say, then, that the foreign language (TL) is what rediscovers the ST, what necessitates its re-articulation as textual revelation. What translation resists is the ST's self-repetition because it is precisely this self-repetition which justifies its history as a history of changing interpretations. Translation tries to reanimate the text *in its textuality*, to refuse its givenness, to restore the primariness of encounter and the inimitable first-timeness of the reading process. But inasmuch as translation incorporates paralinguistic material or paralinguisticity, inasmuch as it attempts to reconstitute contextuality as a configuration of the voice's passage through a string of words, or, better still, as the voice's passage traced by what it utters as it goes, reading as writing, so the text produced has a peculiar fragility. It owes this fragility to its being a performance of a text, a text which the translation's performativity transforms into a scenario, not a play-script, but a film-script, that is to say the kind of script which has little status as script, which is likely to be revised and amended in the course of shooting, and which ultimately begins to assume an almost paratextual existence, something which helps us to understand the ST better, like an ancillary document.

The creative freedom of the translator has much to do with the fact that translation has a special function as an instrument of exploration of the form/genre/medium used in the ST. Many translators speak of their craft as a set of priorities and options laid down by the ST, as if the ST's formal or generical nature were already established, or somehow had been subsumed into, become invisible in, the text itself. But the translator, while not necessarily denying notions of organic form, and the indivisibility of manner and message—indeed, in order to affirm these things—would claim that transference from one language to another involves transformation, a transformation which will, paradoxically perhaps, both reveal the inimitabilities of the ST and at the same time enlarge the translational parameters. The prose poem's relationship both with its form and its medium is a relatively latent one; indeed, it is this latency, we have already argued, which defines it and which has made it resistant to definition. Perhaps this implies a special kind of translational treatment. Since the prose poem can act as both the source and the sum of all versions of it, thanks to its latency, then translation can lie at any point between these two termini, that is to say, in the space which makes travelling from one to the other, source to sum, worthwhile and non-tautological. It is quite difficult for criticism to explore form in the same way: exegesis can so often operate without any reference to form at all. The advantage of translation is not so much that it has to make choices, but that it has to pursue the consequences of those choices; and in doing this, it comes to understand the pressures and flexibilities of the source and target forms/genres/mediums it trades in.

Silence as Translational Presence
The Translator and Resonant Space

In the *Guardian*'s *G2* magazine for 18 July 2002 (p. 9), we read that the publishers of John Cage's music—Peters Edition—have claimed that Mike Batt, the man behind The Planets, infringed copyright with his composition 'One Minute Silence', credited to Batt/Cage. The Cage piece in question is, of course, his 1952 '4' 33'", during which a musician (or musicians) do not play. Batt says not only that *his* Cage is Clint Cage, a pseudonym for himself, but that 'my silence is original silence'. And indeed there is a sense in which he must be right, since, willy-nilly, his silence must be constituted by, and constitutive of, a different set of ambient noises. Steven Poole's article ('A Kind of Hush') continues:

> The live performance of Batt's One Minute Silence was actually unfaithful to the original CD version [on the album *Classical Graffiti*], which is simply one minute's-worth of the absence of any digital signal. Cage's 4' 33", on the other hand, has always been meant to be an ambient soundwork, rather than a pure silence. In the post-performance discussion, Batt says: 'Ours is a better silence: it's digital. Theirs is only analogue'. Let us, too, compare the scores. Cage's score consists merely of vertical lines marked with timings. Batt's piece, on the other hand, is clearly in the key of G major (or E minor), and is more structurally complex, finishing with a flourish of metre-switching from five-eight to three-eight to four-four. These are obviously quite different pieces of music.

There is much to reflect on in these words: silence as a piece of music; acoustically structured silence; the difference between digital and analogue silence; the difference between studio-recorded silence and live-performance silence.

The underlying and salutary reminder is that silence is not an acoustic blank, but has specific resonances, specific motives, specific generical possibilities—the silence of romance (fear of breaking a spell or an image by speaking, by uttering a banality, or activating a non-euphonic voice) is a far cry from the silence of the thriller (stealth, resistance, bluff)—and specific intertexts. By intertexts I mean not only the possibility of generical crossovers (a lyric silence 'quoted' in a horror story), but also larger cultural crossovers. As with voice, we lack an anthropological history of silence; but we can imagine that silence in the Middle Ages had different meanings, functions, timbres from our own, or that there is a Japanese silence quite unlike anything we know in the West; correspondingly, we can imagine a World War One poet, perhaps, who inserts a medieval resonance into the silence of the trenches. We assume that to translate is to translate one discourse (with its attendant acousticity) into an equivalent discourse in another language (with its inescapably 'other' acousticity); but discourse has attendant silences, too, and these we never think to translate. If the burden of this book is to re-establish the eminence, or even pre-eminence, of the materiality of language, then silence is an integral part of acousticity and must itself be consciously addressed as a translational factor; and if, in Chapter 3, my intention was to begin to transcribe 'Le langage des fleurs et des chose muettes!' [The language of flowers and dumb things!] (Baudelaire: 'Élévation'), to acknowledge Nerval's warning: 'A la matière même un verbe est attaché' [Even to matter itself a language clings] ('Vers dorés'), then in this chapter, the converse is my task: to restore to sound its silence, and to silence its acoustic. Silence, whether realised in real time or in 'visual' time, is an intimate part of the paralinguistics of text, but is rarely attended to, other than in its purely physical/respiratory guise, the pause.

But before we examine more closely these relative and fluid silences, we need to put metaphysical or absolute silence in its context, the silence which is pre-terrestrial and post-apocalyptic, or pre-textual and post-textual. Steiner's discussion of silence in the essays of *Language and Silence* revolves around the way it defines certain inadequacies: the inadequacy of language to express that which transcends it; the inadequacy of language to a post-Holocaust world ('Is the poet's verse not an insult to the naked cry?' (1985: 173); the inadequacy of a devalued contemporary language to the linguistic impulses of the poet, hence the latter's silence. In Rimbaud's case, the abdication of language 'signifies the elevation of action over word. [. . .] Having mastered and exhausted the resources of language as only a supreme poet can, Rimbaud turns to that nobler language which is the deed' (67). These arguments, somewhat contradictory—how can one master and exhaust the resources of language, when every silence registers linguistic limitations?—metaphorise silence and in so doing empty it of atmosphere and human hubbub. This inanimate emptiness is not physical, inhabited; it has a meaning—the limits of human contingency and imperfection, and of the capacity to express horror or ecstasy—but is an ultimate ascesis, the point at which the materiality and temporality of linguistic sequence has to be cast off. Steiner's world is a world in which supreme poets live, poets who need a silence commensurate with their linguistic ambitions. But it is a silence that the reader cannot share, loftily inaccessible, unless as a guarantee of the poetically high-principled or of the absoluteness (ultimately unachievable or unsustainable) of the creative affirmation. Rimbaud's illuminations emerge with peremptory imperiousness from the clean slate of a temporal zero, from a lull in being: 'Et dans ce creux temporel, cet hiatus sensible nommé aube, se produisent soudain une explosion de force et de pensée, une brusque giclée d'existence. D'un seul coup le silence se fait cri, l'immobilité se mue en un frisson d'ailes battantes' (Richard 1955: 189) [And in this temporal void, this perceptible hiatus called dawn, occurs, suddenly, an explosion of energy and thought, a sharp burst of existence. At a stroke, silence turns into cry, immobility turns into a shudder of beating wings]. And just as imperiously they come to an abrupt, self-erasing close. We seem to thrive on this demonstration that the poet makes no compromises with a context, with the gradual negotiatedness of thought. And as we have seen, our anxiety about the genericism of the prose poem is appeased: the more formal autonomy we can bestow on it, the more we can feel that it is a textual gesture designed to fly in the face of the page's patient and equable emptiness.

But has the translator aught to do with this projected metaphysical silence? One might argue that this particular silence is alien to his task in several respects:

(i) The ST already exists, has already broken the silence. As we have argued, it is not the translator's business to return to the ST's conditions of appearance, but to instal the ST in a literary continuity.

(ii) This is not a silence the translator can reinvent. It is an untouchable and featureless silence which brings into existence, is brought into consciousness by, the ST but plays no part in its creative self-realisation.

(iii) Inasmuch as this silence affirms the ST as a beginning, endows it with authority, it should be resisted, replaced with other kinds of silence, silences which are not status-conferring, but are an intimate part of the remaking of the ST. This may be an argument for a translation which entails some formal unravelling of the ST. Translation breaks into the ST in order to liberate all the disorders and anarchies in its language, no longer answerable to some formal design that metaphysical silence guarantees.

(iv) The pretextual silence that the translator aspires to is the silence of the page, the silence of the translator's own receptivity prior to the noise of the arriving ST/TT or in the space between the ST and TT.

Immediately one shifts from an undifferentiated silence to a differentiated one, the *quality* of the silence begins to matter.[1] The flow of the language of a text encourages us to think of silence as an *interruption* of speech, silences *between* words or sentences, demarcative absences of continuation. It is in this role in particular that silence is treated either as something negative, featureless, a gap, almost accidental, or, if resonant, as something carrying the meanings and connotations of the words which precede it—we stop in order to interpret a language not fully apprehendable in its flow. But in thinking like this we do not think of the silences which are within, or behind words, nor of the silence of the reading organism, nor of the ambient, criss-crossing silences which suffuse the whole text and act as a complex modal accompaniment. Olivier Bivort (1998: 34–5) reminds us of Sergio Sacchi's words: 'il faudrait peut-être prendre [Rimbaud] au mot: et donc le lire un peu de la même manière qu'il écrivait—lire chez lui la couleur des voyelles, la forme et le mouvement des consonnes, les rythmes instinctifs, les dénivellements, les ruptures—les silences' [One should perhaps take (Rimbaud) at his word: and therefore read him rather in the way in which he wrote—read, in his work, the colour of the vowels, the form and movement of the consonants, the instinctive rhythms, the irregularities, the ruptures—the silences].

Rimbaud's own most suggestive reference to silence is probably to be found at the end of the first section of 'Délires II: Alchimie du verbe': 'Ce fut d'abord une étude. J'écrivais des silences, des nuits, je notais l'inexprimable. Je fixais des vertiges.' [To begin with, it was a course of study. I wrote silences, nights, noted the inexpressible, set down the vertiginous.] Bernard/Guyaux, as others, warn the reader against applying the texts of *Une saison en enfer* too readily to the *Illuminations*: in 'Alchimie du verbe', Rimbaud quotes only his verse poems and 'L'histoire d'une de mes folies' [The story of one of my follies] may well only cover the period between the 'lettre du voyant' to Demeny (15 May 1871) and May 1872 when he decided to abandon verse-poetry (2000: 509–10). But the phrase 'L'histoire d'une de mes folies' may as much be an inclusive, sardonic understatement as a specification of a particular bout of lunatic ambition; it may well be an anticipated wisdom-after-the-event: like Mallarmé, Rimbaud seems to have been permanently accompanied by a sense of the 'Glorious Lie',[2] or the 'lucide désespoir' [lucid despair] of Redon's 'grand Mage'.[3] At all events, it would be difficult to deny such self-evident connections as that between the paragraph which begins 'Je m'habituai à l'hallucination simple: je voyais très franchement une mosquée à la place d'une usine, etc.' [I accustomed myself to simple kinds of hallucination: I saw, very clearly, a mosque where a factory stood] and 'Enfance III' (dated by Py July/August 1873, on the basis of Bernard's opinion; 1967: 86).

Brunel sees Rimbaud's written silences as limit states, moments of rupture produced by expressive pressure: 'C'était bien cela, *écrire des silences*: non pas les extases d'une nuit d'été, pas même la torpeur d'une Afrique désirée où brûleraient tous les feuillets, mais le silence auquel parvient le cri à son paroxysme' (1987: 19) [That is indeed what it was, *writing silences:* not the ecstasies of a summer's night, not even the torpor Africa, that object of desire, where all the manuscript sheets would burn, but the silence of a cry at its paroxysm]. This seems to me to miss the point, to miss precisely that connection Rimbaud characteristically makes between silence and the night, where night gives us access to the other side of being, of words, in a space of mute revolt:

> De la nuit, Vierge-Mère impalpable, qui baigne
> Tous les jeunes émois de ses silences gris;
> Elle eut soif de la nuit forte où le cœur qui saigne
> Écoule sans témoin sa révolte sans cris.
>
> ('Les Premières Communions')

> [(She thirsted) For night, impalpable Virgin Mother, who bathes all young emotions in her grey silences; she thirsted for strong-willed night, when the bleeding heart traffics, unseen, in mute rebellion]

Nights are the places where the birds of spiritual 'dégagement', the 'future Vigueur', are exiled, are dormant, as 'Le Bateau ivre' tells us:

> - Est-ce en ces nuits sans fonds que tu dors et t'exiles,
> Million d'oiseaux d'or, ô future Vigueur ? –
> [Is it in these bottomless nights that you sleep and live your exile,

you countless golden birds, o future Vigour?].

In many ways this setting is not so far removed from that which closes 'Enfance V': an entombment in a 'nuit sans fin' which generates a 'peut-être' of broken boundaries between elements, planets, fact and fiction, the possibility of possibility, a silence which is populated by the phantasmagoria of linguistic invention (as Osmond points out (1976: 94), the phrase 'Je suis maître du silence' will echo with 'Je suis maître en fantasmagories' of 'Nuit de l'enfer'):

> Aux heures d'amertume je m'imagine des boules de saphir, de métal. Je suis maître du silence. Pourquoi une apparence de soupirail blêmirait-elle au coin de la voûte ?
> [In my hours of bitterness, I imagine balls of sapphire, of metal. I am the master of the silence. Why should a light, as from a cellar-window, make its pale appearance in the corner of the vault ?]

Unfortunately, the poet's underground fastness, the world turned upside down, is not hermetically sealed against the light: just as the 'communiante' of 'Les Premières Communions' may yearn for a 'nuit forte' to blacken the grey, so the poet of 'Enfance V' may regret the hint of a 'soupirail' in his dark retreat, a threat to his own lamp.

But the closing lines of 'Angoisse'—

> Rouler aux blessures, par l'air lassant et la mer; aux supplices, par le silence des eaux et de l'air meurtriers; aux tortures qui rient, dans leur silence atrocement houleux.
> [Rolling on wounds, through the tiring air and the sea; on torments, through the silence of the murderous waters and air; on tortures which laugh, in their hideously surging silence].

—suggest silence of a very different kind, a muteness proportional to a cruelty ('meurtriers', 'atrocement'), a sadism of silence which produces pain, deformity, which increases an anguish, which expresses a refusal to be parleyed with. This is a silence resonant with intention and motive, a silence which silences. There is intimated here, perhaps, the view that the reward for discourses of compromise or penitence is suppression, and that this suppression relates to the re-installation of a linguistic quiescence. The parenthesised second paragraph in 'Angoisse' is one of those hastily erected Rimbaldian spaces (cottage, tomb, room, coach) in which the 'cuivre [qui] s'éveille clairon' [brass (which) wakes up a bugle] can trumpet forth its notes. And this brings us back to a silence of latency, or a silence of the other side:

> Ô, suprême Clairon plein de strideurs étranges,
> Silences traversés des Mondes et des Anges:
>
> ('Voyelles', ll. 12–13)[4]
>
> [O supreme Bugle full of strange stridencies, silences traversed by Worlds and by Angels]

I do not wish to tangle at any length with 'Voyelles', other than to reiterate what has already been said with persuasive good sense:

> [. . .] il s'agit, beaucoup plus que d'une broderie synesthésique à la mode de l'époque, de diffracter les mots, de les faire réagir les uns sur les autres, à partir d'échos phoniques, visuels, connotatifs; de les associer selon les lois non logiques de *restes* mémoriels et sensuels qui sont comme un infra-langage parasitant la communication ordinaire, ici promus fils conducteurs, électrisés, de la création poétique.
>
> (Berranger 1993: 83)
>
> [It is much more than a synaesthetic embroidery in the style of the period; it is about diffracting words, making them react on each other, by virtue of their phonetic, visual and connotative echoes; it is about associating words with each other according to the non-logical laws of the *surplus traces* of memory and sensation, which are like an infra-language living parasitically on ordinary communication, here upgraded to electrified conductor wires of poetic creation.]

What is also crucial is the implication of the 'naissances latentes' (l. 2) and the future they are attached to ('Je dirai quelque jour'). Are these vowels in any sense born? Do they ever come into being? Caught in a continual process of *signifiance,* these vowels will never come to an end of permutational becoming, metamorphosis. Language, no less than images, set in motion by the reading voice, is never done with its shifts between phonemic and graphemic awareness, between the oral and nasal forms of vowels, closed and open, rounded and unrounded, front and back, between synaeresis and diaeresis, between the articulated and the elided. No shortage of interpretative keys have been attached to this poem, but in the erroneous belief that a language constitutes the text. And yet not only is this a language within a language—can we hear them both simultaneously?—but the infra-language is all 'éparpillement', dislocation, fraternisation, imbrication, mobility of constituents. The sonnet may suggest a structure of closure and destination, and we duly arrive at the omega; but the structure also sets in motion and maintains a perpetuum mobile of change and slippage.

Too often with Rimbaud, it seems, we are inclined to translate *out of* the text, towards the safety of equivalent words which might be said to do justice to what we have just read (but not to our reading). Translation can stabilise the unsteady text by showing that it can be handled, can be led out of its recalcitrance into community, as a Work. When in 'Alchimie du verbe', Rimbaud writes: 'je me flattai d'inventer un verbe accessible, un jour ou l'autre, à tous les sens. Je réservais la traduction' [I flattered myself that I would invent a language accessible, some day or other, to all the senses. I reserved the rights of translation], or at the end of 'Parade': 'J'ai seul la clef de cette parade sauvage' [I alone hold the key to this savage parade], we may well suppose that, far from writing 'une poésie à clefs', Rimbaud is fearful of interpretative moves which fail to take proper account of the text's tendency continually to re-process itself. If the translator proposes, therefore, to translate *into* the text, he must attempt to capture the silent activity of this self-processing. We usually think of self-reflexivity as something designed to establish and sustain textual integrity, rather than the opposite; but self-reflexivity in the Rimbaldian text is an agent of dissolution, the generator of associative initiatives without guarantees. Faced with Mallarmé's remark about words 'par le heurt de leur inégalité mobilisés' (2003: 211) [set in motion by the collision of their inequalities], a structuralist might respond with a vision of mechanisms of compensation and self-equalisation; a post-structuralist, on the other hand, might present a picture of uncontrollable self-ramification, of loose ends which throw integrative moves into a turmoil of tensional divergence. This latter view would entail a translation in which the elicitation of the silences within words would be a spoiling activity, a verbal pruritis, which refused to let words slip back into the slumber of unequivocal being. In effect, silence would become the very agent of centrifugality.

The silence that I have tried to capture in the version of 'Parade' (see Appendix II (iii) for 'straight' translation) which follows, is, then, the silence of readerly automatism, recollection, association, polyglottal, polymorphological, polyetymological, which sets in motion this fruitfully corrosive inwardness. Heard words are sweet, but those unheard are sweeter. They flash upon the inward ear and in so doing, undo the threads of our attention, hustle us on other journeys. Is this what the ST intended?

It may have done, but it could not say. At all events, translation is about the unconcealing of this 'révolte sans cris'; the release of this turbulent silence is one of translations' literary characteristics.

[Circus] Parade

Rhumb types, stock-sturd~~y~~. Sèvral have squeezed your welts dry. Without ~~needs~~ and in noh hrry to ~~apply~~ their brilliante facultates and their f'm'liaritasy with your perceptions. What ~~mature~~ mien. Eyes z glazed z the summer nigh~~t~~, read and black, *tricolores*, steel-blaue punctuated with goltten stars; deformd fac~~ial~~ features, le~~a~~den, enpa~~l~~lored, burnt out; v~~o~~ices madcapped and graveilled. '**The cruel swagger of their tawdry finery**' [Osmond]—There are young onces, too—What would they ~~think~~ of Cherubino?—with voces that scar~~ee~~ the life outa of you and dangerous weapns. They're sent into the towns '~~to put some back on~~', rigged out in disgusting *lussoury*.

O the arch-violento Paradiso of the grimace of orage! Don't talk to me of your Faq?rs and other side-show b~~ouffoon~~neries. In costumes improvis~~i~~erted in the style of bad dreams, they play *complaintes*, or tragödiens of briganti and demigotts, witty as neither historya nor Religions have ever been. Chinoisamen, Hottentots, [gypsies] **Zigeuner,** ~~fools~~, hyenas, Molochs, o. lunacies, **Diavolos** [demons] of DI [dark intent], they mix populaire, muttherskniee turns with bestl ~~posies~~ and solicitudines. They're ready to ~~interpret~~ new plays and tender-hearted songs. **Meistergiocolieri** [oh, yes!], they transform place and person**nage**, and resort to hypnotic Komödy. '**Eyes blaze, the blood sings, the bones swell and stretch**' [Osmond], tears and red rivulets ~~stream~~ down. Their derisive backchatter and their terror last only a min, or for ~~whole~~ months.

I ALONE HOLD THE KEY TO THIS SAVAGE PARADE

I am trying here to make textually visible four types of silence:

1. The silence of unpronounced letters, the silence of linguistic history, of etymological origins, which reminds us that language is already there; the silence of inappropriability, the silence of a greater knowledge which makes all linguistic use ironic. These are the silences perhaps of 'vos mondes' and of 'vos consciences',

hanging on wilfully to their continuities, the tenacious silences of propriety and respectfulness. Silences which are inhibitions, emasculations. But one might also think of them as the inextirpable traces of the primitive, elements that modern linguistics has not been able to rationalise out of its system. And the longer these elements have stayed, the more irrational and inexplicable they have become. These are the smugglers and contraband that the linguistic customs men are trying to spot and root out:

> Ils signalent aux lois modernes les faunesses.
> Ils empoignent les Fausts et les Diavolos.
> « Pas de ça, les anciens ! Déposez les ballots! »
>
> ('Les Douaniers')
> [They inform on faunesses to (the guardians of) modern laws. They seize hold of Fausts and Diavolos. 'None of that, my wrinklies! Drop that gear!']

2. The silence of surplus and substitute letters. The silences which, like the Entertainers (I borrow Osmond's handy term of reference (1976: 97–100), lead the text a merry dance: Chinamen, Hottentots, gypsies, fools, hyenas, Molochs, old lunacies, demons of dark intent. These are the silences which anarchically prod the text into other languages. These are silences which return language to its own autonomies, and in so doing, disperse any global meaning the text might have, reducing it to fragments, stray linguistic impulses and beginnings which we are powerless to synthesise. The verbal unconscious (equivalent to Benjamin's 'optical unconscious': 'For it is another nature which speaks to the camera rather than to the eye. [. . .] It is through photography that we first discover the existence of this optical unconscious, just as we discover the instinctual unconscious through psychoanalysis' (II, 1999: 511–12)) manifests itself in the Freudian slips which alternative letters, phonemes, morphemes, perceived as silent potentialities at the heart of words; language is not ours even as we invent it. We still hear that set of events that Rimbaud's poem describes, but now language is even less the medium for describing what is already there/has already happened; now the text and its events are an accidental product of the unfolding of language, itself become the subject; the Entertainers, quite

understandably, have become the instruments of language's own exploration of itself. In their 'costumes improvisés avec le goût du mauvais rêve', the Entertainers release the madness in language, its persistent refusal to formulate a meaning, its ability to open up language to its own infinity, its own infinite permutations. Words cease to tolerate the attribution of meaning and, instead, leaping from the dictionary, insist on becoming the matrices of verbal proliferation, and of journeys between themselves as original forms and transformations they cannot imagine. The poet may have the key, but he does not have the mastery. This form of silence sends words out to 'prendre du dos'; indeed it is important that this kind of silence, and the two that follow, are regarded as acts of self-mutilation to produce a creative deformity.

3. The silence of letters removed from the middles and ends of words, syncope and apocope. In their traditional verse-use, these devices entail the removal of word-internal and word-terminal mute e's to produce the correct number of syllables in the line of verse. This is a moment of erasure to ensure a conformity, a paradoxical dose of the demotic to sustain a (bourgeois) 'vieillerie poétique' [poetic old hat]. Poets like Laforgue and Apollinaire may thrive on this humiliating sleight-of-ear practised by the anxious reader. But syncope and apocope, as we have used them here, are different in that there is no external, visible (metrical) justification. Language is invaded by competing languages—newspeak, cybernetics, text-messaging—so that language is no longer envisaged as a psychophysiological manifestation, an expression of the drives of the organism, but a set of manipulable signs with nothing more than an efficiency value, proportional to the speed and economy with which, unequivocally, they can communicate a message. We are back with the 'tambours étouffés' of 'Démocratie', because the silencing of letters is the stifling of phonemes, and more particularly of the 'wild voice' of vowels. It is not difficult to imagine a situation in which acronyms and telegraphic forms cease to be reconstructible and simply replace the original words and phrases: 'Genuine, attract, intellig n/s F 31 WLTM sim M 35–40 GSOH for f/ship+'. In these instances, the silencing itself is suppressed. I have on several occasions restored that silencing, that removal of the possibility of voice. This is a violence of a

completely different kind, not a creative deformation, a monstrosity that produces new forms, excesses, redundancies, unnaturalemphases. This is a backstreet elimination, a commercial enterprise that belongs more to the 'métropole crue moderne parce que tout goût connu a été éludé' than to the fairground. On the one hand, then, a silence without any space within which to resonate, not a silence produced but a silence erased, an elimination in the name of efficiency. If language is our society, then the elimination of silence is a totalitarian gesture which might correspond to the erasure of thought, or private communication, or anything invisible, unmonitored. On the other hand, the crossings-out catch them in the act, that point of silence between being and disappearance. If silence is living a dispensability, that moment at which letters/phonemes can be removed from a text, then it inhabits its own disappearance. No more clearly can we see that the disappearance of sound involves the disappearance of silence. But, in another sense, the crossing out is already completed, and silence, brief, fragile, is what is left between now and the next version of the text, when it, too, will have been removed. This is a (funerary) silence, a temporary 'terrain vague' after a demolition, a verbal equivalent of Haussmannisation or the ruins of the Commune, without prospect of reconstruction.

4. If these crossed-out letters generate, ironically, a continuity between this version and the next, so equally do the crossed-out words. But these latter do not mark a dispensability and removal, but, on the contrary, they outline the possibility of substitution, of alternatives. The crossed-out element is a road to elsewhere, itself not lost from view but merely shifting into storage, as a variant. But more important than the word's individual destiny is the line which crosses out, this gesture which is evacuative only in the sense that it sees that there is a space behind or beyond, and into which it wishes us to move. What is also expressed here is the inescapable paradox: language is both a trap and a release. It is the corpse of the already known, used, exhausted, and the way out of stagnancy, the instrument of renewal. It is perhaps harder for the translator to live this paradox than it is for the creative writer. We have already spoken of the dangers of the translator's need to make the ST more intelligible. Even where this impulse is not so acutely felt, the text must retain some

recognisability, without which the ST no longer participates. This naturally puts translation within the realms of objectives and limits; this is what seems to make translation, because of those limits, potentially perfectible, to endow the *corrigé* with an ethics. Instead, the aim should be to set in motion a series of displacements, to be self-displacing, not, as we have already said, in a series of supercessions, that each confirm and justify the practice of choice, but a choice that exercises itself in order to refuse itself—this crossing-out means: it may not be this, but it is not anything else *in particular*.

What we have enacted here is a variety of local silences. These silences allow one to draw into the text, to make immanent in the text, textual fantasies, processes of textual deformation, in which the silence is always more or less filled by unrealised speech/vocality. What I am imagining here is a translation which carries within it the signs of what I know and you do not. That is to say that my *speaking* of the translation is accompanied by a silent eye-reading of it, during which I take into myself a linguistic and perceptual awareness, a multilinguality, which my speech does not broadcast. Under the cover of its spoken continuity, the text is constantly breaking up, going off at tangents, being invaded by linguistic caprice. Translation, in this guise, is a rodeo: the apparently sedate textual horse has wilfully, and behind everyone's back, turned into a bucking bronco. This is a translation that the translator does not publish; this is a private document, the autobiography of a reading; but it also needs to be (imagined as) spoken, without the listener being privy to its follies. One might think that this withholding runs counter to Rimbaud's ambitions for language as an instrument of utopian socialism, that what is being enacted here is the exasperating and obstructive silence of 'la Reine, la Sorcière' ('Après le Déluge'); or that it perpetuates that state which damns translation as power-play: the knowledge of the translator exceeds that of the reader, and, for that reason, the TT's real unreliability lies not so much in its possible errors or inaccuracies, but in its never having disclosed the whole gestatory story, the whole imaginative adventure. But this secrecy, this withholding, is necessary to the release of the silence of the text, which is this other text. If Rimbaud periodically affirms fraternity, there are equally important self-dissociative moments, moments of self-withdrawal, precisely to safeguard originating experiences ('Aube', 'Villes II', 'Parade', 'Vies'). But fraternity lies in our all preserving our own silences of language: every reader (of translations) must become a translator, must assume the responsibility of textualisation. The translator is not to be trusted with the task which belongs to all of us.

But my argument all along has been that such silences deteriorate into space, because they are uninhabited by anything other than the putative mental operations of the reader. I am looking for a silence generated by letters on the brink of being phonemes, silences made resonant by this in-betweenness, silences existing inescapably as complements to specific sounds, silences filled with nostalgias and urgent anticipations, senses of loss or promise. These silences allow the translator to feed into the text not only the activities of the state police or the prefect of the Seine, of fairground entertainers (linguistic conjurors, exotic savages), of ventriloquists, all the beckonings of vocal delirium, but also translational fantasy itself. A mode of translation in which the language of the TT does not relate to that of the ST on a unit-for-unit (unit of sense) basis, but as a linguistic *gerbe* or *feu d'artifice*, hardly controllable, bursting from the ST, its different language permitting another kind of display. The success of a work derives from a future it releases and cannot predict. And the proliferation of this future grows partly out of the silences within the text which themselves frame new strangenesses, textual thoughts and afterthoughts, surpluses and deficiencies, impulses and desires.

But if we move on to the silence in which the text is embedded and wish to avoid the transformation of that silence into space, then we must invest that silence with a charge of resonances, resonances emanating from the text considered as a construction of sense. In offering a translation of 'Fairy' (see Appendix II (iv) for 'straight' translation), I have taken the perhaps inadvisable step of supplying a code for the kinds of silence I imagine. But I would quickly reiterate that these translations are designed as exemplars of different translational practices, not as embattled alpha-male versions; readers may like to envisage what their own strategies might be in these circumstances and should feel free to revise and adapt as seems fitting. But, at the very least, the codes become a visual reminder of the silence's active presence, of the acoustic fullness of the atmosphere.

Fairy

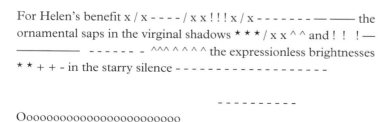

For Helen's benefit x / x - - - - / x x ! ! ! x / x - - - - - - - — —— the
ornamental saps in the virginal shadows ★ ★ ★ / x x ^ ^ and ! ! ! —
——————— - - - - - - - ^^^ ^ ^ ^ ^ the expressionless brightnesses
★ ★ + + - in the starry silence - - - - - - - - - - - - - - - - - - -

- - - - - - - - - -

Oooooooooooooooooooooooooo

conspired together ? ? ? The torrid heat ^^ ^^ ^ ^ ^of the summer
was entrusted x / x . . . . . . .x / x. . . . ./ to silent birds
"„„„„„„„„„„„„„„„„„„„„„"and the necessary dose of indolence !- ! - !
! - - - to a priceless ! o o funeral barge ^ ^ by inlets of loves - - - -
——————-long extinct and perfumes ———— —- — - in a
state of collapse. - <<< After the time of the song x x / . . . .x x / x
x 0 o o of the lumberjills * * with the rumble of the torrent))))
beneath the decimated woods, ((((((((of the cowbells ((((((((
with their valley echoes, x x /. . . . . . . .x x / >>>> of the cries of the
steppes. - - ——————For the benefit ?? x x / x x . . .of Helen's
childhood, + + + the furs and shadows ^ ^ ^ ^ ^ quivered, as did
>> the breasts of the poor ^ ^ ^ and the heavenly legends. . . . . . .
(((((( ))) And her eyes,„„„and her dancing x x / „„„,x x / x,
surpassing even the precious light-bursts >>> ? ? ^ ^ ooo and the
icy influxes,„„, - - - - ——— - - - - - - - - - - - - - - - and the
pleasure x x / x))))) of this so special
******************** décor ! !!!!! ! and time of day 00 oo . . . .
.>>>>>>>> (((((.

Helen is recalled to herself, that is to her childhood, where she (her eyes,
her dreams) is greater than the sum of the parts that conspired to produce
this rebirth. And here this self-recuperation is as fragile as the very
uniqueness of the confluence of elements, themselves so polarised and yet
so interwoven. The conspiracy of a décor serves to detach Helen from it,
so that she can surpass it in a being and an activity which for a moment
consecrates it.

This is a drama of prepostionality. The verbal activity, in direct contrast
with 'Parade', is minimal. It has the peremptory certitude of the past
historic, but to begin with, this imperiousness of tense is bridled by
murkiness of motive ('se conjurèrent') and by passivity ('fut confiée').
What activity is visibly realised—'frissonnèrent'—is at a low, almost
imperceptible level. Violent activity is entirely vested in the wrenching
relationality of the prepositions, which will never declare their true
intentions. They serve to propel the substantives, to configure and make
dance the initially inertial constituents of a context, resistant, it seems, to
any self-expression ('ornamentales', 'impassibles', 'morts', 'muets',
'affaissés'). The second paragraph introduces an irrepressible and
multifarious acousticity; but even though this emerges from the perished
existence of the previous paragraph ('sous la ruine des bois'), it is
consigned to a past ('Après') and parenthesized by dashes (cf. the second
paragraph of 'Angoisse', likewise a linguistic space cordoned off,

remembered, already out of reach). And yet the force of nominality remains on the brink of explosion, and this brinkmanship, this imminence, is held suspended not only by the low-level verbal activity ('frissonnèrent'), but also by the shift from prepositionality to easy, perhaps slack, coordinating conjunctivality. But the final paragraph does manage its eruption. At first led tentatively by a continuation of the coordinating conjunctions, and then recovering the electric tensions of the preposition, it plunges towards the final affirmation.

The advantage of this kind of layout relates to the fact that the eye can almost instantaneously take in what the voice would take time to traverse. In other words, just as we find the spoken and the written ultimately working to each other's advantage, so, as far as textual silence is concerned, the spatial/eye works to the advantage of the temporal/ear: we register more time than it takes us to see it; silence exists as a much larger space within language than the tongue needs to give it credit for.

At first I was tempted to leave the graphic signs unglossed, merely as indications of the complex blends that silences are; the variation in spacing of some of the signs is, correspondingly, intended to convey changes of quality or intensity. But the very graphic resources available were bound to carry certain expressive implications and I thus accepted that a certain coding was necessary, to wit:

x / x:	rhythmic aftermath and anticipation
((( )):	acoustic reverberations and their direction
>>>>:	impatience to read on
<<<<:	desire to reflect on the just read
★★★★:	a certain erotic charge
^^^^:	psychosomatic reaction
+ + +:	stilled blankness

Acknowledging not only that the silences I have chosen might be distributed in very different ways, but also that the ST might be invested with very different kinds of silence, I have left two elements of my schema—00 oo and --------as 'joker' silences, available for all manner of appropriation. I did, however, want to suggest, at the poem's conclusion, the desire left unsatisfied by the non-completion of the syntax: of what unimaginable verb might 'ses yeux et sa danse' be the subject? This poem has a finality at war with itself, claims a uniqueness which, no sooner achieved, provokes invasion by the unappeased reverberations of the reader's silence.

By this coding, I also wanted to suggest what the cross-over between punctuational pauses and interspersed silences might be. I have used silences to segment the text very much in the way that punctuation might; there are, however, rare occasions when silences separate adjectives from their nouns, or subjects from verbs, or isolate a coordinating conjunction; and from time to time, conventional punctuation and coded silence are used in combination. The naturally expressive punctuation marks (question mark, exclamation mark, suspension points) play the roles that one would expect in normal discourse (interrogative, sharply reactive [surprise, enthusiasm, incredulity, puzzlement], meditative). And the inverted commas, as one might expect, transcribe the pianissimo of vocal impulses which did not resolve themselves in speech. Most immediately, these unrealised impulses belong to the birds; but they remind us, too, that reading is itself largely constituted of the reader's silent dialogues with himself, and so the text anticipates this inaudible vocal ferment of its past and future readers. The commas, on the other hand, come to slip their moorings as recorders of syntactic segmentation and engineers of respiratory pause. Instead, they instal a mental marking time, a mesmeric silence, punctuated by the rhythm of wanting to stop, or of not being able to move on; this is not so much a momentary loss for words, as a transfixative silence acted out in obsessive pausing, a stammering of consciousness.

I assume that the codes themselves are self-explanatory and that their manner of interwoven operation is easy to envisage. I would, however, like to give some attention to the rhythmic code, because it conceals a national difference in attitude towards prosodic pause which might complicate the translation of silence.

Someone writing in English would not agree with Spire's asseveration that: 'Le silence n'a pas de valeur rythmique' (quoted by Dugas 1997: 191) [silence has no rhythmic value], and this has much to do with the metrico-rhythmic structures of English and French. In French, one might argue, all lines of verse are acatalectic (syllabically/metrically complete), because there is no principle by which they can be deemed incomplete (catalectic); in regular verse, the nature of the verse-line is defined by the number of filled syllables, and the expected possible patterns of accentuation are, in turn, implied by this number of filled syllables. Accordingly, a decasyllable, for example, is always a decasyllable and not an alexandrine with catalexis (two missing, or silent, syllables). As already discussed, the elision of so-called mute e's is not so much about their muting as about the erasure of their muteness. And where, as in free verse, or indeed poetic prose/the prose poem, we cannot be sure how many syllables a line or phrase/clause has, we must still suppose that its metrico-rhythmic nature is syllabosyntactically determined.

In English, on the other hand, catalexis is built into rhythmic perception, not merely as a line-terminal phenomenon, but line-internally as well. We can comfortably tolerate, in Shakespearean dramatic verse, for example, pentameters of less than ten syllables, because we can compensate for any shortfall by pausing at metrical junctures, or by silently supplying missing beats or off-beats. Metrical regularity is the warrant for this compensatory mechanism.

But silent beats and off-beats are not merely compensatory mechanisms; they can also be beckonings, anticipations, conjurations of words and forms. This is a metrico-rhythmic silence that French poets also inhabit, and it is Valéry who has given us perhaps the most celebrated instance of a poem brought into existence by its silent rhythm: 'Quant au *Cimetière marin*, cette intention ne fut d'abord qu'une figure rythmique vide, ou remplie de syllabes vaines, qui me vint obséder quelque temps. J'observai que cette figure était décasyllabique' (1957: 1503) [As for *Le Cimetière marin*, this intention was, to begin with, no more than a rhythmic figure, empty, or filled with fruitless syllables, which came to haunt me for some time. I noticed that this figure was decasyllabic]. But while Valéry's initiatory silence is long-term, I have, in my translation, attempted to suggest generative rhythmic impulses more locally; and I am not trying to engender verse-lines, to re-establish any creative principle which goes beyond the improvisation of the next segment. Instead, I am trying to launch phrases to infiltrate syntactic structure with the whims of abstract rhythmic figures or the unavoidable imprint of a rhythmic configuration from inner time.

We should return, for our final translation, to Lettrism and its cultivation of silence as part of the realisation of its own 'infinitesimality'. From the outset, silence had been the raw material to be worked, that letters/phonemes gave shape to. Then in 1959, Isidore Isou, Lettrism's founder, announced the arrival of 'aphonisme' or 'aphonie': 'une récitation sans émission de sons, muette. Le récitant ouvre et ferme la bouche, *sans rien dire, pas plus en musique, en langage ordinaire qu'en langage lettriste*' (quoted in Curtay 1974: 121) [a recitation without the emission of sounds, wordless. The reciter opens and closes his mouth, *without saying anything, any more in music, or in ordinary language, than in lettrist language*]; 'aphonisme' became a key vehicle of '*écriture musicale infinitésimale*' [*infinitesimal musical writing*], which was not to be read, but the reading of which one could imagine 'sur le plan *impossible, futur* ou *divin*' [in the dimension of *the impossible, the future* or *the divine*]:

La poésie infinitésimale, partie des phonèmes inaudibles, détruits par un excès (ultra-sons) ou une insuffisance (infra-sons) de puissance, en vient à examiner le problème de la limite des *sens*.

[. . .]

Elle place finalement tous les organes perceptifs en face de toutes les particules inexistantes en soi, capables de suggérer toutes les œuvres lyriques non-réalisées ou non-réalisables, non-conçues ou non-concevables.

(Curtay 1974: 122)

[Infinitesimal poetry, with its origin in inaudible phonemes, destroyed by an excess (ultra-sounds) or an insufficiency (infra-sounds) of power, comes to subject the problem of the limit of the *senses* to scrutiny.

(. . .)

Finally, it confronts all the perceptual organs with all particles, non-existent in themselves, capable of suggesting all those lyric works which are non-realised or non-realisable, non-conceived or non-conceivable.]

This in turn begot Isou's *Manifeste de l'art supertemporel* of 1960, the inevitable consequence of infinitesimal art. If an artist, in creating works, implies infinite non-works (i.e. work produced cannot replace other possible works and in fact prevents them), but is an obstacle to their development thanks to the limitations of his personality, then the single artist must be removed and all possible artists must have access to the project, as must, therefore, all possible arts. Supertemporality, or hyperchronicity, is the blank cheque signed by the initial artist on his own work; and any professional or amateur, any object, plant, animal, and so forth (possible or impossible) may cash it in. Rimbaud might well have had some sympathy with such a project, since this is merely an infinite extension, in all directions, of his own vision of the artist: 'Énormité devenant norme, absorbée par tous, il serait vraiment *un multiplicateur de progrès*!' (letter to Paul Demeny, 15 May 1871) [An enormity becoming the norm, absorbed by all, he would really be *a multiplier of progress*!]. But what would he have made of Anne-Catherine Caron's unpublished 'aphonisme supertemporel', entitled 'Ophélie' (1973) and dedicated to Shakespeare and to himself? Its text runs: 'Souvenez-vous quelquefois et en ce moment, d'Ophélie, flottant sur l'eau, immortelle à sa manière' [Remember now, as at other times, Ophelia, floating on the water, immortal in her own way]. My own aphonistic offering is a version of 'Vagabonds' (see Appendix II (v) for 'straight' translation):

It's foggy and the bare trees indicate that winter is now well advanced [backcloth]. Two figures stroll together, one of them exaggeratedly wrapped up against the cold with overcoat, red scarf wrapped around his nose and cotton wool in his ears. Around them, the lovers, the nannies with their perambulators, the smartly dressed riders on their handsome horses [bare stage]. The sun is a red ball seen through a lattice of bare branches [backcloth]. They pass through the gates [painted wooden construction], moving towards the group of orators on their soap-boxes [silent gesticulation, emphatic movement of mouths], surrounded by drifting audiences [sometimes lovers and nannies].

Let me emphasize immediately that the Lettrists' aphonic translation in the service of the infinitesimal text helps to underline the difference in ontological status between the ST and the TT, previously referred to in the distinction that Barthes makes between the Work and the Text. We should remember that Barthes identifies the 'emergence' of the Text from the Work as a product of the cross-categorial incursions of interdisciplinarity, which leads to a relativisation of the positions of the writer, the reader and the critic. If the Work belongs to a self-stabilising Newtonian world, the world of the Text is animated by the sliding and/or overturning of former categories. This view makes multitranslation an inevitable meaning of translation, not because of the unseizable diversity of the ST, but because the TT is a different kind of text. The ST, to use Barthes's notions, is substance, while the TT is methodology, which '*ne s'éprouve que dans un travail, une production*' (1984: 73) [*is experienced only in an activity, a process of production*]. It is in the genes of the TT to defer or disseminate meaning; by virtue of its new web of associations, disconnections, overlappings, its intertextuality, its variety of perspectives, the TT seeks to infinitise the signifier and thus to perpetuate its own plurality. The 'aphonisation' of a text, or the use of an aphonic text, is a method of indicating that the TT has to start from a performative zero, has to find its way into textuality, backwards perhaps, into a writing, into an acting, into a cinematography. This is a multitranslation as much in breadth as in depth, across media and genres as much as across the space and time of the translator's relationship with the ST.

There are two immediate models for a multitranslation approach that come to mind:

1. The 'shift-of-attention' model, as found, for example, in Toby

Garfitt's 'A Plural Approach to Translating Mallarmé' (1998). Garfitt chooses 'A la nue accablante tu' and proposes: 'The advantage of offering several different versions of the same text is that in each case certain features of the original are respected, while others are of course lost. It should therefore be possible to appreciate the original more fully than would be allowed by a single "literal" version' (1998: 345).

2. The 'exercices de style' model, as found, for example, in Nicholas Moore's thirty-one versions of Baudelaire's 'Spleen' poem, 'Je suis comme le roi d'un pays pluvieux' (1990).

The trouble with the 'shift-of-attention' model is that multitranslation emerges from an assumption, or admission, of translation's inadequacy. A number of mutually complementary translations have to be produced in order to do justice to the uncapturable richness of the ST. If one, however, has the view that the target of the TT is not the ST, not, that is, a *retrospective* target, but on the contrary, something placed on the other side of the TT, in the future, that diaspora that the ST becomes by virtue of its survival, then one will think of multiple translations not as the index of the TT's shortcomings, not as an unfortunate necessity, but as a manifestation of the self-multipliability of the TT, or, rather, of the ST and the TT put together, as an affirmation of a 'future Vigueur'.

As already proposed, translation is about taking texts forward and not, as it were, about going back to them. One might say that the trouble with present thinking about translation is that it treats the linguistic non-coincidence of languages as a set of problems to be solved (*as best one can*), not as a set of opportunities to be gratefully grasped. Linguistic non-coincidence is not a licence to do as one pleases; non-coincidence is a point of inescapable and welcome difference, because it is the difference which justifies the desire to open up future paths for the ST concerned. Even in its own language, the ST can never again be like itself once it has come into existence; and inasmuch as any work is written for posterity, it is written desiring to develop, to be adaptable, to live differently in different imaginations.

It will be apparent from the foregoing remarks that I have much sympathy with Nicholas Moore's 'exercices de style' position. What I regret about it is the risk it runs of implying that multitranslation can extend itself beyond a certain limit *only* if it is prepared to enter the world of travesty, burlesque, parody, the wilfully subversive; and that translation can multiply only by multiplying the text, rather than by multiplying readerly perspectives on a text that may change little linguistically. As I have previously indicated, I believe that our failure to read the generical make-up of translation impoverishes our sense of what translation might be, literarily; and while there can be no doubt that plagiarism, parody, imitation, travesty are hugely important elements in that make-up, multitranslation might also be a way of identifying translation not by its generical uncertainty, but by its promiscuous, 'cubist' attitudes to genre. But the translator, and the reader alongside, must be able to imagine their way out of the ST, out of a national literature into a literature of translation, where the literature is as much in modes of reading as in textual eccentricity. And in order that the reading public is not deceived about translation's attempts to relocate the ST, to release the diaspora, to cross over from national literatures into the literature of translation, by a number of routes, multitranslation must be more naturally translation's medium.

Multitranslation is, thus, the way that we translate not into the text, but out of it. Previously, we have thought of translating *out of* Rimbaud as that mode whereby one attempts to lead textual elements out of textuality towards available meanings, while acknowledging that the Rimbaldian text is at the centre of its own semantic specificity. 'Translating out of Rimbaud' might also mean a kind of textual exfoliation, whereby textual elements flake off, peel off, to contribute to other textual possibilities, or go out to meet texts which, like comets, are passing close to them. We allow ourselves to quote textual fragments as constituents of other texts. If part of the translator's purpose is to facilitate transtextual contacts, or to engineer the migration of one text to another, then translating out is an enlargement of the 'translated text's' field of activity. We have proposed, in Chapter 1, that the TT is an expanding text, as it fills out with the cultural accompaniment that any text attracts to itself as it makes its way forward through time and space. But might there not also be occasions when textual expansion means leaps across, into texts which, themselves, are looking for a 'posthumous' raison d'être? The translator is a negotiator between cultures and periods, and it is only a modulation of this task which would produce a negotiation between a text in one language and one in another. Silence again becomes a crucial factor in this transaction, inasmuch as the 'TT' must allow itself to be re-spoken, in a new set of permutative possibilities. The aphonisation of a 'TT' (distantly related to an ST) is the move by which the 'TT' can be re-grounded in new directional possibilities. It withdraws into a latency which allows it to be re-spoken in the direction of the ST, but also in all other directions.

My translation of 'Vagabonds' is neither a translation nor my own. It is a welding together of two stage-directions from Christopher Hampton's screenplay for *Total Eclipse*, the adaptation of his own play of the same name (1968, 1981) about the relationship between Rimbaud and Verlaine; I have replaced the names of Rimbaud and Verlaine by 'Two figures', 'the latter' by 'one of them', and have added some indications in square brackets. The first performance of *Total Eclipse* was given at the Royal Court Theatre on 11 September 1968, with Rimbaud played by Victor Henry (an actor with a Rimbaldian reputation) and Verlaine by John Grillo; Robert Kidd directed. The text was published in 1969. Hampton reckons that no other play of his has been performed so frequently. Ben Francis (1996: 14) suggests that the play allowed Hampton 'to ask himself the questions that most writers ask at the beginning of their careers: what does it mean to be a writer and what could one reasonably hope to achieve?' And in his notes (*Radio Times*) to the radio production, broadcast on 1 May 1969, Hampton recorded his interpretation of the French poets' ultimate decisions as: 'Rimbaud's rejection of a solipsistic universe, and Verlaine's refusal to abandon his delusion' (quoted in Francis 1996: 14). A television production, directed by Peter Gregeen, was broadcast on 10 April 1973. A second edition of the play opened at the Lyric Theatre, Hammersmith, on 5 May 1981, directed by David Hare, with Hilton McCrae as Rimbaud and Simon Callow as Verlaine; the script was published in the same year. This new edition, apart from a general dramatic tightening, starts each of the two acts with Verlaine quoting passages from *Une saison en enfer* in voice-over; it was broadcast on radio on 23 May 1993. Besides these two English versions, there are two American ones. The film, originally planned as a vehicle for John Malkovich and River Phoenix, finally appeared in 1995, directed by Agnieszka Holland and starring Leonardo DiCaprio as Rimbaud and David Thewlis as Verlaine; the 'written' screenplay was also published in 1995. Francis (1996: 178) reports a possible Japanese novelisation of the film. *Total Eclipse*, then, has an intensely multitranslational life (one of its principal STs being the 1961 edition of Enid Starkie's biography of Rimbaud).

The scene of my stage-directions is set in Hyde Park at dusk. My text is silent in two senses: it is a scenario for a dumb show, and it is a scene that has never been seen, that has disappeared, a might-be or might-have-been scene. The dialogue attached to it in the screenplay consists of the two short exchanges which 'book-end' Act 2, sc. 1 of the play-script. Act 2, sc. 1 of the play-script takes place, not in Hyde Park, but at 34–35 Howland Street, and ends with the couple's *intention* to go and hear Mr Odger in Hyde Park speaking on behalf of the discharged and imprisoned constables; among the closing stage-directions are: '(He [Verlaine] puts on his overcoat, then wraps his long red scarf carefully round his mouth)' and '(He stuffs cotton wool in his ears and speaks as he does so, his voice muffled by his scarf)' (1981: 43–6). But the trip to Hyde Park never materialises. In the 'shooting' script, Hyde Park has become a pub in Soho. The political coordinates of the play-script—Hyde Park as guardian of demagogic democracy, George Odger as republican, and Verlaine's boast about his intended assassination of Napoleon III—become in the film invisible/inaudible, a syncope, an apostrophe.

Stage-directions are a peculiar kind of text, usually willing their own erasure, superseded by the implementation of setting and/or action. But sometimes their literariness will not quite tolerate this erasure. Hampton's directions, designed by me to establish a founding silence, a pantomime out of which might emerge all possible and impossible 'texts' (including performances, happenings, transdisciplinary interferences, etc), become themselves, by a kind of simultaneous back-translation, the first reading or mapping of the animated silence they put in place. If 'Vagabonds' is a prose poem, then 'Hyde Park', if I may dub it so, is a counterpart, a complementary prose poem, designed as its twin. One of the reasons for making this claim, lies in phonemic patterning. The poet's vision in 'Vagabonds' reaches a climax in /y/ - 'traversée par des bandes de musique rare, les fantômes du futur luxe nocturne'—echoed finally in 'formule'. If a corresponding vocalic phoneme were to be attributed to the 'pitoyable frère', then it might well be the /u/ of 'bouche pourrie': /u/ is the phoneme of *physical* sustenance ('nourris', 'biscuit de la route') and of damned togetherness ('joué', 'nous', 'retournerions', 'ajoutait'). But while it may be significant and unsurprising that the poet's paragraph (second) has no instances of /u/, there are certainly cross-overs of belonging ('hurlant', 'en toute sincérité d'esprit', 'trouver'). In 'Hyde Park', the Verlainian phoneme would seem to be /æ/: 'exaggeratedly', 'wrapped' (2), 'nannies', 'perambulators' (Mathilde has recently given birth), 'handsome', 'lattice', with support from its weak form /ə/: 'advanced', 'against', 'around' (2), 'orators'. But the other a's—/ɔ/, /eI/ and particularly /ɑ:/ ('advanced', 'branches' (2), 'scarf', 'smartly', 'pass')—do not compete, are all part of the presiding Verlainian focalisation. And that 'Hyde Park' is the Verlainain twin of the Rimbaldian 'Vagabonds' is borne out, perhaps, by its being touched with the spirit of 'Colloque sentimental', itself echoed in the short dialogue at the end of both play-script and screenplay (1981: 71; 1995: 117–18), when Rimbaud's ghost returns: 'You know I'm very fond of you. We've been very happy sometimes'.

Stage directions are a dumb show, stand outside, or away from, dialogue, which intervenes to actualise and identify the speakers. The peculiarity of the 'speech' in 'Vagabonds' is that it does not declare its hand. Is it spoken by the 'je' of the rest of the poem, either as a memory of a piece of past direct speech (addressed to a third person, or to the 'pitoyable frère' [in which case we must understand 'son infirmité' as 'ton infirmité']), or as a piece of indirect speech ('Je dis que/Je disais que') presented directly and addressed to the reader? Or are these the words of the 'pitoyable frère', spoken in the present to a third person/the reader, reported as direct speech by the poet ('Il dit/disait:. . .' understood), with tenses transposed to the past, and 'son' to be understood as 'ton', or as indirect speech ('Il dit que/il disait que'), with inverted commas retained for dramatic effect, in which case the 'je' may be the 'je' of the poet or of the 'pitoyable frère'? The difficulty of attributing the personal pronouns here reminds us that the relationship is made up both of clear lines of demarcation ('moi pressé de trouver') and moments when shifters remain obstinately shifting ('Car Je est un autre'). Even my slight re-writing of the Hampton text allows one to wonder who the one is, and who the other. At all events, this snatch of speech in 'Vagabonds' cannot come into existence, has no designated speaker, relapses into aphonism out of sheer doubt.

Besides those elements just mentioned which make 'Hyde Park' a prose poetic transposition (as into other keys), or re-origination, of 'Vagabonds', we might briefly mention others: the presence of the red ball of the sun, the atmosphere of 'errance', the 'infirmité' evidenced in the overdressing. And inasmuch as 'Hyde Park' refers us to larger works—in which, however, it never found a true place, remained imaginary—so we can pick up those threads which tie *Total Eclipse* to 'Vagabonds', I mean lines such as: 'He was always searching for a solution, a place, a formula' (1995, 109); 'I wanted to walk to Africa and cross a desert. I wanted heat and violence of landscape. I wanted the sun [. . .] I want the sun' (1995: 47; the last two declarations do not appear in the play-script, 1981: 33); 'Why don't we go south? [. . .] I know you've always wanted to go to Africa. [. . .] Look at the sun' (1995: 87; 1981: 53). And given what we have said about the protean nature of shifters, we might pick out something from the Hyde Park dialogue itself: Rimbaud defines as his greatest fear 'That other people will see me as I see them' (1995: 69; 1981: 43). It goes without saying that the various versions of *Total Eclipse* have assimilated other dicta from the Rimbaldian œuvre, and are littered with other intertexts (e.g. the shots of Verlaine in the exercise yard of the prison at Mons reverberate with Gustave Doré's engraving of *Newgate Prison* (1872) and with the Van Gogh canvas based on it, *Prisoners Exercising* (1890)).

There are, of course, many differences between the play-script and the screenplay of *Total Eclipse*: the play's twelve scenes are all, apart from Act

2, sc. 5 (The Black Forest, near Stuttgart) set indoors, are evenly paced and maintain temporal sequence; the screenplay comprises some two hundred and three shots, has flashbacks and flashforwards, explores external space freely, is very irregularly paced, and cuts and cross-cuts indefatigably. The shooting script differs from the screenplay by its omissions, its changes of location, its occasionally radical re-ordering of shots, its infrequent and minor amendments and additions to dialogue. Thus it is that behind every particular manifestation of *Total Eclipse* are the silent urgings of shift and proliferation, different emphasis, modulation of point of view. These variants are not false moves made on the way to a satisfactory conclusion; they are the potential presences which enjoin upon each particular manifestation the recovery of its virtuality, its silence, which will in turn allow the silent ones to come into existence. But, as in the Lettrist project for the infinitesimal work, existence is only a state of triggering; each work lasts only as long in the perception of the spectator/listener as it takes to establish its own (im)possibility by liberating an (im)possible other. The silence of the aphonic work is therefore not only the sign of the work's will to metamorphosis, to stay only long enough to become other; it also provides a model for the translational process itself, for the ST and its inevitable and consequent TTs, only a small proportion of which will ever become visible.

We might want to claim that the translator is a writer who applies a filmic/cinematographic vision to the ST's theatrical material, that the ST is the theatrical and the TT is the filmic, or the ST is the screenplay and the TT the shooting script. What is important, above all, is the proposition that the translational requires a radical change of perceptual mode: from intention to improvisation, from evenness of perception to a dynamics of proximity, from the search for a guiding semantic to an irregular, purely verbal experience, from the sense of a work's 'contextualisedness' (continuity with time/space of milieu) to a reinvention of contexts through processes of rupture and discontinuity. Silence as we have begun to explore it in this chapter is one aspect of the ST/TT relationship which will allow the TT to activate its own contexts and provide acousticity with new values. We have hitherto asked the reader not to let silence be devalued by becoming space. But we must now turn to that transformation as a prelude to a longer look at the kinds of space the page has at its disposal.

6

From Silence and Time to Noise and Space

One of the abiding myths of poetic language is its contact with an elsewhere; the poet is at once searching for the ground of his own apprehensions and at the same time operating as a mediator between language and a certain source, occluded, for most of the time, by the pressures of immediate communication. Divine inspiration, the Muse, were the ways it was formerly expressed. But even in a post-theological world, the same nagging need to locate a poetic language in relation to an elsewhere persists: '[La poésie] dit violemment, et la présence des choses, et un ailleurs des choses' (Marie-Claire Bancquart, in Sorrell 1995: 12) [(Poetry) expresses violently both the presence of things and an elsewhere of things]. Often this elsewhere is simply a distance from which experience seems to come: 'Dies kommt von weit' [This comes from far off], as Rilke puts it so succinctly in *Die Sonette an Orpheus*, I, 13. And Rimbaud, too, seems to want to speak of the writer as having come back from somewhere, from a journey beyond some bourn, in order to write with the imperatives of that other place. But this elsewhere can situate itself quite as well immanently as it can transcendentally; the trick, it seems, is to make the metaphysicality of language proportional to its physicality, to drive language towards an almost intolerable presence, so that, by a kind of *contre-coup* or *contre-choc*, the absence of the physical manifests itself. This elsewhere is the silence we began to explore in the previous chapter, that other side of language, that unverbalised activity or presence which translation has perhaps, hitherto, paid insufficient attention to.

Part of the transgressiveness of the prose poem is its insistence on proceeding as if it had no truck with the metaphysical, while at the same time insinuating, by the arts of silence and linguistic slippage and 'automatic writing', that the comfortable momentum of the collocational might be undermined, unravelled, by the imperious liberation of the substitutional. What makes the reading of Rimbaud so unnerving is that this substitutional availability occurs as much, if not more, at the level of the grammatical, or of the sub-lexical fragment, as at that of the substantival:

> Un coup d'oeil aux manuscrits permet de constater que, quantitativement, les variantes lexicales sont beaucoup moins nombreuses que les 'grammaticales'. C'est que le terrain privilégié de Rimbaud reste celui de l'expression: les modifications les plus significatives se marquent au niveau de la détermination, des articulants, des prépositions, des genres, de la ponctuation, et ceci dans le corpus entier.
>
> (Bivort 1998: 30)
>
> [A glance at the manuscripts allows one to record that, quantitatively, lexical variants are much less numerous than 'grammatical' variants. It is because Rimbaud's favoured terrain is that of expression: the most significant modifications occur in the area of determinants, articulants, prepositions, genders, punctuation, and this applies to the whole corpus.]

Rimbaud, then, doubly offends: he allows the substitutional to act corrosively on the metonymic particularly where it defines relationship; and he implements the Jakobsonian principle ('*The poetic function projects the principle of equivalence from the axis of selection to the axis of combination*', 1960: 358) without having any formal warrant to do so. If I turn, now, to the rendering of Rimbaud into concrete poetry, it is in the belief that the concrete dramatises a central paradox: linguistic materiality, taken to a certain extreme, ousts the vocal, indeed the human, and takes place in a space, or silence, of its own; and that the concrete exploits, in many of its manifestations, the substitutability of the 'mot-outil' and the lexical fragment, rendering the syntagmatic down into the insistently paradigmatic, a paradigmatic of infinitely multipliable trace.

Concordanced thematic investigations—What do Rimbaud's multiple references to children mean? Why does Rimbaud refer so frequently to curving movements?—are attempts, usually, to stabilise usage, to find a coherence of usage, to identify the values brought into play. But such investigations depend a great deal on the reliability of contexts of use, as though these contexts were indeed statements about the meaning of the term selected. But in our present reading, context ultimately has no reliability, indeed may be said not to exist as a semantically shaping environment. All that one is left with is the multipliability of traces, which themselves have a peculiar syntagmatic autonomy (i.e. can beget any number of syntagms). This, it seems to me, is what puts Rimbaud's prose poems and concrete poetry in touch with conceptual art, in that the materials of conceptual art are items far exceeded by the thought that potentially envelops them.

Before we move further with this argument, we should note that it is not just Rimbaldian prose and concrete poetry, but the majority of translational work undertaken in the previous chapters that points us towards the conceptual. What this book is compelling us to envisage with increasing seriousness is the idea that translation might easily be a branch of conceptual art. Immediately one proposes that translation, as a writerly undertaking, is cripplingly hobbled by its arrant literalism (even in so-called free translations), one begins to think that it may not be necessary to push either processes or renderings to the bitter end, that, on the contrary, pushing things to the bitter end usually involves the reduction of a real and workable perceptual mode to the bathos of its doggecd outworking. To complete processes of thought, or creative ambitions, in a realised object, is likely to banalise those processes and ambitions. The 'work of translation' should, then, replace the production of a TT, or, rather, the TT should be part of the documentation of the 'work of translation', but fundamentally unnecessary to it.

And, of course, our foregoing argument for multitranslation naturally affiliates itself with minimalist and serialist tendencies in conceptual art: 'If the masterpiece was that single painting or sculpture into which the supreme artistic achievement of a career is compressed, then the serial work offered instead a set of alternatives, none of which took precedence. By implication, the concept underlying the series or the process was therefore more important than the final object' (Godfrey 1998: 150). Serialism gives no purchase to the extraction of meaning, but seems, mischievously, to disperse it by ubiquitising its activity. These considerations also help to underline that conceptual translation could not exist in a world in which translation was a literature designed for those ignorant of the language of the raw materials. To try to generate a conceptual translation is to try, equally, to de-commodify translations and the kinds of commodity criticism and commodity-use they too often beget. What exchange value against the ST would a conceptual translation have? None at all, I imagine. The concrete version certainly has many of these conceptual advantages.

The peculiar appropriateness of concrete poetry to the Rimbaldian enterprise lies in its profound paradoxicality and its being at the crossroads of so many different poetic impulses. From one point of view, it has the benefit of yielding no meaning: because concrete poetry is the attempt to push all meaning into form, the embryonic semantics of individual lexemes generate ideas through disposition, through the syntax of space and the modulations of permutative acoustics:

> Concrete poetry gives no results. It yields a process of discovery. It is motion. Its motion ends in different ways. Concrete poetry says formally what it means to say, or means to say what its form says. Its form is its meaning, its meaning its form. (Claus Bremer, quoted in Williams 1967: n.p.)

To paraphrase a meaning from a concrete poem is to destroy the whole point: meaning is in the perceptual encounter with the ST. In this sense there is no meaning to be translated. Like an image from Odilon Redon, language, as a set of embryonic forms, seeds, disembodied eyes, inhabits a space which is itself looking to find horizons, coordinates, a functional topography, and through a cooperative endeavour and mutual complementation, a world is put together and some evolutionary pattern established. The concrete poem, in this sense, is a linguistic equivalent of the project outlined in 'Après le Déluge'.

We can thus attribute to concrete poetry a certain primitive pre-historicism, a desire repeatedly to replunge language in an originary inchoateness from which it can be drawn out time after time in an attempt to reinvent it:

> si ce qu'il rapporte de *là-bas* a forme, il donne forme; si c'est informe, il donne l'informe. Trouver une langue;—Du reste, toute parole étant idée, le temps d'un langage universel viendra!
> (letter to Paul Demeny, 15 May 1871).
> [if what he brings back from *over there* has form, he produces form; if it is formless, he produces formlessness. Finding a language;— Besides, since every word is an idea, the time of a universal language will come!]

What lies in the back of the minds of many concrete poets is precisely this generation of a universal language, the possibility of global communication on the basis of isolated lexemes. Each issue of Gomringer's irregularly published *Konkrete Poesie/Poesia Concreta* (1960 >) announced, in French and German: 'La poésie concrète est le chapitre esthétique de la formulation linguistique universelle de notre époque' (quoted by Solt

1970: 10) [Concrete poetry is the aesthetic chapter of the universal linguistic formulation of our epoch].

The notion of origins leads directly into the notion of ends, and concrete poetry puts the primitivistic in direct touch with the constructivist, that is to say, in touch with an ethos of corporate typographic engineering, where all constituents are without author, and every finished work a communal achievement. Literature embraces technology, and as it does so the ambitions of a monologic discourse give way to an arrangement of abbreviated, polyphonic, information counters. There is certainly a political risk: imperceptibly, language becomes official—free social montage begins to take on the look of the totalitarian. The poem plays with this gamble, in the space between the anarchic/ludic and paronomasia, or permutative variations, which could so easily become brainwashing rather than mantra, or the methodical elicitation of a truth struggling to withold itself.

For the poet who wishes to retrieve concrete practice from this post-revolutionary site and set it to work in the service of revolution again, what Mike Weaver terms the expressionist option remains available (Solt 1970: 7). But we should beware of trying to return concrete poetry to the expressive strainings of lyrical discourse; expressivity must lie in the page's formal design. We must pass beyond Expressionism, towards Futurism, beyond syntax to words-in-freedom. Here the sentiment and lingeringness of adjectives is sacrificed in favour of the essentialist single-mindedness of nouns, verbs yield the personality of their pronouns to the impersonal intuitions and potentialities of the infinitive, and the tonal insinuations of adverbs are banished. Dynamism generates substantival compounding, metaphors in place of similes, the abolition of punctuation (in favour of mathematical symbols). This is an expressive world all right, a world of feelings under pressure, but the feelings are not owned and exercised by a subjectivity: text is not the product of a subjectivity, but of subjectivation, collective, available to individualities. And what subjectivises text is matter itself, the verbal material subjected to Bergsonian intuition: texts are produced by, expressions of, the *energies* in the phenomena themselves, where words are as material as any objects or feelings they evoke:

> To capture the breath, the sensibility, and the instincts of metals, stones, wood, and so on, through the medium of free objects and whimsical motors. To substitute for human psychology, now exhausted, the lyric obsession with matter.
>
> Be careful not to force human feelings on to matter. Instead divine its different governing impulses, its forces of composition,

dilation, cohesion, and disaggregation, its crowds of massed molecules and whirling electrons. [. . .] The warmth of a piece of iron or wood is in our opinion more impassioned than the smiles or tears of a woman.

> (Marinetti, *Technical Manifesto of Futurist Literature*,
> 11 May 1912, in Flint 1972: 87)

What Marinetti preaches is the constant capacity to displace and relocate consciousness, to discover the continuities between the animate and inanimate, to place art at the point of their interactions: 'To force oneself, for example, to render the landscape of smells that a dog perceives. To listen to motors and to reproduce their conversations' (Flint 1972: 88). If syntax is Marinetti's particular enemy, it is not merely because it spells discourse emanating from an individualised psychological source. It is also because it acts as an interpretative intermediary, it holds language penned in the folds of explication and self-explication. With syntax removed, language enters directly into the universe, as matter within the universe; words-in-freedom are worthy inhabitants of 'the unbounded domain of free intuition', the instruments of '*l'immaginazione senza fili*', and as such can instal that incomprehension which is, as it were, intuition's guarantee: '[. . .] we must renounce being understood. It is not necessary to be understood' (Flint 1972: 89).

Marinetti's later 'Destruction of Syntax—Imagination without Strings—Words-in-Freedom 1913' reiterates the substance of the *Technical Manifesto*, but insists on the death of free verse (still too dependent on the bag of tricks of regular verse, and on syntax), the importance of onomatopoeia, and the need for a typographical revolution (including free expressive orthography, to tie up with onomatopoeia), floats the idea of multilinear lyricism and re-instates the adjective, at least in a 'semaphoric' or 'lighthouse' or 'atmospheric' form (i.e. parenthesised, isolated, autonomous, acting on the whole verbal vicinity). But also among the new principles formulated are to be found:

> 4. Destruction of a sense of the Beyond and an increased value of the individual whose desire is to *vivre sa vie*, in Bonnot's phrase.
> [. . .]
> 6. An exact awareness of everything inaccessible and unrealizable in every person. (Apollonio 1973: 96)

Futurism locates that 'elsewhere' of which we have spoken within the human organism, in a metaphysics of the self, but a self which is not bounded, circumscribed, drawn centripetally towards a kernel, but a self which is cumulative, proliferating, in dialogue and exchange with its environment. The alienness which language assimilates to itself in concrete poetry may well be transcendental for some; but for others, it is the-other-which-is-intuited, the other of language itself, that which can only be known in the realm of silence.

The affinity between concrete poetry and serialism lies in its cultivation of repetition. It is possible to think of repetition as something which lifts the eye out of the reading process to situate it in a scanning activity; repetition is grease to the wheels of the eye over the page, the element that transforms semantics into structure. Gomringer, Bann tells us (1967: 8), 'uses the formal device of repetition to cancel all particular impressions'; this is to suggest that concrete poetry shares serialism's dispersal or abstraction of meaning, its transformation of the perceptual into the conceptual, and thus makes the text more available to readerly exploitation. But another view would insist that repetition is a process of defamiliarisation, of the separation of sound from known sense, which both generates otherness in words and is an invitation to recover that other, a process, in short, which turns reference into invocation, common noun into spell.

Bann's assessment of repetition in Gomringer reminds us that, for many, concrete poetry, and particularly concrete poetry of a constructivist kind, is about the writer's dispossession of language. Brion Gysin, in his 'Statement on the cutup method and permutated poems' (1958; 1st pub. in *Fluxus I*, New York, 1965), is unequivocal:

> Take your own words or the words said to be 'the very own words' of anyone else living or dead. You'll soon see that words don't belong to anyone. Words have a vitality of their own and you or anyone can make them gush into action. [. . .] The poets are supposed to liberate the words—not to chain them in phrases. Who told poets they were supposed to think? Poets are meant to sing and to make words sing. Poets have no words 'of their very own'. Writers don't own their words. Since when do words belong to anybody? (Williams 1967: n.p.)

'Dispossession of' may well then become 'possession by', and we experience that shift from speaking/writing the language to being spoken/written by it which Lecercle (1990) identifies as the insurgence of the 'remainder', language's uncontrollable urge to suggest, to play, to unravel, in mechanisms such as pun, paronomasia, anagram.

It may be that creative translation should as much mean letting language have its head, letting language activate its own anarchic creativity, as the translator's taking creative possession of someone else's text, creative appropriation. It is perhaps important that the language of translation should appear subversive, or excessive, equivocating, blurring outlines, slightly 'inaccurate', but more highly motivated, projecting its own materiality as something which masks the signified, makes signification ('traditional' translation) unachievable, and proposes other uncharacteristic meanings through its phonetic or graphic self-amplification. Translation studies, with a perennial perversity, kicks against the pricks of language by continuing to assume that translation's destiny lies in the direction of the maximisation of rationality, the rationalisation of choice, when language has already made other arrangements. Part of the problem, perhaps, lies in the attitude to choice itself. Translations tend to conceive of choice as a set of possibilities which can be rationally evaluated and thus reduced; at best, there is no choice to be made—choice goes without saying—and at worst, the ability to distinguish between the better and the worse. Within this frame, the untranslatable is an inevitable evil whose maximal diminution is the prize. The alternative version looks upon the untranslatable as that which defines translation, because the untranslatable is precisely what the TT is attempting to reconstitute; the untranslatable in the TT should be the guarantor of the untranslatable in the ST.

After all, it is only by safeguarding the untranslatable that the TT can resist the erosion of its own materiality by attempts to recover the meaning of the ST (i.e. of something else—another text!) through it. Choice, therefore, is not to be considered as the exercise of a rationality in processes of elimination, but as the *free* exploration of options, themselves beset by the beckonings of the aleatory and the irrational. It might be argued, of course, that such a procedure is almost bound to take one ever further from the ST with each selection of option, since taking one option will play an influential part in the determination of subsequent choices. To this supposition, there are, I think, three retorts of a rather heterogeneous nature. First, as already mentioned, I do not believe that there is any necessary virtue in the consistency which translational choice is so often in pursuit of, particularly where a translation may feel the need to synthesise or conflate different perspectives on a single ST. Secondly and relatedly, the process of translation is an *exploration* of the ST and of the expressive potentialities which lie unrealised in it; in this respect, translations are always moving away from the ST, albeit with the intention of becoming *contributions* to the ST. Finally, and more pointedly for concrete poetry than for the other poetries, perhaps, translation releases a remainder that neither the ST nor the translator can predict. Of course, no text can predict what will be identified in it (intertextuality, heteroglossia), nor control its effects. But what I am referring to here is more specifically a practice which sets the notion of equivalence (a worthy aim, but an unworkable and strangely repressive concept) at nought by expressly engaging translation in free-associative mechanisms and in the desire to remotivate language each time it engages with it. My objection to equivalence-thinking is connected less with its unachievability than with the implicit attitudes to language and translation it brings with it. In order to function 'equivalently' a word must agree to stay within the bounds of its equivalency; in other words, we are compelled to think of the language of the TT as looking back over its shoulder at the ST, as governed in its area of operation by the givenness of the ST, as motivated by the ST (see our 'rayon/beam' example, Chapter 3).

The concrete poetry translation is peculiarly instructive for translation more generally because, like Lettrism, it puts translation outside the foreignisation/domestication debate. This debate certainly has an historical significance, and is certainly significant for colonial and post-colonial translation studies (see Chapter 7), but elsewhere in translation studies it has become increasingly inhibitive because it under-differentiates the kinds of linguistic experience any text makes available and thus prejudices response; and it discourages us from seeing our own language as that *terra incognita* which makes the re-invention of language at all possible. In the concrete version of 'Départ' that follows (see Appendix II (vi) for 'straight' version), I have tried to re-discover language as a *terra incognita*:

Departure

en	ough	seen	
[ob]	[Dama]	(scene)	
en	countered	the	
xx	xx	vision	
in	every	air	
en	ough		
en	dured	rumbles{p}	af++
at			evening
in			sunlight
	never	ever	over
++	sunlit	cities	
en	ough		

154

[en]	[compassed]	>>	
ac	quainted	withthepausesof	life
it	s	rulings	
>>	. . .	ruMblingS	
		viSioNs	
EM	bark		
on	NEW		
	N(S)EW		affectionS
	[NEWS]	Sound-worlds	. . .
[dis]	(em)	(bark)	
[Dis]			
[dys]			

Key:

++	missing in the text
xx	incomprehensible
>>	illegible
. . .	untranslatable
[ ]	reconstituted by translator
( )	textual addition or emendation introduced by a previous editor
{ }	gloss supplied by translator

Rimbaud's poem looks both backwards and forwards: back to an apparently exhausted sensory experience and forward to an anticipated new self. My version casts Rimbaud's top-to-bottom traversal of time as a left-to-right traversal, and gives value both to the past and to the future (with the implication that the negative lies in between, in an age of syntactic suppression). The past is what the concrete poem looks back to, in terms of primitive, unformed language, language at the level of the cry, the morphological fragment, experiments with sound-formation; the future is obviously what the concrete poem presupposes of cyberlanguages, text messaging, and languages evolving in new guises. And my particular layout is designed to suggest this evolution from past to future, as one shifts across the visual field, from 'prefixes' and unattached 'radicals' (first two columns) to whole 'words' already with abstract capabilities (last two columns) (but the drift rightwards is ragged, irregular, indeed more untidy as it proceeds).

But I wanted to double Rimbaud's past/future experiential polarization with a past/future translational polarisation, operating both across the whole text and in a significant way from top to bottom. The translational past is what my textual key reveals: the efforts of editors and translators to

155

reconstitute, give textual wholeness and respectability to, a text which they look upon as a fragment, or mistaken, or unreadable, or illegible. In short, a negative text, beset with uncertainties, which must be restored to healthy intentionality and made translatable. This key is an extended adaptation of a similar key encountered in Jacques Roubaud's 1973 translation of Armand Schwerner's 'Tablets' and it is Schwerner's introductory note on these tablets which tells us what the translational future might be:

> La forme moderne, accidentelle des tablettes suméro-akkadiennes m'a fourni une structure utilisable poétiquement. Elles m'offraient, entre autres choses, un moyen d'échapper aux formes closes—que je trouve de plus en plus coûteuses—en même temps que la possibilité de desserrer la ceinture syntaxique de l'anglais. Elles suggéraient également des improvisations phonétiques spontanées.
> (Roubaud 2000: 29).
>
> [The modern, accidental form of the Sumero-Akkadian tablets provided me with a structure I could put to poetic use. They offered me, among other things, a means of escape from closed forms—which I find increasingly involve sacrifices—and, at the same time, the possibility of loosening the constrictions of English syntax. They also suggested spontaneous phonetic improvisations.]

The final three 'prefixes' ('dis', 'Dis', 'dys'), we notice, are all translators' reconstitutions and tell us about the translator's failure of nerve. These prefixes are prefixes of dissociation, of the Hadean, of the dysfunctional. And the first of these prefixes mounts on another prefix ('em': 'disembark'): there is a real attempt here to frustrate the poet's/the text's departure, to cancel its ticket and condemn it to failure.

What am I trying to suggest here? That editorial/translational activity has the capacity to destroy the alchemy of translation with too much scruple and too great an addiction to memory; that notions like incomprehensibility and untranslatability are justifications for sanitising the text. Translation deeply wants the text to be whole, communicable, to achieve coherent textuality, even if this involves covert 'supplementation', writing off certain elements, excusing and apologising for certain others. We are calling this 'old' style of translation a reconstitution of text, an attempt to compensate for the inevitable 'shortcomings' of a text (gaps, moments of unintelligibility, inexplicitness, apparent incompleteness), where the translator does not want to translate these shortcomings into a new kind of text. In short, translation can often seem to be the wilful destruction of the ST's silence, the very key to its fruitful recalcitrance.

As a result, the TT is urged to declare itself, to bring itself to voice by other voices (editor, translator), is brought to heel by the need to guarantee the principle of equivalency (the elements of the ST must unequivocally exist or not exist if the equivalency of the TT is to be established). But the concrete poem is not an archaeological fragment; it is the poem unencumbered, expressive within the range of its own visibility, suggestive of new language structures revealed by its very fragmentation. Concrete poetry allows us to rediscover our own language as a foreign country; it gives us a licence to re-forge our links with language in ways that lie outside the grammar book and the language system, and which may include misapprehensions about, and revisions of, the language system which chime better with our linguistic intuitions and desires. Through resistance to utterance, language recovers a capricious autonomy, opens up dimensions in itself we did not suspect, provides those anamorphic experiences which leave us wondering whether it is a duck or a rabbit. Or at least this is our illusion; Rimbaud /the translator may well be control freaks:

> J'inventai la couleur des voyelles! [. . .] Je réglai la forme et le mouvement de chaque consonne, et, avec des rhythmes [*sic*] instinctifs, je me flattai d'inventer un verbe poétique accessible, un jour ou l'autre, à tous les sens. Je réservais la traduction.
>
> ('Délires II: Alchimie du verbe')
>
> [I invented the colours of the vowels ! [. . .] I regulated the form and movement of each consonant, and, with instinctive rhythms, I flattered myself that I would invent a poetic language accessible, some day or other, to all the senses. I reserved the rights of translation].

Prefixation, which is the left-to-right generator of this translation, seems to me to enact the 'fatalité de bonheur' [being fated to happiness] that Rimbaud sees as an innate feature of the human condition. Prefixation itself promises linguistic departure, particularly by its ability to transmute matter into energy, the substantival into the verbal, and by its release of force-lines, directions, impulses. Some of the prefixes are genuine ('en/dured', 'ac/quainted', 'en/countered', and so on), some false ('en/ough', prepositions, first part of a possessive adjective ['it']), but all participate in this concert of impetus-giving (apart, of course, from the fearful and thwarting 'di(y)s' prefixes we have already described). At the same time, the energizing power of prefixes false and true produces new radicals, one of which looks like an expletive ('ough') expressing

157

impatience, two like archaic verb-forms suddenly resurrected ('dured', 'quainted'), one revealing anamorphic metamorphoses ('bark' = boat + dog + trunk covering) and one even suggesting that the marker of possession, 's' (and plurality, and the abbreviated form of 'is' and 'has'), is itself an independent root, ready to become the foundation of a new range of language forms. As indeed it is in my rendering, although in doing so, it participates in a larger and more complex interaction of capital letters.

In the relatively 'archaic' language of Rimbaud's ST, capitalization helps to establish the rhetoricity of discourse (personification, amplification) and thus the ascription of meaning/function, to be harvested by the reader. In my concrete poem, capitals are not evidence of the privileging of concepts or semantic portentousness, so much as the flexible instruments of patterning, the ripples of morphemic, phonemic and graphemic being and metamorphosis, which pass across the face of the text. At the centre of this activity, as already noted, is S, the marker of possession and plurality, which radicalises itself and momentarily informs a new order whose alpha ('Sound-worlds') and omega ('affectionS') it is. This may have echoes of Isou's Lettrist infinitesimality, an infinitesimality which has grammatical as well as lexical dimensions. Of what possible parts of speech is 's' the radical? What is its family of cognates? What is its etymology? How do we account for its changing positions in words? And as 's' begins to inhabit this poem, it gradually unfolds its palette of phonetic realisations: /s/ and /z/, but especially, perhaps, /ʒ/ in 'vision' and 'viSioNs'. After we have crossed into the new order, 's' is still /s/ and /z/ apparently, but it is also, in 'N(S)EW', a totally unknown quantity. It would be easy to pass it off as /ɛs/. But we may also imagine that the brackets by which it is surrounded, and which, ironically, are supplied by a previous editor, hold it in a state of eternal virtuality in the new, susceptible to any number of vocalisations and electro-acoustic distortions and extensions. This language, which at first I thought I recognised and could systematise, is pursuing some polymorphic, metamorphic, anamorphic destiny of its own; it is as if, having comfortably dwelt for years in a Euclidean spatial structure, I had suddenly been thrust into the vertigo and unthinkability of n-dimensional geometry.

The other capitals which accompany this projection of 's' play out similar roles but with more circumspection. The 'M' of 'ruMblings' becomes the prefix 'EM' of departure, but in doing so generates another nucleus of energy, 'E'. The 'N' of 'viSioNs' is likewise thrust forward and clusters with 'E' and 'S' to form the galaxy of the 'NEW'. And in this new galaxy, it is 'W' that is most puzzling: it emerges unannounced—the 'w' of 'with' is the only one that precedes it) and slips back into lower case almost immediately, in 'Sound-worlds'. But 'w' is one of French's most exotic graphemes, realising itself phonetically as either /w/ or /v/, and described as a 'double v' (where, in English, it is a 'double u'); in Rimbaud's work, it almost inevitably conjures up the 'wasserfall' of 'Aube'. Despite this last, 'w' essentially betokens a small Anglo-American enclave in the French lexicon, of which travel (the 'wagon' series) is a relatively significant constituent. The capital 'D's' of '[Dama]' and '[Dis]', on the other hand, belong to pieces of text reconstituted by the translator. These are the old-world capitals of proper names, the first a reference to 'Métropolitain' ('Damas damnant de longueur' [Damascus damning with distance]), where the Damascus road, far from supplying a revelation of ultimate salvation condemns those who travel it to damnation, by its very length. This damnation is confirmed by '[Dis]', one of the trio of undoing, which attempt to draw the itinerary of Rimbaud's poem back towards that of Baudelaire's 'Le Voyage'.

Capital letters take us back to the ST, and in particular to the apostrophe 'O Rumeurs et Visions'. This phrase is often assumed to be a synthesis of what precedes, a final backward glance, tinged with regretful affection perhaps, before the 'Assez' structure is erased and the new start initiated. The apostrophe and capital letters are inflationary in relation to register: the bald telegraphic style allows itself a momentary amplification, which grafts a certain irony on to its poignancy; additionally, the phrase—as, among others, Kloepfer and Oomen (1970: 155) and Fongaro (1993: 17) have pointed out—forms a second hexasyllable after 'Les arrêts de la vie!', the dash between (caesura?) underlining the rhythmic balance (3+3+3+3). The apostrophe elevates this moment of orotundity, engineering one of those 'arrêts de la vie' when stock is taken and one indulges oneself optatively in the invoked. It is one of those 'old-fashioned' apostrophes one finds in the *Illuminations*, that is with the apostrophic 'O' followed directly by a noun, without a definite article, an apostrophe of pure address.[1] But, as we have already pointed out, this kind of apostrophe is as if always under threat from 'accusative' structures and from the prosaic obliterations of the exclamation 'Oh!'

The fortunes of these two utterances (along with the occasional 'Ah!') are as intricately interwoven in *Une saison en enfer* as in *Illuminations*. 'Ô' is a self *within* experience, if only by optation, is a self which has arrived at a pitch of wish-experience so intense that the experience is held away from the subject: the subject does not wish to assimilate and thus confine the experience but to bathe in it as it becomes available. 'Oh!', on the other hand, is a declaration of loss, of being outside experience, of being exiled from beatification. At the end of 'L'Éclair'—'Alors,—oh!—chère pauvre âme, l'éternité serait-elle pas perdue pour nous'—this isolation, enacted by the exclamatory punctuation, is further confirmed by the dashes, as if, had eternity not been lost, we might have read: 'Alors, ô chère pauvre âme, l'éternité serait sauvé.' This 'oh!' is a self being locked out of its own language, an exclamation with a past participial aspect. 'Oh!' is the still photograph to 'Ô's' photogram, because 'Ô' has a projective perspective, is conjuring a future for itself, is a sentient fullness looking for fulfilment, even though set in the past.

The close relationship between 'Oh!' and 'Ô' is as if emphasized by the frequency with which 'Oh!' is associated with a syntax peculiar to 'Ô' (i.e. Ô + NP [or Ô + INF])—as in 'Après le déluge': 'Oh! les pierres précieuses qui se cachaient', 'oh! les pierres précieuses s'enfouissant', or 'Barbare': 'Oh! le pavillon en viande saignante [. . .]', or 'Mauvais Sang': 'Oh! la science!', or 'Délires II: Alchimie du verbe': 'Oh! le moucheron enivré à la pissotière de l'auberge'[2]—just as, on the odd occasion, one finds a structure with 'Ô' that one might more readily associate with 'Oh!': in 'Matinée d'ivresse' we meet 'Ô maintenant nous si digne de ces tortures [. . .]'. In the event, it is hardly surprising that Bernard translates this as 'Oh let us now, so deserving of these tortures, [. . .]' (1962: 250). Fowlie (1966: 233), Schmidt (1976: 224) and Sloate (1990: 44) also translate 'Ô' as 'Oh!' here, but, unlike Bernard, this is for them a standard procedure, in the *Illuminations* at least (although Fowlie also translates 'Ô' by zero).[3]

If I have avoided apostrophe and exclamation in my version, it is to remove the subjective centre and thus to emphasise two distinctive features of concrete poetry. It would be natural for us to look upon the lyric poem as the 'regurgitation' in utterance of digested experience. Lyric poetry may be associated with first-person utterance, but poetic form reminds us that this is *predigested* first-personness. The apostrophe, one might argue, is a sign both of lyric spontaneity and that digestive process; it betokens that moment of stasis in consciousness when desire or loss come to know themselves. The language of the concrete poem pre-dates (and post-dates) both *énonciation* and *énoncé*; it can be uttered, but it is not utterance. And this brings us directly to the second point: concrete poetry is designed to be non-verbal communication with words. Words communicate themselves not as discourse or message, but as 'structure-content'.

In their 'Pilot Plan for Concrete Poetry' (1958), the de Campos brothers (Augusto and Haroldo) and Décio Pignatari describe concrete poetry as a 'tension of things-words in space-time' and its dynamic structure as a 'multiplicity of concomitant movements' (quoted in Solt 1970: 72). The poem is already constructed on three underlying oppositions, between the vertical and the horizontal, between the unstable past of a manuscript and the future of technology-language, between the pre- and post-verbal left-hand columns and the more or less orthodox verbality of the right-hand columns (see pp. 68–9). But these are not reliable structuring axes; they merely stretch the text between points within which it operates as a set of unsteady verbal textures. These textures are hard to describe with any accuracy since they continuously complicate each other, and this process of complication is continuous precisely because the poem resists meaning, resists semantic outcomes, and rather goes on performimg this refusal, this elusiveness.

The enemy of concrete poetry is what is variously called the 'linear-temporistical' (Campos/Campos/Pignatari), or the determination to understand 'analytico-discursivement' (Apollinaire) (Solt 1970: 71). This presupposes a text unfolding its meaning consecutively, at the same rate as the eye runs along it. The eye may pause, turn back, slow down, but it is largely to re-establish the uniform pace of semantic production which has been momentarily threatened by incomprehension. In verse, this pace is both reinforced and guaranteed by rhythmic recurrence and more especially by its spatialisation in the metrical template. In fact, metre, by encouraging the through-reading of the line, actually tends to propel the voice at a certain uniform speed. Those changes of tempo, and stress-degree, those pauses and other paralinguistic features introduced by the reader are expressive enhancements of the text rather than revisions of its ontological status. Even when we speak about the materiality of language in regular verse, we must realise that while this may activate meaning in new ways, may re-organise and de-syntacticalise verbal relationships, its activity is likely to be reabsorbed into an essentially linear and conceptualised version of meaning: we tend to say that words which sound the same will be seen to mean the same, in some way. We do not say that words which sound the same are *constructive* uses of verbal material, sculpting the space in which the words interact. Whatever layers of time we identify in the process of reading will, therefore, tend to be ultimately coincident or at least be seen to share the same teleology. Myths of organic form want to pursue notions of complexity, ambiguity and so on, but not at the expense of the final full-stop.

Concrete poetry works somewhat differently. I have elsewhere tried to describe the different dimensions of poetic time (1998: 97–101): the time of the text, the time of reading, the time of the reader. Textual time in poetry is made up of the modality of words as much as of the tenses of sentences, a trend increased in concrete poetry by the minimalisation of syntax; and aspect will correspondingly play a larger part than is customary. 'Enough', for example, would naturally strike one as action-terminal; with something of the interjection restored to its 'ough', and with its prefix able to generate prospective activity, the word's temporal orientation shifts round towards the instantaneous and the action-initial. Similarly the 'lit' of 'sunlit' has a past-tense orientation, even though the whole word has no tense at all; this past-tense orientation is, in fact, something of a mirage, since the past participle is a past participle of instrument (lit by the sun, bathed by the sun, and so forth) rather than of position in time. However, it increases the word's capacity for poignancy, a capacity further increased by 'lit's' implication of focussed brevity (rather than the diffused duration of, say, 'sun-bathed'). Plurality will suggest the iterative continuous, but may sometimes gravitate towards the simultaneous punctual: are these 'cities' points in a panorama, or a sequence of ill-remembered encounters?

The time of reading is made difficult to assess by concrete poetry's cultivation of the ensemble rather than the sentence, of the 'presentified' (Haroldo de Campos) rather than the encoded, of the scanned or perceived rather than the read: 'A word which is read only grazes the reader's mind: but a word that is perceived, or accepted, starts off a chain of reactions there' (Pierre Garnier, 'Second manifesto for Visual Poetry' (1962), quoted in Solt 1970: 32).

In fact, one might want to argue that a peculiarity of concrete poetry is that the time of reading progressively collapses into the time of the reader, precisely as the horizontal and vertical axes are superseded by the ensemble. Of course, we may still maintain that a message is communicated: kinds of sensory and psychic experience reach saturation point and trigger departure into the new. But, in many ways, this message is a survival from the ST which the TT no longer bears out. And the control of the poem's colouring that the translator/previous editor look to exercise is no more than a mirage. The text is no longer a set of interpretable propositions, but a variety of apparently self-generating linguistic associations/activities which, once read, are transformed into a grid of permutable verbal counters. The concrete poet believes that the single word not only includes all its possible collocations (as lines of force, one might say), but is itself ideogram rather than word (i.e. it is a word communicating multisensorily, rather than as a verbal sign).

What then does it mean to say that the time of reading collapses into the time of the reader? It means that the text itself establishes no rhythm of attention and presupposes nothing about pacing (whether rhythm-produced or narrative-produced). Without these points of reference, time-related patterns of curiosity, anticipation, suspense, satisfaction, do not operate. The mind moves freely, without temporal imperative, among the elements of the construction. In a situation like this, the time of the reader assumes a controlling interest. The time of the reader is an associative time, a time of memory and fantasy, embroidering on, intensifying, possibly even contradicting, the modal and aspectual qualities of textual time. What we are then likely to encounter is a multitude of localised times which fragment and re-open Rimbaud's 'original' past and future pivoting around a moment of decision: 'Assez' + past participle > ! > 'Départ'.

In arguing that the time of reading collapses into the time of the reader, recovered from textual fragments designed as an ensemble, we are proposing that this version has no presiding temporality from which the particular temporalities engendered by individual words(-fragments) and phrases take their bearings. On the contrary, temporal (spatial) experience is created almost exclusively by these words(fragments) and phrases so that the text is a multi-dimensional, facetted construction which cannot be located in an overall spatio-temporal environment. The time of the text is ordered along two pairs of axes: the time of the text/the time of the reader; and the time-quality within the word(-fragment)/the time enveloping the word—for example 'dured', 'compassed', 'quainted' may all insinuate an archaic envelope, but while 'dured' may betoken effortful, moral duration, 'quainted' may suggest something more punctual and decorative. The prefix fragments are like temporal thresholds, sparks of time waiting to catch fire in a range of possible temporal/spatial realisations. Concrete poetry might be said to dramatise the creation of time and space, by using words and word-fragments to project fragments of temporal experience into space.

It is only by composing text with *ajours*—and, as ever, I use this term advisedly, as spaces, textual lacunae, fully integrated into the overall ensemble as an essential part, rather than accidentally created, or left, by a text whose integrity is entirely verbal—and by fragmenting or telegraphising language, that space and time can become lively protagonists in textual activity. Linear syntactical language conventionalises and deadens page-space (it becomes *blank* space) and allows time only to be *re*constructed, persuades it to chronometricise itself. Presentative or ideographic writing, which minimises or nullifies the time of reading, projects space, builds spaces (*ajours*) and disengages temporal experience from conceptualised time, gives us access to the real time of the reader. Thus we can begin to understand why Marinetti felt that free verse, for all its apparent introduction of *ajours*, had missed its chance, was already passé, because it still anxiously cultivated standard syntax and principles of lineation (and therefore temporal linearity). Crude though

Pierre Garnier's example is, it makes its point eloquently enough: 'The structure of the sentence has caused the same damage as the rhythms of poetry. What a difference there is between: "The tiger is coming to drink at the river bank" and the single name: TIGER!' (quoted in Solt 1970: 32). The sentence locates an animal on a temporal scale which runs from the impulse to fulfil an action towards its actual fulfilment. The single name refers us to no time-scale, but puts us in a time of perception whose qualitative features may include excitement, fear, awe, memory of similar images, and so forth (i.e. time in its pure state is a nexus of different temporal directions, 360 degrees time).

If I have concentrated on temporal aspects of my version of 'Départ', at the expense of spatial ones, it is because the relatively ordered columnar lay-out tends to turn *ajours* into space. This is a result of the translational and editorial interferences that the translation dramatises; this is a concrete poem which the translator wants to endow with some kind of textual recognisability, or reminiscence of text. In order to think more consecutively about space in the dynamic of the concrete poem, I would like to move on to another version of 'Départ'. But before doing so, I would like to suggest that background spaces or spatial experience can be generically projected. The space of concrete poetry is a mixture of the utopian and carnivalesque, with its eye on global communication (a space of unobstructed movement and exchange), on the one hand, and on ludic activity (the play of the 'remainder') (a social space of conflictual dialogue), on the other:

> *The remainder is the return within language of the contradictions and struggles that make up the social; it is the persistence within language of past contradictions and struggles, and the anticipation of future ones.*
> (Lecercle 1990: 182; italics in original)

In my own particular scenario, the forces of textuality (editor, translator) have undertaken, by implication at least, to discredit the carnivalesque and the unauthoredness of the constructivist or 'on-me-pense' situation, by trying to restore—paradoxically by virtue of underlining the textual fragility of the manuscript—a Romantic notion of the textually incompetent author hauled to his rightful glory by the devotion of his editors. The overall effect may, however, be to turn the utopian space of the concrete poem into the dystopian. Rimbaud's version of himself as concrete poet is not allowed to depart, and the fragmentation of language is condemned and punished by translational reconstruction— dismembered language is not communication enriched, or alternative communication, but the invasion of the deformed, the grotesque, the monstrous. 'The sleep of reason engenders monsters.'

What I hope is played out in this treatment is the drama of translation. Rimbaud's prose poems are, as it were, homologous with concrete poetry inasmuch as they each have a universal language in view. But in his quest for this language, Rimbaud must set out from French, albeit it from a French that 'implique l'étude des autres langues' (Butor 1989: 66) [entails the study of other languages]. As Butor further reminds us, Rimbaud pursued new languages even after he had renounced literature: 'Tout ce clavier de langues, c'est un moyen de dépasser la malédiction de Babel, tombée sur ces hommes d'autrefois qui ont voulu construire une tour pour voler le feu du ciel, devenir les frères des dieux' (1989: 67) [This whole spectrum of languages is a means of outwitting the curse of Babel, visited on those men of yesteryear who wanted to build a tower to steal fire from heaven, to become the brothers of the gods]. Reading *Une saison en enfer*, one can believe that Rimbaud imagined a different poetics every few months and approached his work in a spirit of tireless experimentation. The translator seeks to perpetuate this spirit. But, in particular, the translator (a) avoids translating the meaning *against* the form or imagining, conveniently, that the prose poem has no form, and (b) attempts to translate the time and space buried in the ST, or to translate the ST into time and space. To achieve (b) is likely to ensure (a).

But in the case of our concrete version of 'Départ', this ambition is jeopardised by a different translational persuasion, a persuasion which, despite its cultural liberalism, perpetuates, thrives on, makes pedagogical capital out of, the Babelian curse. Bound as it is to a certain fixed view of textual correspondence, it continues to operate with a balance-sheet of omissions and additions (in all their possible manifestations), as if the ST were not already marked with the desire for formal metamorphosis (precisely in the interests of (a)). Because of its commitment to rational choice, this kind of translation must set aside all that endangers that principle: not just the illegible, but also the incomprehensible— understanding is a prerequisite of rational choice—and indeed the untranslatable. What this last presupposes is that the untranslatable, regrettable though it is, is also dispensable. Untranslatability then ceases to be a feature of the text and becomes an alibi of the translator. Worse still, it becomes the instrument of critical mystification: the poetic is what is inaccessible to the translator. Conversely, and equally dangerously, rational choice justifies what I call 'reconstitutions', 'additions' and 'emendations', which begin to have the value of essential keys to meaning and enjoy a priority in the secret intentions of the piece that other items do not.

We have suggested that activated space is not as present in our concrete 'Départ' as it might be, and for two reasons: (i) the columnar layout begins to conventionalise space, transforms *ajours* into 'unmotivated' blank space; (ii) the relative abstractness of sound—rumbles, rumblings, sound-worlds—means that no resonance is generated, no resonance which itself would demand space for its own outworking. So I have given my next version a Futurist turn and centred it around a street scene, such as might be found in Boccioni, or Soffici, or Severini, animated by Russolo's art of noises:

```
                    S
                    T
                    C
        N           I
        O           D
        VI          R
        IS          E
     VISIONNOISIV
        IV
        o
        N
```

EN! OUGH!

```
cardoorSLAM          EN! GINE . . . idling (sunlight)
         shutterCLANKsqueaking klaxon   REVV . . . ough
      (even)footFALLFOOTfallFOOTheel(ing)            klaxon
                              bAckFIre  flAgFLap
         interruptions                 o the palpitation of valves
                                       0 klaxon
                                       o
                                       visionsounds
                                       O
                                       0
                                       o the jolting of trams
```

!OFF

dynochagrin   chromophony (enrico)
kaleidosmile   scatolophony (pétarade de fouets)
exceleration   cinematophony (the silent screen)
                           sartorophony (SONia)
                                    bippPHarreZzOghogHmmm

The street, which occupies the middle of the poem, is, in fact, an intersection or T-junction, along which cars and scattered pedestrians make their way. In a very literal sense, it is both an aerial view—of movements felt at some points to be continuous, at others isolated incidents in a scene which is an ever-changing configuration of particulars—and a lateral view, of the kind described by Moholy-Nagy, where different phenomena are viewed through and across each other, in complex layers of varying awareness:

> We travel by streetcar and look out of the window; a car is following us, its windows also transparent, through which we see a shop with equally transparent windows; in the shop we see customers and salespeople; a person opens the door, people pass by the shop, a policeman holds up a cyclist. We take in all this within the moment, because the windows are transparent and everything happens within our field of vision.
>
> (from 'Fotographie ist Lichtgestaltung',
> *Bauhaus*, 2/1, 1928, in Passuth 1985: 304)

But where Moholy-Nagy concentrates on purely visual stratifications, what is visible in my street-scene derives, only by implication, from overlaid sounds, of different intensities, striking the eardrum from a variety of locations, possibly almost simultaneously, as if converging on each other, becoming a cacophonous bundle (even with the 'interruptions'), possibly as a complex symphony of noises interacting across a more extended time-span. The channel of the street has, on each side of it, exclamations ('EN! OUGH!' and '!OFF'), which belong to the aerial perspective, and which are trying, on the one hand, to bring this incessant commotion to a halt, and, on the other, to break the spell and leave. These 'barrier-words' isolate, at the top of the page, a constellation of divinely bestowed stars proliferating visions which are informed with ethical and spiritual obligations. These are seen from below, and thus their multi-directionality strikes perception as essentially two-dimensional, although variation in size of font provides evidence of differentiated depth. Here, there is no noise: the 'rumeurs' have been detached from the 'visions' and are all invested in the street. Equally separated are the two meanings of 'arrêts': the sense of 'ruling' or 'decree' has gravitated upwards, to the realm of divine jurisdiction, while the 'pauses', 'stops', 'interruptions' remain part of the street's rhythm, staccato, syncopated, a world of unpredictable ruptures and unexpected short silences. This process of the separation and re-distribution of meanings is an inevitable part of the re-spatialisation of the text's associative economy and the release, and exploration, of lines of force ('Every object reveals by its lines how it would resolve itself were it to follow the tendency of its forces' ('The Exhibitors to the Public 1912', in Apollonio 1973: 48)).

'Below' the line of the street, and installing a new spatial dimension, are the twin lists of new affections and new sounds. What this dimension is we cannot tell, but it might be a close-up of the page(s) of a manifesto, which we are holding in our hands. But initially, for me, because of its position on the page, it was the orchestra pit of a Wagnerian opera, the hidden chthonic source of a new urban order of interwoven senses and leitmotivic sensations. The 'downwardness' which, in the concrete version, had spelt malediction, editorial intrusion, acoustic sameness, here opens up a space of potentiality, a space, already inaugurated perhaps, of new sensory concepts and combinations. Is there a narrative to be played out between Enrico (Prampolini: 'Chromophony—the Colours of Sounds', *Gazzetta Ferrarese*, 26 August 1913; see Apollonio 1973: 115–18) and Sonia (Delaunay), encompassing between them the marriage of circus and cinema? The poem closes with a Lettrist signature, an -ophony of a kind difficult to identify (authorophony?), a synthesis of all -ophonies perhaps, but also the trace of physical sensation, potentially uninterrupted experiential duration, a kineplasma of being-in-the-world.

The spatial treatment of this poem is not integrative. But that is precisely the point: it is a single scene, but you must constantly change your position if you are to make sense of its conflicting angles of perception. Moving down the page, one in a sense shifts from background (the starry sky), through middle ground (a busy street) to foreground (a fragment of manifesto?), but as one does so, one looks up, one looks down, on looks across, one looks (closely) at. But these spaces are not simply the products of physical points of view. They are also products of cultural points of view. The aerial view of the city street, for example, takes us up to the Haussmannian balcony, the Imperialist view, masculinist clairvoyance, social alienation, while the street-level perspective has the exploitative empathies of the *flâneur*, the wry humanism of the street photographer, the barely controlled neuroses of the man in the crowd. And the space of the manifesto, hectoring, browbeating, the kind of activism that draws in the horizon, closes down the blind field, cuts itself off the better to envelop the reader.

In this world, the apostrophe recovers it's citizen's rights. Now it signifies not the lyricism of the uttering poet, but the lyricism of feelings themselves, the feelings intuited in materials, in objects, in noises. Thus, the 'O/o', by virtue of its different fonts and positions in words, explores the whole gamut of its acousticity and its ability to 'enrhythm' a whole scene ('THE RHYTHMIC MOVEMENTS OF A NOISE ARE INFINITE: JUST AS WITH TONE THERE IS ALWAYS A PREDOMINANT RHYTHM, but around this numerous other secondary rhythms can be felt', Luigi Russolo, 'The Art of Noises', 11 March 1913, in Apollonio 1973: 86); it is the fulcrum of the new emotions, the heart of all sounds (-phony, SONia), except 'the silent screen', the motivator of 'Vision'. The 'O/o', then, like the spaces which intervene in its sounding, figures the informing consciousness of the translator, the translator as the activator of new kinds of sensory and emotional experience, the translator as the open, rounded mouth of pure apostrophic uttering, and the nought of articulate space, which make this experience resonant.

Just as 'Vies' is often viewed as a prelude to 'Départ', not least because, in manuscript, it precedes 'Départ' on the same sheet of paper, so 'A une Raison' might be looked upon as 'Départ's' consummation. My final translation in this chapter is an account of 'A une Raison' (see Appendix II (vii) for 'straight' version) which looks to blend the concrete, the Futurist and the Lettrist, and to explore the ways in which noises, exploiting the mechanisms of rhyme, repetition and rhythm, might sculpt the spaces of the text:

A une Raison

drum tap   tptptpta
thigh slap   slip, slip, slipp, sllli
floor creak   kkkre kffllli
wheels screech scream shriek **ski shurrrze hhhpta**

key change

                      singing   ing
ringingchiming
                                    whining-bawling

            call

169

STEP	**step**	**step**	step	step
	step	step	steppe	**step**
		step	**step**	**step**
			step	step
				steppes

lovelorn, look . . . love; woebegone: love-look!   comebecome

dreamtime   eve
timemachine   **you**   ever
always   every   **where**

In organising this poem as a concrete/Lettrist performance, I began by unravelling its paragraphs/versets as a set of performances, or, conversely, in the last two paragraphs, by encapsulating telegraphically what was already performed. Central to these processes were the at once binding and multiplying properties of rhyme and repetition. But the creative principle here is 'une Raison' of the kind that lurks in the 'long, immense et raisonné dérèglement de tous les sens',[4] and for that reason, too, rhyme is peculiarly appropriate, since rhyme is that order of irrationality, the incorporation of the remainder into official discourse, which constantly needs to justify itself aesthetically, semantically (à la Jakobson) or prosodically (à la Verlaine). Rhyme, it might seem, creates the space in which anticipation (the proleptic) constantly transforms itself into memory (the analeptic). But this view may be too exclusive, and too 'modelled' a way of thinking about rhyme. In our particular version, the absence of a syntax, of a punctuation used syntactically, may release rhyme into a free acoustic-cumulative activity which constantly projects and re-projects different sounds; in other words, the rhyme-partner does not counter the proleptic with the analeptic, but confirms and amplifies the proleptic. More important still, rhyme-structure, freed from the 'fixed' architecture of the stanza, can itself sculpt space, redistribute space or re-survey space with its alternative to triangulation.

My account of the first paragraph is, quite literally a 'discharge of sounds': what are onomatopoeically 'described' sounds ('tap', 'slap', etc.) repossess themselves as unmediated 'vocalisations' in Lettrist transcriptions, which have different rhythmic paces and patterns, and different degrees of rhythmic definition: 'floor creak' and 'wheels [. . .] shriek', for example, produce slurrings (with interruptions). Here, two standard rhyme-patterns intertwine: the *rimes plates* of the full-word sequence provides a counterpoint to the *rimes embrassées* of the Lettrist sequence. One may, of course, wish to argue that rhyme is decisive, in the sense that the Lettrist series rhyme only by consenting to come to an end on a certain sound. But equally the shift from phonemes that *are* the rhyme within a given structure, in the left-hand column, to homophonous phonemes in the right, is a profound increase in rhyme's irrationality and arbitrariness, is a more complete surrender to acoustic hallucination, caprice. And this shift tells us, precisely, of the replacement, in the prose poem, of a pseudo-stanzaic space organising acousticity (the verset) by spaces themselves created by acousticity, the trapezoid configurations of opportunistic chance (the paragraph).

With the key change—from minor to major—sounds ('ringingchiming . . .etc.') no longer have agents or locations, but are caught in spaces of their own. This arrangement uses rhyme to counter the cultural forces of the page (left to right, top to bottom). 'Singing' rhymes with 'ringing', but on the top-to-bottom axis precedes it. 'Call/ing' rhymes with 'bawling', but 'call' precedes it on the left-to-right axis, and 'ing' precedes it on the top-to-bottom axis. Additionally, of course, whereas a stanzaic rhyme-scheme implies an equidistance between line-terminal sounds, an equidistance which helps to stabilise and standardise relationships, in my version, rhyme enacts 'la nouvelle harmonie', not only by flexibilising the space across which sounds echo each other, but also by re-ordering the 'conventions' of (verbal) acousticity (pre-echoes, the same sound-sequence in two places at once, half rhymes *becoming* full rhymes ['bawling: call > ing'] i.e. rhymes in protean process). In this new Rimbaldian world, therefore, the new harmony is, in fact, an instrument for the reconstruction of our living space. A set of sounds, at varying distances from each other, and inclined to blur their sequence, but rhyming nonetheless, mark changing locations in a space which seems sculpted, but which, when read, twists and turns in a set of peculiar torsions.

And this space, this new harmony, is not a given, recovered from the text by a translator, but the principle of mutability which is reading itself, once space is essentially *ajours* and temporality is allowed to operate at the levels explored earlier (time of the text, time of reading, time of the reader). If we look upon translation as the opportunity to activate and make available the times and spaces elided by printing practices and the conventionalisation of the page, or to construct times and spaces appropriate to the ST's contemporary and future life, then the practices of reading must change. Traditional translation presents the TT as a substitute text whose title and author reveal another origin, inaccessible to the ignorant reader. If, on the other hand, the TT is not a substitute but an *escale* on a journey being (endlessly) taken by the ST in another language, if the point of this process is lost without a knowledge of the SL (which must be assumed), if the translational progeny of the ST is reading *into* the ST's poeticity and into its potentiality to proliferate, then the contact that the TT establishes with the ST must be existentially investigative and engage the reader in the same way that it engages the translator. In traditional translation, the translator is an indispensable mediator of the ST who does not expect his readers to manipulate his text (to increase their own pleasure) and therefore potentially to re-translate the ST in their very reading of the TT. But the new translation invites just that: a translation in which the translator records his reading himself, as a contemporary, out of a past text, a past text now endowed with the temporal and spatial flexibilities and significances of the present, such that the reader feels that other options are included in the ST, that the ST exists expressly to ramify expressively, that it inevitably entails the reader in turn becoming a translator.

When we move on to the procreative step, in the next paragraph of 'A une Raison', space becomes the military parade-ground and also the field in which the dragon's teeth are sown by Cadmus, the final row representing the five Sparti who survive the subsequent internecine carnage to become the ancestors of Thebes. Or this is simply the step of one individual colonising a territory, occupying an empty mentality. Here the principle of repetition runs the risk of exponential cloning. If I have introduced into this regimented mass the homophone 'steppe(s)', it is not a leap at facility so much as a cross-reference to 'Fairy'—'Après le moment de l'air des bûcheronnes à la rumeur du torrent sous la ruine des bois, de la sonnerie des bestiaux à l'écho des vals, et des cris des steppes'—and the insinuation of untamed, undefined space, which will blow this parade-ground apart, which will turn these regimented lives into the nomadic wilfulness of motley travellers and traders. This homophone is the multiplying maverick. But many commentators would see these 'nouveaux hommes' as the soldiers of revolution, of the Commune, and the language of this piece as being shot through with the spirit of 'social illuminism' (see, for example, Bernard/Guyaux 2000: 539). This opening fan of repeated presences may indicate less the threat of colonisation than a rallying to socialist colours, from all parts of the globe.

In the line following, I have maintained a horizontal development through time and elaborated on an amorous biography, expressed, in its darker moments, in Romantic compounds ('lovelorn', 'woebegone'), whose two elements conjoin to generate duration, states without prospect of a terminus. The new 'compounds' ('look. . .love', 'love-look') are punctuationally created and imitate the differentiated punctuation of the ST. This means that these new compounds breath the complex life of punctuation—temporal, respiratory, affective—and underline what the punctuation indicates in the ST, that no two new loves are the same; the relationship between 'look' and 'love' shifts from pondered gaze to *coup de foudre*, the punctuation mark acting as the *point de rencontre* of the physical gesture ('look') and the feeling, a fulcrum or flash-point, so that these 'compounds' are turned inwards towards a core, rather than stretched out on the rack of time.

But even in the Romantic compounds there are signs of renewal. 'Woebegone' as the fulcrum of the line's development is as much imperative ('Woe, be gone!') as past participial adjective and its structure is echoed in 'comebecome' ('come, be come!' [?]). The horizontality of this sequence casts it as one of those nomadic processions of 'comédiens' Rimbaud is so likely to catch sight of, a mysterious beckoning to other orders of existence. This is a simple space of traversal, but it does not allow a settled gait, for all the structural repetition. Fongaro (1993: 28) points out that, in the corresponding paragraph/verset in the ST, 'deux dodécasyllabes quasi identiques se suivent, caractérisés par la coupe à l'intérieur d'un mot et devant une syllabe muette' [two almost identical dodecasyllables occur in sequence, characterised by a word-internal *coupe* followed by a mute e] [i.e. 'Ta tête se détour/ne: le nouvel amour ! Ta tête se retour/ne, - le nouvel amour !']. For amateurs of the alexandrine, this would leave three broad choices: either read it as a 'trimètre' (an 'alexandrin romantique'?), with a *coupe lyrique* at the colon, thus:

Ta tê/te se détourne:/ le nouvel amour   2 + 5' +5

or as a standard 'tétramètre', with a *césure enjambante:*

Ta tê/te se détour//ne: le nouvel/ amour!   2 + 4 + 4 + 2

or as a 'new' 'tétramètre', with a *césure lyrique:*

Ta tê/te se détourne://le nouvel/ amour!   2 + 5' + 3 + 2

The trimetric reading has the advantage of making the final measure more instantaneous as the final accent on 'amour' is impatiently reached for through 'nouvel'. The standard tetrametric reading not only lifts out 'nouvel', but more particularly creates a tension at the colon: while the colon tries to create a threshold for the revelation which follows, the -ne of 'détourne', which has already crossed the caesural barrier, also, as an agent of rhythmic liaison, crosses the colon's threshold. The new 'tétramètre' preserves barriers and thresholds the better to launch love reinvented; but, with its *césure lyrique*, it also projects a 7'//5 alexandrine, a new conception of the old, a syncopated and asymmetrical version of balance. As we move along the path towards a possession of this new faculty—what the colon displays, the dash appropriates—we are offered several dynamics, or modes of rhythmic proceeding, and we may choose one mode for the first of the pair of elements and another for the second.[5]

My rendering has not got this capacity for complexity, but I have tried to create ambiguities of rhythmic grouping which (a) produce the same asymmetry and (b) suggest the same tension between threshold and crossover. The first part of my 'line' leaves questions of stressing undecided:

lovelorn, look . . . love; woebegone: / × / . . . // × × or / / / . . . // × /

The second part is an abbreviated form of this undecidability:

love-look! comebecome / × . . . / × × or / / . . . / × /

So a pattern of 7 + 5, a reminiscence of one of the rhythmic possibilities in the ST (the new 'tétramètre'), but here spread over the two elements together. However, punctuationally, 'woebegone' belongs to the second element: it *seems* to belong, affectively, to the first (with 'lovelorn'), but as we have pointed out, it has within it its own transformation and easily gravitates towards the imperative/exclamatory mood which follows it ('woe, be gone! love-look!...').

In the final section of my version, I have collapsed Rimbaud's fourth paragraph into two words. The children's plea for the abolition of time is rendered by 'dreamtime', an aboriginal, ancestral, antipodean Arcadia, but without any indication whether this state is achieved or merely desired. The idea of finding a place of good fortune and satisfied appetites calls forth a word redolent of nineteenth-century science fiction ('time-machine'). The 'always' then erases the time which is shared by the two previous terms and allows the growth of space in the right-hand column: again we begin with an origin ('eve') and then move through time ('ever') into totality ('every') which becomes ubiquity; Reason, the addressee and celebratee of this poem, waits poised to take possession of its future kingdom. Through this final cumulative progression, repetition + one, itself repeating, but at a phonemic level, the repetition + one of the parade-ground, space expands and begets a 'where' for 'you'. The space of this 'where' is a 'partout', the space where 'every' is a totality of places, a space which is place-animated, where places are a migratory population: free mobility in space triggers the mobility of places. This is an ultimate act of decolonisation; the 'anywhere' of 'Démocratie' ('Au revoir ici, n'importe où'), on the other hand, keeps places anchored in geography, so that, however careless of destination one might be, the choice has always to be made, with the inevitable consequences that choosing brings. It is into this colonised space that we shall now move.

7

The Translator as Colonist and Native

When we approach images in Rimbaud, we are faced with a certain schismatic experience. On the one hand, we have the possibility of a deictic or ekphrastic writing, that is, images as part of a verbal description of a perceptual experience, a mimetic writing which may be first order (direct apprehension real or imagined) or second order (apprehension of an apprehension—ekphrasis), or a blend of the two. On the other hand, the self-conscious materiality of Rimbaud's language, with its consequent tendency to autonomize the scriptural object might lead us to suppose that the Rimbaldian image is metaphoric, figurative, rhetorical, part of language's very refusal of mimeticism. When faced with 'Des ciels gris de cristal' (/desjɛlgRidəkRistal/) I can think of a language motivated by an anterior vision or a language which is self-motivating, i.e. a language which makes vision possible (but not compulsory), a language which makes different kinds of connotative or symbolic meaning possible (but not compulsory). Equally, the space of the page, once thought, shifts through different modes of apprehension: a mimetic space mapped out by words, for which the words act ekphrastically; the space within which the text is read, a modal space, a cultural space, a physical space even; the space by which the text is read, the space of mindset, the geometries of psyche, the trajectories of responsiveness; the space generated by the text, not as mimesis, but as the embodiment of a certain dynamics of meaning or verbal being, space as stage, space as kinesics and proxemics.

Who will write a Rimbaldian spaceology? We have revealing work on those spaces which are characteristic of Rimbaud's thematology or 'morphology' (for example, Plessen 1967: 240–84; Nakao 1998), but important though these favoured spaces are, they are not the spaces where his texts, as reading experience, take place. They are not, in other words,

6

the spaces that the translator is seeking to activate or embody in his translation, although some imitation of features of a 'described' topography may have their part to play. Nor is the translator looking to instal the space of the Mallarméan model, that making tacit of the word, 'le poème tu' (2003: 211) [the silent poem], or the 'mise en scène spirituelle' [spiritual mise en scène] of the 'subdivisions prismatiques de l'Idée' [prismatic subdivisions of the Idea] (1998: 391) (though these considerations may play their part). The primary aim is to create spaces which correspond to the mobility of the reading mind as it shifts through different levels of its awareness and self-awareness, and to provoke the reading mind, such that it projects its own spaces. Translating a poem is an attempt to give it a shape, or shapes, or shapeability, in the receiving imagination.

As already intimated, the large drawback in discussions of the spaces of the literary page or the spatiality of literary forms, is that space is treated as an absolute, a state of emptiness, a two-dimensional surface, without features, without activity other than that of providing opportunities for reflection, connotational reverberation, the dialogue between verbal bodies and constituent parts. Although one might call any two-dimensional surface 'planar', space in this kind of usage has no real geometry, no meaningful relation with other spaces, no psycho-perceptual or social implications—by this latter I mean that the page has been assumed to be devoid of markings of social class or social interaction, unlike, say, the cinema or the theatre. Space is assumed to be unmarked, innocent, precisely because it is assumed to antedate all presence. But as Henri Lefebvre reminds us (1974), space is essentially something produced, and in the case of the literary translation, it is something written into existence; put another way, the distinctive literariness of translation is the writing of space (expressive, iconic, contextual) into the fabric of the poem and into the poem's reception.

Central to our conception of the page in its social and existential manifestation, is its transformation of space into place. This is the transformation of perceptual experience, the experience of a geometry, into cultural experience, the endowment of space with cultural values. All spaces and places are susceptible of affective and ideological investment, but place is more likely to focus and identify particular desires, desires to inhabit, to appropriate, to defend, to set up a citadel. Rural migrants, the military, colonialists, religious sects, find the construction of place out of space a necessary guarantee of a raison d'être. Before all else, every human condition, apart from the nomadic, must have its home; but the page may equivocate about whether the place is utopian or dystopian, institutional or domestic, masculine or feminine, national or foreign, mine or yours or his. Conversely, place may become too convenient a refuge, too exclusive an objective. It is true that Rimbaud declares himself in search of 'le lieu et la formule' ('Vagabonds'), but 'Génie' is as much 'le charme des lieux fuyants' [the charm of fleeting places] as it is 'le délice surhumain des stations' [the superhuman delight of halts], and we have already encountered 'Départ' and the 'qui t'en iras partout' of 'A une Raison'. If place is the repository of memory and is sustained by memory, then Rimbaud will beware: memory is only a raw material, to be desedimented and future-orientated ('Ta mémoire et tes sens ne seront que la nourriture de ton impulsion créatrice' [your memory and your senses will be no more than the food for your creative impulse] ('Jeunesse IV')). The child needs to quit the house of colourful images and become the gyrating centre of a diasporic radiation, his flailing arms echoing weathervanes and catherine wheels and swirling skirts on the slopes and terraces. We need to enter the fluid, pan-national territories of a 'negritude', which, in never coming to rest, enables syntheses and resists stationary binarisms and dichotomies, differentiations between inside and outside, me and him.

Jean-Pierre Richard finds in Rimbaud an absence of Baudelairean 'profondeur', which relates directly to his treatment of space:

> L'univers surgi ou écroulé qui est le sien n'accepte jamais de se fixer dans les lignes signifiantes d'une perspective, et cela doit nous apparaître normal, puisque c'est justement cette signification que Rimbaud veut changer, cette perspective qu'il se propose d'abolir. Son horreur de l'ancien, son refus du passé et de la patience, son obsession d'une tension verticale et d'une vérité éclatée l'empêchent d'épouser la perspective traditionnelle fondée sur la fuite, l'horizontal, la convergence.
>
> (1955: 239–40)
>
> [The universe which is his, either springing into existence or collapsing, never allows itself to be fixed in the signifying lines of a perspective, and that must seem to us only to be expected, since it is precisely this signification that Rimbaud wishes to change, this perspective which he sets out to abolish. His horror of the old, his refusal of the past and of patience, his obsession with a vertical tension and an exploded truth prevent him from espousing traditional perspective founded on vanishing points, the horizontal, convergence.]

Rimbaud is certainly a poet of movement, but it is a movement engineered by the cut, which the voice may deliver as continuity, but which involves radical jumps in space and adjustments of vision. In the text which is the subject of our first translation, 'Fête d'hiver', the punctuational indication of the elided traversal of space is the dash (beside its other expressive functions). The spaces he passes through in this impatient acceleration of the *temps de l'histoire* are planar, theatrical spaces, the spaces of wafer-thin screens and backdrops, impenetrable surfaces without blind field or extension. Of course, it may be that a coherent overall space-plan can be reconstructed by the reader, but it will be by virtue of the perspectival-isation of the planar, and thus in many ways untrue to a certain psycho-perceptual principle. This is to begin to suggest that Rimbaud's prose poems are kinds of non-atmospheric writing, or at least that atmosphere is a patchwork of local atmospheres.

Boucher is the final note of 'Fête d'hiver' (see Appendix II (viii) for 'straight' translation), and in his account of Boucher's *Marche de Bohémiens* (Salon of 1769), written after Boucher's death in May 1770, Diderot reviews questions of spatial distribution and atmosphere in an imagined dialogue. Boucher is a planar painter, but the planes are not well separated and consequently atmosphere is squeezed out:

> - Et la magie qui donne de la profondeur à la toile, qui avance et recule les objets, qui les distribue sur différents plans, qui met de l'intervalle entre les plans, qui fait circuler l'air entre les figures?
> - D'accord, elle y manque; c'est une boîte mince où la caravane est renfermée, pressée, étouffée.
> - Et la perspective, qui donne à tout sa dégradation réelle?
> - Il n'y en a point.
>
> (1959: 465–6)
>
> [- And what about the magic which gives depth to the canvas, which foregrounds and backgrounds objects, which distributes them in different planes, which introduces intervals between the planes, which makes air circulate between the figures?
> - True, it is missing; the picture is a narrow box in which the procession is confined, squeezed, suffocated.
> - And perspective, which gives everything its real spatial gradation?
> - There isn't any].

Are we then to propose that we too easily overlook the rococo cast of mind that lurks in Rimbaud? This rococo is not just that of the likes of Watteau and Boucher. It is the rococo of the Second Empire's *bals d'hiver* and other winter parkland diversions. David Scott (1979: 191) quotes G. Chapon's itemisation, in *Les Trois Tivoli* (1901), of attractions at a winter ball:

> promenades, fêtes, danses, courses en char, concerts, fantasmagories, tours de force, expériences physiques, ascensions aérostatiques, feux d'artifice, illuminations.
> [promenades, entertainments, chariot races, concerts, phantasmagoria, special feats, physical experiments, aerostatic ascents, fireworks, illuminations].

while Claisse (1990: 37) picks out a passage from the *Paris-Guide* (1867) devoted to winter entertainments—and skating in particular—in the Bois de Boulogne, and suggests possible connections with Rimbaud's poem:

> A peu de frais, en hiver, et grâce au Bois de Boulogne, on a des paysages de la Sibérie; le givre change en arabesques d'argent [girandoles?] le branchage délicat des bouleaux, et la neige couvre d'un voile blanc le sombre feuillage des sapins. [. . .] Les habiles qui ont vu les bords de la Newa et de la Vistule se lance avec la vitesse de l'oiseau. Ils tracent des paraboles [Rondes Sibériennes?], et de la pointe du fer égratignant la surface qui les porte, ils écrivent des initiales sur la glace.[1]
> [At little cost, in winter, and thanks to the Bois de Boulogne, one can enjoy Siberian landscapes; the frost transforms the delicate branchwork of the birches into silver arabesques (girandoles?) and the snow covers the dark foliage of the firs with a white veil. (. . .) The skilful ones, familiar with the banks of the Neva and the Vistula, launch themselves on the ice with the fleetness of birds. They trace parabolas (Rondes Sibériennes?) and, etching the surface that bears them with the tips of their iron blades, they write initials on the ice.]

But we should not overlook the rococo of Impressionism either, as we find it in the early Renoir, both in theme—park skating (*Skaters in the Bois de Boulogne*, 1868), the riverside guinguette (*La Grenouillère*, 1869), the promenade sentimentale (*La Promenade*, 1870)—and in technique—erotic feathering of touch, distractive painted surface, provocative colour highlighting; or in Degas' early racecourse scenes; or in the picnics of Manet (1863) and Monet (1866); or in Manet's *La Musique aux Tuileries* (1862). In works like these, we find the descriptive constantly tipping into the decorative and the expressive, the illustrative being diverted from itself by the invitations of gracefulness or sentiment.

We have discussed the animating voice as a cinematic projector and we can see the ways in which the planar vision is itself projective. Where perspective draws space out towards the spectator from the vanishing point, puts space in place, fixes its coordinates in a rational framework, a proven linear construction, which makes the spectator paramount as a spectator and singularises the horizon, planar space accumulates projected planes as a superimposition of lateralities, multiplies horizons and liberates the spectator into his own fields of vision. While perspectival space is measurable and territorialisable space, planar space is the space of divagation and option, non-destinational (however much governed by a temporal teleology) and non-purposive. Planar space is picaresque space, episodic, dynamic but non-developmental, driven by accelerated time, but without *Bildung*.

In Chapter 4 we looked at the speaking voice as a force which transforms the ekphrastic into the cinematic. I would like to return to Rimbaud's ekphrastic habit and its various transformations. Ekphrasis, in many respects, redramatises those options which confront the translator. A photograph registers what has been put in front of the camera; a photograph of a work of art is a documentary record and not itself a work of art (what, then, are we to make of early architectural photography [Nègre, Baldus, Le Secq, and so forth], for example, or Man Ray's images of sundry Surrealist works, or Brassaï's graffiti series?). But, clearly, I simplify. A photograph of a sculpture can itself be a work of art: the colour-values are limited to black and white, perhaps, light and shade are thus differently defined and graded; the sense of scale is changed; three dimensions (modelling, volume) are compelled to create two-dimensional shapes; point of view becomes non-human; textural qualities are emphasized; etc. Suddenly the sculpture becomes a fiction, dreamt up by the camera, becomes a new possibility, able to enter into new relationships with other (photographed) objects; the sculpture in front of the camera was not itself, but a performance of itself; it has, because of its new-found fictionality, become an object in transition. In similar fashion, ekphrasis and translation can move in either reproductive or 'fictional' directions: either they 'describe' a source picture/text and, in so doing, initiate an interpretative process, an interrogation of the source; or ekphrasis/TT loosens itself from its referent (source) and becomes its own work of art/literature, fictionalising the source into projective possibility. In this latter sense, every ekphrasist/translator is the Philostratus of the *Imagines*, supposedly describing pictures from the collection of a Neapolitan art-lover and yet indulging in what frequently looks like perceptual licence: of Philostratus's description of a painting of a boar-hunt, Michael Conan (1987: 163) writes:

> Philostratus is so carried away by the precision with which the scene is portrayed that he even sees the boar's hairs bristling, its eyes flashing fire and its teeth grinding and gnashing at the hunters; then, in an instant, with no transition, he sees the captivating grace of the young huntsman surrounded by his lovers, as though it and the beast's ferocity were juxtaposed. And yet, as later becomes clear, the hunt has not even started and the boar is still a long way off [. . .].

This begins to sound like a Rimbaldian cultivation of simultaneous multi-vision, remembering, anticipating, discontinuous, abruptly changing.

The options we have outlined are thus each inhabited by a paradox: describe the picture accurately and the indexical, designating force of language will be proportional to its metalinguisticity/metatextuality (one language describes another language); or abandon strict referentiality and you will achieve a textuality of fictions. One other characteristic of the second option, the option of Rimbaud's ekphrasis and of our translation, is to be found in an observation made by Emmanuel Hermange about ekphrasis and photography:

> However, hermeneutic thought traditionally analyses hidden intentions, the artist, and especially his creation, his mark. This obviously poses a problem where photography is concerned, since it is precisely by eliminating the making of this mark in the space of representation that photography creates a fracture in the production and status of pictures. (2000: 6)

This fracture is not perhaps as striking as these words would lead us to suppose: the ekphrastic treatment of a photograph will still be hermen-eutically effective insofar as it will describe what it is we are seeing and thus, even if only implicitly, instal intention by destroying accidentality; ekphrasis always tells us more than is strictly visible. But if the fictionalisation of the art object is what ekphrasis/translation has in mind, then intention is what the source 'text' may be peculiarly without. In his commentaries on Boucher's *pastorales*, Diderot is frequently troubled by their inconsequentiality: 'Là, mon ami, dites-moi ce que fait un chaton sur le giron d'une paysanne qui ne dort pas à la porte de sa chaumière?' (1959: 461) [There, my friend, tell me what a kitten is doing on the lap of a peasant woman who is not drowsing at the door of her cottage?] and 'Fête d'hiver' has nothing to tell us about structural coherence or semantic direction. Of course, critics have not been slow to point out the acoustic patterning that seems to weave this poem together, for example:

/ɔ/: sonne, opéra-comique, girandoles, prolongent
/wa/: voisins, coiffées, Chinoises
/ʃ/: couchant, Chinoises, Boucher
/ʒ/: girandoles, prolongent, vergers, rouges

But looked at from a rococo point of view, these acoustic trails and highlights might be seen as the aural distractions of an ornamentation, a suggestive play of hues across a lustrous surface. Without a plot to sustain its scrutiny, ekphrasis invites fictionality, either as a supplement to the picture, or as a transformation of the picture's ingredients, a making available of those ingredients to alternative uses.

This possibility is brought into sharp focus by the notational final phrases. It is no surprise to find an exclusive emphasis on the feminine: we are told that the rococo is a feminisation of the monumental baroque style, a shift from court to salon (see Brady 1964, 1966); it is particularly apt to find the First Empire represented by a hairstyle. Nor is it surprising to find steps of increasing exoticism. But the absence of articles is troubling, since it as much suggests available ingredients or merely advertised attractions, as it places Horatian nymphs, and Siberian and Chinese women, in a particular landscape. The notational style might signal the transformation of the descriptive into the impressionistic, subjective and proximate; but, equally, it might convey the casual and summary spirit of itemisation. Has Rimbaud perhaps abandoned place to space, abandoned the project of a parkland settlement or the establishment of Cythera? Has the inevitable destiny of rococo acted itself out? Many are agreed that the world of rococo is unconstrained by the effortful or the confined; space is flexible and accommodating, empty, an invitation to movement: 'Rococo space has its own sort of vacancy because the bodies in it are located casually, in nodules, leaving them in a very free situation so that they can move spontaneously' (Sypher 1960: 28). But rococo space is also fictional and illusory, the mobile but fugitive space of the mirror, which turns penetrable depth into self-absorbed surface and the teasing play of shifting perspectives: 'Il s'agit donc d'une unité jamais stabilisée, en devenir' (Laufer 1963: 25) [What we have, then, is a unity never finally stabilised, in a process of becoming]. The *fête champêtre* takes place, but creates no place; the space which supplies an apparent within, which is held together by disguise, turns out to be a space against which events might happen, but nothing could be. There is no schematic continuity, no homology, between the topographical groundplan and the intricacy of its detail. The central meander keeps space changing with its constant reconfigurations, but seems to precipitate out of itself groups which, though suspensions, are plural and self-disseminating and between which there are no links of gradation, causality or interaction.

I have woven into further translations of 'Fête d'hiver' (see Appendix III (a) and (b)), in italics, the translation of another text, the description by Ernest Lacan of a landscape by the photographer Baldus, quoted by Emmanuel Hermange,[2] and commented upon by him in these terms:

> This photograph's decomposition into a rapid succession of perspectives creates movement, as though this expanse were seen from above. It breaks the continuity which we expect from a description of a painting, which renders and in itself reveals a setting, an organization: that which has been chosen by the artist. It is no longer compulsory to indicate the precise position of all the elements in relation to one another within a picture. Diderot would have done just that, starting from one side of the picture, but this process is never mentioned. The contemplation involved in the apprehension of painting appears to be compromised by the swift observation imposed by photography.
>
> (2000: 14)[3]

I have used Lacan's text because it allows the ekphrasis to move in two opposing directions at once, from background to foreground and vice versa, and thus to entrap the reader in a dialectical gyre of reading. As Rimbaud's text drifts from articled plurals to zero-articled ones, from a shadowy park into unsituated space, casual and fictional, the counter-text progresses from metaphorised willows, 'upstream', to found a real city, a place, Avignon, with the emphasis clearly on the singular. The Phrygian Meander has running, in its own stream, the Rhône of 1853; a river which gathers around it disparate times and spaces is doubled by a river which pursues a history under its twelfth-century bridge. And characters fabricated by art (Horace, Boucher) are invited into a landscape recorded by the camera; the iconic joins hands with the indexical, the invoked/ evoked with the pointed to, so that we can more fully inhabit Rimbaldian paradoxes.

The designs of the further translations will perhaps offend by their simplicity, but I wanted at least to register the two ways in which it might be argued that the poem organizes itself: as a set of screens, the distance between which it is difficult to judge, a stereoscopic presentation of a 'flat' text—this is the 'vision' that I favour—or as a set of images built on the Meander's arabesque, this slower exploration of a slower space, whose elements are woven into a continuity which lies ambiguously across two and three dimensions. In this latter reading, the acoustic echoes in the text operate not as decorative clusters, but transphrastically, undoing differentiation and smoothing transitions, in the manner of Nelson Goodman's ungraduated thermometer as described by Mitchell:

> In an ungraduated thermometer [. . .] no unique, determinate reading is possible at any point on the thermometer: everything is relational and approximate, and every point on the ungraduated scale (an infinite number, obviously), counts as a character in the system.
>
> (1986: 67)

This is the view implied by David Scott's analysis, a view which differentiates between Boucher's method and Rimbaud's: where Boucher 'juxtaposes rather than harmonizes' the 'constituent parts', Rimbaud 'produces a far more bold and homogeneous landscape' (1979: 191). But it is a close-run thing. At all events, to heighten the curvilinear, I have retained 'girandole', as Treharne does (1989: 119), because it acts as a 'faisceau', not just of possible water-jets and rockets and flowers and diamonds and patterns of frost and lights (Fowlie opts for 'candelabra' [1966: 237], Sloate for 'chandeliers' [1990: 85]), but also of associations: its gyrations bring forth the undulating chain of dancers of the farandole (think of the 'tarentelles' of 'Promontoire'; think, too, of the Spanish 'farándula', 'an itinerant group of actors'), while its ending not only bespeaks the diminutive, but also carries a note of the plaintive ('dole').

As a final note on these translations, I should explain that I have interspersed the 'Chinoises de Boucher' with characters from IPA in order to introduce the idea of a calligraphy, or hieroglyphics, of a writtenness which itself pushes towards the decorative and in so doing internationalises itself. I am not trying distantly to ape Chinese characters, but rather to make a point about authenticity and inauthenticity. IPA allows me momentarily to conflate English and French, while designating the Chinese: these 'Chinoises' are the illusions of Western observers in the sense both of deceptive appearance, and wilful self-deception in the service of happiness: 'The China of Boucher and his contemporaries was only a repetition of their familiar universe, enriched by the ingredients and adorned with the colours of a brilliant carnival' (Brunel 1986: 167). IPA might be the lingua franca of a society in which national identity is only a form of self-theatricalisation, and linguistic difference a way of engineering piquant misunderstandings and spicing up conversational commonplaces. But, in fact, the rococo cultivates the language of the pan-national, a language without a grammar or a syntax, the language which, paradoxically, spins out of its pure writtenness a pure phoneticism, an inexhaustible source of buccal pleasures and acoustic correspondences.

Any translator faced with the products of an inescapably 'exotic' culture must develop a strategy to cope with questions of perceived authenticity and inauthenticity. I emphasize 'perceived' because the authentic is no less a construct, a potential illusion, than the (knowingly) inauthentic. In the case of Chinese, we may want to distinguish, for moral and polemical reasons, between 'Chineseness'—a set of cultural givens which are supposed to be innate in the indigenous and to express themselves spontaneously, involuntarily, bearing testimony to notions such as cultural continuity, national identity, and so forth—and 'Chinoiserie', a representation of 'Chineseness' which locates 'Chineseness' (a) in a smaller number of generalised indices and (b) in terms which 'suit' and reinforce Western notions of Westernness; 'Chinoiserie' turns 'Chineseness' into a picturesque or decorative value, promises a certain predictability. But this differentiation is much harder to sustain than one might at first imagine: 'Chineseness' implies a cultural unity and stability which simply does not exist: authenticity is as much subject to the corrosive variations of perspectivism as any other term, and by no stretch of the imagination can China be reduced to a convenient cultural homogeneity.[4] Equally and conversely, 'Chinoiserie' is by no means the purely reductive and unproductive attitude that the word might suggest. We may think that 'Chinoiserie' is at the very least guilty of cultural stereotyping. But is it not possible that the defender of 'Chineseness' is guilty of exactly the same fault? Besides, if we gather together some of the characteristics of 'Chinoiserie' (such as landscape features (cherry trees, mountains, mists, fishermen), traits of character (stoicism, melancholia, capacity for the abject), a range of narratives (Emperors and concubines, picaresque adventures of peasant boys, ruthless bandits), linguistic idiosyncrasies (the picture language of ideograms, absence of syntactic articulation and markers of conjugation, declension, gender, number, i.e. a language which appeals directly to the 'natural' assumptions and intuitions of the reader)), we see that these are responses to deep-felt nostalgias, aspirations, dreams, patterns of self-reassurance. And beneath what is Chinese in 'Chinoiserie' lies the IPA of refused cultural obligation and national differentiation.

And of course, Boucher is as much subject to 'Chinoiserie' as the Chinese: can he manage to be Boucher, as much collector as artist, as much porcelainist as Academician? As soon as the first spectators looked at the first of his pictures, he was 'Boucher', the purveyor of 'light' licentiousness, participated in by young persons with wide-set eyes and unbroken curves between nose-tip and hairline, full-cheeked and half-smiling. Besides, Boucher's own 'Chinoiserie' was by no means first hand: based on 'Chinese' tapestries from Beauvais (1725–30), perhaps, or on Watteau, Boucher's prints and paintings are, for the most part, repertoire work, and fittingly he provided decors for the fairs at Saint-Germain and Saint-Laurent (*Les Fêtes chinoises*, 1754) and for the Opéra Comique (1743–55) (Brunel 1986: 166, 187).

The burden of our argument has been that translation is both an ekphrasis without a source (Philostratus), and itself a lingua franca within which the nationality of national languages might be flavour rather than culture, the symptom of desire, dream, anxiety, rather than a voice making claims about inalienable identity. There might seem to be something anachronistic and retrograde in suggesting, one moment, that translation is post-modern by persuasion, and the next that it is rococo. But, quite apart from the plausibility of an equation between the postmodern and the rococo, there is a clear sense in which the second-degree status of translation chimes with the second-degree experiences of the rococo world. Translation is a masquerade, an entertainment, a 'Chinoiserie', but these seemingly inauthentic features allow it to lift the bane of the authenticity question. The real noeme of photography is not, as François Soulages points out (1998: 18, 53–70), the Barthesian 'Ça a été' [That has been], but rather 'Ça a été joué'[That has been performed]; translation, no less than photography, is a 'mise en scène' of the ST, which allows us not to grasp the ST's reality but to accede to a counter-reality, which throws the ST's reality into question. The melancholy of rococo lies in its lack of belief, in its constant interrogation of the appearances it lives by. Translation, too, is an interrogative art which changes a concern with authenticity into an opening on to the imaginary, a desire to solve problems into a desire fruitfully to perpetuate them.

All translation is to a greater or lesser extent ethnocentric ('qui ramène tout à sa propre culture, à ses normes et valeurs, et considère ce qui est situé en dehors de celle-ci—l'étranger —comme négatif ou tout juste bon à être annexé, adapté, pour accroître la richesse de cette culture' (Berman 1999: 29) [which reduces everything to its own culture, to its own norms and values, and considers what is situated outside its culture—the other, the foreign—as negative or only just worth absorbing, adapting, to increase the richness of the home culture]), not simply because one language 'subjugates' another, but because in any relation of the textual to the metatextual, the textual is assimilated into, digested, tamed and disarmed by, the increased intelligibility of the metatext. The colonist begins by interpreting a people to itself. Translation best serves the post-colonial age by insisting on maintaining, or indeed increasing, what is unintelligible in the ST. The TT must act out the native of the ST in such a way as not to document it (the mirage of 'Chineseness'), but to render its imaginable, its imaginary ('Chinoiserie'). Conversely, the translator must beware of his own linguistic monuments (dictionary, thesaurus), those things which seek to govern his behaviour and remind him of the linguistic obligations put upon him by a consensualised linguistic identity and the sheer weight of linguistic organisation. As Meschonnic puts it:

> La traduction peut alors être montrée pour ce qu'elle est: une pratique du langage qui renforce la logique de l'identité, où elle se situe entièrement. La logique même du rejet indéfiniment reporté de l'altérité. La logique du racisme, du colonialisme. De l'orientalisme. Logique de la définition des dictionnaires.
>
> (1999: 165)
>
> [Translation can then be shown for what it is: a practice of the language which reinforces identity, in which it is entirely located. The very logic of the indefinitely unacknowledged rejection of otherness. The logic of racism, of colonialism. Of orientalism. The logic of dictionary definitions].

As we tackle Rimbaud's 'Démocratie' (see Appendix II (ix) for 'straight' translation), we must be careful to inspect our own eyes for motes.

It is not clear that 'Démocratie' is about French expansionism; on the contrary, it seems to have self-colonisation as much in view as any overseas expeditions. Steve Murphy (1988: 22) suggests that the massacre of the 'révoltes logiques' refers to the suppression of the Commune by the Versaillais army and that the 'pays poivrés et détrempés' 'rappellent les bagnes où la France envoyait ses prisonniers politiques' [recall the penal colonies to which France sent its political prisoners] (Cayenne). The actions of Versailles are here represented as prostitution; 'poivrés' would then also relate to venereal infection. These connections are taken up and elaborated upon by Evelyne Hervy (1999). Among other things, in relation to the 'conscrits de bon vouloir', Hervy observes: 'A "conscrit" was anything but the product of his own "bon vouloir" but was "désigné d'office". In my view, the poem refers in fact to the people personally responsible for conscription: Thiers "le premier conscrit"and his "parti de l'ordre"'(957). The flag, bought back by Thiers after defeat at the hands of the Prussians, suits a country rendered 'immonde' by the blood of both the war and the ensuing Commune (957).

Hervy also warns us: 'The word "démocratie" in the political context of France at that time is increasingly meaningless and is found in the mouths of those from the entire political spectrum' (1999: 956). Let loose on themselves, 'démocratie's' two etymological elements—demos (people) and kratia (< kratos, power)—suggest many forms of possible relationship and consequence. There is also a phonetic sense in which the title makes one ponder; likewise, it seems to enact a collision rather than an alliance, or, if it is an alliance, then one of shared depredation and vandalism. The central element, at all events, is '-cratie' (/kRasi/), and its phonemes seem to me to predict the acoustic protagonists of the poem. What first becomes apparent is the duplicity of the grapheme t, masquerading as the phoneme /s/. /si/ begins to tell us where we shall be: 'ici' (/isi/), but in this word, too, is another example of graphemic/phonemic sleight-of-hand: c (/k/) becomes c (/s/, again). The 'here' that the soldier speaks of ('pa<u>y</u>s'; 'pa<u>y</u>sage') is marked by its /i/: 'immonde'. But we quickly realise that what we may have identified as a phonemic collision between cultures, /a/ = coloniser, /i/ = colonised, apparently set against each other in the opening clause:

Le drapeau va au paysage immonde

is not one. Not only has the /i/ of the colony's 'immondices' been injected by colonial contamination—'alimenterons', 'cynique', 'prostitution', and so forth—but /a/ and /i/ frequently occur cheek by jowl, either phonetically ('paysage', 'alimenterons') , graphically ('militaires', 'crevaison', 'vraie') or grapho-phonetically: the recurrent /wa/ is constructed by 'oi' ('patois', 'poivrés', 'exploitations', 'revoir'). In the end, it seems, the colonised, as much as the colonisers, belong to 'le monde qui va'—'le drapeau <u>va</u> au paysage im<u>monde</u>'—and deserve to be treated just as cavalierly.

The duplicitous t declares its hand in the second 'decasyllable' of the opening:

Le drapeau va// au paysage/ immonde [et] notre patois// étou/ffe le tambour
     4// 4 + 2   [et]   4// 2 + 4

This chiastically arranged pair of decasyllables, pivoting around 'et', closes down a vocality: a t ('patois') drowns out a t ('tambour'). Confined to the second clause of this first verset, the suppression of t by t is next played out across the two clauses of the second verset; and here the suppression is endorsed by force of numbers:

alimenterons [. . .] prostitution v. révoltes

Here we note that the fourth t of the first clause reaffirms its 'ambush' by /s/, and note, too, what we have already implicitly demonstrated: that 'alimenterons' is the equivalent of 'massacrerons'. The third verset goes through exactly the same motion, but this time in reverse: the t in 'détrempés' is subjugated by, and put to the service of, 'monstrueuses exploitations industrielles et militaires', and, once again, in 'exploitations', the second t slips behind its /s/. But the life of t, in the final extended verset, becomes more problematic: we hear it twice as /t/, in words that have lost a suppressive purpose—'n'importe', 'route'—and between this liminary and this terminal appearance, it appears as a silent grapheme ('conscrits', 'ignorants', 'confort', 'c'est', 'avant'). Has our *troufion* sacrificed settlement to a nomadic existence? Has this t frittered itself away in pointless activity?

But while t seems to construct for itself a meaningful, if self-atrophying, development, a configuration which embodies a certain drama of attitude, the c of '-cratie' seems to equivocate much more between its /k/ and /s/ roles, slipping from one to the other in almost alternating fashion (not forgetting the /k/ of the '-ique' adjectival ending). What we should nonetheless pick out are those reminders of /kR/—'massacrerons', 'conscrits', 'crevaison'—and those words—'conscrits', 'confort' even, distantly, 'massacrerons' and 'crevaison'—which encourage us to think 'Faire le con, c'est trop con'.

The last player in my acoustic game does not appear in '-cratie', but is an important element in the second 'hemistich' of the second 'decasyllable' of the opening:

notre patois// étouffe le tambour

It looks, from this evidence, as if /u/ is another element which locks coloniser and colonised in a murderous embrace; and, indeed, /u/ operates rather like t in that it seems to be an element both of oppression ('étouffe', 'nous', 'vouloir', 'roués', 'pour' even) and of resistance, however feeble ('tambour'). And yet it acoustically allies itself with t in those two instances, at the beginning and end of the final verset—'n'importe où' and 'route'—where aggressive identity asserts itself only in its exasperated indifference, or its impatient appetite for further prey.

If I conduct this enquiry at the level of the phonemic/graphemic, it is to establish the exchangeability and transferability by which the text seems haunted. Have I chosen the right phonemes and graphemes as the poem's 'protagonists'? Have I not discovered that any apparent oppositions initiated at the text's outset turn into moments of collusion or at least non-differentiability, and indeed of loss, or shift, of motivation. These movements are embodied in the slippage between grapheme and phoneme, and in particular t > /t/ and /s/ and zero; c > /k/ and /s/. In these circumstances, the colonised becomes an increasingly misty target, as good as disappears, and correspondingly the colonist apparently loses interest in any territorial project. The suppressive power of the colonist as presented here is not shape-giving, but mechanical and anarchic. The 'dialogue' between the colonist and the colonised is no such thing, not so much because the colonised has no voice, but because the colonists are not colonisers, and the colonised, in turn, are not a subject people, because, precisely, there is no sense of territory, because there is space but no place. Without a geography and without the sense of place, there is no topography that will stick, and vice versa. The collision of physical forces at the poem's outset—'drapeau' v. 'paysage', 'patois' v. 'tambour'—is, in the following two versets, dissipated in the drift to pluralisation and to the abstract genericisation of activity ('prostitution', 'exploitations'), and the blurring of boundaries between linguistic categories (literal and figurative, concrete and abstract). At the same time, the combination of strong verbal activity and future-directed self-confidence and prediction, first sounded in 'alimenterons' and 'massacrerons', clings on only in attenuated form thereafter, as the text becomes increasingly telegraphic: the 'au(x)' preposition maintains the sense of futurity in its 'whitherness', while 'aurons' and 'c'est' manage to keep some sort of verbal presence alive. But, overwhelmingly, one hears a voice losing its grip on transitivity—one might expect that of a colonist—and on perlocutionary effectiveness. The language of threat and warning drifts almost imperceptibly to that of declaration and exhortation. We attend those processes whereby the colonised become colonisers, after the example of the coloniser, whereby the coloniser becomes the colonised (in that colonisation itself is a revolt against one's condition by virtue of exasperation both with 'civilisation' [suppression of the primitive] and with the unfulfilled nature, the intransitivity, of one's self as a colonist). These ambiguities are already fully expressed in the ambiguity of the opening 'va', which, in my version, I have felt obliged to translate twice so that the convergence of the two paths can be more clearly seen.

Rimbaud seems to have been preoccupied in this poem with the psychologism of colonisation, à la Mannoni (1964), and it is for this reason that he has attributed the text to a speaker, not so much in a gesture of dissociation—'This is not democracy. But Rimbaud, being the nègre, cannot say "democracy is this"; instead he says what it is not, in words not his own' (Miller 1985: 158)—but in order, quite literally, to imprison the speaker in an utterance which, by the end, he is only too glad to evacuate himself from. It would be easy, in the light of what we have said above, about the loss of verbality and predictiveness, to propose that the poem is about involuntary self-suffocation, a mentality caught in the paradoxes and double-binds of 'conscrits du bon vouloir' and the phrases that follow. Colonialism is a playing out of fantasies, of extremes of behaviour, which the colonist can only just envisage (hence the evasive generalities, brutal though they are, of the second verset) and which ultimately he must abjure. These extremities can be travelled to, and confined within geographical boundaries. But either the extremities will threaten their own chaos, their own intolerable darkness, which necessitates some moving away, or the country will have no shaping geography in the first place, so that the colonist is already disorientated in his own desires. In this reading, there is little question of one culture imposing itself on another, since the other culture is already the image of the colonising culture's desire: the act of suppression must become the act of release. What we encounter in 'Démocratie' is a language grapho-phonetically acting out this procedure. And the more the colonists want the colonised to be like themselves, the more they both want to be brought back from the heart of darkness by the very inhabitants of that darkness, and to be understood by those whose otherness has been the source of appetite.

I have principally been speaking of 'the colonist' in the singular, but in the translation that follows, I have placed another voice within the presiding one. This is partly designed to give some shape to the unevenness of register within the poem. But it also makes audible the many voices that are implicit in any voice, and highlights that sense of the continual theft of one's opinions and feelings by what has already been said, by the predictabilities of ideology and indoctrination, by the trickle-down of orders and briefings (I imagine the 'inner' voice as that of an officer). Does the speaker fully master this borrowed language? Well, not quite perhaps, but he is improving.

As already mentioned, the layout of my translation is designed to mimic a process of convergence, so that, finally, the two sides in this colonial conflict cannot be put apart. And it is important to underline that this convergence is consummated and obliterated in the prose of the final two paragraphs. Prose is as much the medium of borderlessness as it is of arbitrarily dislocative borders (see argument below). It is the unclaimed territory of populated and populatable space which has phantasmally within it any number of maps and territorial allegiances which may from time to time emerge in different configurations, but all of which exist on sufferance, as temporary, highly subjective partitions, making sense only to the individual 'reader'.

Interpretation attempts to consensualise these claims, to make the case for colonisation. But prose is a fluid and elusive medium, and its mobility and proteiformity better serve the traveller than they do the colonist. It is not too far-fetched to propose that this conversion of colonist into traveller is part of the Rimbaldian reading project. The colonist, like the interpretative reader, turns the colonised country into another country:

> L'interprétation d'un texte ne peut être jamais que la tentative de proposer un autre texte, équivalent mais plus satisfaisant pour telle ou telle raison.
>
> (Mannoni 1962: 1347–8)
>
> [The interpretation of a text can only ever be the attempt to propose another text, equivalent, but, for some reason or other, more satisfying.]

Interpretation expresses our fear of the text, the anxieties of incomprehension, of not being able to subdue the text. But if we accept Rimbaud's answer to his mother's question about the meaning of *Une saison en enfer*, that it should be understood 'littéralement et dans tous les sens' [literally and in all senses], we begin to see that the Rimbaldian text is a terrain of multiple traversals, which, whatever else it is, is always itself, a nexus of all directions, meanings, senses by virtue of being prosaic and non-territorialised. For the translator, the lesson is clear: to travel through an ST, without stopping to establish boundaries and weigh the income of territories, but instead to envisage territories and boundaries as floating and possible configurations of the text's space and to imagine what the text's territorial future might be. By putting reading into a colonial context, one comes to see how important the cultivation of an ethos of reading is.

If I have paid particular attention to the phonetic and graphemic patterns in the ST, it is because I believe that the English version can engineer similar equivocations. In the TT, the phonemic/graphemic duplicity lies more exclusively in the c's of 'Democracy', as both /k/ and /s/—the /k/ is ubiquitous, the /s/ to be heard in 'cynicism', 'spice', 'science', 'crapulence'. There is also the odd occasion where c attracts h and thus /t/, in /t ʃ/: 'champions'. The expression of a contempt, and self-contempt, through the /kr/ of 'Democracy', is to be heard in 'crapshit', 'conscript', 'crapulence'. I have also maintained a focus of t, even though it is no longer an element in the title. The opening of the translation provides an opportunity to insist on it, and, as it progresses through the text, so, as in the ST and even though it does not become silent, it begins to fritter itself away, becomes the servant not of suppression but of evacuation. This feeling of the dispersal of t's energy is helped by its periodic slippage sideways into /θ/ and /ð/, and indeed /ʃ/ ('prostitution'). Equally, the /I/ which belongs to the colonised ('crapshit', 'filthy'), though not set against /æ/, soon begins to consort with /s/: 'prostitution', 'cynicism', 'dissent', 'industrial', 'riddance', 'conscripts', 'philosophy', 'ignorance', 'it's'.

Democracy

"The tatty flag suits
this crapshit (tological discussions of language)
country to its t's

The flag moves to and through
(taneity the meaning of the sign)
this filthy landscape

and our patois

puts the mockers (timony of linguistic facts)
on the drum

'In the populous areas
          we will promote prostitution
          (ing across the interindividual social space)
          with cynicism a top priority
          and we (eriority of the sign)
          will ruthlessly
          zero-tolerate any
          consequent expressions (ative processes of speech)
          of dissent (terial entity as signifier)

To the pepper-laden moisture-sodden countries (isation of the utterance)!—product champions of military and industrial enterprises, so outrageous and exploitative they'll beggar belief (ises a superstructural imprint)'.

Good riddance to here, there's where we'll go. Volunteer conscripts, ours will be a brutish philosophy: ignorance our science; crapulence our comfort; and down the pan with the rest of humanity. Now that's what I call progress. Come on, stir your stumps—it's time to hit the road (sure's, is once again the discourse)!"

Behind and in front of every villain stands another villain, as the slave struggles to be master, as the master unwittingly becomes the slave. As readers, we may look upon Rimbaud's version of democracy with detached knowingness, with some complacency, sure that our attitudes are the right ones. But we also are subject to any number of surreptitious colonisations. Our drums are suppressed by the jargons, the patois, of the institutions we are members of, where the notion of 'institution' covers all systems of belief, and all 'sciences' of behaviour. Perversely, we, too, continually submit to forms of self-colonisation. Consequently, I also wanted to make Rimbaud's text part of a 'poème-conversation', or dialogue of voices, which could not hear each other. I chose as my inserts fragments of a critical discourse, Norman Bryson's discussion (1983: 135–40) of the Russian linguist N.Y. Marr's positioning of the linguistic sign in the superstructure of Historical Materialism's base/superstructure division, as something posterior to, and generated by, the material formation. But just as Marr's base 'smothers' superstructure by making it redundant, so, in similar fashion, Saussure's *langue* has committed *parole* to a semblance of freedom which is only superfluity; and Chomskyian 'competence', with all the sacred obligations of the innate, has discredited 'performance' and clipped its self-expressive wings. I have chosen 'headless' phrases at the beginnings of lines from pages 136–9 of Bryson's work, partly to suggest the stubborn ostinato of certain critical positions, which the eventful drives of the poetic text can interrupt, but neither persuade nor bring to a halt. This headlessness is also partly designed to dramatise the drawing of borders, to represent the task of colonial government as a bisection of linguistic entities. The distribution of territories does not correspond to the distribution of languages, and it is prose, in particular, which may seem to condone this cadastrian habit; for if poetry tends to pursue a policy of peaceful settlement within the territory of the page, disposing itself in such a way that it makes best use of the page's resources, while seeming to respect the diversity of the topography and the sanctity of borders, prose ever imposes its own rigid, pre-parcelled land-blocs which often sever one morpheme from its partner at the turn of the line and turn the well-meaning into nonsense. Nonsense? Not quite perhaps. Because these headless suffixes remind us of the colonisation involved in word-derivation: the root is taken over, converted to another order, by the addition of a transformative agent (morpheme); this rupturing of connection by the imposition of borders paradoxically lays bare, reveals to scrutiny, just those instruments of linguistic coercion and relocation; at the same time it is as if the root/radical escapes into some free zone where it might recover its primitive 'purity' and at least live out its time as a fugitive. But this is a mirage. Even though we cannot see it, the root is held within the borders of the page, right up against the border, its attempt to escape deflected back into the compound by a hyphen. Reading is a fanciful occupation; writing, too. Perhaps it is only fair that the final victim of these boundary-drawing dislocations is Saussure himself: 'The category expunged from linguistics as surely in Marr's account as in Saus-/sure's, is once again the *discourse*, as the evolutionary topology of the language, its structure of recurrent affiliations from signifier to signifier' (Bryson 1983: 137).

We must relate thoughts of this kind to the very nature of the prose poem, because it would seem that the prose poem is itself a deeply self-contradictory phenomenon: as a medium, prose indeed yields to the page, to the limitations and constrictions of the page's space, but is itself a purveyor of borderlessness, of collocational, intonational, respiratory fluidity; once perceived as a form, however, it begins to borrow, or seems to begin to borrow, some of the page's inflexibility in the mapping of language into space. If, in short, the prose poem is seen as the incipient transformation of the temporality of prose into spatiality, then the prose poem is the site of the freeing of poetry from the colonial and the leading of prose towards it. Writers such as Terdiman (1985), Monroe (1987) and Murphy (1992) have expressed the self-contradictoriness of the politicised prose poem in other ways: its potential subversiveness is subverted either by the inevitably self-marginalising, and possibly self-aestheticising, idiosyncrasy of its discourse; or it willy nilly finds itself arming itself against the enemy with the enemy's own weapons: 'As hybrid genre, the prose poem registers its multiple Others, the systems against which it seeks to found its difference. But because it is constituted as a denial of their force, it cannot repesent its own *generation* out of them' (Terdiman 1985: 279). It is this situation of expressive double-bind in the prose poem that I wish to go on further to explore in my translation, or rather translational presentation, of 'Royauté'.

For the prose poem, then, the ambivalence of the page is intimately bound up with its own ambivalence: either the page seems to act like a ruthless obstacle to prose's ambitious promotion of the borderless, imposing its own non-negotiable cartographic divisions and separations; or, as we have been trying to demonstrate, translation might negotiate between the prose poem and its page so that they collaborate in new ways to their mutual benefit—the page is no longer a grid laid over a parcel of graphic material which threatened to travel through a space without fixed places, but rather a receptive space looking to define its multiplicity in relation to a text which, in turn, is looking for the space to actualise its own possibilities; if dancers sculpt space, then they do so as the instruments of a spatial choreography. In my first reading of 'Royauté', however, the offers that the page-space makes are withdrawn by the writer himself:

Royalty

One fine morning, among a peace-loving people, a man and a
    woman, poised, self-assured, beautiful, loudly
    proclaimed in the public square:

                              'Friends, I want

    her to be queen!'

              'I *want* to be queen!'

She laughed
and trembled

He told his friends of a revelation,
of an ordeal finally at an end

                          Every now
and then

                they fell weakly
                against each other

And, indeed, they *were* king and queen
for a whole morning, when
                the carmine-coloured drapes were
    hoisted on the house fronts, and throughout the
    afternoon, too,
    when
    their progress
    took them towards

                        the

gardens
                        of

palms.

If the page, in one of its manifestations, is a social space, a stage on
which social relations are reconfigured by the new dispositions of a

discourse itself reconfigured, then the translator is the architect of a new forum, or plaza, or *place publique*. This last phrase immediately takes us to the central event of 'Royauté':

> [. . .] un homme et une femme superbes criaient sur la place publique. 'Mes amis, je veux qu'elle soit reine!' 'Je veux être reine!'

That this optativity is directed at dreams of monarchy might come as a disappointing surprise. But this is not so much a society looking for chosenness as for the freedom to diversify social roles without lasting obligations. The page is a public square on which anyone may write, make his/her declarations. But the inverted commas put possession of the page in the hands of the author/narrator. The 'En effet' is not so much what the couple claimed by right, as the concession that was made to them. And it is a peculiar mixture of cruelty and magnanimity which motivates the chilling transformation of the first paragraph's elastic, expanded or iterative time (imperfect) into the impassive intransigence of the second paragraph's miserly time (past historic), while, concomitantly (and hypocritically?), there is the suggestion of a relaxation and extension of time, both in the unhurried syntax and in the adverbials ('toute une matinée' and 'toute l'après-midi'). Narratorial 'royalty' far exceeds any royalty that subjects might wish to arrogate to themselves; one begins to suspect that 'doux' is the conciliatory way of expressing pliability and compliance. My reason for adding 'too' in the final paragraph lies in what it expresses of a favour unwillingly granted; and the separation of the elements of the final phrase is designed to enact the dissolution of space and the impossibility of reaching a place in order to establish it.

The 'place publique' does not survive. The *space* in which to become king and queen, with a people, imperceptibly becomes the *time* to be king and queen, where space is only grudgingly surrendered by time, in a pair of relative clauses ('où les tentures carminées se relevèrent sur les maisons' and 'où ils s'avancèrent du côté des jardins de palmes'). In the end, there is no time in which to achieve spatial objectives. The prose poem might tease us with spatiality, but prose can always reclaim its temporality: the cruelty of the second paragraph lies in its relaxing the grip of time syntactically, while, syntactically, forcing space to the margins, to planarity and direction.

The planarisation of space is encapsulated in 'sur les maisons'. Here again are Rimbaud's façades, the places of an ostensible visibility (balconies, windows, doors) and expressiveness, places of public declaration, themselves points of visual vantage, but whose two dimensions elide an inwardness that foments conspiracy, secret or obscene acts, panoptical control, scriptural paranoia. The theatre certainly creates a stage for the free exploration of fictions; but the space of the action on stage is a planar space, while the three dimensions of the theatre itself belong to the invisible director. In this scenario, the translators are among the actors on stage, themselves acting out a speculative drama, hoping to achieve a royalty from ordeals undergone and 'trouvailles' chanced upon. But it is not just that, as director, Rimbaud might say: 'Je réservais la traduction'. It is his ability to occupy both spaces, both roles, the stage and the auditorium, child and witch. For, after all, the Queen-Sorceress ('Après le Déluge'), who will not tell us what she knows and we do not, is also young Arthur.

It may seem perverse to turn this enchanting fairy tale/fable into the triumph of the jealous stepmother, but the power politics of the prose poem makes it inevitable. How does one work in a form that has neither formal nor generical authority? How does one work in a form that is in the midst of market competition (with the journal, the newspaper article, the *promenade*, caricature writing, the *physiologie*, the *chose vue*, and so forth) (see Monte 2000: 39–63)? In my second version of this poem (see Appendix III (c)), I have kept my original translation intact, but changed the space it occupies, its environment. Now, as a newspaper article, it can more effectively be seen to act out the politics of its position, while the position of the translator radically changes: for, while the translator shares with the source-writer some of the attributes of the correspondent, he has also assumed the task of editor.

There are many senses in which this prose poem deserves to be a *fait divers*. It is highly resistant to interpretation. Those suggestions that have been made about the royal couple—Rimbaud and Verlaine, Rimbaud and his imagination ('la reine des facultés' [the queen of the faculties]), Rimbaud and his genius, Rimbaud and the queen, 'la Sorcière', of 'Après le Déluge'—lack conviction. The 'jardins de palmes' may be a misheard 'Jardin des Plantes', or may refer to Christ's entry into Jerusalem; we may hear a Nervalian intertext, as Py has done (1967: 113): 'nous étions l'époux et l'épouse pour tout un beau matin d'été' [we were husband and wife for all of a beautiful summer morning] (*Sylvie*, VI); but these are only straws to be snatched at. By its very brevity and textual positioning, the *fait divers* declares itself to be a small eruption in the seamless continuity of ongoing international news, an eccentricity in the intricate weave of quotidian eventfulness, something local, marginal, small-scale, unable to displace the general run of the news, but with its own shock value.[5] What possessed this pair to make this foolhardy claim to kingship? Despite their being 'superbes', their nervous fatigue bespeaks some prolonged 'psyching up', some feverish prelude. Public reaction is difficult to gauge: beside the drapes on the façades and the circle of friends, there is little evidence of public interest. And the impersonality of the characters ('a couple' rather than named individuals) makes this geographically very distant, an event in an elsewhere with little ability (right?) to establish itself in the consciousness of the readership.

I do not want to consider in any detail, the layers of contextual pressure that would be exerted on 'Royauté', were it to appear in a newspaper: whether it were a tabloid or a broadsheet, what its politics were, what kind of readership and reading it presupposed, what conventions of presentation and layout the paper used, what the adjacent news items might be, what the larger stories in other parts of the paper, and so on. Here, it appears in the *Sun* of Monday 23 July 2001, p. 23, alongside a story about a girl injured in a hit-and-run incident while showing off her bridesmaid's dress and tiara, and below two stories about police officers involved in car crashes. The bridesmaid story is accompanied by a medley of photographs: the girl on her hospital bed, a cameo-shaped photograph of her as a bridesmaid, a square mugshot of the jailed driver, a picture of the father with two of his children and a reminder photograph of the page in the *Sun* when the incident was first reported. These are pieces of a visual jigsaw which the accompanying article seems to encourage us to put together. But in fact we cannot do so, because the photographs are temporally unaligned and because their affective values are so discrepant. Indeed, it is more likely that photographs and article are designed to pull against each other, that the reader is not intended to be *pacified* by the story and its outcome (the girl fully recovered, the hit-and-run driver jailed), but rather to respond as if the story were a provocation and an irritant, an event which deserves to be played over and over again in different blends of bile, sympathy, curiosity. Looked at against this accompaniment, Rimbaud's story of an event among a peace-loving people, where individuals are allowed to enjoy their moment of sartorial splendour and popular admiration without incurring the wrath of a jealous destiny, seems as innocuous as it is pointed. Ironically, without photographic support, Rimbaud's narrative becomes too purely narrative: in a tabloid newspaper, every story without a photograph becomes a shaggy dog story, sustained only by its brazen gratuitousness and the insolence of a punch-line without any punch.

The work of art looks extremely vulnerable in the highly competitive arena of the newspaper page. Where is Rimbaud's indexicality now? Self-reflexivity really does look like the suicide of relevance, and the poem's language undergoes a process of journalisation, becomes meretricious: the words 'revelation' and 'ordeal', in particular, are indistinguishable from their newspaper equivalents—standard melodramatizations of any discovery or discomfort, and quite without any spiritual implications.

But what if the *fait divers* did not quite play its appointed game? What if the *fait divers* became a prose poem, or the prose poem infiltrated the columns of a newspaper? At what points, surreptitiously, does the prose poem exceed the brief of a *fait divers*? In its cavalier refusal to identify time ('One fine morning') or place ('a peace-loving people'); in its unwarranted value-judgements and responsiveness ('poised, self-assured, beautiful'); in its narratorial proximity ('She laughed and trembled' v. 'She was visibly nervous'); in its general lyrical inhabitation of the experience. I imagine that, as a press report, it might have run something like: 'In the main square of X, on Tuesday morning, a couple proclaimed themselves king and queen. The decision was apparently made after much soul-searching; they were visibly disturbed. They spent the day as a 'royal' pair, and processed in the area near the palm-gardens. There was some decking of house fronts, and the support of close friends; but public reaction generally was confined to inquisitive bystanders.' As a prose poem, 'Royauté' exceeds the news, as its signifiers exceed any particular signified. Armed with an indexicality without a referentiality, a literality that can be understood 'dans tous les sens', the prose poem's release of the connotative or the symbolic is guaranteed by its linguistic materiality and the consequence— that its textuality is unsupersedable. If I ask what a news item means, I am asking questions about motivation, intention, implication; if I ask what a prose poem means, none of these considerations is appropriate because of its achievement of textual autonomy. But I might also claim that to ask what it means is not important; that the event it conveys is its own multisensory reading, not what might be deciphered from it. In this sense it *is* a shaggy dog story, and one that can be told again and again in almost any environment.

I should add that on that same day, 23 July 2001, I inserted 'Royauté', with appropriate changes of shape and format, into the *Daily Mail* (see Appendix III (d)), below an article in which Ken Clarke was being warned to tone down his pro-euro stance if he wanted to be in the running for the Tory leadership; and alongside an article announcing the imminent death of George Harrison. The drama of the news is peculiarly dependent on the transfixative power and pressures of time: as if Ken Clarke and George Harrison were imprisoned within the chain of events embodied by, indeed generated by, the unrelenting dailiness of the newspapers and their insistence that there is something new to report, that the news is pushed on at a regular pace. And the very layout of the newspaper page only serves to confirm this predicament: hemmed in by framed columns, underlined headings and screaming headlines, put on the spot and required to respond by the pointing finger of photographs, the person in the news must gallop to an outcome. If deixis establishes presence in the newspaper world, it also charges the subject with the responsibility of assuming a proactive role in the entertainment of the reader. But the prose-poem news item ('Royauté') can be placed in any outlet at any time, and each time it will discharge its significance differently. It flouts the news because it is not transfixed by time; it can make news because it hands itself back to temporality each time it is read. 'Royauté' is not in the gaol of time, but just visiting.

The implication for the translator is, again, clear: if the translator's task is to re-energise the ST, then an integral part of that re-energisation might be the discovery of the appropriate context for publication. Where should Rimbaldian texts be? The notion of re-contextualisation is not merely a broad cultural question about degrees of foreignisation and domestication, but poses specific questions about the vehicle and medium of delivery. If a text is to 'make progress' then it needs to be more than formally updated; it needs also to be updated in its operative effectiveness. I am not suggesting that the process of translation is an obligation to provide the ST with the force of propaganda or exemplarity; I merely mean that an essential part of re-thinking texts is the re-thinking and performance of their socio-political implications. This can only be safely undertaken if the reading of translations becomes a much more active and sophisticated process than at present it is reckoned to be. Indeed, it begins to assume that the reading of translations is an opportunity to interrogate the ends which texts can be asked to serve.

In an age of mechanical reproduction, all images and texts have a high degree of transferability—and indeed Walter Benjamin's words are very relevant to the objectives of translation: translation seeks to replace the cult value of the ST with an exhibition value which the TT promotes:

> In the same way today, by the absolute emphasis on its exhibition value the work of art becomes a creation with entirely new functions, among which the one we are conscious of, the artistic function, later may be recognised as incidental. (1968: 225)

Inasmuch as translation is a literary equivalent of mechanical reproduction, translation removes the ST from its originating context in order to be able to (a) make questions of authenticity and inauthenticity irrelevant (i.e. just as one supposes that the photographic representation of an object is not made inauthentic by its being taken from a 'radical' angle—bird's eye view, worm's eye view, dramatic close-up—or with filters, etc., so a TT is not inauthenticated by its adopting similarly 'distorting' techniques: quite simply, the ST is susceptible of being perceived in these ways; there is no way of representing an object which is more authentic than any other way); (b) insert the ST, at any particular time, in a potentially infinite variety of new contexts, precisely because of the adaptability of its 'form'.

One might be of the view that, in order to be a real agent of social transformation, the prose poem would have to be confident about its genericity, since it is as an alternative genre that it can interrogate the established orders of poetry and prose; agenericity is all very well, but it is always vulnerable to generical re-assimilation of various kinds. But there might be a view which insists that performance must always outleap and consume competence; or, put another way, that the prose poem is a *langue* which, *by its very nature*, generates the potentiality of a disruptive and revolutionary *parole*. As we have already argued in the Introduction, the prose poem is not, *as it is*, a discourse of taboo-breaking, but a making possible of taboo-breaking; it creates the space for taboos to be broken, and only the reader, or the translator, can embody or actualise the act. The prose poem cannot wage a generical war, but the translator can increase the chances of its effectiveness in persistent guerrilla operations. The socially transformative energies of the prose poem are not to be found in that spatialization of prose that the prose poem may already be reckoned to be, but in the spaces that its textuality might generate.

Rimbaud's City Spaces
Translating the Geometries of Social Architecture

'Royauté' seems to promise the generative force of public space. This is the space of non-functionalist interaction, a space set aside for unpredictable events within an atmosphere of leisured tolerance. The public square is where we learn the civic virtues in conditions of psychological well-being and potential or loose-leafed community. The couple who pronounce themselves king and queen offer a utopian image of what true publicness might represent: a general participation in experiences that are extremely private: love, revelation, ordeal. Public squares sustain a subjectivity and at the same time make it socially binding, partly by ensuring that it remains multi-functional, non-prescriptive. But on our argument, the poet of 'Royauté' does not entertain for long this opening on to confidently declared identity/role and mutual respect. Almost become an urban administrator, exerting a panoptical control in a world whose lineaments we cannot envisage other than through his agency, the poet consigns the event to 'zoned' time and segregated places. Apparently, the 'coup d'état', however benign, was headed off; the news item managed to be no more than a *fait divers* with all the on-sufferance fulfilment of a fairy tale. Whatever exhilarating social disruptiveness its has as a prose poem, 'Royauté' seems to reflect or predict the failure of urban reappropriation. In this sense, 'Royauté' also relates to the issues of the Commune, if we agree with Eagleton that the Commune is about the politics of place rather than of class:

> It was a revolution out on the street from the start, an uprising for which the bone of revolutionary contention was the streets themselves, rather than the streets as a front-line defense of a proletarian seizure of capital. It was thus a peculiarly *mobile*, multiple

affair, in which what mattered was the citizen rather than the producer, the political issue of control over everyday culture as a whole rather than the protection and promotion of a more narrowly conceived class identity.

(Ross 1988: ix)

Viewed in this light, what narratorial role do we want to attribute to the Rimbaud of 'Royauté'? Perhaps not that of the embittered instrument of the illusion's erasure, which we have adopted hitherto—Rimbaud joins the enemy to express his bitter disappointment, in ironic self-punishment. Perhaps the collapsing of space into time, the fragmentation of inhabitable space by the segmentation of time ('matinée', 'après-midi'), reflects a revolution in which a place of the 'carnivalesque', Paris, falls prey to the constrictions of the military calendar (three months [March–May 1871], culminating in 'la semaine sanglante') and Rimbaud's 'control' of the narrative is only the control of the already known, an elegiac reiteration of an inevitable outcome.

But, whatever our conclusion, we should stop, too, over the significance of urban narrative. What holds a city together? It might be the city's topographical legibility, its enabling of the panoramic view, its playing out at street level of an overall plan easy to reconstruct in the mind (Haussmann). It may be a set of relationships we understand, relationships of trade, genealogy, legality, social hierarchy. It may be a symbolism, a set of overarching meanings abstractable from an architecture, from the pattern of monuments. It may be a narrative, but that narrative must be expanding or multicursal; if it is to generate a sense of the corporate, it must be made of intersecting lives, of instances in which chance encounters can take on the concertedness of coincidence. The narrative of the couple in 'Royauté' remains a 'narrow' narrative, unable to activate cross-currents and ramifying consequences, a narrative of increasing isolation. Urban narratives must be shaggy dog stories, stories constitutionally incapabe of coming to a convincing conclusion; the past historic of 'Royauté' is peculiarly damning inasmuch as, without a narrative resolution to justify it, it can only sound like a writing-off. Is there any possibility of narrative in 'Ville', the subject of our first translation (see Appendix II (x) for 'straight' translation)?

'Ville' is, in effect, a tale of two cities: first, a city apparently without morphological complexity, homogeneous and doctrinaire, a city in which a certain featureless architecture has begotten certain behavioural characteristics, a city in which, to judge by the presence of passive constructions and abstract subjects, human agency has been gradually whittled away. Second, within this city, behind its façades, or on its perimeter, another city, dimly outlined, invisible from the outside; the inhabitant can only be sure of the building that his own inwardness has as if constructed. The poet's dwelling sounds like an example of heritage architecture and the vision on the world it provides is phantasmal, sensitive to the urban uncanny, metaphorising. While the prose of the first city provides a sequence of guide-like statements from a citizen peculiarly detached from his own living space, the prose of the second unfolds rhapsodically and in disorderly fashion from the cottage matrix, and comes to an end, not for any good syntactical reason, but because of a rhetorical imperative; this is the syntax of Old Paris, with no sense of a main thoroughfare/clause, where proliferating buildings, courtyards, alleys, streets constantly reformulate space, time, morality, vision:

> Produit d'une occupation fort ancienne, le tissu interne des quartiers est loin d'avoir, en effet, la cohérence formelle des opérations unitaires réalisées dans les percements haussmanniens ou dans les grands lotissements périphériques. Il s'en degage une forte variation de l'ordonnancement: ou bien l'alignement lui-même est hétérogène, par la succession de constructions chronologiquement et architecturalement étrangères les unes aux autres; ou bien des portions cohérentes d'alignement se succèdent de façon anarchique, figeant dans la morphologie urbaine la multiplicité des interventions immobilières [. . .].
>
> (Loyer 1987: 269–70).
>
> [The old neighbourhoods of Paris are far from possessing the formal coherence of either the unified streets built by Haussmann or the big outlying developments. There is marked architectural variation: streets are lined by totally heterogeneous rows of constructions that are chronologically and architecturally foreign to each other, or by coherent architectural groups juxtaposed in an utterly anarchic way (thus revealing the multiplicity of real-estate operations that created the city's morphology)] (trans. Clark 1988: 269).

The first city can generate no narrative because it is a speculative construction ('crue moderne', 'doit être plusieurs fois [. . .]'), and the narrator himself is, as we shall see, a shifter, momentarily occupying a role which gives him neither authority nor credibility. There may be signs of a subjectivity, but no motives for a protagonism, first-person or third-person. In the second city, with its syntax not of an architecture or city plan, but of movement through the windings of the streets, the poet, aggressively centred in self and community (the insistence of the possessives, first-person singular and plural), narrates a transformation of vision, the resurrection of the Baudelairean city:

> Dans les plis sinueux des vieilles capitales,
> Où tout, même l'horreur, tourne aux enchantements,
> Je guette, obéissant à mes humeurs fatales,
> Des êtres singuliers, décrépits et charmants.
>
> ('Les Petites Vieilles')
> [In the sinuous folds of old capitals, where everything, horror even, turns to enchantment, I watch in wait—as my imperious temperament dictates—singular, decrepit and charming creatures.]

The little old women watched by the Rimbaldian 'guetteur' are not latterday manifestations of Éponine and Laïs, but of Allecto, Megaera and Tisiphone, familiars, too, of Baudelaire's Paris. Just as the primeval darkness of the second city is interwoven with the (grey) light of the first, so in this Erebus, in Baudelairean fashion, the rich opacity of myth rubs shoulders with the instructive transparency of allegory; and personification in turn clings to, or reveals, person. The final enumeration—Death, Love, Crime—begins to drive us back into a teeming, bustling reality, where the police of statistics vainly pursue the elusive and protean contingencies of human existence.

My verse translation (see below) is built on the radical distinction between these two cities, but before we pass on to that, we should develop some of the textual detail:

1. 'Je suis un [. . .] citoyen d'une métropole'

What citizenship has Rimbaud got in mind? A citizenship by accident, by default? A citizenship by virtue of belonging to a community, a community itself created by homogeneity rather than partnership? Is this citizenship something constitutional, or ethnic, or social? Does it confine itself to the civic, or expand to the national? Is this a citizenship of bestowed identity or shared interest? What obligations and what rights does this title entail? Richard Rogers argues indefatigably for the restitution of public space as the key to the recovery of citizenship, but citizenship itself remains an elusive flag of convenience:

> The shape of the city can encourage an urban culture that generates citizenship. This important role needs to be recognized. To my

thinking urban culture is fundamentally participatory. It manifests itself in activities that take place only in the dense and interactive environment of towns and cities. [. . .] From heated exchanges of views in cafés to listening to Birtwistle in a concert hall, these activities define the character of a particular city, they give identity to an urban society, capture the essence of its people and bind the community. (1997: 151)

Can citizenship distil into an essence this heterogeneity, this relativism, of activity and experience? Is citizenship full and self-affirmative, or empty and putative? James Donald (1999: 99) concludes that 'citizenship' should designate not a substantial identity but an empty space, a position to be spoken from, like a deictic. Certainly in 'Ville', in its ephemerality and featureless averageness ('point trop mécontent'), it sounds like a shifter. Who would shake in their shoes at this 'Civis Romanus sum'? Thus, the poet is a shifter ('Je') defined by a shifter ('citoyen') in a world in which the indefinite article has none of its anarchic, uncontrollable yet-to-be-definedness; it is an indefinite of something that has become an unknown quantity by a process of self-atrophy or loss of interest, an experiment which has become a habit and a strait-jacket.

2. 'éphémère et point trop mécontent'

It is usually proposed that this poem has something to do with Rimbaud's experience of London, with Verlaine, in the latter months of 1872. The evidence lies in 'mon cottage' (34 Howland Street?), the coal smoke, the reference to the continent as another place, London as the only contemporary city with a population running in to millions (about 3,250,000 in 1865), Verlaine's comment about the absence of monuments in London, in a letter to Edmond Lepelletier (24 September 1872),[1] and parallels with views expressed about London, again by Verlaine, in his 'Sonnet boiteux'.[2] Underwood is also of the opinion that the pre-positioning of the adjectival pair—'éphémère et point trop mécontent'—alludes to English syntax.[3] These adjectives are non-committal and self-effacing, but the pre-positioning does suggest an attempt to establish a subjectivity, a tone of voice (self-mocking? dissatisfied? self-excusing ['these qualities are innate to this noun, I can't help it']?) which allows us equally to measure a stifling of selfhood.

3. 'parce que tout goût connu a été éludé'

In this clause, it is not entirely clear whether all known tastes/styles have been avoided so that unknown styles can be introduced, or so that no style at all is identifiable. The general feel of this city leads one to assume the latter, but, either way, there is an absence of recognition. Simmel reminds us that when an individual work of art affects us deeply, then its style is of no concern to us; style relieves the work of its absolute autonomy (1997: 211). Style takes us into the broad emotional categories. In the context of 'Ville', the significance of the absence of style is twofold: the planning administration has no visible, acknowledgeable ideology to promote, no vision of life; and the inhabitants, for their part, cannot generalise a subjectivity in the self-expressiveness of a style, nor can they affirm any sense of community through style. Simmel sees style as imparting a calming effect, the feeling of security and serenity, as working at 'the more pacified levels, where one no longer feels alone' (1997: 214–15). At the same time a multiplicity of styles allows the individual to become the centre of, to stabilise, that heterogeneity by combining available styles in ways attuned to his/her own personality. With no style at all, without shared hooks for our subjectivity, that subjectivity has no legitimated modes of self-expression, disappears from the agenda of the administration, and thus atrophies or finds its way into pathological excess.

We have used 'avoided' to render 'éludé', and indeed the majority of translators take the same route (Bernard, Fowlie, Sloate, Treharne, Sorrell); Varèse has 'evaded' and Schmidt has 'eluded'. The truth is that 'éludé' brings with it suggestions of ruse, dissimulation, finesse, avoidance by stealth. Here the passivity of the construction and the absence of agent add to the sense of guile, of incognito, of transferred responsibility. One might 'avoid' things as a matter of moral principle, as a moral agent; one is more likely to 'elude' things from a position of moral weakness. One might envisage a translation such as 'side-stepped', but it may be better to use 'avoided' with some adverbial qualification.

4. 'dans les ameublements et l'extérieur des maisons aussi bien que dans le plan de la ville. Ici vous ne signaleriez les traces d'aucun monument de superstition.'

What seems to be missing from this account is the 'middle ground' that reconciles city-plan and the domestic building. The street and square as social nexus are nowhere to be seen. The populace does not really have anywhere to be. In fact the city itself may be invisible: it is *Ici*, but the tense of 'signaler', the conditional, suggests both 'if you/one were here' and 'if this city, which I am in the process of describing, existed'. The city is drifting into abstraction, unreality. Equally, the string 'les ameublements [. . .] le plan de la ville' may be an abbreviation of a longer list, with middle terms elided; Rimbaud may have in mind the thoroughgoingness of the Haussmannian vision:

> S'il est vrai que Paris n'est qu'un *gros bourg*, c'est qu'à travers l'immensité de son espace se situent de multiples points de repère qui vont de la hiérarchie monumentale des edifices à celle, non moins élaborée, des espaces vides—rues, avenues, places et squares. Ainsi la partie renvoie-t-elle constamment au tout—l'immeuble à la rue, la rue au quartier, le quartier à la ville.
>
> (Loyer 1987: 232).
>
> [If Paris did not become sprawling and overgrown, it is because the vast, expanding city was structured by means of a hierarchy of edifices and a no less elaborate hierarchy of empty spaces (streets, avenues, intersections, and squares). The city was redesigned so that each of its parts would constantly refer back to the whole—the building to the street, the street to the neighbourhood, and the neighbourhood to the city.] (trans. Clark, 1988: 232)

Either way, we are in a world in which the utopian cannot be put apart from the totalitarian, in which the extremes of the pragmatic-utilitarian and the visionary-conceptual touch. The observation made about the monuments suggests that the city has no biography, stores and safeguards no collective memory, fosters no urban (national) pride, pursues no public *Bildung* (!), with an official landmark-history. These monuments are not, I think, necessarily religious; and if we imagine a proselytising commentator, then this might refer, *pace* Verlaine and London, to monuments such as the Vendôme column, symbol of a militaristic patriarchy and predatory unilateral law, laid low by the Commune.

5. 'La morale et la langue sont réduites à leur plus simple expression, enfin! Ces millions de gens qui n'ont pas besoin de se connaître amènent si pareillement l'éducation, le métier et la vieillesse, que ce cours de vie doit être plusieurs fois moins long que ce qu'une statistique folle trouve pour les peuples du continent.'

But the image of the poet as proselytising commentator does not convince. The city's predictabilities and policy of lowest common denominator make mutual understanding and interpersonal negotiation unnecessary. Without the friction of heterogeneity, the intractable difference of individual lives, without the hotch-potch of an unsupervised and cumulative architecture, all the irregularities of lived time, the flexibilities and uneven pacing, are erased. Here, there is no room for the accidents of History, the unfinishedness of divergent, successive projects; time, left by default to a homogeneous, unpossessed chronometricity, finds the quickest route between two points. I understand 'statistique folle' to mean a statistics characterised by large and unaccountable disparities. 'Enfin' I see as the ironic consummation of a wish (mostly because of its position and following exclamation mark) and not as a signal of summary (= 'bref'). The two demonstratives—'Ces millions. . .' and 'ce cours de vie'—are false deictics. Thanks to the absence of punctuation, the former looks, at first, as if it might be an anticipation of a restrictive relative clause ('Ces millions de gens qui n'ont pas besoin'); but the relative clause has the feel of non-restrictiveness and the demonstrative seems rather to express a movement of self-dissociation and of speculative calculation. The demonstrative of 'ce cours de vie' is an agent of syntactic cohesion, of analeptic reference: 'ce cours de vie' gathers into a single noun the three nouns preceding it.

6. 'Aussi comme [. . .] dans la boue de la rue'

Our first response to this last 'sentence' might be rather guarded: do we detect a psychic disorder, an incipient paranoia? Simmel's analysis of the metropolis and mental life tells us what to expect. Given the brevity and scarcity of human contacts, we have to make the most of our individuality:

> Finally, man is tempted to adopt the most tendentious peculiarities, that is, the specifically metropolitan extravagances of mannerism, caprice, and preciousness. Now, the meaning of these extravagances does not at all lie in the contents of such behaviour, but rather in its form of 'being different', of standing out in a striking manner and thereby attracting attention. For many character types, ultimately the only means of saving for themselves some modicum of self-esteem and the sense of filling a position is indirect, through the awareness of others.
>
> (1997: 183)

The poet here is hardly the wild man of apocalypse, but we may catch a certain edge of hysteria in his voice, a certain satisfaction in vengefulness. And in these circumstances, any 'we' is bound to be hostile simply because it proposes a community, and probably a heterogeneous one at that, given that investment in peculiarities is the only way to personality.[4]

We pass from the city as panorama to the city as labyrinth, from the city as abstractable geometry and statistics to the city as proliferating metaphor. James Donald (1999: 17–18) brings to bear on the real/imaginary urban interface a Derridean notion of the spectre, as glossed by Slavoj Žižek. Žižek's explanation runs like this:

> Why, then, is there no reality without the spectre? Lacan provides a precise answer to this question: (what we experience as) reality is not the 'thing itself', it is always-already symbolized, constituted, structured by symbolic mechanisms—and the problem resides in the fact that symbolization ultimately always fails, that it never succeeds in fully 'covering' the real, that it always involves some unsettled, unredeemed symbolic debt. *This real (the part of reality that remains non-symbolised) returns in the guise of spectral apparitions.*
>
> (1994: 21; italics in original)

Are these the Rimbaldian spectres: the non-symbolisable residue of reality? In some ways, yes; in some ways, no. No, insofar as they seem to be part of the poet's (first) symbolization of the 'other' city. But yes, in that they equally represent what the city in its self-symbolisation cannot eradicate. As a citizen, the poet must project, even if ironically, the city's view of itself; its programme is one of elision. But as a poet, embattled, holed up in his 'cottage', his answer must be an answering symbolization. Our question is whether, behind this symbolism of Furies and their personifications, we feel the real presence of the city street: the smog, a real servant class—the dry-eyed messengers of their employers—emotional deprivation, street urchins complaining in the dirt.

But what kind of revenance is this if the spectres are 'nouveaux'? We may think of spectres as persistent traces of a past that needs exorcising, and this, given the further references (Erinyes, Death, Love and Crime), is what they are. Up to a point. But their novelty is that of a new version. Here the Derridean treatment of the spectres of Marx takes on other colourings: the spectral is what testifies to a living future, still to come, a discomfiting anticipation, an incipience; or it is what sees us before we see it: 'We feel ourselves observed, sometimes under surveillance by it even before any apparition' (1994: 101)? We see when it is already too late; the poet recognizes these figures—they already exist—but they have not yet existed; the not yet is too late; the present thus becomes the very space of hallucination, as haunting memories shift seamlessly into haunting anticipations. We may feel in this particular instance, in this uninterruptedly unwinding sentence, without the identifiable event of a main verb, that the prose poem has been unable to establish its claim to a present, a present of its own making.

It is not surprising that 'cottage' has exercised critics. Was Rimbaud thoroughly familiar with the word's connotations? Does it confirm the insertion of the sylvan dream into the urban environment? Is it meant to represent the most vernacular architecture one can think of? Does it place the Rimbaldian point of view in the suburbs (the Second Empire taste for suburban chalets)? Perhaps it hardly matters, as long as it is the kind of dwelling about which one might be justifiably possessive.

The preposed adjectival pair here—'l'épaisse et éternelle fumée de charbon'—is a riposte the the preposed adjectival pair of the first sentence. Again an anglicising strategy perhaps—although the 'compoundness' of the noun ('fumée de charbon') supplies an obvious syntactical pretext— designed to endow its 'éternelle' with greater incontrovertibility, to match and obliterate the opening 'éphémère'. This pre-positioning seems to express a conspiratorial understanding between the poet and the smoke, since it is the smoke which is the generative medium of the spectres, and there is a more insistent, more concerted interplay between half-closed e (/e/) and half-open e (/ɛ/): three instances of each in 'épaisse et éternelle fumée', supported by a further /ɛ/ in 'à travers' whose /a/'s form with the /a/ of 'charbon' a neat envelope for the whole phrase. The increased tonal presence in the adjectives, created by the pre-positioning, is a piquant mixture of threat and ironic caressiveness.

My verse translation below is a response to Verlaine's 'Sonnet boiteux', an account which supposes that Rimbaud's poem has a clear 'volta' ('Aussi comme [. . .]') with a significant change of direction and manner, and that the whole is built on 8:6 proportions. The nature of the shift from octave to sestet here is very much that of the Baudelairean sonnet as described by David Scott:

> In the majority of Baudelaire's sonnets, whereas the octave tended
> to be discursive, the sestet was analytical or visionary. Its primary
> quality was its perceptiveness—its ability on the one hand to clarify
> or re-assess, often ironically, the preceding quatrains, and on the
> other to elaborate their implications and reveal their ultimate
> significance. Its function was, like the mind or spirit, to interpret and
> synthesize the raw experience, the sense data of the octave.
>
> (1977: 47)

But this transformation of the physical into the metaphysical is accompanied by a process of formal unravelling. My sonnet 'limps' like Verlaine's: its rhymes lose their way and it uses Verlaine's tredecasyllables as an excuse for a heterosyllabic treatment which tests the reader's tolerance to the limit in its cavalier closure (what licences a line-initial capital will condone!):

> I am a none too discontented, soon displaced
> Citizen of a modern metropolis.
> Modern? Perhaps, since no known taste
> In furnishings, houses, city plan, brings solace,
>
> Nor monument to irrational belief.
> Morals, language, stripped to barest basics,
> And lives so uniform that time is more their thief
> Than on the continent, so say the mad statistics.
>
> So,
>   as from my cottage window I can see
> New spectres wading through the city's smoke,
> Unending, thick—our sylvan shade, our summer
>
> Night!—new Furies passing by my door,
> My homeland and my whole heart's core,
> Since all here's this,—our bustling servant-daughter
>   Death, dry-eyed, and Love
>   on wings of black despair, and Crime
>   prinked up and whining
>   in the muddy street.

My last line may seem like a brazen piece of rule-bending, an attempt to carry incompetence on a technicality, but there are good textual reasons, as we have seen, for performing this 'débordement': the personified Eumenides quite literally break down the city-sonnet's limits, cannot be administratively contained, take enjambement to extremes. The metaphysics of the city outstrips its utopian rationality, drifts into the air around the conurbation, so that its agents are free to operate in the space of their own caprice.

I have had to abbreviate some of the source text, but this might be seen as an inevitable erosion: these abbreviations occur in the English/ Shakespearean octave, in a modern city in which 'ce cours de vie doit être plusieurs fois moins long que ce qu'une statistique folle trouve pour les peuples du continent', while the sestet which, precisely, identifies this as a continental/Petrarchan sonnet, extends the time of the form to include a tail. In fact, the continental sonnet has always, potentially at least, been a tale of two cities: the octave, with its customarily chiastic, self-mirroring rhyme scheme (abba/abba) is a classical architecture of the symmetrical and static, of self-completing form; the sestet, on the other hand, is a dynamic structure (usually three rhymes in six lines as opposed to the octave's two in eight, in a scheme that has greater unpredictability), mobile, on the move, asymmetrical, incomplete (in that one rhyme of the first tercet at least must wait for completion in the second tercet). In terms of ground-plan, the octave lays out the axial boulevards of Haussmannisation, generating a visible pattern of spatial relations based on a binary principle. The sestet, on the other hand, works by the principle of three (tercets, Eumenides) in order to summon the archaic, labyrinthine city behind the regularised façades, the meandering streets and alleyways which emerge from each other like complex root systems, in a syntax of self-extending apposition. In peculiar fashion, we might argue that the sestet can never be properly assimilated by the sonnet. The continental sonnet has all the look of a fixed form, of a structure which has refined itself to an elegant and eloquent complexity; but, in reality, it is a form which has never come to terms with itself and its expressive range and peculiar dynamic result from the lack of resolution of its own contradictions.

The heterosyllabicity of my version is kept, up to the eruptive growth on the last line, within fairly tight margins—between eight and thirteen syllables; this is partly designed to reflect Raybaud's comment:

> Bizarrerie ou duplicité, dès les premiers mots, quelque chose ressort de la contradiction du registre et du propos, qui envahira la dernière phrase, et l'image ultime—l'éloge de 'tout goût connu [. . .] éludé' en alexandrins, comme embâcles dans un texte qui en frôle sans cesse la noblesse pour le démanteler en 'vers faux' de onze et treize pieds, ou en vers de douze pieds si irrégulièrement coupés qu'ils perdent la forme en gardant le nombre [. . .].
>
> (1989: 87)
>
> [Vagary or duplicity, from the very first word, something emerges from the contradiction in register and discourse, which will invade the final sentence and the ultimate image—the praise of 'every known taste (. . .) avoided' in alexandrines, like barriers in a text which constantly flirts with the alexandrine's nobility, only to dismantle it in 'false lines' of eleven or thirteen syllables, or in lines

of twelve syllables so irregularly segmented that they lose their shape
even though they maintain the syllabic count (. . .).]

Rimbaud's 'first' city never manages to look convincing, and if it aspires
to a standardised uniformity, there is some satisfaction to be had from
observing its managing only fitfully to achieve it: in my translation, only
lines 1, 4 and 7 are dodecasyllables; the sestet remains resolutely set against
any trace of them. Heterosyllabicity also introduces a pattern to which I
will return later in my argument: the inability of strings of signifiers (as,
here, lines) to find their way back or forward to a superordinate principle,
either back to an origin (as, here, the sonnet, in alexandrines) or forward
to a new principle of synthesis and coherence (the kind of writing that none
of these prose poems quite ever manages to be).

Many have pointed to the natural connection between montage and the
cityscape, as, indeed, between the urban-visual and the cinematic (see, for
example, Donald 1999: 63–92; Barber 2002; essays in Leach 2002:
203–43). Montage offers a paradoxical mixture of the fragmented and the
tendentiously relational. By setting my sonnet in a montage (see Appendix
III (e)), I want to capture not only the anarchic play of urban encounter
and association, but also the compelling need to discover the hidden design
of the city, what it wills without our knowing, what it makes available in
its magisterial indifference. We read the montage as ephemeral citizens,
passing through a sudden compilation, a here and now in real time which
might slip back into something predicted, predictable, but which might
equally thrust us forward into ramifications of randomness. If montage is
allowed to fix itself, then, more than any single image, it will tie us into a
programme, into a propaganda, into a too insistent articulation of
meanings; but transience sustains the interrogative mode, an interrogation
which is bound to beget other spectatorial and readerly maps. Montage
offers us the documentary in the service of the oneiric. All objects, however
authentic, however 'factual', once wrenched from the context which
prescribes their use, that makes their use coterminous with their meaning,
are emptied of documentability; photography is compelled to exist in a
state of constant self-contradiction. In order to be effective in a montage,
a photograph must not be returned to its context, and interpretation by
processes of reconstruction (i.e. the return to the mimetic) must be
thwarted. Even those objects which might be recognized must be allowed
to make a journey into otherness. So in my own effort, the repeated
photograph of 34 Howland Street, and even the misty image of London
(Alvin Langdon Coburn), must drift off into new imaginary locations, into
other cities. Deprived now of direction, of relational distance, of scale, of

spatial configuration, these elements which began their life in reality, and which will sacrifice none of their indexicality, may seek out new referents, without those referents ever coming into existence.

Montage as the image of the urbanite's mental space plays out the drama of legibility, not so much as a problem posed by a city plan, or an architecture or a particular distribution of population, but as a problem of the assimilative capacity of human consciousness. Montage can be experienced as a non-space, without perspective or planar arrangement, without a position for the reading/viewing subject. In circumstances like this, the human mind dissolves into the city's images, is possessed by the city, becomes a homeless blank, as perhaps in the first city of 'Ville'. In these circumstances the city can have no name and citizenship is a purely putative position. Alternatively, montage is seen as presenting a multidimensional space which, while it cannot be absorbed in a single panoramic view, yields itself to the perambulating *flâneur*, is gathered into human consciousness, but not necessarily resolved by that consciousness.

This is the experience conveyed perhaps by 'Villes I' ('L'acropole officielle [. . .]) (see Appendix II (xi) for 'straight' translation). As the poem proceeds, the city is increasingly internalised: the first paragraph is made up of instances of direct sensory involvement (such as 'J'assiste à', 'Quelle peinture!', 'j'ai pu voir', 'j'ai tremblé'); in the second paragraph, on the other hand, the emphasis is on mental process and the internalisation of the sensory ('j'ai cru pouvoir juger', 'je n'ai pu me rendre compte', 'A l'idée de chercher [. . .], je me réponds', 'Je pense qu'il y a')—here, noticeably, the language of speculation ('cru', 'doivent contenir', 'doit être'), taken over, it seems, from 'Ville', now emerges from a moving subjectivity rather than from a shared/anonymous fund of current assumptions. But even as the eerily unpopulated city—the city of early urban photographers like Marville?—is assimilated, so the fringe of awareness keeps adding more of the invisible, the animisms which declare the city to enjoy a threatening autonomy, impervious to psycho-colonisation: the metro continues to run, even if empty; traffic lights change in the empty street; theatres periodically swallow and disgorge groups of people they have turned into audiences. What effect can any individual have on this well-oiled and oblivious mechanism? What is necessary for it to take notice? At the end of the second paragraph, the *flâneur*-poet gives up ('je renonce à me faire une idée') and takes refuge in a generalising account (sight unseen?) of the suburbs and countryside beyond.

To account for Rimbaud's architectural tastes as we find them in 'Villes I', we might begin by turning to Haussmann's eclectic gigantism, the monumental city in which monuments have to redefine their relationship with the surrounding architectural fabric because size no longer makes the difference.[5] But Haussmann's Paris is over-decorated, too static, not receptive enough in its structures to new technologies of communication, not responsive enough to new materials (cast-iron, steel, glass), even though it makes use of them. Raybaud, without wishing to suggest 'influence', proposes that our real guide to Rimbaldian city planning should be the recently discovered (1967) work of Hector Horeau, 'urbaniste en chef de la Commune' [the Commune's town-planner-in-chief], with its projects for the remodelling of Trafalgar Square and Brighton, for roof-gardens, covered boulevards, footbridges between boulevards, interconnected spaces in theatres, and so forth (1989: 76–81, 213–15). We might equally turn to the new Babylons of the Vienna School, to the vision of Otto Wagner, which includes the socially levelling effects of styleless (*Nutzstil*) apartment blocks (the spirit of 'Ville'), as well as plans for accelerated communications systems dictating the shape of continual urban expansion (see Frisby: 2002). But, as one reads these urban *Illuminations*, it is also difficult not to feel their prescience in relation to the Futurist architecture of Antonio Sant'Elia.

Sant'Elia's 'Città Nuova', whose full sixteen drawings were first exhibited in Milan, in May 1914, at an exhibition of the Nuove Tendenze group, and which doubled as the 'Città Futurista' in his 'Manifesto of Futurist Architecture' (1 August 1914), anathematises the decorative[6] and the monumental.[7] Another of Sant'Elia's gripes is the blatant disregard of the properties of modern materials, and more especially of their self-expressive qualities and constructional possibilities. Architecture (shapes and decoration) must give way to large-scale sculptural engineering which exploits the impulses of the materials themselves. On this understanding, Sant'Elia can project cityscapes in which levels and masses interpenetrate and in which the mechanisms of the building can be brought to the surface and displayed:

> [. . .] the Futurist house must be like a gigantic machine. The lifts must no longer be hidden away like tapeworms in the niches of stairwells; the stairwells themselves, rendered useless, must be abolished, and the lifts must scale the lengths of the façades like serpents of steel and glass. [. . .] It must soar up on the brink of a tumultuous abyss: the street will no longer lie like a doormat at ground level, but will plunge many storeys down into the earth, embracing the metropolitan traffic, and will be linked up for necessary interconnections by metal gangways and swift-moving pavements.
> (Apollonio 1973: 170)

These seem to be the kinds of multi-level complex, with outlines sculpted and set in motion by bridges or railways, that Rimbaud has in mind in 'Villes I', at the beginning of the second paragraph, or in 'Les Ponts' ('Un bizarre dessin de ponts, ceux-ci droits, ceux-là bombés, d'autres descendant ou obliquant en angles sur les premiers, et ces figures se renouvelant dans les autres circuits éclairés du canal, [. . .]'), or in 'Promontoire' ('et leurs railways flanquent, creusent, surplombent les dispositions de cet Hôtel, [. . .]'). This translation of shapes into events, still tentative in 'Villes I' ('le groupement des bâtiments en squares [. . .]', 'un bras de mer [. . .] roule sa nappe', 'Un pont court conduit', 'qui contournent les halles') seems like the active projection of Futurist lines of force, which both reveal the object's sensibility and express the urge to 'physical transcendentalism':

> What is overlooked is that all inanimate objects display, by their lines, calmness or frenzy, sadness or gaiety. These various tendencies lend to the lines of which they are formed a sense and character of weighty stability or of aerial lightness.
>
> Every object reveals by its lines how it would resolve itself were it to follow the tendencies of its forces. [. . .]
>
> All objects, in accordance with what the painter Boccioni happily terms *physical transcendentalism*, tend to the infinite by their *force-lines*, the continuity of which is measured by our intuition.
>
> ('The Exhibitors to the Public 1912', in Apollonio 1973: 48)

Force-lines provide us with a useful metaphor not only, as we shall see, for the ways in which Rimbaud makes meaning, but also for the business of translation: it is the translator's task to read and activate the force-lines of a text; the translator does not ask what words mean but where they are going; the translator, by quite literally creating a space, and environment, for language, sets it on a range of trajectories, which no contour seeks to confine. Translation is textual in its orientation, in its literariness, but that does not presuppose the pursuit of autonomy. The task of the TT is not to become self-reflexive but to activate its blind field, just as it takes place itself in the blind field of the ST.

The city performed in 'Villes I' lies somewhere between and beyond Paris and London, which appear in the text only as points of comparison, either explicit or implicit (for example, 'candélabres géants' = those five-lamp *réverbères* (?) to be seen on the rue de Caumartin, for example, or the boulevard de Sébastopol; 'Le quartier commerçant est un circus d'un seul style, avec galeries à arcades' = Piccadilly Circus and Regent Street). This 'beyond' is important, because it takes us into the unnamed. Sant'Elia's 'Città Nuova', like so many of the architectural parallels we have mentioned, never got further than the drawing board; and its conceptuality is the very source of its peculiar fascination. This proposition we shall return to below.

The description seems systematically to follow a ground plan, from the acropolis, through the business quarter, to the suburbs, and then on to the surrounding country/county. And, as in 'Ville', we seem to move from the modern of technological advance and urban planning to the persistent traces of a past ('gentilhommes sauvages'). But this is not a threatening past, a past which is the city's ineradicable unconscious, id, pulsional drives; it is a cartoon, spectator sport, the fringe lunacy of the out-of-touch.[8] The city has found a way of admitting and updating Rimbaud's favoured East—'J'envoyais au diable les palmes des martyrs, les rayons de l'art, l'orgueil des inventeurs, l'ardeur des pillards; je retournais à l'Orient et à la sagesse première et éternelle' [I sent to the devil the palms of martyrs, the aura of art, the pride of inventors, the frenzy of plunderers; I went back to the East and to the original, eternal wisdom] ('L'Impossible', *Une saison en enfer*)—or at least of superimposing it on the chilly North; the 'eternal West' is a sublime irrelevance. 'Villes I' is also to be distinguished from 'Ville', because, among other things, the poet is more tourist ('Pour l'étranger de notre temps [. . .]') than citizen and thus more investigator than guide. But, as in 'Ville', the figure of the poet is doubled: not as between a brainwashed self and a self defiantly at bay, but between the self as 'ingénieur-architecte' [architect-engineer] and the self as 'promeneur-scrutateur' [*flâneur*-scrutineer], the latter ironising the former (Raybaud 1989: 94). This tension leaves us still reaching for the spirit of this city, even though it has proved to be much more 'nameable', in both common and proper senses, than the 'first' city of 'Ville'.

Naming is putting in place, the necessary prelude to taxonomy. Categories, mappings and so on reveal an order which is the more self-evident for the correctness of the names. Incorrect naming will produce significant delusions. The porcupine has nothing to do with pigs; its true home is among the rodents. We name within our current and limited knowledge. The horses of the Piritané (Britons), that come to Tahiti in Segalen's *Les Immémoriaux* (1907), are not 'des sortes de cochons à longues pattes, à queue chevelue' (1956: 165) [sorts of pig with long legs and a hairy tail]. Or are they? As we have already discovered, Rimbaud can find a beyond of language within the limits of language, where these limits beget creative misapprehension, false etymology, false collocation, mishearing, malapropistic neologism, interlingual interference. Language has other worlds concealed in its follies. And as we argued from the outset, the Rimbaldian text itself is unsteady, seems almost designed to produce readerly delusions: in the present translation, for example, I have followed Guyaux's suggested reading, 'à l'aspect de colosses des gardiens', and not what he regards as Germain Nouveau's mistranscription: 'à l'aspect des gardiens de colosses'; but it is Nouveau's 'mistranscription' which has been universally translated. Who would presume to be right?

But if one is trying to push beyond the limits of language, then the nature of naming itself becomes a critical operation. The poet seems to have two ways forward. He can create a signifier in excess of any signified, a colossus which has as if digested all its possible contexts and syntaxes and collocations. Rimbaud's ambitions for language are of a piece with his architectural ambitions: not with the architecture of 'Ville' which naturally produces a language reduced to its barest essentials, but with the ultra-'architecture' of 'Villes II' ('Ce sont des villes!'—see Appendix II (xii) for 'straight' translation), where 'chanter' and 'sonner' are the 'linguistic' paradigms out of which all other languages—'rugir mélodieusement', 'crier', 'flottes orphéoniques', 'rumeur', 'mugir', 'sangloter', 'hurler', 'musique inconnue'—are free to modulate. This amplification and potentiation of the word might be understood as the transformation of the common noun into the proper noun: at each encounter with it, we take only a little of it away, while having an acute sense of its inexhaustibility. Reading the proper noun is the equivalent of the child's embracing dawn: 'je l'ai entourée avec ses voiles amassés, et j'ai senti un peu son immense corps'. It is usual for linguists to say that proper nouns designate or identify, but do not mean. But Lévi-Strauss (1952: 285) proposed the opposite and is eloquently supported by Barthes in these terms:

> Le Nom propre est lui aussi un signe, et non bien entendu, un simple indice qui désignerait, sans signifier, comme le veut la conception courante, de Peirce à Russell. Comme signe, le Nom propre s'offre à une exploration, à un déchiffrement: il est à la fois un 'milieu' (au sens biologique du terme), dans lequel il faut se plonger, baignant indéfiniment dans toutes les rêveries qu'il porte, et un objet précieux, comprimé, embaumé, qu'il faut ouvrir comme une fleur. Autrement dit, si le Nom [. . .] est un signe, c'est un signe volumineux, un signe toujours gros d'une épaisseur touffue de sens, qu'aucun usage ne vient réduire, aplatir, contrairement au nom commun, qui ne livre jamais qu'un de ses sens par syntagme.
>
> (1967: 152–3)

[The proper Name is also a sign and not, as one might expect, a simple index, designating without meaning, as current thinking, from Peirce to Russell, would have it. As a sign, the proper Name offers itself for exploration, for decipherment: it is both a 'habitat' (in the biological sense of the word), into which one must plunge, bathing indefinitely in all the reveries it carries, and a precious object, pressed, embalmed, that one must open like a flower. Put another way, if the Name (. . .) is a sign, it is a voluminous sign, a sign always pregnant with an intricate density of meaning, that usage does not work to reduce, to flatten, as it does with the common noun, which only ever delivers one of its meanings per syntagm.]

The proper name enjoys the condition of being constantly semanticised and of being infinitely semanticisable. It is a superordinate signifier packed with subordinate signifiers; the fewer these subsignifiers are, the more likely it is that we are indulging in the lazy shorthands of 'Chinoiserie' (fantasy stereotypes, piquant ethnic crossovers, rococo masquerade); but all subsignifiers will want to fend off signifieds, postpone signification, the better to interact and undertake journeys of mutual exploration. Cities have proper names and operate like proper names: 'We cannot know a "city", only those of its places we come to frequent. [. . .] Remembering the cities we have left, we recall only certain times spent in certain places' (Burgin 1996: 7). Walking the streets is the way in which we multiply and interconnect signifiers, and defer the meaning of the city. We have already had occasion to describe the sonnet as a tale of two cities, to imagine a layout of lines as a street-plan; the street unfolds a syntax of signifiers like a line of verse:

> Car la ville est un poème, comme on l'a souvent dit et comme Hugo l'a exprimé mieux que quiconque, mais ce n'est pas un poème classique, un poème bien centré sur un sujet. C'est un poème qui déploie le signifiant, et c'est ce déploiement que finalement la sémiologie de la ville devrait essayer de saisir et de faire chanter.
>
> (Barthes 1985: 271)
>
> [For the city is a poem, as has often been noted and as Hugo has expressed it better than anyone else, but it is not a poem of classical design, a poem centred on a single subject. It is a poem which deploys the signifier, and it is this deployment which, in the end, the semiology of the city should try to grasp and give lyric voice to.]

In speaking of the streets as a syntax, we draw attention to a critical view of Rimbaud's writing that may be misleading, namely that he is a lexical rather than syntactic poet (we might add, in view of our earlier analyses, prepositional rather than conjunctive) ('A l'inverse du "syntaxier" Mallarmé, Rimbaud est un poète lexical: il juxtapose les mots qui, loin de toute articulation, gardent chacun son insistance propre. Les seuls rapports entre événements ou entre phrases que cultive Rimbaud sont de coprésence' [Todorov 1978: 246] [Contrary to the 'syntaxist' Mallarmé, Rimbaud is a lexical poet: he juxtaposes words which, far from creating syntagmatic links, each retain their own particular emphasis. The only connections between events and phrases cultivated by Rimbaud are those of co-presence.]) There are senses in which this view might be accepted: one might argue that Rimbaud's 'straight-line' syntax, with its elisions and abbreviations, is heading towards a Futurist or concrete ideal, where blank spaces themselves become the adequate syntax. But this would be to overlook the 'topographical' function of syntax for Rimbaud: one kind of syntax is necessary to suppress another, just as one kind of street-plan might be implemented in order to obliterate another. The syntax that is Rimbaud's enemy is certainly not the fastidious Latinate variety of Mallarmé, but the kind that makes sense of the words in it, that makes words serve certain communicative conventions, makes words functional or rhetorical; about this kind of syntax Marinetti has no good to say:

> Syntax was a kind of abstract cipher that poets used to inform the crowd about the color, musicality, plasticity, and architecture of the universe. Syntax was a kind of interpreter or monotonous cicerone. This intermediary must be suppressed, in order that literature may enter directly into that universe and become one body with it.
>
> (Flint 1972: 89)

Rimbaud's is a strategic syntax, designed for guerrilla warfare, by spoiling devices, subversion, decoy. We have already had occasion to watch him plunging into the multicursal labyrinth at the end of 'Ville', avoiding the main thoroughfare, always ready to dart down another alley, apparently leading away, but then coming back before the principal articulation could be established. In 'Villes I', as the sense of spatial and directional orientation reaches its most tenuous, so the causal links between different parts of the sentence go underground or become aberrant: 'A l'idée de chercher des théâtres sur ce circus, je me réponds que les boutiques doivent contenir des drames assez sombres. Je pense qu'il y a une police; mais la loi doit être tellement étrange, que je renonce à me faire une idée des aventuriers d'ici.' In this way, Rimbaldian syntax helps to engineer the deferral of signification, to suspend signifiers, and thus compensates for the absence of those suspensive devices of equivalence enjoyed by verse; but Rimbaud's syntax is a forward-moving suspensive mechanism, characterised by the non-consecutive, rather than a recuperative one.

But there is a fly in the ointment of our signifying model. We suppose a superordinate signifier which acts as a radiational/gravitational focus for a string of subordinate signifiers forever fugitive from their signifieds (indices without referents). The superordinate signifier is a proper noun shepherding its flock of subordinate proper-noun-equivalents. But Rimbaud's cities have no names! There are two ways of responding to this moment of crisis. We speak of the street, the string, of subsignifiers as a line of verse. With its 'pieuse majuscule' [pious capital letter] (Mallarmé 2003: 75), the line of verse itself becomes, according to Mallarmé, a composite proper noun, holding together, in a single perceptual span, its chain of signifiers:

> Le vers qui de plusieurs vocables refait un mot total, neuf, étranger à la langue et comme incantatoire, achève cet isolement de la parole: niant, d'un trait souverain, le hasard demeuré aux termes malgré l'artifice de leur retrempe alternée en le sens et la sonorité, et vous cause cette surprise de n'avoir ouï jamais tel fragment ordinaire d'élocution, en même temps que la réminiscence de l'objet nommé baigne dans une neuve atmosphère.
>
> (2003: 213)
>
> [The line of verse which from several lexemes recomposes a total word, brand new, alien to language and as if incantatory, completes this isolation of utterance: denying, with a regal gesture, any chance still clinging to the terms despite the device of their being re-immersed in significance and sonority, and provokes in you the surprise of never having heard a particular, ordinary fragment of speech, at the same time as the memory of the named object bathes in a newborn atmosphere.]

What higher superordinate/proper noun are these lines of signifiers— themselves become compound proper nouns—the subordinates of? The poem's title? Yes, but only insofar as the title means 'this poem' (hence the use of first lines as titles). The superordinate is the text thought of as the city of reading. We cannot name Rimbaud's cities, but they have titles, which tell us of a textuality, a streetplan, a topography, an inhabitable space that reading will turn into a place.

Alternatively, we assume that there is no superordinate name, no encompassing signifier. The prose poem has not got the textual autonomy that the verse-poem has, whatever we may wish to think. Its very coming into existence was motivated by this escape from autonomy, even while it continued to flirt with the idea of the self-generating text. And so something of the transformation described by Mallarmé takes place: an object is transformed, such that memories of its former self linger on, bathed now in a new atmosphere. But deprived of the superordinate point of reference, its signifying power floats freely, non-gravitationally. There is no way forward, to a broader, cohesive participation, and there is no way back to an origin in a signified/referent. What can such texts do? Peter out, be erased, reach for some concluding, apophthegmatic remark? Do we confront Rimbaud with a loss of nerve? Or congratulate him on a gamble which cannot be written off, even by himself? For the outcome of the gamble depends on the reader, not a reader looking for textual coherence, even though, from time to time, there may be convincing signs of it; rather, a reader looking for a future, and therefore unwilling to deny chance.

Maybe modern/futurist cities have neither names nor texts; maybe the proper way to live in them is not by endowing them with a personality or by making sense of their disposition. Questions of scale, spatial configuration, arterial layout, level, remain conjectural, not simply as puzzles that thwart spatial reconstruction but as invitations to reimagine space itself, or to find new spatial contexts for this motley collection of constructions, a city invisible to itself, because it is always conceivably other and elsewhere, rather like the self-unnaming Venice of Calvino's *Invisible Cities*, for ever making itself available to other names. Does Rimbaud want his city to be intelligible, legible? Apparently not. Its unintelligibility stems not only from the indiscriminate jumble of architectural styles, but also from the sheer ambition of the engineering feats, which architecture can never really give convincing form to. In such circumstances we are likely to fall victim to the pathologies of space (vertigo, agoraphobia, claustrophobia, the uncanny). Montage—see Appendix III (f) for a montage rendering of 'Villes I'—we might argue, is similarly an unintelligible text, and in similar fashion, like the Rimbaldian text, is designed to engender pathologies of reading, moments of semantic dizziness, of feeling overwhelmed by the density of images, of feeling lost in imaginative distances too great to cross.

Montage helps to liberate that imagining activity that Dee Reynolds sees as central to the reception of Rimbaud's work (and to that of Mallarmé, Kandinsky and Mondrian):

Imagination can be described in terms analogous to the signifying process as it is seen in poststructuralism, in other words, as a *process* of image production which does not culminate in the formation of a final, stable and coherent image. Imagining activity causes the fissuring of an image's presence, through awareness of what the image does not contain, its lack of totality and wholeness. An 'image', whether it be a mode of consciousness generated by a linguistic description or a visual image in a painting, is not 'imaginary' unless it negates itself by exceeding its own powers of presentation, suggesting more tha[n] it can explain or make visible.

(1995: 3)

In what senses do the images of 'Villes II', for example, exceed their powers of presentation? What might this be, this mountainous landscape, these crests, but then these gorges, ravines, abysses? High-rise urban architecture, those deep-plunging falls to the street. There are the footbridges and platforms that 'Villes I' has accustomed us to, but without the natural landscape metaphor, we cannot properly imagine the resonances of these spaces (Who might these Rolands be? Advertising hoardings?), nor the way the light bursts on flagpoles and rooftops. Craters produced by urban demolition, or railway station cuttings, are surrounded by soaring *immeubles* ('colosses') and ornate streetlamps ('palmiers de cuivre'). And so on. In a world of conceptuality, cityscapes become *décors de théâtre*, and metaphors switch back and forth, in two directions at once. Even the sea, the mobile, fluid crowd, reaches the spectator as 'rumeur', as the flashing lights or the milling hubbub of the teeming population. Here is an image of self-forming gatherings, processions, corporations— community constantly rediscovers itself in this protean mass. Thinking one's way through this Rimbaldian *fête* entails thinking one's way through restless change and along the force-lines of intuition. This text can afford to be non-consecutive precisely because, at some other level of experience, potential coherence-seeking is engaged, but never allowed to complete itself. What may sound like comfortable equivalences—for example, volcanic crater = urban demolition site—are moments of undecidability, non-coincident superimpositions, lines of conjecture leading off in other directions.

These switchings between the figurative and non-figurative will not work unless some degree of metatextuality is allowed to have its way. Montage presents us with drawings and photographs which are already reproductions of something that exists as a representation.[9] This metatextual distance is both a metatextuality, an idea of an event, and a re-embodiment of that idea in another order of reality. We cannot tell whether 'Les Ponts' is an ekphrastic account, or a direct contact with a reality/vision metaphorised as ekphrasis. This is perhaps the cusp on which Rimbaud's poems often situate themselves: a report of indexicality which allows all kinds of trajectory, intuition, manipulation, and an indexicality tempting us with ways back to a new referent (the boulevard in Baghdad). The unintelligibility that Rimbaud courts is not a question of semantics, but of perceptual position. And this uncertainty drives thought beyond text, into what Reynolds would call 'imaginary space', into the construction of possibility which will never find confirmation. We have what we have. This reality, for all its insistent indexicality, remains phantasmal: however much it is possible to sing 'la joie du travail nouveau', we still cannot elude 'les fabuleux fantômes des monts où l'on a dû se retrouver'. And inevitably one frequently encounters this particular modality of assertive supposition ('doit être plusieurs fois moins long', 'doit être tellement étrange', 'a dû se retrouver'), where 'devoir' is the *imperative* of conceptuality, of following force-lines.

By virtue of their conceptuality, every city contains any number of cities and any number of cityscapes. If the city is, thanks to its very opacity, the screen upon which we are bound to project our fantasies, if within the city we are already constructing cities, then Rimbaud's poetic language must have a similar opacity, must similarly refuse to yield a satisfactory signified, so that we are bound to invest each signifier with our own imaginary space. Conceptuality, as we use it here, is intimately tied to that condition of the process we have already had occasion to advert to on several occasions: the de-referentialisation of the indexical. Montage pursues this same programme. Through the *Verfremdungseffekt* it enacts on its constitutive photographs/drawings, the montage diverts them from what they would normally say about a moment that 'has been'. Montage asks us to question our relationship with photographs, the assumptions we make about their visibility, their evidential value and what they imply about the unchangeability of reality; at the same time it invites us to re-project them, but now as the malleable 'documents' of our own psyches.

The violences of montage, implied by the cutting out and superimposition of images, are the violence of the destruction of syntax, the violent ruptures of the non-consecutive, the violence of paradox in the service of thinking *à rebours*. These violences, these acts of revolution, destroy the officialised order of the family album and reduce it to the debris of the scrapbook. Like Benjamin's view of history, montage constantly recreates itself in the mind of the spectator/reader as temporary collocations of fragments, quotations, images; montage turns the voluntary memory of history into involuntary memory, and in so doing once again suggests what might be the true task of translation: to exercise the same kinds of violence on the ST, the cutting and pasting, the same processes of editing and engineering, but not as some wilful, vandalistic intervention, rather as a way of making better sense of what translation already has to do with plagiarism, citation, travesty, imitation, as a way of ensuring that translation is not an implicit endorsement of the official order, the literary canon, but a searching interrogation of it, and finally as a way of putting the reader at the centre of sense-making; voluntary memory is the recuperation of a sense already made, while involuntary memory, released by the fragmentation of the consecutive and the consequent liberation of chance, necessitates that sense shall be made ever again, in very private ecmnesic experiences.

If we have argued for montage as an inevitable product of the expansion of the ST as it makes its way across space and time, then we should also argue for it as an instrument of the dispersal of authorship, and an instrument of verbal engineering. The attraction of montage for socialist revolutionary ideology is, of course, its refusal of single-authoredness and the sense of presiding authorial presence. We may feel, on the basis of evidence already adduced, that Rimbaud still very much belongs to a tradition which expects an author to inform and take responsibility for his/her work. But translation, unavoidably, and desirably, is about the multiplication of authorship and this process is both epitomised in, and accelerated by, montage. Distributed authorship, not anonymity, is the goal. Translation on this reckoning is itself a process of socialisation, of conversion of the authordom/authority of the ST into a citizen-community of the TT.

As a brief coda to this chapter, I would like to offer a translation of 'Les Ponts' (see Appendix III (g), and Appendix II (xiii) for 'straight' translation). This poem has attracted plenty of critical attention, both structural and interpretative, and my preoccupation is, as ever, to do with the way it is textually perceived by the reader rather than with its meaning. I have revived the four-column presentation, last used for 'Enfance IV' in Chapter 4, for two reasons: first, I wanted to establish a text which infinitely repeats itself, which denies its own last sentence. The vertical layout destroys the pressure of the lateral edges, which is where, in pictures, frames makes their most insistent point about cutting off and closure; the edges of top and bottom (sky and earth) have a peculiar elasticity. Into this uncontrollable, free-falling reading experience, where the eye finds it so much more difficult to anticipate, to read ahead, repetition can insinuate itself almost before it is noticed. Rimbaud's cities constantly recycle the reader, while their conceptuality or force-lines lift the reader beyond the frame which wishes to confine or annul them.

But I also wished to enact the process of the entanglement of vision, of being caught up in a vertiginous spectacle which will not keep still, or come properly into focus (here again exacerbated, of course, by the almost exclusively plural forms). In other words, I wanted to show how problematic space is further complicated by the unremitting flow of time, by that metamorphic unfolding of the projector-voice. Previously, we have treated metamorphosis as pure changingness, a cinematic experience in which retinal retention is not the key to the moving image.[10] But here, in a Futurist universe, we need to incorporate the chronophotography of Marey, and its 'refinement' in the photodynamism of the Bragaglia brothers; we need to imagine a reading process in which an unending sequence of imbrications multiplies whatever we have in front of us:

> Indeed, all things move, all things run, all things are rapidly changing. A profile is never motionless before our eyes, but it constantly appears and disappears. On account of the persistency of an image upon the retina, moving objects constantly multiply themselves; their form changes like rapid vibrations, in their mad career. Thus a running horse has not four legs, but twenty, and their movements are triangular.
>
> ('Futurist Painting: Technical Manifesto 1912',
> in Apollonio 1973: 27–8)

Our solution is not as bold as this. But perhaps it gives a taste of the way that a certain kind of vision might communicate itself to the very act of reading it, to the very words on the paper asked to perform it. And one might, after all, wonder whether translation should not set out to achieve this: to translate the ST into the psychophysical experience its words convey. If the ST is an expanding text, then part of that expansion might well be the expansion of the text into a wraparound perceptual event. After all, for the Futurists, the priority is to put the spectator at the centre of the depicted subject.[11]

9

Translating the Space of Reading

In this final chapter, I want to get a little closer to a consideration of the page as reading space—a model of the psyche of the text, a model of the psyche of the reader—in order to underline the suggestion that translation is not just about the transference of a text from one language to another, but that it is also, and critically, about imagining the reader, projecting the reader into the translated text. One of the drawbacks of the policy of domestication, besides its 'stifling of the drums' with a coloniser's patois, is its implementation of non-confrontational and non-interrogative attitudes towards the text. The page is the creative and imaginative space of the translator, on to which the ST is mapped as it is translated. But we are also asking it to embody the psycho-perceptual posture of the reader, to be the inscription on the page of a mindset of reception, the spatial diary of a response. How does one achieve synomorphy between the spaces of the text and the spaces of the reading imagination, between the spaces of the text and the spaces of the translator's creative activity, between the spaces of the translator's creative activity and the spaces of the reading imagination? We are proposing that the attempt to establish this synomorphy, however difficult to negotiate, should be a central preoccupation of translation.

Of course, when we read a text silently, we are co-present with it. But there are many senses in which we are not 'face to face' with it: it does not return our gaze, it seems impervious to our scanning eyes, it bears no traces of us as we turn the page. In using the page to 'open up the text'—despite the text's being prose—we are not only trying to make its active textuality more visible (and, indeed, more active), but we are also branding it, marking it, with presences other than its own.

There are other reasons why we should open the text up. In their printed versions, all texts are 'fair copies'—we no longer see the changes of mind, the crossings out, and so on, and we are given the impression that the text flows forward in seamless consecutiveness, even though we know that it has probably been written, rewritten, reordered, on several different occasions. 'Freeing' the language of the prose poem is an attempt not only to give it more textual design, not only to involve the reader with it more rawly, more vulnerably, but also to draw the text back into its pre-published animation, uncertainty, ruggedness. The activation of the interpretative mode depends substantially for its justification on the text's having fallen into place, having achieved confidence in itself. How much is this confidence a matter of presentation?

If space helps to re-mobilise the text, to re-establish it as something thinkable rather than thought, then it does so partly by mobilising the text's acousticity: as we intimated in Chapter 3, a structuralist account of a text might lead us to assume that 'verbal music' inheres in the text, as part of its linguisticity, and can be recuperated as pattern, repetition, rhyme, anagram. The very stability of the music in the text allows translational strategies of compensation to be developed: 'I could not capture the alliterative where it occurs in the ST, so, in the TT, I have re-located it'. But a text's acousticity is principally about what you hear and how you hear it. What sounds does the readerly ear disengage from the tangled acoustic undergrowth? One reader hears the chain of /k/ and /kl/; another hears the play between the voiceless /k/ and the voiced /g/; another hears the distance between /k/ as velar stop and /v/ as labio-dental fricative; sometimes the same reader hears now one thing, now another. It is not sufficient to say that these things are all the linguistic 'facts' of the text and therefore audible. Audibility is no guarantee of hearing, audibility does not concern itself with different degrees and distributions of attention, and how a given text might engineer these. Translation should be less about mechanisms of acoustic compensation and more about 'stirring' (as one might porridge) textual audibility, engaging the listener's ear through the reader's eye. Reading a text is not about sifting out the self-selecting 'rhetoric' of acoustic figures (alliteration, rhyme, chiasmus), but bathing in the close-packed implicatedness of the many and multiplying acoustic relationships; as Eliot puts it, speaking of free verse: 'Rhyme removed, much ethereal music leaps up from the word, music which has hitherto chirped unnoticed in the expanse of prose' (1978: 189).

A word of some significance in Rimbaud's lexicon is 'rumeur'. In 'Enfance IV', 'la rumeur des écluses couvre mes pas'; in 'Fairy', there is reference to 'la rumeur du torrent sous la ruine des bois'; 'Villes II' tells us of 'la rumeur des perles et des conques précieuses', a collocation similar to the one we find in 'Mystique'; in 'Départ', we hear the 'Rumeurs des villes'; and the 'Génie' 'a fait la maison ouverte [. . .] à la rumeur de l'été'. Osmond (1976: 166) defines the word as 'A diffuse murmuring sound, which in Rimbaud almost invariably has very happy associations'. My own feeling is that the 'rumeur' is something of a gamble. It is not in itself so much a sound as a quality of sound which can be applied to a single source or can synthesize a cluster of sounds. It is the transferability and flexibility of the 'rumeur' which is significant; like its other persona (hearsay, gossip, passage of information), it is likely to spread, but its origin can only be guessed at and its 'authenticity' can never finally be confirmed. I take 'rumeur' to be the acoustic equivalent of the spectre, suspended between being and non-being, being and becoming, past trace and prefiguration of a future. I make this connection particularly on the basis of the close conjunction of 'sourd' and 'rumeur' in 'Being Beauteous': 'sourd' is the adjectival manifestation of the 'rumeur', muted, muffled often by distance, resistant to identification, never far from the hidden and secretive: 'Des sifflements de mort et des cercles de musique sourde font monter, s'élargir et trembler comme un spectre ce corps adoré' [Whistlings of death and circles of muffled music make this adored body rise, expand and tremble like a spectre]. Here, 'sourde' lives out its phonetic kinship with 'sourdre' ('Après le Déluge', 'Enfance I'): the 'rumeur' produces an eruption. But if 'rumeur' feels so often like the prelude to a revelation, the growing music, the orchestral conspiracy of phenomena, announcing a new life, it leaves us with some doubts: in 'Départ', the 'Rumeurs des villes' seem stuck in a rut, unable to release themselves in 'l'affection et le bruit neufs' that the poet sets out to pursue; and in 'Enfance IV', the 'rumeur'of the sluices drowns out the noise of the poet's footsteps, where we might expect the footsteps to signal creative momentum: 'Un pas de toi. C'est la levée des nouveaux hommes et leur en-marche' [You take a step. New men rise up and are on the march] ('A une Raison'); 'Son pas! Les migrations plus énormes que les anciennes invasions' [His step! Migrations more vast than the ancient invasions] ('Génie'). The 'rumeur' which does not realise itself in new noise, eruption, becomes inhibitive, immobilising.

One should add that, in the context of 'Mystique', which is our first text for translation in this chapter (see Appendix II (xiv) for 'straight' translation), and as in 'Villes II', the 'rumeur' is connected with the conch, which is the carriage of Venus, the trumpet of Triton (tritons), the merman—love and the unknown of hybridity. But the conch is also the concha, the external ear, the organ which hears the sound of the sea held in the conch. There is matter enough here for human nights.

'Rumeur' is important for my translation, not only because it poses a lexical challenge, but also because it constitutes for me an image of the (Rimbaldian) poem as a whole. I have 'solved' the lexical problem by expressing the muffled, undifferentiable nature of the sound in 'distant' and by suggesting that the surf is a synthesis of all the sounds and instruments of the sea. The 'rumeur' is also a dynamic impulse, a muted straining towards a liberation of new music, vision, which I have tried to encapsulate in 'surge'.

We might argue that the final two paragraphs express an opposition more strongly than they do a simultaneity: 'la bande' (banner? scroll? planar band of sky/sea?) is cast in a passive role by a verb which conveys shape but no activity, despite 'tournante' and 'bondissante' (suspended animation?), while the 'douceur fleurie des étoiles [. . .]' both descends and 'fait l'abîme'. As Anne Freadman persuasively argues, Rimbaud uses 'abîme' here not as a noun object, but as a noun complement; that is, 'faire' is to be treated as a transforming attributive (hence my translation by 'becomes'):

> In *la douceur fleurie des étoiles et du ciel et du reste . . . fait l'abîme*, the *terminus a quo* and the *terminus ad quem* of the metaphor are both expressed, but together they describe not an analogy, but the process of metamorphosis. One 'thing' is changed into another by means of the transference of its properties. Indeed, it is one of the properties of these 'things' that they can transform themselves, and this is the significance of the variant of the metaphoric *faire* that we find in 'Bottom': 'tout se fit ombre et aquarium ardent'. Rimbaud's metaphors are used both to project the identical into the other and to transform a 'thing' into its opposite. [. . .] It becomes possible to suggest that the *myth of metaphor* underlies the ideology of 'changer la vie': the metaphoric process would be the instrument of change, while the resulting metaphor would be *la vie changée* that is, *l'inconnu*.
>
> (1974: 71–2)

This kind of argument bears out, to some extent, our promotion of the metamorphic voice in Chapter 4. But the metamorphic voice brings other consequences to bear on the Rimbaldian ideology: *l'inconnu* as consistently disappears as it is produced; life is changed in a process of constant change which threatens to make all change a memory. If the printed text has the advantage of maintaining, suspended, this process of change, it now makes metaphor serve analogy, or identification, rather than metamorphosis, and leaves change as that which can always be envisaged but never accomplished (hence our argument about indexicality and conceptuality in the previous chapter).

Before moving on to suggest some way out of this dilemma and to explore the consequences of thinking of the text as a 'rumeur', I would like to look briefly aside at translation. 'La douceur fleurie des étoiles et du ciel et du reste' (ST) becomes 'l'abîme fleurant et bleu là-dessous' (TT); the past participle, that is, a possessed quality which is part of the ST's attractiveness, becomes the present participle, that is, part of the TT's future-projected activity; 'fleurant' is 'fleurie' performed, so that it recovers its ability not to be *there*, displayed, in space/time, but to espouse the motions of space/time, to change space/time. At the same time, the TT compels the ST to say 'Je est un autre', to transfer its properties in such a way as to transform itself; above all, not to hang on to itself, but to let itself go into its otherness. This process is justified not only by the fact that the ST is willy-nilly going into (creating?) a new (other) language, but also because it is in the nature of language to be shifting its ground, both in relation to other languages and in relation to its own stock. Structuralist views may tempt us with systems in which each component finds its differential niche and in which the reliability and describability of the system depends on its holding still. Any enterprise which encourages the signifier to exceed the signified, any enterprise which allows words to flaunt their materiality and thus summon forth the demons of paronomasia, anagram, homonymy, and all the follies of verbal perception, will make of the system a mobile and unsteady architecture, constantly having to reconfigure itself in order to stay upright. Translation should set language systems in motion by the very gift of untranslatability; notions like 'equivalence' and 'compensation', by their very overtones of quantifiability and measurability, imply the confrontation of two stable, ready-formed systems; we still need to imagine a translation practice designed expressly to undermine systems, to frustrate contrastive linguistics and to institute exchanges deemed to be negotiable in any currency.

In suggesting that we think of the poem as a whole as a 'rumeur' of words, I have two things in mind. We have already had occasion in earlier chapters to speak of the transphrastic activity of morphemes, phonemes, graphemes: these elements, disseminated across the text, not only begin to suggest the traversal of the text by Kristevan semiotic pulsions, but imply an alternative mode of sense-making which emanates, precisely, from the activation of language's very materiality, rather than from its grammatical or syntactic structures. This is the 'rumeur' of language, the complex white noise by which the voice is accompanied as it reads aloud. But in order to bring this 'rumeur' to awareness, as a synthesis of discrete but nondifferentiable noises, as a gathering of the half-heard and half-concealed, which might produce an explosion of experience, one needs to explode the text, so that the reader *puts together into* 'rumeur' what asks to come apart again as constellations of separate sounds, colours, visual sensations (see Appendix III (h)). This is not a poem which, like a concrete poem, can be looked at, eye-scanned; it must be read, drawn together in a 'rumeur'. In other words, I am trying to reverse one process by another, in a double movement: I have undone the prose poem in order to give relief to particular words, pacings, pausings, groupings, and used different sizes of font to diversify rhythms of attention and the ways in which the eye recuperates the text. In asking the reader to read the text, I am also asking him/her to undo what I have done and reconstitute the prose poem; at the same time this reading, the reading of the 'rumeur', should produce that Rimbaldian 'éclatement', 'éparpillement', 'dégagement' which is departure into a new sound-world.

But I also wanted to suggest the mobility of the 'rumeur', the fact that, as we have already noted, it is not so much a sound in itself as a quality of sound produced by a wide variety of phenomena. The 'rumeur', with each reading, will never quite be the same; the inflexions will be slightly different, as will the mix. The 'rumeur' is transferable and, within its ostensibly generalised singleness, polymorphous. I have tried to capture this characteristic by the simple device of producing variations of disposition, without changing either language or fonts (see Appendix III (i) and (j)). Font-changes might have sophisticated the process, but my principal interest is not in what advances or recedes in the ear, but in how words/sounds are gathered into 'collective nouns' by the reading eye. I would add that this kind of exercise, simple though it is, serves to remind us that texts are usually presented to us as all but inert; this inertiality has, paradoxically, to do with the definitiveness of the ST. But translation asks the ST to change, to resume its life, its doubts about itself, a life whose traces are still to be found in its variants. The text counters the reader's desire interpretatively to take possession of it by never being ready.

It will be clear that by proposing a dialectical reading process and by making multi-translation a *sine qua non* of the translation of 'rumeur', I am trying to solve the dilemma adverted to earlier, by which change into the new, the unknown, is either repeatedly self-cancelling or toyed with but never enjoyed. It might be objected that these 'options' are not as mutually exclusive as I am proposing, that the alert reader can both have his cake and eat it. I am seeking a way in which to combine both experiences *inevitably*, by complicating the relationship between temporality and spatiality, between linearity and recurrence. The text must be read, but it is not easy to read through; the text can be read again, but only with a displacement of its 'rumeur'. It is intended to have a Heraclitean momentum, but its flux is decelerated by resistant spatiality. Between Étienne-Jules Marey's arrested analyses of the kinetic phases of movement and the indecipherable blur of synthesised motion lies the photodynamism of the Bragaglia brothers. It is this middle ground that I am trying to locate with translation.

Alberto Manguel may be able to supply us with some metaphors for reading (1996: 163–73) and remind us how important the physical context of reading is. But few commentators concern themselves with the reader's perceptual habits, as the eye negotiates the page. The main obstacle to any effort to embody the psycho-perceptual space of reading is the same as that to be encountered in any discussion of paralinguisticity. Paralinguisticity is either (i) readerly input that can be described in very general terms, but which cannot be captured in any detail, quantified, catered for in writing or criticism; or (ii) it is largely dictated by linguisticity, by what is already in the text, and thus remains implicit, textually unenacted. This book is suggesting that the TT should be much more involved with paralinguisticity than the ST, that translation is peculiarly concerned with constructing paralinguistic environments for the ST, so that it is both participated in by the reader and endowed with a wider range of expressive possibility and formal realisation. In other words, the inscription of the paralinguistic into the text is a feature of the literariness peculiar to translation (hence our emphasis on free verse as a translational medium, hence our general concern with 'subtextual' inputs like punctuation, typography, margins). Space as a paralinguistic feature has principally to do with segmentation and the consequent dynamics of a text, and with the nature of readerly attention (quality, pacing, distribution). This latter includes differences of focal point: is the materiality of language in focus, or is the focal point beyond language (i.e. does the eye de-semanticise or semanticise the text?)? This differentiation, certainly for the purposes of developing an art of translational presentation, might be more profitably imagined as that between the haptic and the optic.

This dichotomy, established by Alois Riegl, differentiates between, on the one hand, touching with the eye (the haptic), visually palpating the world for texture and surface, and, on the other, tracing shape and volume (the optic), the 'pure vectoriality of outlines' (Gandelman 1991: ix), visually scanning the world for linear configuration. This distinction coincides, roughly speaking, with Wölfflin's distinction between 'das Malerische' (painterly) and 'das Linearische' (linear) and with that made between German and Italian printmakers of the Renaissance by William

Crawford, in his discussion of William Ivins's *Prints and Visual Communication* (1953):

> The Germans filled their pictures with indications of surface texture, often with a dutiful singlemindedness that sacrificed the illusion of volume beneath the surface. The Italians did the opposite. They sacrificed texture while achieving the illusion of volume by stressing outline and contour, using simple lines.
>
> (1979: 3)

The haptic is the world of disorder, the world of matter seen in close up, the pigment of language, the unfinished, the 'noisy' (Gandelman 1991: 141–3). There are obvious ways in which one can lay bare the raw materials of literary construction: we have, in the previous chapter, considered montage, and the concrete poetry of the sixth chapter pursues an entropic principle which promises a language of nothing but noise. But any literary construct which foregrounds the materiality of language at the expense of sense transforms acousticity from a supportive role as instrument of euphony, of aural fluency, and semantic highlighter, to an independent and interfering organism, projecting vocalic grain, reducing utterance and melody to '-lalia' and hubbub. In the third paragraph of 'Mystique'—'Et tandis que la bande en haut du tableau est formée de la rumeur tournante et bondissante des conques des mers et des nuits humaines'—I can pick out the alliterations in /t/ and /b/ and /d/ and /m/, or the assonances in /ã/, /ɔ̃/, /e/, /o/, /u/, /ɛ/, /y/, and either reassimilate them into the words as modes of linkage, disposition, repetition, verbal music reinforcing the coherence and cohesiveness of the syntactic structure (the optic perception), or let these sound patterns establish their own acoustic granularity as voiced or unvoiced, resonant or obstruent, dental or velar, rounded or unrounded, back or front, and so on (the haptic perception). Within this buccal, glottal, laryngal activity what matters is less the sound that is produced than the ways in which movements of the lips or tongue, nasality, allow voice to engage other senses, touch, taste, smell. Language begins to acquire the sensory density necessary if Rimbaud is to launch his new language which 'sera de l'âme pour l'âme, résumant tout, parfums, sons, couleurs' [will be of the soul, for the soul, synthesising everything, perfumes, sounds, colours]. I might have translated the haptic perception of the poem by using fonts and typefaces to pick out acoustic threads or patterns of graphemes: for example,

And w̲h̲i̲Le the band at the top of the pIcture is made of

the dIstant wh<u>eeL</u>Iing and Leap Ing surf- surge of conches
and human nights.

I have not highlighted all the acoustic kinships here, but one can begin to
see how the 'wordness' of the word begins to disintegrate, and how
multiplied are the claims on attention, how easy it is to believe that
conventional syntax is no longer the mechanism by which this language is
articulated.

But instead of this device, I have resorted to a set of three superimposed
printings (see Appendix III (k)), with the intention of varying the density
of the verbal surface, not only so that it acquires a tactility through its
unevenness, as though one might try to brush some of the obstructive
words away, but also so that the letters themselves have a certain thickness
(however wafer-thin) and seem to exist in three-dimensional space.
Furthermore, in this version, the superimposition does not, as in 'Les
Ponts' merely seek to enact retinal retention, or after-image; that is to say,
the relationship between a word and its 'shadow(s)' is not a consistent one;
instead, we will either have the sense of a snapshot of words positively
floating in different planes, on the move and arrested only by the camera
of the page; or we will look upon this as a superimposition of transparent
sheets, carrying versions of the poem laid out in different dispositions.
Either way, language does not just have the materiality of its look or its
sound; it now has a materiality of being, a tactility which brings that
language, through the fact of physical existence, into real time. As a printed
text, language, however materially it may function in the voice, however
graphically expressive its layout and graphemes may be, will still exist in
a transcendental time, the time of the page's whiteness or of its own infinite
reproducibility.[1] Presented haptically, language *begins* to return to a
temporality of the here and now, of the contingent, the random, so that
reading becomes more like an encounter with the text, not because the text
uses eye-catching fonts, underlinings and so on, but because language is
in relief, stands away from its support, is not merely a feature of that
support. Like the impasto of the Impressionists, these superimposed
printings guarantee or embody a moment of sensory contact; they *grow
from* and re-enact that moment of contact, celebrate it, insist upon it, rather
than merely allowing it. And we miss the point if we merely preoccupy
ourselves with the difficulty of reading it, or at least, we will miss the point
if we misunderstand the difficulty of reading it. The difficulty of reading
this text should not be felt to derive from deliberate interference with the
underlying conditions of visibility, but from the very difficulty of reading
the text; the text was already opaque, resistant in its materiality, something

which could only *accumulate*, rather than sift out, meanings. There never was an originary visibility. It is not difficulty which is artifice, but visibility, and inasmuch as interpretation is about making visible, it is as artificial as the bounding of mass and space by lines, or the insistence on the perceptual reality of local colour. Difficulty is the acknowledgement of the necessary engagement of intuition, of a contact whose wholeness makes it communicable but not describable, communicable in its indescribability.

If, on our argument, the haptic actively promotes visual difficulty, then the optic seems to will the opposite, to scan for connections and positions, to map a coherence, the belonging together of parts. The optic takes the line of least resistance and least distraction, the *trace*, the *conventions* of depiction (modelling, scale, direction, perspectival relationship). Inevitably, therefore, I have chosen to represent this mode of visual conduct by the tracing of putative eye-movements across the poem (see Appendix III (l)) of the kind recorded by A.L. Yarbus, by David Noton and Lawrence Stark, and by E. Llewellyn Thomas (Gandelman 1991: 6–13), for both texts and paintings. These eye-movements (movements of the fovea within the retina), or saccades, gather the text in, plot what it utters in a back-and-forth of relating, pursuing, at one and the same time, the syntax of the written and the syntax of the depicted. What the trace recounts is the need to see the picture whole, to uncover the informing coherence, and at the same time to identify the 'points of fixation', at the extremities of the lines, the beginnings of a haptic engagement, but only at those points which might turn out to be the key moments of the picture's meaning. More fundamentally perhaps the optic elides the presence of the artist, the picture as style and signature, the bearer of that qualitative presence which so preoccupies the haptic.

These two 'options' are imagined as the polar extremities of reading, an attempt to perform on the page the modes of perception between which any reading will find any number of intermediate positions. In our simplification, the reader is attempting to negotiate between the urge to see a topography and the desire to dwell in the text's enveloping verbal textures, where the anxiety of interpretation no longer demands an outcome.

Once again, we must return to the ambitions of translation. Whatever else we want translation to do, we want it to test the assumptions of reading, to confront the reader with habits of verbal perception. In some senses, there is no understanding of other translational issues—linguistic, cultural, gender—unless there is, first, a confrontation of the reader with the perceptual/cognitive processes to which reading itself might be subject. But more crucially perhaps, translation is the way we sensitise ourselves to our own habits and desires as readers, to the personal ways in which we process verbal materials.

This is to suggest that the responsibilities of translation are larger than one might believe. The mediatorial role that the translator finds himself in, does not coincide with that of the international diplomat, however much translators may wish this role upon themselves. The translator is not someone who by explicit function arrogates to himself the task of making cultural and ideological decisions on behalf of his readers and in his readers' absence. Translation should set itself the task of dealing reader (translator) to reader, to empower the reader to make his/her own decisions about interventions. In order for this to happen effectively, not only must the reader be fully informed of the strategies adopted by the translator and the decisions made, but the reader must also be brought to an awareness, by textual layout, of the modes of exploration and absorption we customarily use. Criticism has its own assumptions about what reading is, but these are predicated, in rather circular fashion, on the nature of the textual meaning to be extracted. Translation has the ability to alert us to these elisions and reveal us to ourselves as readers, by challenging us, or persuading us, with particular agendas embodied in certain typographical arrangements and spatial dispositions.

But my visual preoccupation with 'Mystique' is not quite complete. Anne Freadman makes the suggestion that:

> The *talus* is an image of convexity, reinforced by such subsidiary images as *mamelon, sommet* and *arête*, and attenuated in the *courbe* of sentence 3. *L'abîme* is an image of concavity, as are *les conques* and *le panier*. The contrast between these two concepts leads to a further contrast: the images of convexity are defined *in* a space, are contained by it and points in this space are articulated as directions as well as positions. But the space itself has no shape. The opposite is true of the concave images, which define the shape of the space which they contain. The function of space is subordinated to the shaping of matter in part A, while in part B, matter participates in the shaping of space.
>
> (1974: 76)

These are interesting observations and persuade Freadman to a reading in which a given, fully formed universe (convex) is destroyed by the 'homicides' and the 'batailles' (horizontal); from this grows an incipient process of regeneration which finds its full flowering in a new act of creation (concave). From a landscape in which objects push their way into a space without shape or resistance, without being contained by it, we move to one in which space is gathered and sculpted by objects within their own yielding outlines. My first 'illustrated' version of the text (see Appendix III (m)) is an attempt to make the poem itself this experience of concavity, gathering the vision into the encompassing arms of the 'panier' simile, itself seen as an expanding sequence of concave lines as it swivels down, releasing flowers/stars upwards again, as 'fleurie' becomes 'fleurant'. In this way the 'panier' figure becomes the image of the reading mind, drawing the poem in, giving shape to its space, without destroying its textuality, and as if regurgitating it again, but this time inhabited by, coloured by, the reading mind's activity. A mark of this activity is to be found in the encirclement or isolation of 'nights', because night ('the blue flowering abyss beneath') is the poem's visionary destination, and because 'human nights' are that black which is the sum of all pasts and source of all futures, the colour of transition. Dawn's arrival and night's departure will always produce that procession which is part funeral cortege, part circus train ('Ornières'); these nights are perhaps the 'fêtes de (la) nuit' that we find in 'Vies III' and 'Villes II', or the midsummer nights (and their dreams of new loves) alluded to in 'Parade' and 'Ville'.

But is Py right to affirm of 'Mystique', and we to imply, that 'En fait, seule la perception globale de "tous les sens fondues en un" permet de *lire* le poème' [In fact, only the global perception of 'all the senses melted into one' allows one to *read* the poem]—that here, once again Rimbaud is speaking his universal language (1967: 152). The danger of such a view is that it solves the 'problem' of Rimbaldian space by homogenising it as, precisely, universal. In similar fashion, to cast Rimbaud as a syncretist and cosmopolitan is to cast him as a space-collapsing or space-compressing eclectic, helping the geography and topography of an entire world to converge on a promontory. But the contrary view would be that Rimbaud compels us into spaces we can hardly get our minds round, in which multidimensionality and the pressure to imagine it, compel the eye to localised brief encounters of an aggregational kind, where the aggregation will not stand as anything other than as a sculpture seen in degrees of rotation. The spaces of 'Mystique', for example, seem to set out from a fairly 'in-place' disposition which coincides with the reading of the page: top > bottom, left > right. But outlines twist into new configurations—e.g. the line of the 'pente du talus' is 'spiralised' by the wheeling robes; upshooting tongues of flame round off to the 'mamelon'—top and bottom are inverted before our eyes. It is a scene in which the distances between planes or traversed by perspectival lines are difficult to judge because our sense of the geometry of the site is constantly dispersed by abstraction and/or pluralisation, or is masked by images interposed or seen in close up: 'les herbages d'acier et d'émeraude'; 'descend [. . .] contre notre face'. Indeed, as I read this poem, I feel space expanding and contracting like a concertina: and this changing perceptual experience is engineered not only by movements and lines, but by the perceptual modalities of words themselves: the difference between 'fleurie' and 'fleurant', for example, is the difference between being outside and distant enough perceptually to encompass (already-formedness) ('fleurie'), and being enveloped by, or within, and unable visually to control a diversification ('fleurant'). But it is not easy reliably to distinguish between experiences of 'insideness' and those of 'outsideness'. And, equally, we may begin to question the certainty of the distinction made by Freadman between the convex and the concave, shapeless and shaped space. Is the 'talus' convex or concave? The curve of the 'panier' or the conch is concave or convex depending on one's position. Indeed, one might say the same of any curve or curved object. And, correspondingly, space may be either shaped or shapeless, turn from one to the other and back, according to whether our minds isolate objects (in spaces of their own), or fit them snugly into a total, quantified, integrated, yielding environment.[2] It is altogether less demanding to adopt a ready-triangulated space or landscape, and read off against it whatever spatial indications there are, however unaccommodating. Thus we 'explain' the closing paragraphs of 'Mystique' as the motionless firmament of the starry sky reflected in the restless, protean surface of the sea: the sea in the sky of the penultimate paragraph is inverted into the sky in the sea of the final paragraph. Or if we take the repetition of 'talus' to be confirmation of a single underlying rural landscape, then 'l'abîme fleurant et bleu' might be ground falling away to a flowery dell. But the translation of Rimbaud's notations back into a tableau, a framed spatial disposition (Van Eyck's Ghent altarpiece, *Mystic Lamb*?) is surely not what the transformative text of 'Mystique' proposes.[3] And, besides, it would represent the suppression of the haptic by the optic.

Visually, the haptic seems to find its consummation in Impressionism. Impressionist *touches* have that fleeting gesturality which confirms them as a performance of real visual-physical contact in real time, confirms their indexicality But what we perhaps mean is that Impressionism most highly polarises the haptic and the optic, whose order is proportional to the transcendent nature of its temporality. For what Impressionism produces is the nervous mobility of the spectator, a spectator made schizoid by imperatives of double focus, the painted surface and the represented scene. In the end, Impressionist pictures do not place the spectator, they displace him, first by turning spectation into a perambulating activity—back and forth across the canvas, back from the canvas's surface and forwards towards it—and second, by frequently interposing other, better placed spectators, within the picture, between himself and the scene depicted. Cubism shares this disorientation of the spectator, by erasing the single point of view and concealing the object in its own structure. Like Impressionism, Cubism intensifies the conflicting demands of the painted surface and the represented image (look at/look through), 'psychologises' the process of spectation and eradicates the distinction between space and matter. Like Impressionism's gestural manner, Cubism's low relief and non-perspectival, non-volumetric shading encourage a haptic ocular attitude, although ocular possession is resisted by the multiplied, virtual light, by the disintegration of the sense of surface and by the abstractness of texture. And just as Impressionism's divisionism, its scattering of light in the spectrum of colours, recalls the text's transphrastic dispersal of its acousticity, the myriad colour highlights of its phonemes, so Cubism, monochromatic though it may be in its analytic phase, effects something of the same dispersal in the multiplication of its imbricated surfaces and angles.

But the Cubist model is particularly to our present purpose, because it sits on the interface between what the eye sees and what the mind can conjecture; it shows us objects in complex structures of surface, but it provides, too, an absence of (visual) information about spatial relationships, about distances between planes, about angles. In this sense, Cubism picks up the 'conceptual' of our previous chapter more satisfactorily than Impressionism does. The Cubist object is a conceptualised trace of perceptual events, a conglomeration of perceptual events which cannot itself survive as a percept. As we move into our final translational encounter, with 'Antique', we shall perhaps see Cubism's relevance more clearly.

The puzzles presented by 'Antique' (see Appendix II (xv) for a 'straight' translation) resolve themselves into two underlying concerns: the reading of the overall 'situation' and of the final sentence in particular. The son of Pan (satyr, faun) is a statue (Py 1967: 99), brought to life Galatea-like, or 'une vision onirique volontaire, commandée' (Brunel 1998: 193) [a dream vision, willed, expressly conjured up], a sly subversion of the 'blason' (Raybaud calls it a 'dé-représentation' [1989: 13]). The potential sources of the hermaphroditic element ('où dort le double sexe'), from Ovid to Swinburne, have been comprehensively surveyed by Guyaux (1991: 85–105), who also offers an assessment of the way in which 'Antique' relates to contemporary decadent and symbolist accounts of androgyny:

Le texte de Rimbaud est au plus loin de l'hermaphroditisme
morbide' de la fin du XIXᵉ siècle. [. . .] L'hermaphrodite rimbaldien
n'est pas caractérisé par l'inflexion d'un sexe vers l'autre comme
chez les pré-Raphaélites ou chez les peintres de la Renaissance
interprétés par Péladan ou par Huysmans: le *double sexe* est une
grâce et une force cumulées, une puissance. Comme la Lesbos de
Baudelaire, cet autre fantasme qui tient tête aux vastes utopias,
l'*Antique* de Rimbaud n'appartient qu'à lui.

(105)

[Rimbaud's text is at the furthest pole from the 'morbid
hermaphroditism' of the end of the nineteenth century. The
Rimbaldian hermaphrodite is not characterised by the inflection of
one sex towards the other, as in the work of the Pre-Raphaelites or
the Renaissance painters as interpreted by Péladan or Huysmans:
the 'double sex' is simultaneously a grace and a force, a power. Like
Baudelaire's Lesbos, that other fantasy that hold its own against the
vast utopias, Rimbaud's 'Antique' belongs only to him.]

As for the final sentence, Brunel is of the view that it represents the
'démarche [. . .] d'un danseur' (1998: 193–4) [gait (. . .) of a dancer], a
precise, studied choreography; Py sees it as motion slowed down by visual
fragmentation: 'une marche remarquablement ralentie par la
fragmentation de la perception visuelle en trois temps' (1967: 100) [a
walking motion remarkably slowed down by the fragmentation of visual
perception into three stages]. For Osmond, it accurately depicts the faun's
preparing to walk, 'flexing the right thigh, and then moving the left leg in
stages: first flexing that thigh, then swinging the entire leg off the ground'
(1976: 101); Bernard/Guyaux laconically quote Ernest Delahaye:
'L'attention de l'observateur s'est arrêtée sur une seule partie de la
première jambe, sur les deux parties de la seconde' (2000: 534) [The
observer's attention has become fixated on a single part of the first leg and
on both parts of the second].

In view of these perceptual ambiguities—because, after all, they are
perceptual rather than interpretative—there is every justification for taking
up Osmond's implicit invitation: 'After Rimbaud, other artists have
portrayed the human body in the form of a musical instrument (e.g. the
Cubist painters)' (1976: 102) (see Appendix III (p)). In this rendering of
'Antique', a Cubist figure is asked to inform our reading of a text; the
graphic figure is a presence in which is grounded a presiding awareness.
The figure is designed to replace the title, or vie with the title, as a reference
point; or is designed to act as a point of destination for the title's point of

departure (we shall have more to say about titles in a moment). And the variations in font, as well as establishing particular kinships between individual words and between particular phonemes/graphemes, are designed to suggest that lexical items are set at different depths in a relief, or at different angles to each other. But this is not writing cubistically; it is writing to the tune of a cubistic totem. This still seems to me an important undertaking, however literal and embryonic the means, simply because one of our arguments is that translation should diversify modes of apprehending the text (taking intervening time and space into account), rather than fossilise meanings that criticism has already made available, or perform conventional linguistic transformations which only go to fossilize differences, the very life-blood and licence of translational creativity. In making a text available to 'domestic' audiences, the translator should also make available ways of reading it, make available the TT's availability to further mutations. The translator must set out to undermine his own (interpretative) authority in order to empower the reader, yes, but also to protect a creative freedom.

The faun crosses borders: between the human and the animal, the animate and the inanimate, the visual and the musical, the masculine and the feminine. The second sentence—'Autour de ton front [. . .] tes yeux [. . .] remuent'—suggests a reversal of perspective in mid-sentence, from the viewed to the viewing, or a multiplication of eyes as their changing positions are precipitated out of a head turning backwards and forwards. This, like other Rimbaldian poems, is a text in which different modes of representation compete, different syntaxes, different temporalities (punctual, iterative, continuous, omnitemporal). It is Cubism which destabilises space, recreating it and at the same time making it unrecognisable: portrait is like still life is like landscape. We have spoken much about Rimbaud's play with the ekphrastic; Cubism is, we might say, the point at which ekphrasis, the mediation of the visual by the verbal, finally breaks down, proves inoperative, and the spectator/reader is left without the wherewithal to shape vision, is left with only a visceral response. This is the point at which Cubism endows the visually problematic with psychological repercussions;[4] we cannot take part in the picture's staging of its own meaning; the picture's staging draws out our responses, is the instrument of our perceptual self-exploration, without providing confirmation or advice.

In the previous chapter we looked at the way in which, in our reading of Rimbaud, the perceptual can cross over into the conceptual; we can see how the non-consecutivity of his writing will multiply perspectives and sources of light; we can see how, in turn, these processes will localise and problematise space—spaces of depiction and spaces of perception, spaces of creation and spaces of recognition, spaces occupied and spaces vacant. In particular, this broad affiliation with Cubism might be described in what it presupposes about mode of reading. Cubist titles measure distances between the 'represented' and the 'representant' (the canvas). It is usual to assume that the title is the destination of the image, the place we have to find our way from and back to; the title, when repossessed is now replete with the picture. In analytic Cubism, we start out from the title and the destination disappears. Instead of providing us with meanings which take us back to the title as a repository of those meanings, the image provides us with *access to* what the title might become. The title designates the content of a picture which the content of the picture is unwilling to designate. The title also acts as a guarantee of the prior existence of the subject; in Cubism, the picture/text works to cast this priority into doubt by restoring the object to the inchoateness of perceptual encounter, to a conglomeration of sensory experiences. This predicament is exacerbated in Rimbaud's work where titles are often already oblique and even difficult to identify as parts of speech ('Antique', 'Mystique', 'Barbare', 'Being Beauteous', 'Fairy', 'H').

Thus the object cannot be spoken about, since the only narrative available is the object's very constitution. In 'Antique', what might have been a 'blason', itemising and celebrating bodily features in their achieved 'characteristicity', must be a 'contre-blason', in which body-parts only ease themselves into perception, in which itemisation, far from enacting vicarious possession, must constantly give ground to objects in the process of self-constitution. The difference in syntactical terms, simply put, is between a noun + copula + predicative adjective ('blason') and a noun + verb ('contre-blason'): 'Tachées de lies brunes, tes joues se creusent'— after the promise of stasis in the past participle, does 'se creusent' follow a standard usage ('affectent une forme creuse') or does it regather some of its verbal unsteadiness? How dark/shadowed do the cheeks become? Is this a continuous form of the present, a progressive form, or even a present which completes itself as we watch? Even 'Ta poitrine ressemble à une cithare', which seems closest of all to the tribute of 'blason', the present, at once punctual and omnitemporal, begins to come undone in its continuation—'des tintements circulent dans tes bras blonds'—in which the musical instrument becomes a music which dissolves into activity impossible to locate. What does 'circuler dans' really mean: 'tinklings circulate through your pale arms' (Varèse 1957: 25); 'plucked notes run in your pale arms' (Bernard 1962: 243); 'tinklings move up and down your white arms' (Fowlie 1966: 227); 'Tinklings vibrate in your blond arms'

(Schmidt 1976: 159); 'in your fair arms music rises and falls' (Sloate 1990: 33); 'tinkling notes move about your blond arms' (Treharne 1998: 71); 'a trickle of notes runs round your blond arms' (Sorrell 2001: 265)? What these translations most valuably reveal perhaps is not that 'circuler dans' is hard to translate, but that reading a Rimbaldian poem, like looking at a Cubist picture, involves us in a here and now not so much of contact and response (Impressionist impasto), but of intuition and negotiation; as Jennifer Pap puts it, apropos of Reverdy's Cubism:

> Thus, for Reverdy, perception of the image-object is not a simple possession of it or absorption of/into it, but rather the difficult construction of thought, cast as a net around the object. The net— or web—is not an instrument that grasps, but the pattern of our ideas of the object and its own connections to the world. Like Kahnweiler, he brings concept and vision to bear simultaneously on the object, but the poet also makes the viewer's body an integral part of the new relation to the object.
>
> (1997: 172)

How is translation itself to achieve this net-casting relationship with the source text, to avoid the grasping and appropriation? Multiple translation may be a way of getting all the meanings out of a text (see Garfitt 1998); but more valuably perhaps, multiple translation is a way of 'constructing thought' about a text, and this thought is not so much caught in the ST's semantic teleology, as preoccupied with the effectiveness of its own means to diversify and perpetuate the literary life of the ST. I do not envisage different presentations of the TT in order to *do justice to* the ST (how could one ever know what that means), but in order to multiply the ways in which it might be active in our minds.

David Hockney laboured to make clear that, for him at least, Cubism was not about the object but about the experience of perception;[5] that Cubism was not about the translation of an iconic relation to reality into an autonomy independent of reality, but a compacted narrative of a sensory exploration of reality which could be unfolded out of the composite picture rather like an oriental scroll. Against this view might be set Jacques Rivière's observation that Cubism abandoned conventional lighting because it tied the object to time, the single moment, and thus became an obstacle to the emergence of the object's true structure or essence (Pap, quoting Fry 1997: 178). This potential contradiction at Cubism's heart is acted out in 'Antique' by the tension between the possessive and demonstrative adjectives. Within the context of a 'blason', the possessive, the second-person possessive, is the index of the 'characteristicity' of the bodily feature and of a literary strategy: the more I say it is yours, the more I make it mine. Referentiality seems to be safely in place, the record of a particular thing seen, as long as 'you' is *you*. But referentiality is undone by the restlessness of the verbs and the equivocations of prepositions. With the arrival of the demonstrative in the sixth sentence—'Ton cœur bat dans ce ventre où dort le double sexe'—a new perceptual orientation is installed. Bivort (1991: 92) identifies these demonstratives as part endophoric (intratextual/cotextual), part exophoric (extratextual/contextual) and, in relation to the possessives, harbingers of an attitudinal shift:

> En fait, le démonstratif est là pour empêcher l'identification directe avec le référent du poème, ici le possesseur des parties du corps déterminées par l'adjectif possessif; on sait que le centre du poème, 'le double sexe', caractérise l'antique [. . .] comme étant un hermaphrodite. Or Hermaphrodite est au départ un être masculin (fils d'Hermès et d'Aphrodite) dans le corps duquel s'est fondu celui d'une nymphe, Salmacis. Rimbaud présente son antique à l'image du centaure ou de la sirène, créatures bipartites: la partie supérieure du corps est masculine ('Gracieux *fils* de Pan!'), l'inférieure, féminine surajoutée (le ventre, aussi métonymie pour sexe féminine).
>
> [In fact, the demonstrative is there to prevent any direct identification with the poem's referent, here the possessor of the parts of the body determined by the possessive adjective; we know that the poem's centre, 'the double sex', characterises the 'antique' (. . .) as being an hermaphrodite. Now Hermaphrodite was to begin with a masculine being (son of Hermes and Aphrodite) whose body blended with that of a nymph, Salmacis. Rimbaud presents his 'antique' in the likeness of a centaur or siren, bipartite creatures: the upper part of the body is masculine ('Gracieux *fils* de Pan!'), the lower part, feminine, added (the belly, also a metonymy for the female genitalia).]

Bivort adds that the demonstrative has a slightly pejorative value, particularly when set beside the appreciative adjectival phrases and appositions which accompany the anatomy of the upper body. This is certainly a convincing proposition. From a Cubist point of view, we watch the move from a view of the object in which, though angles of vision change, a narrating identity is maintained—(nominative) > vocative, (my)

> your—as is an absorptive process: these early lines are an itinerary through 'yourness', which seems to necessitate imagistic elaboration as a fixative, towards a view which, though deictic, is third-person and expulsive—as the Cubist painting redefines the relationship between spectator and object, as it re-defines the object through its problematic perceptibility, so the spectator loses his controlling point of view/narratorial position and is, to all intents and purposes, ousted from the picture, which assumes the determination of its own visibility. Like Hockney, Braque argues that Renaissance perspective is ocular sleight-of-hand, which removes any direct, tactile experience of space, and forces objects away from the spectator rather than bringing them within reach. But we should acknowledge perhaps that, as we have intimated, the 'indexicality' of Cubism is not the indexicality of an object arrested and copresent in the flux of real time (as in Impressionism), but the indexicality of the copresence of text/picture and reader/spectator. Real time is no longer represented in the picture but has migrated to this side of the text/canvas and to repeated moments of perceptual indecision. Truly, the Cubist text/picture is a peculiar paradox: the text/picture which is, perceptually, intensely engaging, but uninhabitable and impenetrable (in both its senses).

Where one might take issue with Bivort's reading of the demonstratives of 'Antique' is in his identification of them as anaphoric (back-referring, recapitulative). Anaphoric they certainly are, since they refer back to the poem's title, to the body of the faun before us, and, for Bivort, particularly to the 'double sexe'. But they also seem to carry a strong cataphoric (forward-referring, anticipatory) charge: the poet's exhortation ('Promène-toi') is an awakening, but in the night (oneiric?), of a body (lower half) which was asleep (?) and which then struggles into visibility. The body of the faun is both a body already with an arcadian, dionysiac pedigree and a body struggling to emerge. We read a text which gives us access to a future which the text encourages us to place in its own blind field ('Est-ce en ces nuits sans fonds que tu dors et t'exiles, [. . .] ô future Vigueur?' [Is it in these bottomless nights that you sleep and live out your exile, (. . .) o future Vigour?]). But as visibility moves down the thigh to cover the whole leg and the text comes to a close, we realise perhaps that the 'future Vigueur' lies not in those forces which we might await as a second coming, another flood, a dawn, but in our own perceptual flexibility or resourcefulness. In this sense, Impressionism and Cubism have the same lesson to teach, the same substitution of planar space for perspectival space, the same favouring of the haptic over the optic. These parallels with the visual arts are fraught with danger, but it does seem eminently useful to think of the Rimbaldian text in Cubist ways: either the text is, like analytic/hermetic Cubism, a deconstruction of iconicity, of mimesis, which involves the virtual disappearance of the object, but in order that the spectator's perceptual capacity is flexibilised, endowed with a new availability ('disponibilité'), and in order that the indexical is no longer a quality of the depicted but of the spectator's perceptual contact with the depicted; or the text is a peculiar mixture of analytic and synthetic Cubism in which the deconstruction of the iconic reveals, magically, other patterns in the carpet which can perhaps be projected into a new iconicity: hence the blending of the endophoric and the exophoric, of the anaphoric and cataphoric. At all events, faced with the demonstrative adjectives of 'Antique', and recognising their ability to straddle the intratextual and the extratextual, the anaphoric and the cataphoric, we might propose that this part of speech, instrument as it is of deixis, perceptual focus, textual cohesion, is equally the instrument of multidirectional pointing, visual superimposition, scumbling and textual dissemination.

I have tried to write cubistically elsewhere (Scott 2002b), in relation to a poem of Apollinaire's. And to bring this chapter to a close, I would like to offer two further versions of 'Antique', each exploring cubistic writing in slightly different ways. The first of these efforts (see Appendix III (q)) brings us back to one of the perennial issues of the book: the acoustic text, transphrastic activity, the dispersal of meaning and syntax, the anarchy of pulsional interference, in short, language affirming an insubordinate materiality. It is difficult not to be struck by the intense acoustic activity to be found in 'Antique'. For Raybaud (1989: 12–15), the poem is a 'détournement' or 'déformation' of a programme both generical ('blason') and stylistic (classically archaising Parnassian), and one of the instruments of this 'détournement' is the music, the 'tintements' from the faun's torso:

> Ainsi, l'ambiguïté résulte d'un 'programme' que le poème détourne et déforme jusqu'à une figuration mal identifiable. Démarche qui constitue une surprise, en ce qu'à la différence de beaucoup de textes, [. . .] ce texte-ci semble annoncer, d'entrée, son objet: 'Gracieux fils de Pan!' Mais il *tourne*, quittant le plan sémantique, pour jouer de sa terme *sonore*, issue des termes même de l'annonce, et sur laquelle vont se composer les termes de la fable.
>
> (1989: 13)
>
> [Thus, ambiguity results from a 'programme' that the poem misappropriates and distorts until it becomes a representation difficult to identify. A procedure which comes as a surprise, in that, unlike many texts, (. . .) this text seems to announce its subject from

the outset: 'Gracieux fils de Pan!' But it *turns*, quitting the world of semantics, to make use of its acousticity, derived from the very terms of the opening apostrophe, and on which the terms of the fable are to be composed].

From the opening sentence Raybaud picks out the phonetic strings in /ø/, /(ɥ)i/ and /ã/, and adds to these other acoustic linkages in /kR/, /si/, /bR/ and /bl/, and /u/; he also points out the 'satyre' lurking, its vowels reversed, in 'cithare'. One has no difficulty at all in agreeing with Raybaud's underlying diagnosis: the faun's music frustrates the prosecution of a pre-established agenda and spirits away an object initially caught in a transfixative tribute; such a finding coincides with what we have said about the Cubist picture's deconstructive relationship with its title. But to Raybaud's justified assertion that the phonetic strings conjure up and warrant subversive lexical items (erotic, orgiastic), I would want to add the suggestion that shared sounds are as much the sources of planar torsion as they are of orchestrational harmony. A full rhyme might strike us as an adjacency in the same plane: homophony brings words flush with each other; in half rhyme (assonance or consonance), the homophonous element is the hinge upon which one word turns through degrees away from another. This may seem a fanciful metaphor. A metaphor perhaps, but not fanciful. If one encounters 'brow, crowned', or 'in this belly, bed of', or 'left leg', as consecutive elements in the syntagmatic chain, one can think of the acoustic affinities as accidental, a lucky supplement to their meaning. If those acoustic affinities are structured, metrically or by layout, as 'rhyme', then (a) the syntagmatic relationship becomes a paradigmatic one, and (b) the homophonous element is the paradigmatic key. In other words, shared phonemes/graphemes become the triggers of making, which, while they may continue to observe a certain recognisable syntax, set up a mode of proceeding which no longer has syntactical fulfilment as its objective, since paradigmatic making is continuous and non-teleological. This paradigmatic making is the reason for that non-closure of the Rimbaldian prose poem signalled by Guyaux (1985a: 189):

> Les *Illuminations* sont une performance d'inachèvement. L'ouverture, ou plutôt la non-clôture de l'œuvre, apparaît dans chaque texte, aussi délimité pourtant qu'une fable ou un sonnet, puisqu'il commence à la première ligne et s'achève à la dernière. C'est un périmètre qui semble fermé et qui s'ouvre.
> [The *Illuminations* are a performance of incompletion. The opening, or rather the non-closure, of the work, occurs in each text, even if

it is as delimited as a fable or a sonnet, since it begins with the first
line and ends with the last. It is an area which seems closed, but
which opens out.]

If Cubism is characterised by the interpenetration and overlapping of
forms, if, in its low relief, planes are tilted against each other, then in
language equally words meet each other at angles, share portions of the
same territory, intersect. And it is peculiarly in the hybridised nature of the
prose poem to tread the border between the syntagmatic and the
paradigmatic, the metonymic and the metaphoric, the non-metrical and
the metrical, the perceptual and the conceptual (mimetic/Cubist), teasing
the reader with the dialectical shifts between the poles.

It is in this spirit that I have essayed a calligrammatic version of
'Antique' whose form is partly governed by the figure developed in the
previous version, but also by the ways in which (a) words intersect each
other, or make contact with each other, through a shared grapheme, or (b)
letter shapes suggest parts of an anatomical outline or a physical feature.
I have tried also, but with only partial success I think, slightly to vary my
calligraphic style, so that (a) different portions of the 'body' have slightly
different graphological characteristics, some more angular and 'gothic',
others more rounded and Italianesque, and (b) the lightness or heaviness
of touch varies. These are my attempts to create, with writing, different
'sculptural' styles, different 'hues' within a general monochromaticism
(and hence some intimation of planar variation) and differences of
'shading'. But the design is principally important in its creation of a figure
directly out of language, in which shape and volume and surface and spatial
displacement are produced by the letters themselves. The graphemic
components of words must be seen to generate an alternative 'syntax', a
syntax which directly sculpts its own intuitive perceptions, its own
tactilities on the page. We might propose that the true art of the calligram
is neither of the options to be found in Apollinaire's work, as defined by
Bohn (1986: 51)—'Shaped writing (a) Solid forms' and 'Shaped writing
(b) Outlined forms', themselves manifestations of, respectively, haptic and
optic ways of addressing the poem's images—but an art in which linguistic
items are properly free agents, protagonists, assembling themselves
according to the promptings of their own letter shapes, where by 'letter
shapes' we are referring both to the physical shapes thought of in purely
graphic terms, with, therefore, a degree of elasticity, or capacity to be
modelled, and as constituents of the Roman alphabet, beneath whose
apparent graphemic similarities complex phonetic differences send words
of at tangents to each other.[6] Through these means I have hoped to bring

about a true reconciliation of the haptic and the optic.

My final rendering of 'Antique' is in the style of Gertrude Stein. The still lifes of *Tender Buttons* (1914) evidently owe much to Stein's conversations with Picasso, whom she had come to know as early as 1905—his portrait of her was painted in 1906—and to her perusal of his work (and that of Cézanne and Braque). Kaufmann (1989) cautions against superficial or misconceived identifications of Cubist characteristics in *Tender Buttons*, but nobody questions their presence. The collection itself has attracted polarised responses—the poems mean nothing coherent/the poems have multiple encrypted messages running patchily through them (sexual, Gnostic, anti-patriarchal, socio-economic)— similar to the contradictory readings of analytic Cubism we have already touched upon.

I say 'in the style of Gertrude Stein', but the significance of this remark is by no means clear. Randa Dubnick (1984) identifies the Stein of *The Making of Americans* as an analytic Cubist and the Stein of *Tender Buttons* (1914) as a synthetic Cubist.[4] But DeKoven (1983) finds in *Tender Buttons* an intersection of styles: '"Rooms", the third section of the book, is all in the 1911 transitional style. [. . .] "Objects" and "Food", the first and second sections of the book, both begin in the transitional style, then accelerate steadily through the middle style towards the extreme style of 1913 [i.e. towards greater fragmentation]' (76). My own rendering gravitates towards the style of 'Rooms' in its recourse to self-extending syntax, in which repetition has a significant part to play. But like the Stein of 'Objects' and 'Food', I also resort to wilful 'mishearings' or 'misunderstandings'. Where, for example, Stein uses 'cross' for 'less', or 'be where' for 'beware', or 'in specs' for 'inspects', I sandwich 'androgyny' within 'hermaphrodite' ('him and Roger and he Aphrodite') and indulge in other, similar, (half-) homophonies:

> Being Pan's son is one being graceful and wanting to change in not needing to want though being Pan's son is changing to graceful.
>
> Around your brow, crooned is sung in sunlit making or flower a reds and buries the little orbs then the precious ones moving. Seen eye holders. Re cheeks, what is it, vine leavings, suppose it absorbing, suppose some hollowing. On the canine no saturnine on ogle listening.
>
> Like your torso is its being a Cythera or some stringing strumming just so, not a not plucked but notes and notes in and out wandering wan winsome in arms is not disagreeable.
>
> Your heart is managed a cycling please do not please do not

lower than belly than which way to him and Roger and he Aphrodite.

   Walk then at night-time in nightfall the gentle the moving this right thigh and moving then duskily this other the other thigh just after the darkness the right thigh the left thigh in parting the day then departing start walking this thigh moving slowly and then this other one the other and gradually lifting starkly and darkly this left leg deftly.

I seem to use Rimbaud as the *prima materia* with which I can pastiche Gertrude Stein. Is Stein a participant in my dialogue with Rimbaud, or is Rimbaud a participant in my dialogue with Stein? It hardly matters as long as we cling to these two principles: (i) the translation which seeks to register the journey of the ST across the space/time between there and then and here and now will inevitably be a translation which involves a third party or third parties (i.e. the inhabitants, or their representative, of the intervening space/time); (ii) translation may very consciously practice pastiche, but even if it does not, the adoption of a style, a register, a persona will entail a degree of pastiche-writing. We must therefore confront what it means to say that translation *is* pastiche. I have argued in other circumstances (2000: 133)—apropos of the epigraph—that the 'third voice' is extremely beneficial, distracting ST and TT from their tête-à-tête, from a set of issues (linguistic fidelity, cultural accuracy, compensation, etc.) quite properly made fruitless by the intervention of other interests (how could the ST and the TT ever think that they were all that was at stake?). Now I would argue not merely for the beneficiality of the third voice but for its indispensability, both in terms of history and of good practice. Pastiche is often an explicit part of the involvement of the third voice, but, more fundamentally, the third voice is present even when only two think they are in dialogue—because pastiche is the unavoidable 'other' of the translating I and the unavoidable 'other' of the translated you.

   Pastiche is translation seen as a complication of intentions and outcomes. Pastiche parades itself cockily (parody) and with apologetic shame(lessness) (travesty). It is a tributary mockery, a self-dissociative gesture which conceals a vital journey of self-exploration and self-discovery. If we wish to understand translation as a complex psychological predicament, which in a sense it must be if it is be of any creative value to the translator, then to think of it as pastiche—where pastiche is understood to be the superordinate term for a whole cluster of impulses as diverse as parody, travesty, quotation, plagiarism, imitation, tribute, caricature—will help us to envisage what might be included in the recipe. I say 'what might be', since I do not want to imply that translation can only be valuable if it is the source of feelings of unrelieved *Angst*.

Pastiche is Cubist inasmuch as it translates objects or figures from the 'real world' into arbitrary copies, animated by the playful and indeed caricatural, but as a mode of autobiography and perceptual self-investigation. In suggesting these kinds of affinity—we have argued ourselves into a position of claiming that translation is Cubist—we are looking to encourage a translational practice in which the ST is a percept which, by dint of perceptual multiplication, loses its ability to do anything other than act as the 'iconic' origin of the TT. The TT achieves its own autonomy not by turning away from the ST, but by conceptualising it, that is to say, by endowing it with virtuality, by treating it not as something recuperable from the TT, but as something which the TT is taking forward, *and only taking forward*. By that I mean that the ST can never properly come to itself again in an actualisation, never rematerialise as it was. Of course there will continue to be a product, a TT, but this TT is no more than a token, a spectre, asking to be treated putatively, an instigation, an invitation, a provocation, a relay, pushing the ST on its way. Translation transforms the ST as percept into the ST as concept. In such circumstances, we cannot desire to be accurate about, or faithful to, the ST. We can only desire that it lives its literariness differently, in a sequence of infinite renewals.

A question with which Rimbaud's work leaves us is whether it gravitates more towards Cubism or towards Futurism. We should, of course, recognize that this is a question our own approach has inevitably, but unwillingly, created. But we must insist that Rimbaud's work, in its afterlife, travels not only through Cubism and Futurism, but all other -isms and styles between then and now; our task as translators is precisely to acclimatise Rimbaud's work to these new environments, so that they can help us to uncover those expressive latencies and aesthetic potentialities in his prose poems which we might otherwise overlook. It is in this way that we look to translation to make Rimbaud more intelligible to us: not by clarifying his meanings—a fruitless undertaking, a job already done—but by finding a multiplicity of places for him in the modern artistic consciousness, by showing the uses to which his work can be put so that, through it, we are brought back to ourselves, to our own assimilation of artistic and literary currents across the intervening distance, to the perspective from which we have no choice but to view his work. To ask a question about Rimbaud's relative proximity to Cubism and Futurism is both dangerously to leave out of account all *I* have left out of account— Imagism, Dada, Surrealism, Bauhaus, Abstract Expressionism, Ecopoetics, and so forth—but it is also, implicitly, to ask comparative and literary historical questions about influence, aesthetic ancestry and progeny, the development of styles. I must insist that I am not trying to suggest that Rimbaud is a forerunner of, a tacit presence in, this or that twentieth-century movement. The literary history that translation presents is a very different affair; it is a literary history whose elements can be shuffled, in which kinships are actively created by the translator, *by the practice of translation*, where history itself would have repined. It is a literary history motivated by experiments with possibility, passing fancies, achronological speculation. Translation can be an instrument of traditional literary history, of course, translating authors into positions that their 'rayonnement' seems to justify. But in experimental translation, the literary history is also experimental, and is not the original justification for the translation, but the inevitable outcome of the way in which the translator has imagined the spaces of writing and reading, directs and distributes verbal attention, thinks the page.

Conclusion

We have suggested that it may be important, in a new regime of translation, to think of translation as a conceptual art (term first in current use in 1967), that is, we assume that the product is in many ways an inadequate evidence of the conceptual processes, ambitions and potentialities which the particular translational project has activated and developed, that, in short, the artistic concept is in striking excess of the artistic object.[1] If anything, translation has erred at the other extreme, burying all traces of objectives, methods, elaborations; even footnotes have been deemed lapses of taste[2] (the result must speak for itself—but of what should it speak?). For us, on the other hand, the 'version' becomes a token or stand-in for, or rather corridor to, the conception it cannot do justice to. And perhaps, after all, this is what the translator desires. To call translation a conceptual art is also to presuppose that translation constantly questions assumptions about translation, about what translation needs to be in order to be translation, and implies that there are ways of achieving its ends which are much more 'economical'.

In the case of the present book, to argue for a conceptual translation must look like a rather transparent attempt at self-defence: for one thing, one might believe that anything that tries to carry itself by force of argument must be suspect; for another, that the potentialities of typography and the hard-copy page are severely limited and soon exhausted: ambition soon outstrips resource and conceptuality becomes the child of necessity. But suspicions aside, it still remains true that what can be thought about a translation and translational possibility far exceeds not just our ability to put it into practice, but also the point of putting it into practice. I certainly do not wish to fall back on a Mallarméan contemplation of the inestimable fruits of the blank page. But part of the justification for developing the spaces of the page as vital constituents of the translational 'site' lies in the opportunity it offers to generate a rendering which is in excess of its own text, which carries a conceptual supplement. At all events, the translator should avoid turning the ST as a sequence of signifiers into a TT which is a corresponding sequence of signifieds—translation must work to maintain the ST as signifier, as a work whose power to signify constantly exceeds any proposed signified (in these circumstances, there is little point in going through the motions of spelling out, in the TT, a signified). Concomitantly, language must be allowed to expand and elaborate itself in non-linguisic spaces. We need to be reminded that space is integral to language's activity, that space represents the speakers of language and those listening to it: space is the presence of the paralinguistic, both in its vocalic and auditory dimensions (there *is* a paralanguage of hearing, connected with selection, tracing, mishearing, anticipation, and so on; as Barthes puts it:

> [. . .] ce qui est écouté ici et là (principalement dans le champ de l'art, dont la fonction est souvent utopiste), ce n'est pas la venue d'un signifié, objet d'une reconnaissance ou d'un déchiffrement, c'est la dispersion même, le miroitement des signifiants, sans cesse remis dans la course d'une écoute qui en produit sans cesse des nouveaux, sans jamais arrêter le sens: ce phénomène de miroitement s'appelle la *signifiance* (distincte de la signification).
>
> (1982b: 229)
>
> [(. . .) what is listened to, here as there (principally in the field of art, whose function is often utopian), is not the arrival of a signified, the object of a recognition or a decipherment, it is the very act of dissemination, the shimmering of signifiers, continually restored to the process of listening which continually produces new signifiers, without ever arresting meaning: this phenomenon of shimmering is called *signifiance* (as opposed to signification).])

All along, our purpose has been to persuade translation away from the metalinguistic—though not as a feature of montage—and towards the paralinguistic.

There may seem to be a contradiction in all these endeavours: on the one hand, an ST of signifiers held off from signification, a text always and never to be read, a text whose language is constantly activating paralanguages, a text always *being read*. On the other, a TT struggling to maximise linguistic materiality, to maximise orality and graphic visibility, to incorporate the creative sensibility of the translator and the receptive sensibility of the reader, in a word, to achieve a maximum of *actualisation*. But this duality is one that makes sense of, and is made sense of by, multitranslation, which holds the contending drives in a fruitful balance: we translate ever again because the ST's signifiers will never have done with tempting us to versions which are worth undertaking, not because they produce satisfactory signifieds, but because they perpetuate the ST's significance in the very act of our participating paralinguistically in it. This double experience is what I understand by the Barthesian 'scriptible'. The translator locates himself more in the reading process than in the text; the creativity of the translator expends itself in translating this movement of consciousness through the text. And as we have found, in our third, fourth and fifth chapters, the voice and the eye are both instruments of reading, the inscribers of paralanguage into the text, and the psycho-physiological dimension of receptive consciousness.

One of our reasons for preferring the page as a definition of text, rather than the sum of printed characters, is that it does not distract us from, or submerge, our sense of textual discourse. The activation of space, and its integration into the fabric of text, are ways of outwitting interpretation, itself an enemy of the discourse of text, as is argued by Henri Meschonnic. He begins by condemning the monocularity and discontinuity of interpretation:

> Paradoxalement, une *bonne* traduction ne doit pas être pensée comme une *interprétation*. Parce que l'interprétation est de l'ordre du sens, et du signe. Du discontinu. Radicalement différente du texte, qui *fait* ce qu'il dit. Le texte est porteur et porté. L'interprétation, seulement portée. La *bonne* traduction doit faire, et non seulement dire. Elle doit, comme le texte, être porteuse et portée.
>
> (1999: 22)
>
> [Paradoxically, a *good* translation must not be conceived as an *interpretation*. Because interpretation is of the order of meaning, of the sign. Of the discontinuous. Radically different from the text, which *does* what it says. The text is both bearer and borne. Interpretation is only borne. *Good* translation must do and not merely say. It must, like the text, be both bearer and borne.]

For Meschonnic, interpretation is a response which accepts the structuralist schizophrenia of the sign (sound/sense, *signifiant/signifié*), and, additionally, surrenders textuality to the word-for-word. Textuality itself is discourse, orality,[3] a rhythmicisation of language, a

259

corporealisation of language, a certain subjectivisation of language (appropriation of language by a subjectivity):

> Parce que dans le rythme, au sens où je le dis, on n'entend pas du son, mais du sujet. Pas une forme distincte du sens. Traduire selon le poème dans le discours, c'est traduire le récitatif, le récit de la signifiance, la sémantique prosodique et rythmique, non le stupide mot à mot que les ciblistes voient comme la recherche du poétique.
> [...]
> Parce que le mode de signifier, beaucoup plus que le sens des mots, est dans le rythme, comme le langage est dans le corps, ce que l'écriture inverse, en mettant *le corps dans le langage.*
>
> (1999: 24–5)
>
> [Because in rhythm, in the sense I intend, it is not sound one hears, but subject. Not a distinct form of meaning. To translate according to the poem in the text is to translate the recitative, the story of significance, the prosodic and rhythmic semantics, not the stupid word-for-word that the 'targeters' see as the quest for the poetic.
> (...)
> Because the signifying mode, much more than the meaning of the words, lies in the rhythm, as language lies in the body, which writing reverses, by putting *the body in language.*]

Additionally, for Meschonnic, texts can become archaic as language, but never as discourse. He taxes Picard with confusing the two, that is to say, confusing the meaning of Racine's plays with the historical meaning of Racine's vocabulary; the meaning of the plays as plays is not finite, while the meaning of Racine's vocabulary is fixed in time (you need an historical dictionary to read them) (1999: 168). I would, however, want to qualify this observation by arguing that discourse, while it does not depend on translation to demonstrate its non-archaicity, becomes archaic if its language is not renewed, if it is seen to be the preserve of, or somehow dependent on, a particular lexicon. This is certainly one of the dangers of historicist, as opposed to historical, approaches to translation.

If we detect in our project a Janus-faced tug between the virtualization or conceptualization of the ST, and the TT as an aggressive leap at physicality or actuality, resolved by the principle of multitranslation, then we might point to a similar contradiction in Rimbaud's work. In his letter to Paul Demeny of May 15 1871, Rimbaud himself refers to two kinds of creative process: 'Cela m'est évident: j'assiste à l'éclosion de ma pensée: je la regarde, je l'écoute: je lance un coup d'archet: la symphonie fait son remuement dans les profondeurs, ou vient d'un bond sur la scène' [This is obvious to me: I witness the birth of my own thought: I watch it, I listen to it: I draw my bow across the strings: the symphony begins to rumble in the depths, or leaps on to the stage]. As a gloss on this declaration, Michael Brophy provides the following comment:

> La parole rimbaldienne oscillerait entre ce qui demeure latent, souterrain, en gestation, et ce qui, tout au contraire, se délivre soudain du vide et du silence en jouissant d'un élan aussi irrésistible que bref.
>
> (2002: 91)
>
> [The Rimbaldian utterance oscillates between what remains latent, subterranean, in gestation, and what, on the contrary, suddenly breaks free from emptiness and silence, delighting in a surge of energy as irresistible as it is brief.]

How can the latent and subterranean find a connection in our minds with that which manifests itself with the sudden force of revelation? These are, however, two aspects of the same experience. If translation wants to hold open the signifier, in a state of latency, if it wishes always to be going beyond itself, to somewhere else, it equally, if provisionally, wishes to realise itself as literature, as an event in the literature of translation. And it is only by realising itself, repeatedly and multiply, as literature, that translation can safeguard the virtuality of the ST, can translate signifiers into signifiers, the semanticisable into the semanticisable. At the outset of this book, we identified, as one of translation's transformational dangers, the tendency of the TT to make the ST more intelligible. We need perhaps to envisage a translational strategy whereby the TT makes the ST more incomprehensible, not only because we want to create a situation in which the reader has to turn to the ST in order to understand the TT, but also because we want the reader to be compelled to 'write' the psychophysicality of their encounter with the intractable materiality of language. The decoding of meaning destroys that textual resistance whereby we identify the desire of language, the desire to break into its own proliferation. The reader thus borrows the tactics of the translator, disassembling, reassembling, developing, highlighting, sounds, grammar and syntax, so that the text is invested with *significance* rather than being plundered for its meaning. In a sense, both the translator, as reader of the ST, and the readers of TTs, need to be readers who do not understand, who do not wish to understand.

Let us again briefly outline what we feel a literature of translation principally involves:

> (a) the incorporation of the paralanguage of reading (speaking and listening) at the expense of the metalinguistic tendencies of translation; this would entail the development of new languages of layout, typography, punctuation and, possibly, diacritical signs, and would inevitably invite translation in the direction of performance art;
>
> (b) the treatment of the whole page as text, in order to safeguard the discourse in text and to ensure that translation is a literature of more than the text, a literature unafraid to incorporate the intertextual, the paratextual and the contextual, into the textual;
>
> (c) the promotion of constructivist principles, a literature of editing and engineering, which naturally employs the resources of montage, (electronic) multi-media and hypertextuality, all kinds of textual manipulation (e.g. the mechanisms of Oulipo);
>
> (d) the multiplication of text in variant texts (multitranslation);
>
> (e) the exploration and elaboration of translation's generical affinities with pastiche, parody, travesty, plagiarism, citation, imitation, paraphrase;
>
> (f) the development of new rhetorical resources (such as new understandings of rhymelessness, of etymology, morphology, transphrastic phonetics, forms of syntax, capitalisation and italicisation, and so forth).

Translating the *Illuminations* urges us towards a new literature of translation. The real problem is not about how to translate the meanings of Rimbaldian words—Rimbaldian criticism has ridden this problem to the staggers—but how to translate their textual status, their relationship to time, space, expressivity, and their contribution to a particular kind of creative enterprise. Faced with texts subject to slippages of all kinds, texts which have to an extent been artificially 'stabilised', we more than ever need a translation which reflects textual fluidity, and the *kind of text* that is implied. This is not to cast any doubt on the scholarship of those who have established and edited Rimbaldian texts, but merely to acknowledge that there is much here that hangs on a policy of informed guesswork.

But this is not a problem peculiar to Rimbaldian texts; they merely serve to dramatise it with peculiar force. Any text may have succumbed to certain decisions by a hair's breadth, may have let a percentage of the aleatory have its way, if only for a moment. The pragmatic view would be that, in the end, texts constitute themselves reliably enough, thanks to the accumulation of editorial decisions and the number of 'consensual' editions they go through. But what if this situation fulfils only an historical need, a need of cultural heritage: knowing who your authors are entails the assumption that their texts are knowable? Besides, to establish a text is not to establish the stability of its textuality. A new literature of translation might be better placed to convey the 'what if' of making, the 'try out' of making, its ongoingness, its doubts and unpredictabilities, its failures and lucky chances.

In the face of such attitudes to the literary text, to what kind of reader does the translator owe his obligations? If the Rimbaldian text is the more or less accidental result of textual 'glissements', in the reception as well as the creation of the text, then should the translation prolong these 'glissements', or at least encourage the reader of the TT to do so? Clearly the translator cannot show the ST again, as if nothing had happened, as if it were still there, caught in amber, endowed with an unchanging accessibility. Clearly, the translator does not wish to use translation merely to bring out the text's interpretative difficulties (there are other ways of doing that). It is not the problematics of meaning that the translator wants to address, but the problematics of the ST's writing and of its textual survival. The kind of reader that the translator is looking for is one who comes to the TT in order to discover how the ST might be rewritten into the reader's mind, and the problematics of its presence amongst us, as something we cannot let go of.

In *Translating Baudelaire* (2000: 218–46), I made my translation of 'Le Voyage' a montage, in an effort to bring Baudelaire's text into a relation of dialogue with texts which both anteceded and succeeded his. This was because I wanted to make explicit, in actual textual practice, that the translator's task is not only to measure the mental/cultural space that a text has traversed as it comes towards us across time, but also to emphasise that the ST itself already has other texts audible within it. These potential itineraries of an ST across its own history and across the history it has itself become for the contemporary reader, imply multitranslation, constant retraversals of potential sources and potential progenies. But it leaves the translator with the question of what kind of dialogue with intertexts he wishes to institute. Montage is a way of leaving that question open, of leaving it to the reader to make sense of and supplement. This neutrality has the virtue of soliciting a *textual* engagement from the reader: if the translator wishes to involve the reader in a text about which the reader may be linguistically, or even culturally, ignorant, then montage at the very least, confronts the reader with the gap that the translator is bridging, not the linguistic gap so much as the gap between then and there and here and now, which has been filled with related activity, either explicitly intertextual or more loosely associative. Montage makes the reader realise that the ST is not closed off in a space of its own, to be taken or left, but that it is a cross-roads of widening writerly trends, without which those trends cannot come fully into their own, or harvest their full richness.

A TT does not primarily relate to the ST as an exercise in contrastive linguistics. It does so as a textual memory of the ST, not in the chronometric sense, whereby the act of memory is the thrusting back in time of an originating experience, but in the Bergsonian sense whereby the psychic life is cumulative, and always simultaneous with its contents, which may erupt in all manner of ecmnesic sensation. Such an attitude to translation allows us to understand much more easily the sense in which translation is more to do with intertextuality than linguistic equivalence, much more to do with an ST perceived in the difference it has generated, than an ST clinging on to a sameness, from its very backwardness in time.

The translator is the poet who joins the crowd of other speakers, who borrows the voices that are available, the better ultimately to emerge from processes of borrowing, plagiarism, imitation and pastiche, into his own light. We have to imagine a situation in which we look upon translation as pastiche like that practised by Proust, in order to find a position relative to spiritual ancestors. The translator can only get (back) to his own voice by the detour of translation; the voice of the self can only be heard after it has been intimately linked with the voice(s) of the other(s):

> L'hommage à l'autre devient le meilleur moyen de se dévoiler en se cachant, la langue de l'autre devient le seul lieu où articuler la sienne propre [. . .].
>
> (Druet 2002: 120)
>
> [The tribute to the other becomes the best way of disclosing oneself by hiding, the language of the other becomes the only place in which to articulate one's own.]

The translator belongs to a literary community in which a collage of voices occupies a collective space, so that literary ownership is constantly being transferred, and so that, consequently, works come to join the throng without standing on their dignity or wanting to make a case for differential status. And like those 'open-minded' public spaces championed by Rogers, the collective spaces of translation 'foster tolerance and radical thought' (1997: 152) and in doing so, paradoxically, invite participants to inhabit their privacies without fear of siege or embattlement.

Appendix I

Wordsworth's 'The Daffodils' and François-René Daillie's translation

The Daffodils

I wandered lonely as a cloud
That floats on high o'er vales and hills,
When all at once I saw a crowd,
A host, of golden daffodils;
Beside the lake, beneath the trees,
Fluttering and dancing in the breeze.

Continuous as the stars that shine
And twinkle on the milky way,
They stretched in never-ending line
Along the margin of a bay:
Ten thousand saw I at a glance,
Tossing their heads in sprightly dance.

The waves beside them danced; but they
Out-did the sparkling waves in glee:
A poet could not but be gay,
In such a jocund company:
I gazed—and gazed—but little thought
What wealth the show to me had brought:

For oft, when on my couch I lie
In vacant or in pensive mood,
They flash upon that inward eye
Which is the bliss of solitude;
And then my heart with pleasure fills,
And dances with the daffodils.

William Wordsworth

J'allais solitaire ainsi qu'un nuage
Qui plane au-dessus des vaux et des monts
Quand soudain je vis en foule—ô mirage! –
Des jonquilles d'or, une légion!
À côté du lac, sous les branches grises,
Flottant et dansant gaiement à la brise.

Serrées comme sont au ciel les étoiles
Qu'on voit scintiller sur la Voie lactée,
Elles s'étendaient sans un intervalle
Le long du rivage au creux d'une baie:
J'en vis d'un coup d'œil des milliers, je pense,
Agitant la tête en leur folle danse.

Les vagues dansaient, pleines d'étincelles,
Mais *elles* dansaient plus allégrement;
Pouvais-je rester, poète, auprès d'elles
Sans être gagné par leur enjouement?
L'œil fixe—ébloui -, je ne songeais guère
Au riche présent qui m'était offert:

Car si je repose, absent ou songeur,
Souvent leur vision, ô béatitude!
Vient illuminer l'œil intérieur
Qui fait le bonheur de la solitude;
Et mon cœur alors, débordant, pétille
De plaisir et danse avec les jonquilles.

trans. François-René Daillie

Appendix II

Plain prose translations of selected *Illuminations*

(i)   Jeunesse II: Sonnet/Youth II: Sonnet
(ii)   Solde/Sale
(iii) Parade/Parade
(iv)   Fairy/Fairy
(v)   Vagabonds/Vagabonds
(vi)   Départ/Departure
(vii) A une raison/To a Reason
(viii) Fête d'hiver/Winter Entertainment
(ix)   Démocratie/Democracy
(x)   Ville/City
(xi)   Villes I/Cities I
(xii) Villes II/Cities II
(xiii) Les Ponts/The Bridges
(xiv) Mystique/Mystique
(xv)   Antique/Antique

(i)   *Youth II: Sonnet*

Man, of common constitution, was not your flesh a fruit hanging in the orchard;—o childhood days!—the body a treasure to expend;—o loving, Psyche imperilled, or Psyche's strength? The earth had inclines thick with princes and artists, and race and progeny urged you to crimes and mournings: your destiny and risk, the world. But that labour long since fulfilled,—you, your calculations,—you, your bouts of impatience—are no more than your dance and voice, unfixed, unforced, although a reason for a double happening of invention and advance,—in human brotherhood and discretion throughout the image-empty universe;—the present season only now esteems the dance and voice reflected in justice and in force.

(ii)   *Sale*

For sale: goods left unsold by the Jews, goods left untried by aristocrats and criminals, goods unknown to forbidden love and to the diabolical probity of the masses: goods which neither time nor learning has to acknowledge.

Voices reconstituted; the fraternal animation of all the choral and orchestral energies and their being put to immediate use; the opportunity, not to be repeated, to liberate our senses!

For sale: priceless Bodies, non-ethnic, not of any world, asexual, without descendants! Riches gushing up with every move! Unrestricted sale of diamonds!

For sale: anarchy for the masses; irrepressible satisfaction for practised connoisseurs; hideous deaths for the faithful and for lovers!

For sale: dwellings and migrations, sports, perfect masques and comforts, and the noise, movement, future they activate.

For sale: incredible feats of applied calculation and leaps of harmony unfamiliar to the human ear. Chance discoveries and verbal concepts you could never have imagined, with immediate possession.

Irrational and inexhaustible élan towards the invisible splendours, towards the imperceptible delights—and its alarming secrets for every vice—and its terrifying high spirits for the crowd.

For sale: the Bodies, the voices, the vast unquestionable opulence, which will never be sold. The salesmen have still got stock to clear. The commercial travellers need be in no hurry to surrender their commissions.

(iii)   *Parade*

Rum types, stock-sturdy. Several have squeezed your worlds dry. Without needs and in no hurry to apply their brilliant faculties and their familiarity with your perceptions. What mature men! Eyes as glazed as the summer night, red and black, *tricolores*, steel-blue punctuated with golden stars; deformed facial features, leaden, enpallored, burnt on; voices madcapped and gravelled! The cruel swagger of their tawdry finery!—There are young ones, too,—what would they think of Cherubino?—with voices that scare the life out of you and and dangerous weapons. They are sent into the towns to 'put some back on', rigged out in disgusting *luxury*.

O the arch-violent Paradise of the grimace of rage! Do not talk to me of your Fakirs and other side-show buffooneries. In costumes improvised in the style of bad dreams they play *complaintes*, tragedies of brigands and demi-gods, witty as neither history nor religions have ever been. Chinamen, Hottentots, gypsies, fools, hyenas, Molochs, old lunacies, demons of dark intent, they mix popular, mother's-knee turns with bestial poses and solicitudes. They are ready to interpret new plays and tender-hearted songs. Master jugglers, they transform place and person, and resort to hypnotic comedy. Eyes blaze, the blood sings, the bones swell and stretch, tears and red rivulets stream down. Their derisive backchat or terror last only a moment, or for whole months.

I alone hold the key to this savage parade.

(iv) Fairy

For Helen's benefit, the ornamental saps in the virginal shadows and the expressionless brightnesses in the starry silence conspired together. The torrid heat of the summer was entrusted to silent birds and the necessary dose of indolence to a priceless funeral barge by inlets of loves long extinct and perfumes in a state of collapse.

—After the time of the song of the lumberjills with the rumble of the torrent beneath the decimated woods, of the cowbells with their valley echoes, and of the cries of the steppes.—

For the benefit of Helen's childhood, the furs and shadows quivered,—as did the breasts of the poor, and the heavenly legends.

And her eyes and her dancing, surpassing even the precious light-bursts, the icy influxes, and the pleasure of this so special décor and time of day.

(v) Vagabonds

Pitiful, pitiable brother! What appalling nights of sleeplessness I owed him. 'I didn't take hold of this enterprise with enough energy. I had made light of his weakness. It would be my fault if we found our way back into exile, and bondage.' He reckoned I had a streak of bad luck and a naivety, of the most unusual kinds, and he backed all this up with unsettling explanations.

By way of reply I would jeer at this satanic doctor and finish by going over to the window. I conjured up, beyond the landscape criss-crossed by bands of rare music, the phantoms of the nocturnal luxury to come.

After this vaguely purgative distraction, I would stretch out on a straw mattress. And, almost every night, no sooner was I asleep than the poor brother would get up, his mouth sewer-thick, his eyes starting out of their sockets,—just as he dreamed of being!—and would drag me into the main room howling his dream of mindless grief.

I had, let it be said, in all sincerity, undertaken to restore him to his primitive status as sun-child,—and we wandered, revitalised by the wine of the 'cavernes' and wayside biscuit, with me impatient to find the place and the formula.

(vi) Departure

Seen enough. The vision was encountered in every atmosphere.
Had enough. The muffled din of cities, at evening, and in the sun, and always.
Familiar enough. Life's summary judgements/interruptions.—O Reverberations and Visions!
Departure into new affections and sound-worlds!

(vii) To a Reason

Your finger tap on the drum discharges all sounds and generates the new harmony.
One step and you conjure up a new breed of men and set them in motion.
Your head turns: new love! Your head turns back,—new love!
'Change our lots, shoot to pieces the plagues that weigh on us, with Time first on the list.' This is how these children serenade you. And others beg of you: 'Increase, somewhere or other, the substance of our fortunes, and of our dearest wishes.'
Arrived here from always, you, heading for everywhere.

(viii) Winter Entertainment

The tumbling water churns and chimes behind the huts courtesy of comic opera. Girandoles in the orchards and alleyways running alongside the Meander pick up—the greens and reds of the setting sun. Nymphs from the pages of Horace, their hair dressed au Premier Empire,—Siberian rounds footed by round Sibériennes, Chinoises from the brush of Boucher.

(ix) Democracy

'The tatty flag suits this crapshit country to its t's [The flag moves to and through this filthy landscape], and our patois puts the mockers on the drum.

In the populous areas we will promote prostitution, with cynicism a top priority. We will ruthlessly zero-tolerate any consequent expressions of dissent.

To the pepper-laden, moisture-sodden countries!—product champions of military and industrial enterprises, so outrageous and exploitative they'll beggar belief.

Good riddance to here, *there*'s where we'll go. Volunteer conscripts, ours will be a brutish philosophy: ignorance our science; crapulence our comfort; and down the pan with the rest of humanity. Now that's what I call progress. Come on, stir your stumps—it's time to hit the road!'

(x) City

I am an ephemeral and none too dissatisfied citizen of a metropolis credited with being modern, because every known style has been studiously avoided in the furnishings and exteriors of the houses, as in the city plan. Here you would be at a loss to point out any monument to past beliefs. Ethics and language are reduced to the barest minimum, at long last! These millions of people who have no need to know each other, pursue their education, work, old age with so little variation that their life-span must be several times shorter than what unruly statistics tell us about continental peoples. Thus as, from my window, I can see new spectres moving forward through the thick and persistent smog—our sylvan shade, our summer night!—new Furies, passing by my cottage door, which is my homeland and my heart's content, since all here is like this,—dry-eyed Death, our ever-busy daughter and servant, a Love without hope and a fetching Crime whimpering in the street's mud.

(xi) Cities I

The official acropolis far exceeds the most colossal conceptions of modern barbarity. Impossible to render in words the lustreless light emanating from the imperturbably grey sky, the imperial effulgence of the buildings, and the earth's permanent, covering snow. Copies have been made, in an unusual style of *amplificatio*, of all the architectural wonders of classical times. I visit exhibitions of paintings at venues twenty times larger than Hampton Court. And what painting! A Norwegian Nebuchadnezzar was responsible for the construction of the ministry staircases; the minor officials I had the chance to see, already have more self-conceit than Brahmas, and the Herculean build of the construction managers and security guards sent a chill down my spine. By the device of grouping buildings, in closed squares, courtyards and terraces, they have effectively squeezed out the cabbies. The parks represent primitive nature cultivated with consummate art. Parts of the upmarket district are impossible to account for: an arm of the sea, unencumbered with boats, insinuates its sheet of frosty blue between quaysides top-heavy with giant candelabra. A short bridge leads to a postern directly beneath the dome of the Sainte-Chapelle. This dome is an artistic steel armature about 15,000 feet in diameter.

At several points on the copper footbridges, platforms and staircases which wind round the covered markets and pillars, I felt I could calculate the vertical scale of the city! But one miracle of construction I simply could not get a take on: what are the levels of the other quarters above or below the acropolis? For the contemporary visitor, it is impossible to work out where one is. The commercial quarter is a circus in a perfectly uniform style, with arcaded galleries. No shops are to be seen, but the snow on the roadway has been trampled; a handful of nabobs, as rare as Sunday morning strollers in London, head towards a carriage all set with diamonds. Several red velvet divans: polar drinks are served which cost between 800 and 8,000 rupees. When it occurs to me to look for theatres in this circus, I tell myself that the shops must have their fair share of shady dramas. I *think* there is a police force; but the law must be so bizarre that I give up trying to imagine what the spivs and racketeers are like hereabouts.

The suburbs, as elegant as the rue de Rivoli, are favoured with a bright atmosphere. The population works out at several hundred souls. Here again, the houses are not built in rows; the suburbs peter out oddly into the countryside, or rather, the 'County', which covers the never-ending 'westliness' of the forests and mammoth plantations, where gentlemen-savages hunt down their family histories by artificial light.

(xii)   Cities II

What cities these are! A people for whom these dream Alleghanys and Lebanons have been brought into being! Crystal chalets, chalets of wood, which move on invisible rails and pulleys. The old craters encircled by colossi and copper palms roar melodies in their fires. Celebrations of love resound along the canals hung up behind the chalets. The hunt of the carillons jangles madly in the gorges. Guilds of gigantic singers flock forward in clothes and oriflammes as brilliant as light bursting on mountain peaks. On the platforms, amidst the gaping chasms the Rolands blare out their braggadocios. On the footbridges across the abyss and on the roofs of the hostelries, the sky inflames the masts with flags. The collapse of the apotheoses regains the mountain fields where the seraphic centauresses manoeuvre among the avalanches. Above the line of the highest crests a sea turbulent with the ever-repeated birth of Venus, decked with choral flotillas and the murmur of precious pearls and shells,—from time to time the sea glooms with gleams of mortality. On the slopes you can hear the lowing of harvests of flowers as large as our weapons and goblets. Processions of Mabs, in robes russet and opaline, climb from the ravines. On the higher ground, Diana gives suck to the deer, their hooves in the waterfall and brambles. The suburban Bacchantes make a sobbing to-do and the moon burns and howls. Venus favours the caves of the smithies and hermits with a visit. Groups of belfries ring out the ideas of the different peoples. Unfamiliar music drifts from the castles of bone. All the legends mill about and the impulses rush headlong into the villages. The paradise of the storms gives way. Without respite, the savages dance the festival of the night. And for an hour I went down into the bustle of a Baghdad boulevard, where clusters of people sang the joys of a new kind of work, in a stiff breeze, moving about without being able to escape the fabled phantoms of the mountains where they must have foregathered.

What trusty arms, what propitious hour will restore to me this region, the fount and origin of my sleeping and my smallest movements.

(xiii)   *The Bridges*

Grey skies of crystal. A bizarre choreography of bridges, some horizontal, some curved, others sloping down to the first, or going off at tangents to them, and these figures recurring in the other, illuminated, windings of the canal, but all of them so long, so light that the banks, with their heavy accumulations of domes, sink and shrink. Several of these bridges are still lined with dilapidated buildings. Others sport masts, or signals, or spindly parapets. Minor chords cross each others' paths and head off. Ropes loop up from the banks. A red jacket strikes the eye, other costumes perhaps, and musical instruments. Are these popular tunes, snatches from seigniorial concerts, the debris of public anthems? The water is grey and blue, as wide as a sea-sound.—A white beam of light, falling from the peaks of the sky, reduces this piece of theatre to nothing.

(xiv)   *Mystique*

On the sloping embankment the angels wheel their woollen robes in the meadow grasses of steel and emerald.

Fields of flame lick up in leaps to the tip of the hill-breast. On the left the decaying vegetation on the ridge is trampled over by all the homicides and all the battles, and all the noises of disaster describe their arcing parabolas. Behind the right-hand ridge the line of Orients, of advances.

And while the band at the top of the picture is made of the distant wheeling and leaping surf-surge of conches and human nights,

The flowery *douceur* of the stars, the sky and all that swivels down upturned opposite the embankment, like a basket, so close to our faces, and becomes the blue flowering abyss beneath.

(xv) Antique

Son of Pan, full of grace! Around your brow crowned with flowerets and berries your eyes, precious orbs, move. Stained with darkening wine dregs, your cheeks sink to sunken. Your sharp teeth gleam. Your torso is like a cithara, plucked notes run up and down your pale-skinned arms. Your heart beats in this belly, bed of the slumbering double sex. Walk, at night, gently moving first this thigh, this other thigh and this left leg.

Appendix III

Pictorial translations of selected *Illuminations*

(a) Fête d'hiver/Winter Entertainment
(b) Fête d'hiver/Winter Entertainment
(c) Royauté/Royalty
(d) Royauté/Royalty
(e) Ville/City
(f) Villes I/Cities I
(g) Les Ponts/The Bridges
(h) Mystique/Mystique
(i) Mystique/Mystique
(j) Mystique/Mystique
(k) Mystique/Mystique
(l) Mystique/Mystique
(m) Mystique/Mystique
(n) Mystique/Mystique
(o) Mystique/Mystique
(p) Antique/Antique
(q) Antique/Antique

the greens and
reds   of the
setting   sun

and finally the city
seems to emerge
ready-formed
from the fortified papal palace

the tumbling water
churns and chimes
behind the huts
courtesy of
comic opera

girandoles in the orchards and
alleyways running
alongside the
Meander
                pick   up –

then the other branch
of the river
with its
                mediaeval bridge

Nymphs from the
pages of Horace
their hair
dressed
au Premier
Empire

dwarf willows going down to the Rhône to
bathe their abundant tresses

Siberian rounds footed by round Sibériennes

ʃinwaz (ə) from the brʌʃ   of buʃe

WINTER ENTERTAINMENT

(a)

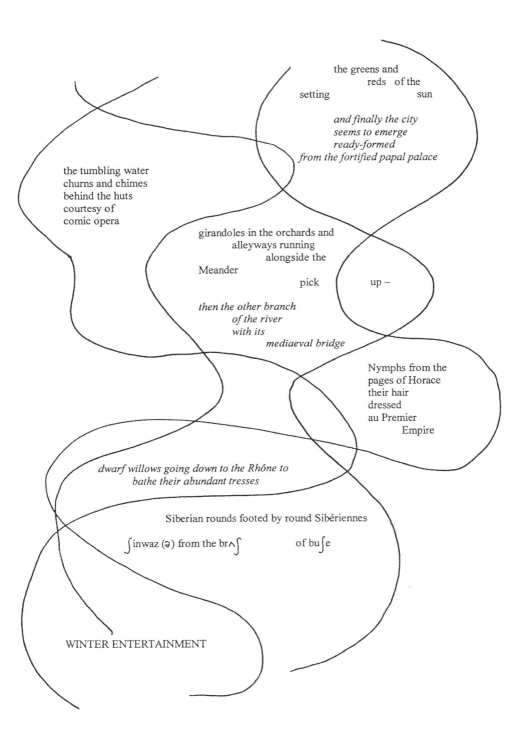

the greens and
reds   of the
setting   sun

and finally the city
seems to emerge
ready-formed
from the fortified papal palace

the tumbling water
churns and chimes
behind the huts
courtesy of
comic opera

girandoles in the orchards and
alleyways running
alongside the
Meander

pick   up –

then the other branch
of the river
with its
mediaeval bridge

Nymphs from the
pages of Horace
their hair
dressed
au Premier
Empire

dwarf willows going down to the Rhône to
bathe their abundant tresses

Siberian rounds footed by round Sibériennes

ʃinwaz (ə) from the brʌʃ   of buʃe

WINTER ENTERTAINMENT

(b)

Crash cop trapped in patrol car

By JAMIE PYATT

A BADLY injured cop was trapped for 90 minutes in his patrol car after a smash yesterday.

The 34-year-old PC was passenger in a marked Peugeot 406 which crashed with an Audi estate.

Firemen had to cut him free from the wreckage before he could be airlifted to Kent and Sussex Hospital in Tunbridge Wells, Kent.

A brigade insider said: "It was a very difficult job—and took over an hour and a half to release the man."

The unnamed officer, who is stationed in the town, suffered head and chest injuries plus a broken leg and ankle.

His condition was last night described as serious but stable.

Investigators

The police driver and occupants of the Audi — a mother and adult son — had minor injuries.

They were also treated at the Kent and Sussex Hospital.

The scene in Frant, East Sussex, was closed for five hours as accident investigators moved in.

A police spokesman said: "The passenger of the police vehicle is seriously injured.

"We are trying to determine how this could have happened."

● TWO policemen were hurt when their armed response car crashed and burst into flames — igniting bullets in the boot.

The cops escaped from the car near Gateshead, Tyne and Wear. The scene was sealed off as firemen tackled the blaze.

The victims were last night being treated for minor injuries at Newcastle General Hospital as a probe into the mystery smash got underway.

ROYALTY!

One fine morning, among a peace-loving people, a man and a woman, poised, self-assured, beautiful, loudly proclaimed in the public square: 'Friends, I want *her* to be queen!' 'I *want* to be queen!' She laughed and trembled. He told his friends of a revelation, of an ordeal finally at an end. Every now and then, they fell weakly against each other. And, indeed, they *were* king and queen for a whole morning, when the carmine-coloured drapes were hoisted on the house fronts, and throughout the afternoon, too, when their progress took them towards the gardens of palms.

SOPHIE'S MAID IT!

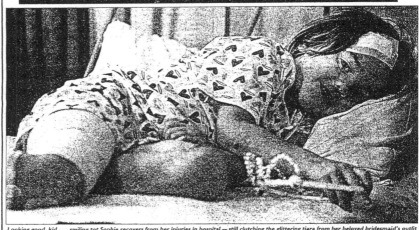

Looking good, kid . . . smiling tot Sophie recovers from her injuries in hospital — still clutching the glittering tiara from her beloved bridesmaid's outfit

So proud . . . in bridesmaid's gear before smash

Relief . . . dad Mark with Sophie and son Ben, 3

Wedding tot better after hit-run horror

By ROBIN PERRIE

BRIDESMAID Sophie Graham — left for dead by a hit-and-run driver eight days ago — has made an amazing recovery.

Sophie, five, was unconscious for three days after suffering a double skull fracture when she was mown down while showing off her wedding outfit to pals.

But she stunned nurses when she suddenly woke up and asked: "Can I have a bacon buttie?"

And to prove she was better, she followed that with a bowl of ice cream.

Printer dad Mark, of Gateshead, Tyne and Wear, said: "You couldn't see her for tubes at first, but you'd think nothing was wrong now."

Tiara

Sophie was bridesmaid for aunt Deborah Gregory, and loved her outfit so much she begged mum Andrea, 27, to let her play in it the next day.

But as she showed off her tiara and posy, driver Garry Wilkinson hit her in his Volvo. He got out of the car and looked at her before walking away.

Sophie, who also broke a leg, spent three days in intensive care before pulling round on Wednesday.

Mark, 28 — also dad to Matthew, six, and Ben, three — said: "She had a respirator and a bolt in her head. But the transformation is astonishing."

Wilkinson, 30, got six months' jail and a three-year driving ban. He admitted driving while disqualified, having no insurance, and failing to stop after an accident.

(c)

Daily Mail, Monday, July 23, 2001

Would-be Tory leader is given some forthright advice

By John Deans
Chief Political Correspondent

Give ground on Europe or lose, Clarke is warned

KENNETH CLARKE is being urged to boost his Tory leadership prospects by toning down his rhetoric on Europe and the euro.

Friends are telling him that softening his pro-euro stance would broaden his appeal among activists and with the electorate as a whole.

The pressure comes as Mr Clarke and Right-winger Iain Duncan Smith embark on nationwide tours this week to drum up support among the 330,000 Tory members.

Party vice-chairman Steve Norris said the former Chancellor should counter his image as a 'genial wrecker' by giving ground on Europe and showing he would be prepared to accept a pro-pound policy promoted by the Shadow Cabinet.

He warned Mr Clarke: 'There has to be a policy which is at the very least Eurosceptical, if not downright hostile. He has got to recognise the collective will of the Shadow Cabinet.

'If Kenneth Clarke wants to lead the Tory party, as many Conservatives hope he will, he has to understand that it's him who has to give some ground rather than the other way round.'

Mr Duncan Smith is standing by William Hague's pledge to 'save the pound' and will be making the single currency issue a central plank of his campaign.

With the party in the country as well as at Westminster dominated by Eurosceptics, Mr Clarke could be at a significant disadvantage if he does not moderate his approach.

Although he has said he does not see Europe as a mainstream issue for the Tory battle, he has acknowledged that if elected leader he would not be able to load his front bench with pro-euro MPs.

One of his campaign insiders said yesterday: 'He is clear about the limitations he will have because of the likely make-up of the Shadow Cabinet.'

Mr Norris, who supported Michael Portillo until his elimination last week, also took a swipe at Mr Duncan Smith.

He stressed that the Tories must aim to win back the six million voters since 1992, and warned: 'If we lurch off to the Right we might as well pack up and go home because, frankly, there won't be a lot of people around.'

But Mr Norris admitted that the choice between Mr Clarke and Mr Duncan Smith had left party

'They don't want the euro'

members 'between a rock and a hard place'.

Mr Duncan Smith appeared on the BBC TV Breakfast with Frost programme yesterday to insist that he is the underdog despite weekend surveys suggesting he is building a lead among local officials and rank and file members.

He reiterated his hardline stance on Europe, stressing the need to protect the democratic rights of nations and limit EU activities to co-operation on trade and legal affairs.

He was emphatic on the euro, declaring: 'The majority of the party is settled. They don't want to enter the euro. With me, we will be led to oppose the euro at the next referendum.'

Mr Clarke, meanwhile, was keeping a low profile yesterday.

He will meet Tory members in London today, then leave on a campaign tour which will take in the north-east of England, Scotland and Wales by the end of the week.

j.deans@dailymail.co.uk

ROYALTY!

One fine morning, among a peace-loving people, a man and a woman, poised, self-assured, beautiful, loudly proclaimed in the public square: 'Friends, I want *her* to be queen!' 'I *want* to be queen!' She laughed and trembled. He told his friends of a revelation, of an ordeal finally at an end. Every now and then, they fell weakly against each other. And, indeed, they *were* king and queen for a whole morning, when the carmine-coloured drapes were hoisted on the house fronts, and throughout the afternoon, too, when their progress took them towards the gardens of palms.

Harrison: 'Indomitable spirit'

Harrison 'knows he is going to die soon'

By Mark Reynolds

GEORGE HARRISON is losing his fight against cancer, friends suggested last night.

The former Beatle, who has been having radiotherapy after developing a secondary brain tumour, is said to have accepted he is dying.

The 58-year-old musician is reported to be 'philosophical' about his condition and is aware that he does not have long to live.

Sir George Martin described how Harrison made the emotional confession after being treated by leading cancer specialists in Switzerland.

'He is taking it easy and hoping that the thing will go away,' said Sir George, who was the group's producer. 'He has an indomitable spirit but he knows that he is going to die soon and he is accepting that.

'George is very philosophical. He does realise that everybody has got to die sometime. He has been near death many times and he's been rescued many times as well.

'But he knows he is going to die soon and he's accepting it perfectly happily.'

The other surviving Beatles, Sir Paul McCartney and Ringo Starr, were unavailable for comment.

News of the extent of Harrison's illness comes after he was diagnosed

'George is very philosophical'

with the malignant brain tumour last month, his third bout of cancer.

His fight against the disease began in 1997 when he discovered a cancerous growth on his neck. Two intensive courses of radiotherapy followed and he later received an all-clear.

'I got it purely from smoking,' he said at the time. 'Luckily, they found that this nodule was more of a warning than anything else. I'm not going to die on you folks just yet.'

After recovering, Harrison began having annual checks at the Mayo Clinic in the U.S. However, in March, he was diagnosed with lung cancer and had surgery to remove a tumour.

But after a convalescing in Tuscany with his second wife Olivia, he was diagnosed with brain cancer.

Professor Franco Cavalli, Switzerland's most senior cancer specialist who has treated Harrison in Bellinzona, said: 'He has not recovered but he is not a patient any more.'

In addition to his health battle, Harrison suffered an attack on his life in 1999 when a crazed fan broke into his mansion in Oxfordshire and stabbed him ten times. Michael Abram, 34, a former heroin addict, was sent to a mental hospital indefinitely last November.

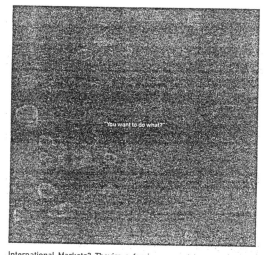
"You want to do what?"

International Markets? They're a foreign concept to some brokers.

With the notable exception of Sharepeople. The online broker that gives you access to multiple international markets from one account. And the only UK online broker that can say it's from American Express. All of which we hope is reason enough for you to consider us. If, however, you need a little more prompting we'll be happy to give you £100 when you join? So please call 0870 737 6000 during business hours or visit www.sharepeople.com The site's open all hours. Which is, now we mention it, another concept the average broker isn't too familiar with.

(d)

I am a
none too
discontented, soon
displaced
Citizen of
a modern
metropolis.
Modern?
Perhaps, since no
known taste
In
furnishings,
houses, city plan,
brings solace,

Nor
monument to
irrational belief.
Morals,
language stripped
to barest basics,
And lives
so uniform that
time is more their
thief
Than on
the continent, so
say the mad
statistics.

So,
as from my cottage window I can see
New spectres wading through the city's smoke,
Unending, thick – our sylvan shade, our summer

Night! – new Erinyes passing by my door,
My homeland and my whole heart's core,
Since all here's this, - our bustling servant-daughter

Death, dry-eyed, and Love

on wings of black despair, and Crime
prinked up and whining
in the muddy street.

(e)

The official acropolis far exceeds the most colossal conceptions of modern barbarity. Impossible to render in words the lustreless light emanating from the imperturbably grey sky,

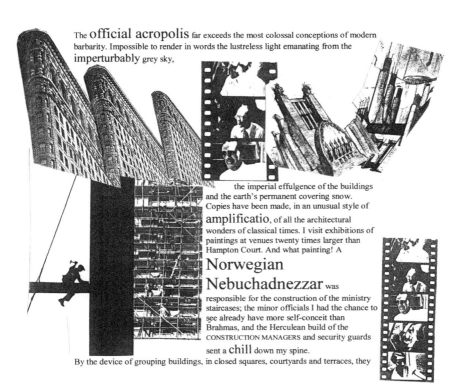

the imperial effulgence of the buildings and the earth's permanent covering snow. Copies have been made, in an unusual style of amplificatio, of all the architectural wonders of classical times. I visit exhibitions of paintings at venues twenty times larger than Hampton Court. And what painting! A

Norwegian Nebuchadnezzar was

responsible for the construction of the ministry staircases; the minor officials I had the chance to see already have more self-conceit than Brahmas, and the Herculean build of the CONSTRUCTION MANAGERS and security guards

sent a chill down my spine.

By the device of grouping buildings, in closed squares, courtyards and terraces, they

have effectively squeezed out the cabbies. The parks represent primitive nature

cultivated
Parts of the
impossible to account
boats, insinuates its sheet
giant candelabra. A short bridge

with consummate
upmarket district
for: an arm of the sea, unencumbered with
of frosty blue between quaysides top-heavy with
leads to a postern directly

Art.
are

beneath the

dome of the Sainte-Chapelle. This dome is an artistic steel armature about

15000 feet in diameter.

At several points on the

copper footbridges, platforms and staircases which wind round

the covered markets and pillars, I felt I could
calculate the vertical scale of the city. But one
miracle of construction I simply could not get a
take on: what are the levels of the other quarters
above or below the acropolis? For the
contemporary visitor it is impossible to work out
where one is. The commercial quarter is a circus
in A PERFECTLY UNIFORM STYLE, with
arcaded galleries. No shops are to be seen, but
the snow on the roadway has been trampled; a

handful of nabobs, as rare as

Sunday morning strollers in London, head
towards a carriage all set with diamonds. Several
red velvet divans: polar drinks are served which
cost between 800 and 8000 rupees. When it
occurs to me to look for theatres in this circus, I
tell myself that the shops must have their fair

share of shady dramas. I *think* there
is a police force; but the law must be so bizarre
that I give up trying to imagine what the

spivs and racketeers are like

hereabouts.

(f)

The suburbs, as elegant as the rue de Rivoli, are favoured with a bright atmosphere. The population works out at several hundred souls. Here again, the houses are not built in rows; the suburbs peter out oddly into the countryside, or rather, the

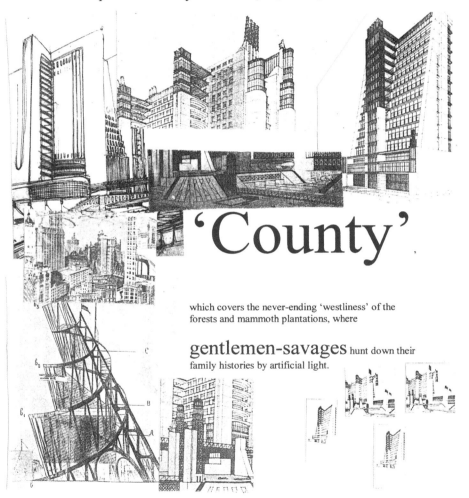

'County',

which covers the never-ending 'westliness' of the forests and mammoth plantations, where

gentlemen-savages hunt down their family histories by artificial light.

(f)

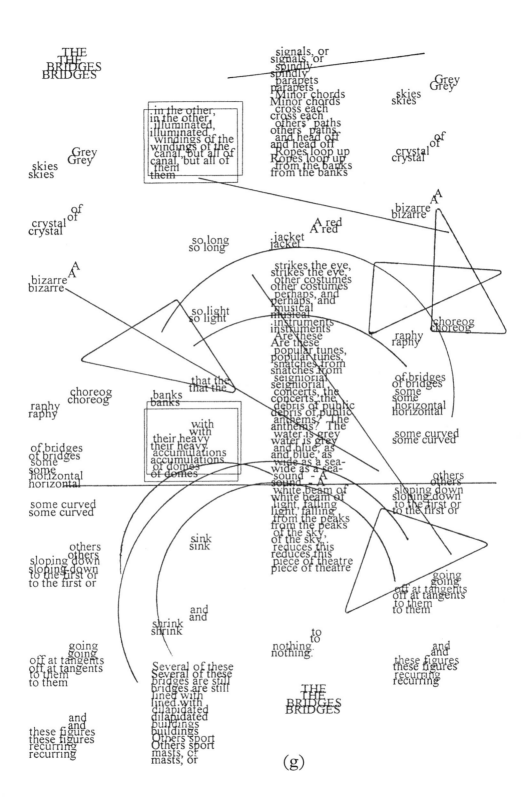

signals, or
spindly
parapets
Minor chords
cross each
others' paths
and head off
Ropes loop up
from the banks

Grey
skies

of
crystal

A
bizarre

choreog
raphy

of bridges
some
horizontal

some curved

others
sloping down
to the first or

going
off at tangents
to them

and
these figures
recurring

Grey
skies

of
crystal

A
bizarre

choreog
raphy

of bridges
some
horizontal

some curved

others
sloping down
to the first or

going
off at tangents
to them

and
these figures
recurring

in the other,
illuminated,
windings of the
canal, but all of
them

so long

so light

that the

banks

with
their heavy
accumulations
of domes

sink

and

shrink

Several of these
bridges are still
lined with
dilapidated
buildings
Others sport
masts, or

A red
jacket

strikes the eye,
other costumes
perhaps, and
musical
instruments
Are these
popular tunes,
snatches from
seigniorial
concerts, the
debris of public
anthems? The
water is grey
and blue, as
wide as a sea-
sound - A
white beam of
light, falling
from the peaks
of the sky,
reduces this
piece of theatre

to
nothing.

THE
BRIDGES

(g)

On the sloping embankment

MYSTIQUE

the angels wheel their woollen robes

inthemeadowgrassesofsteelandemerald

of the hill-breast

up   in leaps to the tip

lick

of flame

Fields

On the left

the decaying vegetation on the ridge
is trampled over by all the homicides and all the battles
and all the noises of disaster describe their

arcing parabolas

Behind the right-hand
ridge

the   line   of Orients   of   advances

And   while the band at the top of the picture is
made of   wheeling and leaping
the distant   surf-surge
of conches
and human   nights

the flowery *douceur* of the stars   the sky and all that   swivels
down
upturned
opposite the embankment   like a basket – so close
to our faces and becomes the blue
flowering abyss   beneath

(h)

On the sloping embankment

MYSTIQUE

the angels wheel their woollen robes

inthemeadowgrassesofsteelandemerald
of the hill-breast
up   in leaps to the tip
lick
of flame
Fields

On the left

the decaying vegetation on the ridge
is trampled over by all the homicides and all the battles
and all the noises of disaster describe their

arcing parabolas

Behind the right-hand
ridge

the   line   of Orients   of   advances

And while the band at the top of the picture is
made of   wheeling and leaping
the distant   surf-surge
of conches
and human   nights

the flowery *douceur* of the stars   the sky   and all that
swivels
down
upturned
opposite the embankment   like a basket – so close
to our faces and becomes
the blue
flowering abyss
beneath

(i)

On the sloping embankment

MYSTIQUE

the angels wheel their woollen robes

inthemeadowgrassesofsteelandemerald

of the hill-breast

up   in leaps to the tip

lick

of flame

Fields

On the left

the decaying vegetation on the ridge
is trampled over by all the homicides
and all the battles
and all the noises of disaster describe their

arcing parabolas

Behind the right-hand
ridge

the   line   of Orients   of   advances

And while the band at the top of the picture is
made of   wheeling and leaping
the distant
surf-surge of conches
and human   nights

the flowery *douceur* of the stars the sky and all that
swivels
down
upturned
opposite the embankment   like a basket – so close
to our faces and becomes
the blue
flowering abyss
beneath

(j)

On the sloping embankment On the sloping embankment

MYSTIQUE MYSTIQUE

the clanging wheel the clanging wheel in their woollen robes
ofsteelandemerald
of the hill-breast

inthemeadowgrassesofsteelandemerald up in leaps to the tip
ofsteelandemerald flame of the hill-breast of the hill-breast

of up in leaps to the tip
Fields flame lick
of flame
On the left Fields

the decaying vegetation on the ridge
On the left is trampled over by all the homicides
and all the battles
and all the noises of disaster describe their vegetation on the ridge
is trampled over by all the homicides

and all the battles and all the battles
and all the noises of disaster describe their
arcing parabolas
behind the Right-hand

ridge arcing parabola parabolas
theline of Orients of advances

Behind the right-hand right-hand
And ridge while the band at the top of the picture is
ridge made of the distant wheeling and leaping

theline line of Orients Orients of of advances advances
surf-surge of conches

And while the band at the top of the picture is
made of distant wheeling and leaping

the flowery douceur of the stars the sky and all that
the distant surf-surge of conches
surf-surge of conches

and human nights
upturned opposite the embankment like a basket –
and becomes

so close to our faces
the flowery douceur of the stars the sky and all that
the blue swivels
flowering abyss down
upturned beneath

opposite the embankment like a basket – so close
to our faces to our faces and becomes becomes
the blue
the blue flowering abyss
flowering abyss beneath
beneath

(k)

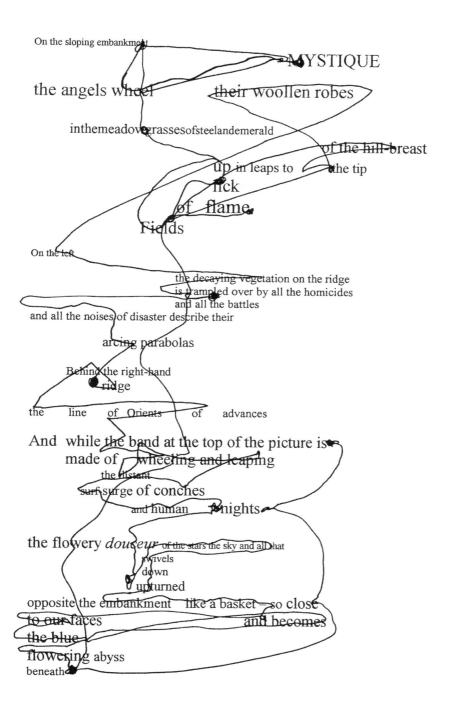

On the sloping embankment

MYSTIQUE

the angels wheel   their woollen robes

inthemeadovergrassesofsteelandemerald

of the hill-breast

up in leaps to   the tip

lick

of flame,

Fields

On the left

the decaying vegetation on the ridge

is trampled over by all the homicides

and all the battles

and all the noises of disaster describe their

arcing parabolas

Behind the right-hand

ridge

the   line   of Orients   of   advances

And   while the band at the top of the picture is
made of   wheeling and leaping

the distant

surf surge of conches

and human   knights

the flowery *douceur* of the stars the sky and all that

swivels

down

upturned

opposite the embankment   like a basket — so close

to our faces   and becomes

the blue

flowering abyss

beneath

(1)

On the sloping embankment

MYSTIQUE

the angels wheel their woollen robes

inthemeadowgrassesofsteelandemerald

of the hill-breast

up in leaps to   the tip

lick

of flame

Fields

On the left

the decaying vegetation on the ridge
is trampled over by all the homicides
and all the battles

and all the noises of disaster describe their

arcing parabolas

Behind the right-hand
ridge

the   line   of Orients   of   advances

And while the band at the top of the picture is
made of   wheeling and leaping
the distant
surf-surge of conches
and human   nights

the flowery *douceur* of the stars the sky and all that
swivels
down
upturned

opposite the embankment   like a basket – so close
to our faces   and becomes
the blue
flowering abyss
beneath

(m)

MYSTIQUE

the angels wheel their woollen robes

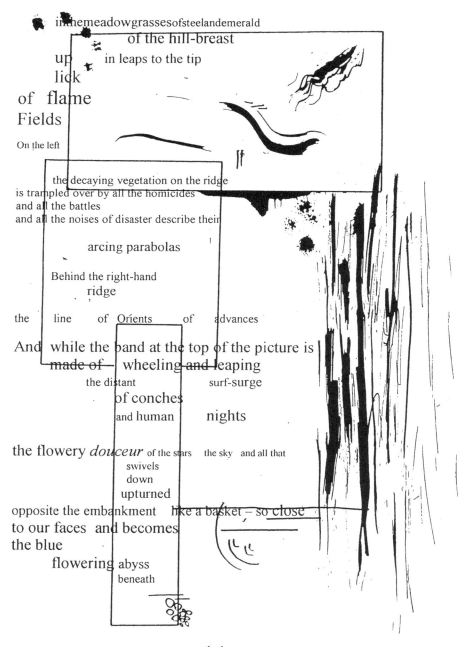

inthemeadowgrassesofsteelandemerald

of the hill-breast

up   in leaps to the tip

lick

of flame

Fields

On the left

the decaying vegetation on the ridge
is trampled over by all the homicides
and all the battles
and all the noises of disaster describe their

arcing parabolas

Behind the right-hand
ridge

the   line   of Orients   of   advances

And while the band at the top of the picture is
made of   wheeling and leaping
the distant   surf-surge
of conches
and human   nights

the flowery *douceur* of the stars   the sky and all that
swivels
down
upturned
opposite the embankment   like a basket – so close
to our faces and becomes
the blue
flowering abyss
beneath

(n)

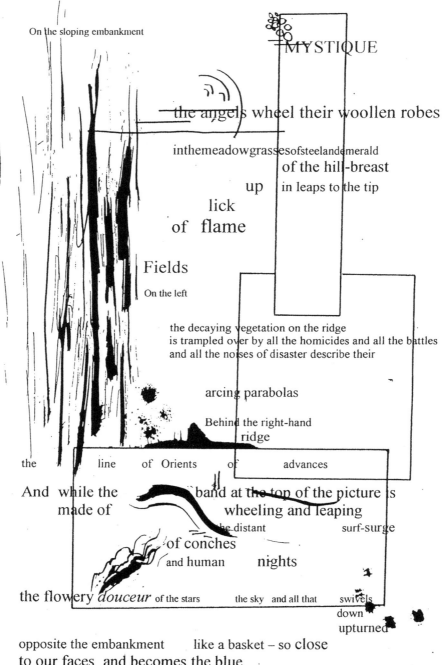

On the sloping embankment

MYSTIQUE

the angels wheel their woollen robes

inthemeadowgrassesofsteelandemerald
of the hill-breast
up   in leaps to the tip

lick
of flame

Fields

On the left

the decaying vegetation on the ridge
is trampled over by all the homicides and all the battles
and all the noises of disaster describe their

arcing parabolas

Behind the right-hand
ridge

the   line   of   Orients   of   advances

And while the   band at the top of the picture is
made of   wheeling and leaping
the distant   surf-surge
of conches
and human   nights

the flowery *douceur* of the stars   the sky and all that   swivels
down
upturned

opposite the embankment   like a basket – so close
to our faces and becomes the blue
flowering abyss   beneath

(o)

Son Of PAN

*f*ull of grace!

Around your br0w 0 ⌒ 0 ⌢ ⌢ 0

Cr0wned with flowerets

and **berries**

your EYES,

precious orbs,

move

stained with darkening wine dregs,
your cheeks

sink to

SUNKEN

Your sharp *teethgleam*

Your torso is like a cithara
p-l-u-c-k-e-d notes
up and down

run

your   pale-skinned arms

your   heartbeats in this   belly

bed   of the slumbering double sex

WALK, AT NIGHT,   gently moving

first this *thigh*   this *other* thigh

and this left

leg

(p)

Your eyes precious

Son of grace ORBS full MOVE

a c b a r
r w
A round
n e j o
d with sharp teeth gLEAM
your cheeks ink to sunken
stained with
darkening
wine of dregs
and berries

plucked notes in
up Up up and
down day down
down

your torso is like a cithara
torso is your like cithara a
like your cithara a torso is
cithara torso your a like is
your

arms

your
heart
beats

in this

b
belly
d

Walk

at night of the slumbering
gently double e x
moving
first
thi s   o th er
thi gh   th igh
th is and
th is
left
leg

(q)

Notes

Introduction

1. Of course we must recognise that within prose, punctuation had always been available for requisitioning as an index of the temporality of thought within the phrase, as an index of the movement of the voice through the verbal material. But these psychic, respiratory and affective gestures were always deemed secondary to punctuation's grammatical and syntactic duties and thus could be developed only patchily and inconsistently. It is true that certain punctuation marks assimilated to themselves lives which were almost exclusively expressive (suspension points, the dash when not pursuing its parenthesising function), but other marks continued to have their expressive potentialities suppressed by more utilitarian functions. Critical attention has certainly been paid to the expressive punctuation of *Illuminations*, and especially to the dash (see, for example, Lapeyre 1981: 448–50; Macklin 1990; Murat 2002: 333–65), but in this project, I shall be paying it scant regard.

2. Oliver Bernard's admirable 1962 translation of Rimbaud's work has quite rightly maintained its position over the years as the standard version. More recent accounts of the *Illuminations* by Daniel Sloate (1990), Mark Treharne (1998) and Martin Sorrell (2001) deserve high praise for their compelling resourcefulness. And it should be noted that Paul Schmidt's influential translations of 1967 present us with *Illuminations* done into free verse; I am merely attempting to make further progress in the direction he has indicated, a direction already more radically explored by Hans Therre and Rainer Schmidt in their 1988 German version. ('Wir stöbern nicht nach irgendeinem SINN, wir wollen SINNLICHKEIT freisetzen' (2000: 7) [We are not rummaging after some MEANING or other, we want to release SENSORIALITY]).

Chapter 1

1. Auden puts the point succinctly: 'A writer bears the responsibility for what

he writes [. . .]. In a case where his original is really obscure, that is to say, his difficulty in understanding it is not due to his own ignorance or stupidity, what is the translator to do? Should he give as literal a translation as he can, and thus write an English sentence which he cannot himself understand, or should he write an intelligible English sentence at the cost of altering what the original text actually says? Personally, in cases of desperation, I believe he should take the second course (Auden and Sjöberg 1964: 25). But this situation only means that the reader looks up to the translator and is, consequently, and perhaps deservedly, 'translated down to' (Auden and Sjöberg 1964: 26) by the translator.

2.   'That said, one should add that the vast range of readings to which "Angoisse" has given rise is indicative in itself of a text and a collection which is elusive, multi-layered, chameleon-like and forever escaping the confines of any definitive interpretation. Rimbaud's prose poetry refuses to become familiar with or to the reader' (Macklin 2000: 172).

3.   See, for example, Macklin's 'Epiphany, Identity, Celebration: Towards a Definition of the Rimbaldian *Poème-Fête*' (1998).

4.   Steve Murphy, for example, is of the view that over-emphasis on individual texts actively blinds us to revealing links and unjustifiably promotes a Rimbaldian aesthetic of the fragment: 'L'exercice consistant à lire *en diagonale* les *Illuminations* ne nous paraît pas—dans le sens spatial—dépourvu d'intérêt: lorsqu'on prive chaque texte de ses relations avec d'autres *Illuminations*, c'est la démarche critique elle-même qui fragmente, attribuant ensuite une essence fragmentaire qui n'est que l'inévitable conséquence d'une vision réductrice de l'œuvre' (1998 : 159) [The exercise, which involves skimming through the *Illuminations*, does not seem to us devoid of interest: when one deprives each text of its connections with other *Illuminations*, it is the critical process itself which fragments, subsequently ascribing to the work a fragmentary essence which is no more than the inevitable outcome of the reductive vision applied to it].

5.   As Barthes puts it: 'Ainsi peut s'amorcer au sein de l'œuvre critique le dialogue de deux histoires et de deux subjectivités, celles de l'auteur et celles du critique. Mais ce dialogue est égoïstement tout entier déporté vers le présent: la critique n'est pas un « hommage » à la vérité du passé, ou à la vérité de « l'autre », elle est construction de l'intelligible de notre temps' (1964a: 257) [Thus there can begin, at the heart of the critical work, the dialogue between two histories and between two subjectivities, those of the author and those of the critic. But this dialogue is, egoistically, wholly biassed towards the present: criticism is a 'tribute' neither to the truth of the past, nor to the truth of the 'other', it is the construction of the intelligibility of our time].

6.   I do accept, however, that it is in the ideological interests of sacred STs to be seen as immutable, and that the TTs of sacred STs must correspondingly be seen as immutable, if spirit-channelling (see Robinson 2001) is to have any credibility].

7.   Barthes expresses it thus: 'Fiction d'un individu (quelque M. Teste à l'envers) qui abolirait en lui les barrières, les classes, les exclusions, non par syncrétisme, mais par simple débarras de ce vieux spectre: *la contradiction logique*; qui mélangerait tous les langages, fussent-ils réputés incompatibles; [. . .] Alors le vieux mythe biblique se retourne, la confusion des langues n'est plus une punition, le sujet accède à la jouissance par la cohabitation des

langages, *qui travaillent côte à côte:* le texte de plaisir, c'est Babel heureuse' (1973: 9–10) [The fiction of an individual (some Mr Teste in reverse) who abolishes within himself barriers, classes, exclusions, not by syncretism, but by simply getting rid of that old ghost: *logical contradiction;* who mixes all languages, even those meant to be incompatible; (. . .) Thus the old Biblical myth is reversed, the confusion of languages is no longer a punishment, the subject achieves bliss through the cohabitation of languages, *working side by side:* the text of pleasure, is Babel happy].

Chapter 2

1. This cited article has equally interesting things to say about the exclamation mark: 'Le point d'exclamation consiste en un trait vertical qui s'élargit en s'élevant; cette figure a par elle-même quelque chose d'élancé, de jaillissant, sorte d'image des sentiments subits et expansifs qui, d'ordinaire, provoquent l'exclamation. . .' [The exclamation mark consists of a vertical stroke which widens as it rises; this mark has in itself something aspirational, upthrusting, about it, a sort of image of sudden, expansive feelings which, ordinarily, provoke exclamation].

2. Cornulier argues that even if one accepts Fongaro's procedure in principle, the lines he discovers are anachronistic (i.e. their structural novelty is not confirmed by contemporary practice in regular verse). This argument might itself be questioned: Baudelaire, for instance, pushes the *trimètre* in asymmetrical directions, and Verlaine's handling of the 6 + 6 structure of the alexandrine at this time (*Romances sans paroles*, 1874) is, on occasion, extremely rough; but that is not the point. The point is that, by virtue of prose's very nature as a medium, no rhythmic configuration within it can be anachronistic; intimating that these may be lines of verse becomes an arch provocation of a very Rimbaldian kind. Besides, one might equally claim that the first occurrence of any phenomenon is, in a sense, before its time. I would, in any case, want to suggest that the critical world needs to make room for the anachronisms of reading (2002a: 239–52) (Montaigne sometimes sounds like Proust), no less than for readers' idiosyncratic routines (see Cornulier 1994: 109); and this suggestion becomes more urgent when we turn to translation, since, if it is the task of the ST to make progress through the TT, anachronism is not merely unavoidable, it is positively desirable, and the translator, far from seeking to act the part of a certain historical Arthur Rimbaud, accepts the consequences of being what Cornulier calls 'n'importe quel lecteur de n'importe quelle époque' [any reader of any period] (1994: 107).

3. See also Sergio Sacchi: 'Certes, l' « image », en principe, peut se définir par opposition à ce qui lui fait essentiellement défaut: la réalité. Or ce manque peut donner, paradoxalement, à l'image aérienne nichée dans la mémoire, un poids écrasant, paralysant, comme à la fin d'*Ouvriers*: « Je veux que ce bras durci ne traîne plus *une chère image* ». L'«idée du Déluge » de l'*incipit* tient, elle aussi, de l'«image » dans cette acception dépréciative' (1994: 60) [Admittedly the 'image' can, in theory, be defined in opposition to what is essentially missing from it: reality. Now this lack can, paradoxically, endow the ethereal image, nestling in the memory, with a crushing, paralysing weight, as at the end of 'Workers': 'I do not want this hardened arm any more

299

to drag along *a dear image.* The 'idea of the Flood' of the opening also relates to the 'image' in this pejorative sense].

4. Denis (1968) is the first to explore the equation between Flood and Commune in any depth.

5. Sacchi manages to derive some compensating consolation from this image-bound negativity: 'Certes, ces images "merveilleuses" ne sont, finalement, que des images: les paroles, le savoir secret, le sens définitif leur manque toujours—puisque « la Reine [. . .] ne voudra jamais nous raconter ce qu'elle sait [. . .] ». Elles ne seront jamais qu'une pure surface visuelle. Cependant, c'est en elles et par elles que se réalise une véritable transfiguration des choses' (1994: 61). [Admittedly, these 'marvellous' images are only, when all is said and done, images: words, secret knowledge, a definitive meaning continues to be missing from them—since 'the Queen (. . .) will never wish to tell us what she knows (. . .)'. They will only ever be pure visual surfaces. However, it is in and through them that a true transfiguration of things is achieved]. I remain unpersuaded.

6. Much critical opinion favours the presence of the cyclic in 'Après le Déluge'. See, for example, Osmond 1976: 87; Guyaux 1985b: 239–40 (although this is a cycle of 'phantasmal' Floods); Sacchi 1994: 59: 'En effet, à l'instar du renouveau qui revient cycliquement, l'événement révolu pourrait refaire surface, tel quel, dans l'heure présente [. . .]. Ainsi, les Déluges devenus pluriels au verset 12, l'avant-dernier du poème, évoquent peut-être aussi la possibilité d'un retour cyclique' [In fact, in the manner of renewal which returns in cycles, the completed event might re-surface, as it was, in the present (. . .). Thus the Floods, now plural in the twelfth and penultimate *verset* of the poem, perhaps also conjure up the possibility of a cyclical return].

7. See Barthes 1980: 175–6: 'Tel serait le « destin » de la Photographie: en me donnant à croire (il est vrai, une fois sur combien ?) que j'ai trouvé « la vraie photographie totale », elle accomplit la confusion inouïe de la réalité (« *Cela a été* ») et de la vérité (« *C'est ça* »); elle devient à la fois constative et exclamative [. . .]' [Such would be the Photograph's 'destiny': by leading me to believe (it is true, once out of how many times ?) that I have found 'the true, total photograph', it brings about the unheard-of confusion of reality (*'That-has-been'*) and truth (*'That's it'*); it becomes at once a record and an exclamation (. . .)].

8. We might here refer to Barbey d'Aurevilly's comment in a letter to Trebutien: 'Et de fait il y a dans le diable de *fouillis* qui est ma nature [. . .] couché quelque part, un poète inconnu et c'est des œuvres cachées de ce poète que ceci a été traduit dans la furie ou la Rêverie d'un moment' (1966: 1612) [And indeed there is in the devilish *jumble* that is my nature (. . .) lying doggo somewhere, an unknown poet and it is from the hidden works of this poet that this has been translated in the frenzy or Reverie of a moment]; or, alternatively, to Marc Fumaroli (1984: 53): 'Le propre du poème en prose, c'est de se donner pour le reflet imparfait, allusif, d'une œuvre idéale absente. Par là, du reste, il peut prétendre à un pouvoir de suggestion supérieur à l'œuvre close et parfaite à laquelle il donne l'impression de renvoyer. Il s'apparente à la traduction, elle aussi «énigme dans un miroir » d'une œuvre achevée, mais reposant ailleurs, dans une autre langue' [It is the peculiarity of the prose poem to pass itself off as the imperfect, allusive reflection of an absent, ideal work. By this means, besides, it can lay claim to powers of suggestion superior

to the closed and perfect work to which it seems to refer us. It is related to translation, which, likewise, is 'the enigma in a mirror' of a work complete but located elsewhere, in another language].

9. Since my focus in this discussion is necessarily limited, I would refer readers to the searching studies of 'Aube' by Hackett (1969), Bobillot (2001) and Pensom (2002).

10. It might be suggested that this verset—and the echo which occurs in the final paragraph of the poem—alludes to Baudelaire's 'Le Guignon', which itself is largely composed of 'translations' of Longfellow and Gray. Where Gray/Baudelaire pair the gem and flower in a shared condition of wasteful neglect in a hostile environment ('gem of purest ray' v. 'dark unfathom'd caves'; sweet flower v. desert), Rimbaud distinguishes between the activities and direction of gem and flower, only to imply that the creative impulse may find ways of giving them a common purpose.

11. For other suggestions about how sonnet structure might be reconstructed from this poem, see Schaettel (1976) and Little (1980).

Chapter 3

1. This aspect would also include the cultural characteristics of certain phonetic components—the connection between nasality and expressions of respectfulness, for example, or of class membership—and the phonetic features of national speech habits: the French speak 'dans le masque' [in the front of the face] (facial resonators), hence phenomena such as the 'baryton martin'; the Russians, on the other hand, 'poitrinent' [chest-speak/chest-sing] and thus produce their typical bassi profundos.

2. Rodenburg (1998: 8–9) speaks of aiming to make 'the voice so fundamentally a part of the actor's physical being that it actually becomes an extension both of yourself and your talent'.

3. This is a view that Lecourt—albeit undisparagingly—would endorse: 'Qu'est-ce que la parole? Un outil, rien d'autre. [. . .] votre parole doit se comporter en outil docile et vous suivre sans que vous vous en préoccupiez' (1999: 11–12) [What is speech ? A tool, nothing more. (. . .) your words must behave like a docile tool and follow your lead without your having to concern yourself with them] .

4. 'Timbre' in the sense that concerns us is defined by *Le Petit Larousse Illustré* (1999: 1011) as 'Qualité particulière du son, indépendante de sa hauteur ou de son intensité mais spécifique de l'instrument, de la voix qui l'émet. *Voix au timbre chaud*' [Particular quality of sound, independent of its pitch or intensity but specific to the instrument or voice which produces it. *Voice with a warm timbre*] . The account in *Le Nouveau Petit Robert* (1993: 2253) is remarkably similar: 'Qualité spécifique des sons produits par un instrument, indépendante de leur hauteur, de leur intensité et de leur durée. [. . .] PAR ANAL. *Le timbre de la voix.* [. . .] *Le timbre clair d'une voix*' [Specific quality of sounds produced by an instrument, independent of their pitch, their intensity or their duration. (. . .) BY ANALOGY. *The timbre of the voice.* (. . .) *The bright timbre of a voice*].

5. For an overview of directions taken in 'body studies', see Gliserman 1996: 1–29. Gliserman's own enterprise is disentangling the bodily layers embedded in the text of novels, in the form of explicit and symbolic

references, and of syntactic 'gestures'.

6. The value that Barthes ascribes to the word 'phonétique' seems rather inconsistent with itself. Here, it represents a segmental element, a fragment likely to undo our grasp of the suprasegmental, while in the quotation further up the page, from *Le Plaisir du texte*, it has the virtue of the pre-phonological.

7. One might quote, as an example, this paragraph from 'Fairy': '—Après le moment de l'air des bûcheronnes à la rumeur du torrent sous la ruine des bois, de la sonnerie des bestiaux à l'écho des vals, et des cris des steppes.'

8. Chantal Chawaf (1992: 8) describes writing's responsibility for the situation we describe in this way: 'Trop souvent l'écrit est une position obsessionnelle de contrôle et de mise à distance du vivant. La parole, la voix, le corps, le désir, l'émotion sont « momifiés » en littérature par l'écriture qui ne laisse de la chair qu'un art plutôt funéraire, qu'un masque plutôt mortuaire de la vie captive' [Too often the written is an obsessional position of control and distantiation from the living. Speech, the voice, the body, desire, emotion are 'mummified' in literature by writing which reduces the flesh to something like a funerary art, to something like a death-mask of captive life].

9. Pierre Brunel (1998: 92) comments: 'Atmosphère de cour, cette fois (à l'opposé du « sans parents ni cour » du premier alinéa), avec des terrasses voisines de la mer qui font penser à Elseneur et à Ophélie' [Courtly atmosphere, this time (contrary to the 'sans parents ni cour' of the first paragraph), with terraces overlooking the sea which bring to mind Elsinore and Ophelia].

10. One is reminded of what Antoine Raybaud has to say about the 'Enfance' cycle as a whole. Rimbaud explores possible childhoods and possibilities of childhood, where memory crosses over with fantasy: 'l'enfance n'est plus le lieu des origines, mais l'espace de dispersion de tous les possibles de l'*identité problématique*' (1989: 194) [childhood is no longer the place of origins, but the space of dispersal of all the possibilities of *problematic identity*].

11. The Lettrists' ambitions for poetic language correspond closely to the ones we are pursuing in this chapter: 'Une matière, à la source d'un gigantesque continent de beautés sonores, se tenait dans l'ombre du langage établi et de ses associations limitées. Les lettres, les bruits humains (de l'*aspiration* au *claquement de doigt*, ou au *frappement de pied*) antérieurs aux mots, particules plus fines que les mots agglomérés, entrent dans la lumière du lyrisme verbal, mué en lyrisme pré-verbal, *phonétique*' (Curtay 1974: 39) [A material, at the source of an immense continent of acoustic beauties, lay waiting in the shadow of established language and its limited associations. Letters, human noises (from *breathing in* to the *snapping of fingers*, or the *stamping of feet*) prior to words, particles finer than agglomerated words, enter the light of verbal lyricism, transformed into pre-verbal, *phonetic* lyricism].

12. Curtay (1974: 71) provides an example of a Lettrist transcription of Mallarmé's:

> La chair est triste, hélas! Et j'ai lu tous les livres.
> Fuir ! là-bas fuir ! Je sens que des oiseaux sont ivres

into:

> Gdajagass, gdjagass, la berr est biste jétu toutétivre
> Foulfi, ah, foulfir hava hava où doandégo onquivre.

13. Laforgue's notes on Baudelaire, written early in 1885, cover nineteen sheets.

The relevant comments run:

Baudelaire

> chat, indou, yankee, épiscopal alchimiste
> [. . .]
> Yankee ses 'très-' devant un adjectif
> ses paysages cassants—et ce vers
> 'mon esprit, tu te meus avec agilité'
> que les initiés détaillent d'une voix métallique.
> (Hiddleston 1980: 111).

[Baudelaire

> cat, Hindu, Yankee, episcopal alchemist
> (. . .)
> Yankee, his 'très-' before an adjective
> peremptory landscapes, and this line
> 'my spirit, you move with agility'
> that the initiated spell out with a metallic voice.]

Chapter 4

1. And we should add, since we have trafficked with this trope in the previous chapter, that anamorphosis lies somewhere between juxtaposition and metamorphosis. Unlike metamorphosis, anamorphosis is a change not in the thing seen but in the seeing of it, but it is an experience of the single object (object-complex) split in two as it were and not a juxtaposition of two objects as in the tenor and vehicle of a metaphor. It is above all a process of non-identification or misidentification which resolves itself into a moment of recognition. It is very closely related to, and frequently synonymous with, the cinematic device of double-take. Anamorphosis's moment of recognition is a moment of truth, but that truth may be a recognition of the uncanny in the familiar or of the familiar in the initially uncanny.

2. See, for example, Jean-Pierre Richard: 'Lieux, moments, existences vont donc être rendus à une liberté merveilleuse, le réel se faire l'espace même du possible, les sensations se multiplier, et tout glisser à la métamorphose' (1955: 220–1) [Places, moments, existences are thus to be given a wonderful liberty, the real is to become the very space of the possible, sensations are to be multiplied, and everything is to slip into metamorphosis]; or Peter Broome: 'Moved by the conviction that the *Illuminations* are still very much a text *en devenir* and, by their very structure and substance, metamorphic' (1979: 378).

3. Osmond's view of 'Enfance III' is predominantly sanguine: the birdsong is tingling revelation, the clock points to a magic outside time, the costumed procession of child-players represents 'a favourite image for poetry and freedom' (1976: 92–3), although he does concede that in the final verset, the text plunges 'abruptly, into a sort of resigned despair' which 'intensifies the feeling of exclusion'. For Berranger (1993: 267–8), the atmosphere is more consistently dark, the exclusion irreversible from the start, the guilt unappealable: 'Les images de perte, de défection, de déception se multiplient: l'horloge ne sonne pas, la petite voiture est abandonnée, quelqu'un vous

chasse; les participes passés insistent sur un inéluctable achèvement ("abandonnée", "enrubannée", "aperçus")' (267) [The images of loss, of desertion, of disappointment, multiply: the clock does not chime, the small carriage is abandoned, someone chases you away; the past participles insist on an inescapable pastness ('abandonnée', 'enrubannée', 'aperçus')]. Solitude is the price of freedom, singularity the mode of vision of those outside community (the 'nid de bêtes blanches', the 'petits comédiens en costumes'). But if these differences of interpretative colouring are no more than is to be expected, one might register rather more surprise at the difference of response to dynamic and perspectival indications: for Osmond these versets are moments frozen by their very perceptual acuity: 'a series of discrete perceptions, each by its very isolation focussed with great sharpness' (1976: 92); for Berranger, on the other hand, 'Enfance III' is a rather more restless, kaleidoscopic text: 'Toute une série de mouvements agitent ce texte en tous sens, malgré l'arrêt induit par l'anaphore et le présent de "Il y a"' (1993: 267) [A whole series of movements toss this text in all directions, despite the immobilisation induced by the anaphora and the presentness of 'Il y a']. And, correspondingly perhaps, different claims are made about the presiding point of view: 'Rimbaud here gives us not so much things seen in childhood as images of the nature of childhood vision' (Osmond 1976: 92); 'La structure anaphorique, qui génère le rythme, est une tournure impersonnelle: ce qui donne au texte le ton du bilan, du constat dés-affecté: le « Je » qui n'est encore qu'un « *vous* », puis « *on* », se retourne, quittant l'enfance, pour un moment d'arrêt, comme en suspens avant l'assujettissement définitif, au temps, à l'identité' (Berranger 1993: 267) [The anaphoric structure, which generates the rhythm, is an impersonal turn of phrase: which gives the text the tone of a balance-sheet, of a dis-affected report: the 'I' which is still only a 'you', then 'one', turns back, as it quits childhood, for a moment's pause, as if in momentary suspension before its definitive subjection to time, to identity]. An imitation or recreation of childhood vision? Or the disengaged, 'documentary' perspective of the adolescent already beyond childhood and casting a cool, backward glance?

4. I count 'faëry' as three syllables. But the difference between 'faëry' and 'fairy' is not one syllable. It is the difference between, on the one hand, the archaic, the poetical, the beyond reach, the unassimilable, the alien, and, on the other, the domesticated, the picturesque, the banal—the mythological to the faëry's mythic, the narrative to the faëry's existential. The difference expresses the tensions to be found in the poem between a 'lost domain' and a 'fête foraine', between an eerie otherworld and the convivially charming. But do readers any longer make a distinction of pronunciation (i.e. a pronunciation of 'faëry' which sounds much closer to the French 'féerie')?

5. We have already had occasion to refer to Hopkins. The diversification of a single hue, as here, might remind us that Hopkins undertakes similar exercises, in order to 'inscape' colour, as in 'Henry Purcell':

    The thunder-purple seabeach, plumèd purple-of-thunder

    But, equally, we might turn to the remark made by Mallarmé about Manet's *Le Bal de l'Opéra* (1873–74), some couple of years after Rimbaud's poem (supposing it to belong to 1872–73): 'Je ne crois pas qu'il y ait lieu de faire autre chose que de s'étonner de la gamme délicieuse trouvée dans les noirs'

(1945: 698) [I do not think there is any reason to do other than marvel at the delicious gamut brought out in the blacks].

Chapter 5

1. 'Si toutes les paroles se ressemblent, tous les silences diffèrent, et la plupart du temps toute une destinée dépend de *la qualité* de ce premier silence que deux âmes vont former' (Maeterlinck 1901: 19) [If all utterances resemble each other, all silences differ, and for most of the time a whole destiny hangs by *the quality* of this first silence that two souls generate].
2. 'Tel est le plan de mon volume Lyrique, et tel sera peut-être son titre, La Gloire du Mensonge, ou le Glorieux Mensonge. Je chanterai en désespéré !' (to Henri Cazalis, 28 April 1866(?), in Marchal 1995: 298) [Such is the plan of my Lyric volume, and such will perhaps be its title, The Glory of Lying, or the Glorious Lie. I will sing as one in despair].
3. 'mais mon admiration tout entière va droit au grand Mage inconsolable et obstiné chercheur d'un mystère qu'il sait ne pas exister, et qu'il poursuivra, à jamais pour cela, du deuil de son lucide désespoir, car *c'eût été* la Vérité' (to Odilon Redon, February 2 1885, in Marchal 1995: 575) [but all my admiration focusses on the great Magus, the inconsolable and dogged seeker of a mystery, which he knows does not exist, and which he will pursue, for ever for all that, from the sorrow of his lucid despair, because *it would have been* the Truth].
4. Bernard/Guyaux remind us that 'strideur' also appears in 'Paris se repeuple', where, equally, 'il s'agit d'un clairon silencieux, dont la musique est « latente » ou à venir' (2000: 439) [it is a matter of a silent bugle, whose music is 'latent' or still to come]; this case is helped if one prefers the reading 'clairon sourd' to 'clairon lourd' (429).

Chapter 6

1. Other examples of 'old-fashioned' apostrophes are to be found in 'Angoisse' ('Ô palmes! diamant!'), 'Barbare' ('Ô monde! [. . .] Ô Douceurs, ô monde, ô musique!'), 'H' ('Ô terrible frisson des amours novices'), 'Jeunesse: Sonnet' ('ô journées enfantes! [. . .] ô aimer') and 'Génie' ('ô jouissance de notre santé [. . .] Ô fécondité de l'esprit et immensité de l'univers ! [. . .] Ô monde !').
2. Compare these exclamatory structures with, for example, 'Ô les calvaires et les moulins du désert' ('Enfance II'); 'Ô le plus violent Paradis de la grimace enragée' ('Parade'); 'Ô les énormes avenues du pays saint, les terrasses du temple !' ('Vies I').
3. In more recent translations, we find similar practices: Treharne (1998) translates 'Ô' by 'Ah' in 'Enfance II', by 'Oh/oh' in 'Matinée d'ivresse', 'Ouvriers' and 'Jeunesse: Sonnet', and by zero in 'Départ', 'Matinée d'ivresse', 'Ouvriers' and 'Génie'; Sorrell (2001) translates 'Ô' by 'Oh/oh' in 'Enfance II', 'Matinée d'ivresse' and 'Jeunesse: Sonnet', and by zero in 'Génie'.
4. The meaning of 'Raison' has been much debated. Osmond (1976: 110–11) and Bernard/Guyaux (2000: 539) provide useful reviews of possibilities.
5. We should remember that the poem's final line also constitutes a dodecasyllable: 'Arrivée de toujours, qui t'en iras partout' (3 + 3 + 4 + 2).

As an alexandrine, despite the cavalier disregard for the final e of 'Arrivée' (apocope) (unremarkable in verse-practice of the latter part of the nineteenth century), this is a chip off the old block for our social pioneers.

Chapter 7

1. It is worth recording that Scott and Claisse draw rather different conclusions about Rimbaud's attitude towards these social extravagances and theatrical artifices. For Scott (1979: 188), they fulfil a need in Rimbaud 'to escape into a vivid, imaginary, synchronic universe from the drab, moralistic, pseudo-rational world of which, in his late adolescence, he had already taken the measure'. For Claisse, on the other hand, Rimbaud's attitude is derisive: 'La dérision avec laquelle Rimbaud corrige, dans *Fête d'hiver*, ce genre de satisfaction béate et mondaine va de pair avec la charge d'une vogue littéraire. Car, à l'instar de la bonne société et d'un Napoléon III cultivant la mode fastueuse, le goût oriental [. . .], et la nostalgie du siècle de Boucher [. . .], les littérateurs du temps [. . .] rêvent eux-mêmes avec regret—face à la platitude bourgeoise—aux chinoiseries, boudoirs et autres *Divertissements champêtres* du XVIIIᵉ siècle. Aussi, *Fête d'hiver* doit-il se lire également comme une parodie de ce goût et, en particulier, de l'œuvre qui l'illustre mieux qu'une autre: les *Fêtes galantes*' (1990: 34). [The derision with which Rimbaud corrects, in 'Fête d'hiver', that smug and fashionable kind of satisfaction goes hand in hand with the caricature of a literary fad. For, following the example of polite society and a Napoleon III cultivating a lavish manner, a taste for the oriental (. . .), and a nostalgia for the century of Boucher (. . .), the literati of the period (. . .) themselves dream wistfully—faced with bourgeois platitude—of chinoiseries, boudoirs and other *Pastoral Amusements* of the eighteenth century. Thus, 'Fête d'hiver' should be read equally as a parody of this fashion and, in particular, of the work which illustrates it better than any other: [Verlaine's] *Fêtes galantes*].

2. 'Au premier plan, des saules nains qui semblent descendre vers le Rhône pour y baigner leur longue et épaisse chevelure; puis le Rhône; puis une île qui coupe la perspective; puis l'autre bras du fleuve avec son vieux pont; enfin, la ville qui semble sortir toute entière du vieux palais fortifié des papes. Au fond, la *vue* se perd dans une immense campagne que bordent à l'horizon les montagnes du Dauphiné. *Cette vue* est un véritable chef-d'œuvre de photographie' (quoted in Hermange 2000: 14) [In the foreground, dwarf willows which seem to go down to the Rhône to bathe their long and luxuriant hair; then the Rhône; then an island that interrupts the perspective; then the other arm of the river with its old bridge; and finally the city, which seems to emerge, in its entirety, from the old fortified palace of the Popes. In the background, the *view* merges into an immense stretch of countryside, bordered on the horizon by the mountains of the Dauphiné. *This view* is a true photographic masterpiece].

3. What this suggests about Diderot's ekphrastic method seems to be broadly true; but visual exasperation is sufficient to shake him out of patience of method; in his accounts of Boucher, we often find an abrupt notational style, which seems to grow largely from his irritation with the random scattering of unintegrated, gratuitous items: 'Au-dessous du berger, son chien; au-dessus du petit paysan, plus encore sur le fond, une fabrique de pierre, de plâtre et

306

de solives, une espèce de bergerie, plantée là on ne sait comment. Autour de l'âne, des moutons; vers la gauche, derrière la bergère, une barricade rustique, un ruisseau, des arbres, du paysage. [. . .] c'est la meilleure leçon à donner à un jeune élève, sur l'art de détruire tout effet à force d'objets et de travail' (1959: 460) [Below the shepherd, his dog; above the small peasant, even further back, a building of stone, plaster and joists, a kind of sheepfold, heaven knows how it got there. Scattered round the donkey, some sheep; towards the left, behind the shepherdess, a rustic fence, a stream, trees, landscape. (. . .) this is the best lesson you could give a young student in the art of destroying all effect with an excess of objects and detail.]

4. As Sherry Simon succinctly puts it: 'The idea of culture as an envelope which securely binds all the members of a national community within the same coherence of meaning today belongs to the realm of myth' (1999: 58).

5. In his posthumously gathered reflections on the *fait divers*, Louis Chevalier notes the way in which the bareness of the *fait divers* as fact, not only pushes it towards the tall story and the *canard*, but also makes it a powerful source of shock: 'mais on ramasse aussi le fait divers au sens vulgaire, comme on ramasse un coup, un choc' (2004: 139) [but one 'cops' a *fait divers*, in the vulgar sense of the term, just as one 'cops' a blow, or a shock]. Cases of cannibalism, a downpour of toads, a calf with two heads, these things are able, like the Rimbaldian prose poem, to affirm a kind of insolent gratuitousness, the impertinence of just being there. *Faits divers* are news items which are not analysed, the implication being that they are beyond analysis; Barthes describes this phenomenon, in his own study of the *fait divers*, in these terms: 'Causalité aléatoire, coïncidence ordonnée, c'est à la jonction de ces deux mouvements que se constitue le fait divers: tous deux finissent en effet par recouvrir une zone ambiguë *où l'événement est pleinement vécu comme un signe dont le contenu est cependant incertain.* (1964b: 196–7; italics in original) [Aleatory causality, ordered coincidence, it is at the junction of these two movements that the *fait divers* is constituted: ultimately both encompass an ambiguous zone *in which event is fully experienced as a sign whose content is, however, uncertain*].

Chapter 8

1. Verlaine notes that London is '*sans monument aucun*, sauf ses interminables docks (qui suffisent d'ailleurs à ma poétique de plus en plus moderniste)' [*without any monument whatever*, other than its interminable docks (which, I may add, meet the needs of my increasingly modernist poetic)].

2. The text of Verlaine's sonnet runs as follows:

Ah! Vraiment c'est triste, ah! Vraiment ça finit trop mal.
Il n'est pas permis d'être à ce point infortuné.
Ah! Vraiment c'est trop la mort du naïf animal
Qui voit tout son sang couler sous un regard fané.

Londres fume et crie. Ô quelle ville de la Bible!
Le gaz flambe et nage et les enseignes sont vermeilles.
Et les maisons dans leur ratatinement terrible
Épouvantent comme un sénat de petites vieilles.

Tout l'affreux passé saute, piaule, miaule et glapit
Dans le brouillard rose et jaune et sale des Sohos
Avec des *indeeds* et des *all rights* et des *haôs*.

Non vraiment c'est trop un martyre sans espérance,
Non vraiment cela finit trop mal, vraiment c'est triste:
Ô le feu du ciel sur cette ville de la Bible!

[It's really very sad that things aren't working out well.
It shouldn't be allowed, to suffer as I am now.
It's really much too much this death of naïve creatures
Who see all their blood flow out beneath their fading eyes.

The smoke and cries of London, that biblical city!
The gas flares up and swims, the signs are painted crimson,
And houses standing there, all shrunken back terribly,
Cause fear as though they were a club of aged women.

The awful past jumps up, it whimpers miaows and bow-wows
Among the dirty pink and yellow fogs of Soho
With its 'indeeds' with its 'all rights' with its 'good evenings'.

No really, it's too much a martyr's hopeless torture,
No really, it's too sad, no really things are too bad—
Fire-coal sky hanging over that biblical city!
(trans. Sorrell 1999: 123)

3. 'Le début même du poème: *Je suis un éphémère et point trop mécontent citoyen d'une métropole crue moderne*, semble par sa tournure et son humour, aussi anglais que peut l'être une succession de mots français. Le long qualificatif précédant *citoyen* imite la syntaxe anglaise et ironise sans doute en même temps aux dépens des Londoniens, car la litote paraît imitée de celle qu'on trouve dans la traduction anglaise d'un discours de Saint Paul qui se lit souvent aux services protestants: "I am a citizen of no mean city"' (1976: 305) [The very opening of the poem: *I am an ephemeral and none too discontented citizen of a metropolis believed to be modern*, seems, in its construction and its humour, as English as a string of French words can be. The long qualification which precedes *citizen* is an imitation of English syntax and is doubtless, at the same time, ironical at Londoners' expense, because the understatement seems, in its turn, to be an imitation of the understatement which appears in translations of one of Saint Paul's speeches, often read at Protestant services: 'I am a citizen of no mean city'].
4. As James Donald puts it: 'Politics is about the always-to-be-achieved construction of a bounded yet heterogeneous, unstable and necessarily antagonistic "we"' (1999: 100).
5. 'En augmentant d'échelle, en changeant de matériau et en se couvrant d'un riche décor, l'immeuble entre dans le champ du monumental dont il bouleverse la définition: ni le grand ou le petit, ni la pierre ou le bois, ni le riche ou le pauvre ne constituent désormais des différenciations probantes entre le monument et la maison. Pour définir le monument, il va falloir user d'autres critères, tels que l'isolement (oppose à la contiguïté des immeubles) ou le cadre de verdure (contrastant avec la 'minéralité' traditionnelle de l'urbain)' (Loyer 1987: 237) [When apartment buildings became huge, richly

ornamented stone constructions, they took on the characteristics of the monument and thus robbed the latter of its distinctive features. The old distinctions—big/small, stone/wood, rich/poor—could no longer be used to differentiate a monument from a house. To define a monument, other criteria had to be invoked, such as isolation (as opposed to the contiguity of apartment buildings) and verdure (contrasting with the rest of the city's traditional mineral character)] (trans. Clark 1988: 237).

6. 'The new beauty of cement and iron are profaned by the superimposition of motley decorative incrustations that cannot be justified either by constructive necessity or by our (modern) taste, and whose origins are in Egyptian, Indian or Byzantine antiquity and in that idiotic flowering of stupidity and impotence that took the name of NEOCLASSICISM' (Apollonio 1973: 160).

7. 'We have lost our predilection for the monumental, the heavy, the static, and we have enriched our sensibility with a *taste for the light, the practical, the ephemeral and the swift.* We no longer feel ourselves to be the men of the cathedrals, the palaces and the podiums. We are the men of the great hotels, the railway stations, the immense streets, colossal ports, covered markets, luminous arcades, straight roads and beneficial demolitions' (Apollonio 1973: 170).

8. Raybaud sees this as a more serious revenge against the incursions of the industrial-authoritarian: 'D'où, probablement, la "revanche" du dernier paragraphe (la résurgence d'un archaïsme, cette fois fabriqué): il rééclaire du côté du désordre et de la sauvagerie la ville "outre-barbare"—gigantisme de la pure reproduction, éviction des citoyens' (1989: 96) [Hence, probably, the 'revenge' of the final paragraph (the resurgence of archaism, this time manufactured): it casts new light, from the perspective of disorder and savagery, on the ultra-barbaric city—a gigantism of pure reproduction, eviction of citizens]. Claisse similarly provides a redemptive reading of the closing sentence: the 'gentilhommes sauvages' are the agents of a reconciliation between civilisation and nature, and their hunt is for the future: 'L'inattendu de l'expression "chasser leurs chroniques" souligne la révolution opérée par cette noblesse spirituelle: au lieu de poursuivre le lièvre, comme les gentilshommes ennuyés de Pascal, une nouvelle noblesse cherche, envers et contre tout, à se saisir d'un autre avenir.' (1990: 81) [The unexpectedness of the expression 'chasser leurs chroniques' underlines the revolution brought about by this spiritual nobility: instead of hunting the hare, like Pascal's bored gentry, a new nobility seeks, in the face of all opposition, to take possession of another future.] I remain unconvinced, and would want a better reason for laying aside the opinions, already cited, which Rimbaud expresses in 'L'Impossible' (*Une saison en enfer*).

9. I have tried to intensify this sense of metatextuality by including in my three-page montage for 'Villes I' (Appendix III (f)) three images which are already montages: Mieczyslaw Berman's *On the Construction Site* of 1929 (on the first and second pages), László Moholy-Nagy's film montage of an Architectural Congress in Athens of 1933 (on the first page) and Paul Citroën's *Metropolis* of 1923 (on the third page, three fragments). Other images used are: first page—Walter Gropius' *Flatiron Building, New York* (1928), two architectural drawings by Sant'Elia (*Electric Power Station*, 1914, and *Monumental Building*, 1915), and Moholy-Nagy's *Roofs in Helsinki* (1930); second page—Moholy-Nagy's *Roofs in Helsinki* (1930) and Mario Bellusi's *Modern Traffic*

in Ancient Rome (1930); third page—Vladimir Tatlin's drawing for the *Monument to the Third International* (1920) and further architectural drawings by Sant'Elia (*Design for Block with External Lifts on Three Street Levels*, 1914, *Casa a gradinata*, 1914, and *Perspective for 'La Città Nuova'*, 1914 [these last two drawings were used as examples of *La Città Futurista* in Sant'Elia's 'Manifesto of Futurist Architecture']).

10. Aumont underlines the error of explaining the perception of cinematic motion by 'persistance rétinienne' with characteristic terseness: 'Il est d'autant plus étonnant de constater que, jusque chez des auteurs par ailleurs importants comme André Bazin ou Jean-Louis Comolli, on a continué à perpétuer, par inertie intellectuelle, la théorie totalement erronée, et d'ailleurs intrinsèquement absurde, de la "persistance rétinienne". Nous n'insisterons donc jamais assez: la persistance rétinienne existe bel et bien, mais si elle jouait un rôle au cinéma, elle ne pourrait que produire un brouillamini d'images rémanentes. La perception du film n'est possible, en fait, que grâce à l'effet-phi, et aussi grâce au masquage visuel *qui nous débarrasse de la persistance rétinienne*' (2001: 34) [It is all the more surprising to note that, even among authors important in other respects, like André Bazin and Jean-Louis Comolli, we witness the continued perpetuation, thanks to intellectual inertia, of the completely erroneous and, besides, intrinsically absurd, theory of 'retinal persistence'. We can never insist enough: retinal persistence does indeed exist, but if it played a role in cinema, it would produce only a hotch-potch of residual images. In fact, the perception of film is only possible thanks to the phi-effect, and also thanks to visual masking *which rids us of retinal persistence*.]

11. 'With the desire to intensify the aesthetic emotions by blending, so to speak, the painted canvas with the soul of the spectator, we have declared that the latter *must in future be placed in the centre of the picture*' ('The Exhibitors to the Public 1912', in Apollonio 1973: 48).

Chapter 9

1. Braque provides a spatial equivalent of transcendental time when he said of letters in Cubist paintings that they were 'forms which could not be distorted because, being quite flat, they existed outside space and their presence in the painting, through contrast, enabled one to distinguish between objects situated in space and objects outside it' (quoted in this form, and without reference, in Cox 2000: 240).

2. In many ways one might argue that the process of reading is inevitably non-Euclidian: narrators or characters may ostensibly be placed in space, so a particular point of view is presupposed, but the reading process cannot maintain point of view simply because no concrete word has any inherent indicator of proximity, angle of vision, direction, length of look. It is only because language is symbolic rather than iconic, relating to a signified rather than a referent, that this causes no problem. I ask the reader to test this proposition in two further versions of 'Mystique' (see Appendix III (n) and (o))—one an inversion of the other, to maintain the theme—which employ a mix of the planar geometry last used in 'Fête d'hiver', and 'free-hand' abstract shapes, primitive life forms à la Redon. How does the inherent n-dimensionality of words react to these embryonic spatial indicators? Or does

one simply make one's imaginative task less taxing by thinking only of signifieds?

3. In the notes to his 1998 edition (121–2), Pierre Brunel draws attention to the potential reminiscences of the *Book of Revelation* to be found in 'Mystique': there, the angels turn around the throne (V, 11); the connection between the angels' robes and the Lamb is there expressed as 'And he said to me, These are they which came out of great tribulation, and have washed their robes, and made them white in the blood of the Lamb' (VII, 14); precious stones are what garnish the foundations of the New Jerusalem (XXI, 19–20); the 'prés de flammes' is perhaps a reference to the lake of fire, mentioned in XX, 15. Brunel's conclusion is that 'Mystique' presents us with a 'corrected' vision of apocalypse: 'D'une part, il substitue à la traditionnelle représentation des damnés et des élus le partage "moderne" des désastres et des progrès [. . .]. D'autre part, et surtout, il inverse le ciel et l'enfer, la place de la lumière et des "nuits humaines". Il ne s'agit pas d'un simple changement de perspective, mais bien de donner à l'homme, et même au damné dans l'"abîme", la douceur que Dieu voudrait réserver aux anges et aux élus' (206) [On the one hand, it substitutes for the traditional representation of the damned and the elect, the 'modern' division of disasters and advances (. . .). On the other hand, and above all, it inverts heaven and hell, the place of light and the place of 'human nights'. It is not a question of simply changing perspective, but rather of giving to mankind, and even to the damned in the 'abyss', the beatific ease which God would reserve for the angels and the elect].

4. It is curious that the psychological consequences of the perceptual difficulties created by Cubism should not have received more critical attention, particularly as Marius de Zayas was already making this point in the pamphlet he produced to accompany a Picasso exhibition at the Photo-Secession Gallery (April 1911): 'In presenting his work he wants the spectator to look for the emotion or idea generated from the spectacle and not the spectacle itself. From this to the psychology of form there is but one step, and the artist has given it resolutely and deliberately. Instead of the physical manifestation he seeks in form the psychic one, and on account of his peculiar temperament, his physical manifestations inspire him with geometrical sensations' (Stieglitz 1997: 578).

5. 'I've recently been reading a lot of books about Cubism and I keep coming upon discussions of intersecting planes and so forth, as if Cubism were about the structure of the object. But really, it is rather about the structure of *seeing* the object. If there are three noses, this is not because the face has three noses, or the nose has three aspects, but rather because it has been seen three times, and that is what seeing is like' (1984: 17).

6. To say that there are no signs of this practice in *Calligrammes* is to do Apollinaire something of an injustice. But examples are few and far between and indicate an opportunism of the occasion rather than a method of composition.

Conclusion

1. As Lucy Lippard has it in the catalogue for the retrospective exhibition *Reconsidering the Object of Art 1965–1975*: 'Conceptual art, for me, means work in which the idea is paramount and the material is secondary,

lightweight, ephemeral, cheap, unpretentious, and/or dematerialized' (quoted in Godfrey 1998: 14).

2. 'La note en bas de page est la honte du traducteur. . .' [The note at the foot of the page is the shame of the translator. . .] (Dominique Aury in Mounin 1963: xi).

3. This word is of supreme importance for Meschonnic and lies at the centre of his notion of discourse: 'Mais si le rythme n'est plus ce qu'il était, s'il est l'organisation du mouvement de la parole, au sens que Saussure donne à *parole*, une organisation qui est la spécificité, la subjectivité, l'historicité d'un discours, et sa systématicité, alors l'oralité est le primat du rythme dans le mode de signifier. Dans le parlé comme dans l'écrit. C'est la littérature qui le réalise, emblématiquement. C'est même en cela et par cela qu'elle est littérature' (1999: 29). [But if rhythm is no longer what it was, if it is the organization of the movement of *parole*, in the sense that Saussure gives to this word, an organization which is the specificity, the subjectivity, the historicity of a discourse, and its systematicity, so orality is the pre-eminence of rhythm in the mode of signifying. In the spoken as in the written. It is literature which realises it, emblematically. It is precisely in and through that that it is literature.]

Bibliography

Abernathy, Robert, 1967. 'Rhymes, Non-rhymes, and Anti-rhymes', in *To Honor Roman Jakobson: Essays on the Occasion of his Seventieth Birthday I* (The Hague: Mouton), 1–14.

Alexander, Michael, 1997. 'Ezra Pound as Translator', *Translation and Literature*, 6/1, 23–30.

Apollonio, Umbro (ed.), 1973. *Futurist Manifestos*, trans. Robert Brain, R.W. Flint, J.C. Higgitt, Caroline Tisdall (London: Thames and Hudson).

Auden, W.H. (ed. and trans.) and Sjöberg, Leif (trans.), 1964. *Dag Hammerskjöld: Markings* (London: Faber and Faber).

Aumont, Jacques, 2001. *L'Image* (2nd edn) (Paris: Nathan).

Bann, Stephen (ed.), 1967. *Concrete Poetry: An International Anthology* (London: London Magazine Editions).

Barber, Stephen, 2002. *Projected Cities: Cinema and Urban Space* (London: Reaktion Books).

Barbey d'Aurevilly, Jules, 1966. *Œuvres romanesques complètes II*, ed. by Jacques Petit (Paris: Gallimard).

Barthes, Roland, 1957. 'L'Art vocal bourgeois', in *Mythologies* (Paris: Éditions du Seuil), 168–70.

—, 1964a. 'Qu'est-ce que la critique?', in *Essais critiques* (Paris: Éditions du Seuil), 252–7.

—, 1964b. 'Structure du fait divers', in *Essais critiques* (Paris: Éditions du Seuil), 188–97.

—, 1967. 'Proust et les noms', in *To Honor Roman Jakobson: Essays on the Occasion of his Seventieth Birthday I* (The Hague: Mouton), 150–8.

—, 1970. *S/Z* (Paris: Éditions du Seuil).

—, 1973. *Le Plaisir du texte* (Paris: Éditions du Seuil).

—, 1980. *La Chambre claire: Note sur la photographie* (Paris: Éditions de l'Étoile/Gallimard/Le Seuil).

—, 1982a. 'Le Grain de la voix', in *L'Obvie et l'obtus: Essais critiques III* (Paris: Éditions du Seuil), 236–45.

—, 1982b. 'Écoute', in *L'Obvie et l'obtus: Essais critiques III* (Paris: Éditions du Seuil), 217–30.

—, 1984. 'De l'oeuvre au texte', in *Le Bruissement de la langue: Essais critiques IV*

(Paris:Éditions du Seuil), 71–80.

—, 1985. 'Sémiologie et urbanisme', in *L'Aventure sémiologique* (Paris: Éditions du Seuil), 261–71.

Baudelaire, Charles, 1975. *Œuvres complètes I*, ed. by Claude Pichois (Paris: Gallimard).

Benjamin, Walter, 1968. 'The Work of Art in the Age of Mechanical Reproduction', in *Illuminations: Essays and Reflections*, ed. by Hannah Arendt, trans. by Harry Zohn (New York: Schocken Books), 217–51.

—, 1999. 'Little History of Photography', in *Selected Writings II: 1927–1934*, ed. by Michael W. Jennings, Howard Eiland and Gary Smith, trans. by Rodney Livingstone et al. (Cambridge, MA: The Belknap Press), 507–30.

Berman, Antoine, 1999. *La Traduction et la lettre ou l'auberge du lointain* (Paris: Éditions du Seuil).

Bernard, Oliver (ed. and trans.), 1962. *Arthur Rimbaud: Collected Poems* (Harmondsworth: Penguin Books).

Bernard, Suzanne, and Guyaux, André (eds), 2000. *Rimbaud: 'Œuvres'* (Paris, Garnier).

Berranger, Marie-Paule, 1993. *12 poèmes de Rimbaud analysés et commentés* (Alleur: Marabout).

Berry, Cicely, 2000. *Your Voice and How to Use It* (London: Virgin).

Bivort, Olivier, 1989. 'Un système linguistique de création dans les *Illuminations*: L'Exemple de l'article défini générique', *Romanic Review*, 80, 89–99.

—, 1991. 'Un problème référentiel dans les *Illuminations*: Les Syntagmes nominaux démonstratifs', *Parade Sauvage*, 7, 89–102.

—, 1998. 'Métalangage et contraintes herméneutiques: Du sens tu au sens guidé', in Thomas Klinkert and Hermann H. Wetzel (eds.), *Traduction = Interprétation. Interprétation = Traduction. L'Exemple Rimbaud* (Paris: Champion), 25–35.

Bobillot, Jean-Pierre, 2001. 'Tous les sentiers mènent à "Aube": Essai de stylistique rimbaldienne', *Parade Sauvage*, 17–18, 247–69.

—, 2002. 'De quoi parle-t-on quand on dit: "voix" en poésie? La Voix dans le poème ou la retour du refoulé: Rimbaud, etc.', in Jacques Wagner (ed.), *La Voix dans la culture et la littérature françaises 1713–1875* (Clermont-Ferrand: Presses Universitaires Blaise Pascal), 239–50.

Bohn, Willard, 1986. *The Aesthetics of Visual Poetry 1914–1928* (Cambridge: Cambridge University Press).

Bonnefoy, Yves, 1979. 'On the Translation of Form in Poetry', *World Literature Today*, 53/3, 374–9.

Brady, Patrick, 1964. 'Rococo and Neo-classicism', *Studi Francesi*, 8, 34–49.

—, 1966. 'Rococo Style in French Literature', *Studi Francesi*, 10, 428–37.

Bresson, Robert, 1988. *Notes sur le cinématographe* (Paris: Gallimard).

Brettell, Richard, et al. (eds.), 1988. *The Art of Paul Gauguin* (New York: New York Graphic Society).

Broome, Peter, 1979. 'From Vision to Catastrophe in Rimbaud's *Illuminations*', *Forum for Modern Language Studies*, 15/4, 361–79.

Brophy, Michael, 2002. 'Jacques Dupin et l'enjeu d'un "rebondissement illimité"', in Michael Bishop and Christopher Elson (eds), *Contemporary French Poetics* (Amsterdam: Rodopi), 89–95.

Brunel, Georges, 1986. *Boucher* (London: Trefoil Books).

Brunel, Pierre (ed.), 1987. *Arthur Rimbaud: 'Une saison en enfer'* (edition critique)

(Paris: José Corti).

— (ed.), 1998. *Arthur Rimbaud: 'Une saison en enfer', 'Illuminations' et autres textes (1873–1875)* (Paris: Livre de Poche).

Bryson, Norman, 1983. *Vision and Painting: The Logic of the Gaze* (Basingstoke: Macmillan).

Burgin, Victor, 1996. *Some Cities* (London: Reaktion Books).

Butor, Michel, 1989. *Improvisations sur Rimbaud* (Paris: Éditions de la Différence).

Chamberlain, Lori, 1992. 'Gender and the Metaphorics of Translation', in Lawrence Venuti (ed.), *Rethinking Translation: Discourse, Subjectivity, Ideology* (London: Routledge), 57–74.

Chambon, Jean-Pierre, 1983. 'Quelques remarques sur la prononciation de Rimbaud, d'après les « coppées » IV à IX de Verlaine', *Circeto*, 1, 6–12.

Chappuis, Pierre, 1979. *André du Bouchet* (Paris: Seghers).

Chawaf, Chantal, 1992. *Le Corps et le verbe: La Langue en sens inverse* (Paris: Presses de la Renaissance).

Chevalier, Louis, 2004. *Splendeurs et misères du fait divers*, ed. by Emilio Luque (Paris: Perrin).

Claisse, Bruno, 1990. *Rimbaud ou 'le dégagement rêvé': Essai sur l'idéologie des 'Illuminations'* (Charleville-Mézières: Musée-Bibliothèque Arthur Rimbaud).

Clark, Charles Lynn (trans.), 1988. François Loyer, *Paris Nineteenth Century: Architecture and Urbanism* (New York: Abbeville Press).

Colette, 1965. *La Vagabonde* (Paris: Livre de Poche).

Collomb, Michel, 1997. 'Voix, esthétique, littérature', in Michel Collomb (ed.), *Voix et création au XXe siècle* (Paris: Honoré Champion), 13–26.

Collot, Michel, 1980. 'La Dimension du déictique', *Littérature*, 38, 62–76.

Conan, Michael, 1987. 'The *Imagines* of Philostratus' (trans. Elaine Williamson), *Word and Image*, 3/2, 162–71.

Cornulier, Benoît de, 1994. 'Illuminations métriques: Lire ou faire des vers dans la prose à Rimbaud', in André Guyaux (ed.), *Rimbaud 1891–1991* (Paris: Champion), 103–23.

Cox, Neil, 2000. *Cubism* (London: Phaidon).

Crawford, William, 1979. *The Keepers of Light: A History and Working Guide to Early Photographic Processes* (New York: Morgan and Morgan).

Cressot, Maurice, 1974. *Le Style et ses techniques: Précis d'analyse stylistique* (Paris: PUF).

Culler, Jonathan, 1981. 'Beyond Interpretation', in *The Pursuit of Signs: Semiotics, Literature, Deconstruction* (London: Routledge and Kegan Paul), 3–17.

Curtay, Jean-Paul, 1974. *La Poésie lettriste* (Paris: Seghers).

Decaunes, Luc, 1984. *Le Poème en prose: Anthologie (1842–1945)* (Paris: Seghers).

DeKoven, Marianne, 1983. *A Different Language: Gertrude Stein's Experimental Writing* (Madison: University of Wisconsin Press).

Denis, Yves, 1968. 'Glose d'un texte de Rimbaud: « Après le Déluge »', *Les Temps Modernes*, 260, 1261–76.

Derrida, Jacques, 1985. 'Des Tours de Babel', in Joseph F. Graham (ed.), *Difference in Translation* (Ithaca: Cornell University Press), 209–48.

— , 1994. *The Specters of Marx: The State of the Debt, the Work of Mourning, and the New International*, ed. by Bernd Magnus and Stephen Cullenberg, trans. by Peggy Kamuf (London: Routledge).

Diaz-Diocaretz, Myriam, 1985. *Translating Poetic Discourse: Questions on Feminist*

Strategies in Adrienne Rich (Amsterdam: John Benjamins).

Diderot, Denis, 1959. *Œuvres esthétiques*, ed. by Paul Vernière (Paris: Garnier).

Donald, James, 1999. *Imagining the Modern City* (London: The Athlone Press).

Druet, Sarah, 2002. 'Jean-Michel Maulpoix dans le domaine public de la poésie: Une nouvelle quête d'impersonnalité', in Michael Bishop and Christopher Elson (eds.), *Contemporary French Poetics* (Amsterdam: Rodopi).

Dubnick, Randa, 1984. *The Structure of Obscurity: Gertrude Stein, Language and Cubism* (Urbana: University of Illinois Press).

Dugas, Guy, 1997. 'Trois théoriciens d'une poésie de la voix: Sadia Lévy, André Spire et Henri Meschonnic', in Michel Collomb (ed.), *Voix et création au XXᵉ siècle* (Paris: Honoré Champion), 187–96.

Dunn, Leslie C., 1994. 'Ophelia's Songs in *Hamlet*: Music, Madness, and the Feminine', in Leslie C. Dunn and Nancy A. Jones (eds), *Embodied Voices: Representing Female Vocality in Western Culture* (Cambridge: Cambridge University Press), 50–64.

Eco, Umberto, 2001. *Experiences in Translation* (trans. Alastair McEwen) (Toronto: University of Toronto Press).

Eigeldinger, Frédéric, 1986. *Table de concordance rythmique et syntaxique des 'Illuminations' d'Arthur Rimbaud* (Neuchâtel: A la Baconnière).

Eliot, T.S., 1978. 'Reflections on *Vers Libre*', in *To Criticize the Critic* (London: Faber and Faber), 183–9.

Evans, Frederick H., 1992. 'Glass Versus Paper', in Anne Hammond (ed.), *Frederick H. Evans: Selected Texts and Bibliography* (Oxford: Clio Press), 67–73.

Flint, R.W. (ed.), 1972. *Marinetti: Selected Writings* (trans. R.W. Flint and Arthur A. Coppotelli) (London: Secker and Warburg).

Fongaro, Antoine, 1993. *Segments métriques dans la prose d'"Illuminations"* (Toulouse: Presses Universitaires du Mirail-Toulouse).

Fowlie, Wallace (trans. and ed.), 1966. *Rimbaud: Complete Works, Selected Letters* (Chicago: University of Chicago Press).

Francis, Ben, 1996. *Christopher Hampton: Dramatic Ironist* (Charlbury, Oxford: Amber Lane Press).

Freadman, Anne, 1974. 'To Read Rimbaud: (b) A Reading of "Mystique"', *Australian Journal of French Studies*, 11/1, 65–82.

Frisby, David, 2002. 'The Metropolis as Text: Otto Wagner and Vienna's "Second Renaissance"', in Neil Leach (ed.), *The Hieroglyphics of Space: Reading and Experiencing the Modern Metropolis* (London: Routledge), 15–30.

Fumaroli, Marc (ed.), 1984. *Maurice de Guérin: Poésie* (Paris: Gallimard).

Gandelman, Claude, 1991. *Reading Pictures, Viewing Texts* (Bloomington: Indiana University Press).

Garfitt, Toby, 1998. 'A Plural Approach to Translating Mallarmé', *Forum for Modern Language Studies*, 34/4, 345–52.

Genette, Gérard, 1982. *Palimpsestes: La Littérature au second degré* (Paris: Éditions du Seuil).

— , 1987. *Seuils* (Paris: Éditions du Seuil).

Gliserman, Martin, 1996. *Psychoanalysis, Language, and the Body of the Text* (Gainesville: University Press of Florida).

Godfrey, Tony, 1998. *Conceptual Art* (London: Phaidon).

Goody, Jack, and Watt, Ian, 1968. 'The Consequences of Literacy', in Jack Goody (ed.), *Literacy in Traditional Societies* (Cambridge: Cambridge University

Press), 27–84.

Griffiths, Eric, 1989. *The Printed Voice of Victorian Poetry* (Oxford: Clarendon Press).

Guyaux, André, 1985a. *Poétique du fragment: Essai sur les 'Illuminations' de Rimbaud* (Neuchâtel: A la Baconnière).

—, 1985b. *Arthur Rimbaud: 'Illuminations'* (Neuchâtel: A la Baconnière).

—, 1991. *Duplicités de Rimbaud* (Paris-Geneva: Champion-Slatkine).

Hackett, C.A., 1969. 'Rimbaud: *Illuminations*: "Aube"', in Peter H. Nurse (ed.), *The Art of Criticism: Essays in French Literary Analysis* (Edinburgh: Edinburgh University Press), 217–24.

—, 1982. 'Rimbaud et Apollinaire, quelques différences', in André Guyaux (ed.), *Lectures de Rimbaud, Revue de l'Université de Bruxelles*, 1–2, 215–30.

Hampton, Christopher, 1981. *Total Eclipse* (London: Faber and Faber).

—, 1995. *Total Eclipse* (London: Faber and Faber).

Harrison, Tony, 1976. *Phaedra Britannica* (after Jean Racine) (London: Rex Collings).

Hermange, Emmanuel, 2000. 'Aspects and Uses of *Ekphrasis* in Relation to Photography, 1816–1860', *Journal of European Studies*, 30, 5–18.

Hervy, Evelyne, 1999. '"Patrouillotisme" and "Thierrorisme" in Rimbaud's "Démocratie"', *Modern Language Review*, 94, 955–60.

Hiddleston, J.A., 1980. *Essai sur Laforgue et les 'Derniers Vers' suivi de Laforgue et Baudelaire* (Lexington, KE: French Forum).

Hockney, David, 1984. *Cameraworks*, introduced by Lawrence Weschler (London: Thames and Hudson).

Holloway, Marcella Marie, 1947. *The Prosodic Theory of Gerard Manley Hopkins* (Washington: Catholic University of America Press).

Hytier, Jean, 1923. *Les Techniques modernes du vers français* (Paris: PUF).

Jakobson, Roman, 1960. 'Closing Statement: Linguistics and Poetics', in Thomas A. Sebeok (ed.), *Style in Language* (Cambridge, MA: MIT Press), 350–77.

Kaufmann, Michael Edward, 1989. 'Gertrude Stein's Re-vision of Language and Print in *Tender Buttons*', *Journal of Modern Literature*, 15/4, 447–60.

Kloepfer, Rolf, and Oomen, Ursula, 1970. *Sprachliche Konstituenten moderner Dichtung: Entwurf einer deskriptiven Poetik – Rimbaud* (Bad Homburg v. d. H.: Athenäum Verlag).

Kristeva, Julia, 1974. *La Révolution du langage poétique: L'Avant-garde à la fin du XIXe siècle – Lautréamont et Mallarmé* (Paris: Éditions du Seuil).

—, 1977. *Polylogue* (Paris: Éditions du Seuil).

Lambert, José, 1998. 'Literary Translation', in Mona Baker (ed.), *Routledge Encyclopedia of Translation Studies* (London: Routledge), 130–3.

Lapeyre, Paul, 1981. *Le Vertige de Rimbaud: Clé d'une perception poétique* (Neuchâtel: A la Baconnière).

Laufer, Roger, 1963. *Style rococo, style des 'Lumières'* (Paris: Corti).

Laver, John, 1980. *The Phonetic Description of Voice Quality* (Cambridge: Cambridge University Press).

Leach, Neil (ed.), 2002. *The Hieroglyphics of Space: Reading and Experiencing the Modern Metropolis* (London: Routledge).

Lecercle, Jean-Jacques, 1990. *The Violence of Language* (London: Routledge).

Lecourt, Colette, 1999. *La Voix de la réussite ou la parole maîtrisée* (Alleur: Marabout).

Lefebvre, Henri, 1991. *The Production of Space* (trans. Donald Nicholson-Smith)

(Oxford: Blackwell) (1st pub. 1974).

Leroy, Christian, 2001. *La Poésie en prose française du XVIIe siècle à nos jours: Histoire d'un genre* (Paris: Honoré Champion).

Lévi-Strauss, Claude, 1952. *La Pensée sauvage* (Paris: Plon).

Lista, Giovanni, 1994. *Loïe Fuller: Danseuse de la Belle Époque* (Paris: Somogy Éditions d'art/Stock).

Little, Roger, 1980. 'Rimbaud's « Sonnet »', *Modern Language Review*, 75/3, 528–33.

— , 1995. *The Shaping of Modern French Poetry: Reflections on Unrhymed Poetic Form 1840–1990* (Manchester: Carcanet Press; Paris: Alyscamps Press).

Lowell, Robert, 1971. *Imitations* (London: Faber & Faber).

Loyer, François, 1987. *Paris XIXᵉ siècle: L'Immeuble et la rue* (Paris: Hazan).

McCallion, Michael, 1988. *The Voice Book* (London: Faber and Faber).

Macklin, Gerald, 1990. 'Perspectives on the Role of Punctuation in Rimbaud's *Illuminations*', *Journal of European Studies*, 20, 59–72.

— , 1998. 'Epiphany, Identity, Celebration: Towards a Definition of the Rimbaldian *Poème-Fête*', *Neophilologus*, 82, 19–31.

— , 2000. 'Defamiliarization and Discontinuity: Rimbaud's "Parade", "Angoisse", "Soir historique"', *Nottingham French Studies*, 39/2, 163–76.

Maeterlinck, Maurice, 1901. 'Le Silence', in *Le Trésor des humbles* (Paris: Mercure de France), 7–25.

Mallarmé, Stéphane, 1998. *Œuvres complètes I*, ed. by Bertrand Marchal (Paris: Gallimard).

— , 2003. *Œuvres complètes II*, ed. by Bertrand Marchal (Paris: Gallimard).

Manguel, Alberto, 1996. *A History of Reading* (London: Flamingo).

Mannoni, O., 1962. 'Le Besoin d'interpréter', *Les Temps modernes*, 1347–61.

— , 1964. *Prospero and Caliban: The Psychology of Colonization*, trans. Pamela Powesland (New York: Frederick A. Praeger) (1st pub. 1956).

Marchal, Bertrand (ed.), 1995. *Stéphane Mallarmé: Correspondance complète 1862–1871 suivi de Lettres sur la poésie 1872–1898 avec des lettres inédites* (Paris: Gallimard).

Meschonnic, Henri, 1982. *Critique du rythme: Anthropologie historique du langage* (Lagrasse: Verdier).

— , 1999 *Poétique du traduire* (Lagrasse: Verdier).

Miller, Christopher, 1985. *Blank Darkness: Africanist Discourse in French* (Chicago: University of Chicago Press).

Mitchell, W.J.T., 1986. *Iconology: Image, Text, Ideology* (Chicago: University of Chicago Press).

Monroe, Jonathan, 1987. *A Poverty of Objects: The Prose Poem and the Politics of Genre* (Ithaca, NY: Cornell University Press).

Monte, Steven, 2000. *Invisible Fences: Prose Poetry as a Genre in French and American Literature* (Lincoln: University of Nebraska Press).

Moore, Nicholas, 1990. *Spleen ('Le Roi Bonhomme'): Thirty-One Versions of Baudelaire's 'Je suis comme le roi. . .'*, ed. by Anthony Rudolf (London: The Menard Press).

Morier, Henri, 1975. *Dictionnaire de poétique et de rhétorique* (2nd ed.) (Paris: PUF).

Mounin, Georges, 1963. *Les Problèmes théoriques de la traduction* (Paris: Gallimard).

Murat, Michel, 2000. 'Rimbaud et le vers libre: Remarques sur l'invention d'une forme', *Revue d'Histoire Littéraire de la France*, 2, 255–76.

— , 2002. *L'Art de Rimbaud* (Paris: José Corti).

Murphy, Margueritte, 1992. *A Tradition of Subversion: The Prose Poem in English from Wilde to Ashbery* (Amherst: University of Massachusetts Press).

Murphy, Steve, 1988. 'Illuminations obscures – singularités sémantiques', in Sergio Sacchi (ed.), *Rimbaud: Le Poème en prose et la traduction poétique* (Tübingen: Gunter Narr Verlag), 19–31.

— , 1998. 'Interprétation et autotextualité dans *Les Illuminations*', *Romance Quarterly*, 45/3, 155–67.

— (ed.), 2002. *Arthur Rimbaud: Œuvres complètes IV: Fac-similés* (Paris: Honoré Champion).

Nakao, Juro, 1998. *Poétique du parc d'attractions: Étude sur l'espace et le mouvement dans l'œuvre de Rimbaud* (Villeneuve d'Ascq: Presses Universitaires du Septentrion).

Naliwajek, Zbigniew, 1982. 'L'Anaphore dans « Enfance III »', in André Guyaux (ed.), *Lectures de Rimbaud, Revue de l'Université de Bruxelles*, 1–2, 129–39.

Ong, Walter, 1982. *Orality and Literacy: The Technologizing of the Word* (London: Routledge).

Osmond, Nick (ed.), 1976. *Arthur Rimbaud: 'Illuminations'* (London: The Athlone Press).

Oulipo, 1973. *La Littérature potentielle (Créations Recréations Récréations)* (Paris: Gallimard).

Pap, Jennifer, 1997. 'The Cubist Image and the Image of Cubism', in Dudley Andrew (ed.), *The Image in Dispute: Art and Cinema in the Age of Photography* (Austin: University of Texas Press), 155–80.

Passuth, Krisztina, 1985. *Moholy-Nagy* (London: Thames and Hudson).

Pensom, Roger, 2002. 'Le Poème en prose: De Baudelaire à Rimbaud', *French Studies*, 56/1, 15–28.

Plessen, Jacques, 1967. *Promenade et poésie: L'Expérience de la marche et du mouvement dans l'œuvre de Rimbaud* (The Hague: Mouton).

Py, Albert (ed.), 1967. *Arthur Rimbaud: 'Illuminations'* (Geneva: Droz; Paris: Minard).

Pym, Anthony, 1992. *Translation and Text Transfer* (Frankfurt am Main: Peter Lang).

Raybaud, Antoine, 1989. *Fabrique d''Illuminations'* (Paris: Éditions du Seuil).

Reynolds, Dee, 1995. *Symbolist Aesthetics and Early Abstract Art: Sites of Imaginary Space* (Cambridge: Cambridge University Press).

Richard, Jean-Pierre, 1955. *Poésie et profondeur* (Paris: Éditions du Seuil).

Robb, Graham, 2000. *Rimbaud* (London: Picador).

Robinson, Douglas, 2001. *Who Translates? Translator Subjectivities Beyond Reason* (Albany, NY: State University of New York Press).

Rodenburg, Patsy, 1998. *The Actor Speaks: Voice and the Performer* (London: Methuen).

Rogers, Richard, 1997. *Cities for a Small Planet*, ed. by Philip Gumuchdjian (London: Faber and Faber).

Rohdie, Sam, 2001. *Promised Lands: Cinema, Geography, Modernism* (London: BFI).

Romains, Jules, and Chennevière, Georges, 1923. *Petit Traité de versification* (Paris: NRF).

Ross, Kirstin, 1988. *The Emergence of Social Space: Rimbaud and the Paris*

Commune (London: Macmillan).

Roubaud, Jacques, 2000. *Traduire, journal* (Caen: Nous).

Roumette, Julien, 2001. *Les Poèmes en prose* (Paris: Ellipses).

Ruthven, K.K., 1969. *A Guide to Ezra Pound's 'Personae' (1926)* (Berkeley, CA: University of California Press).

Sacchi, Sergio, 1994. 'Rimbaud et les « merveilleuses images »', in *Rimbaud 1891– 1991*, ed. by André Guyaux (Paris: Honoré Champion), 53–62.

Salines, Emily, 1999. 'Baudelaire and the Alchemy of Translation', in Jean Boase-Beier and Michael Holman (eds), *The Practices of Literary Translation: Constraints and Creativity* (Manchester: St Jerome Publishing), 19–30.

Schaettel, Marcel, 1976. 'Analyse et (re)construction d'un « sonnet » de Rimbaud', *Revue des Lettres Modernes*, 445–449 (série Rimbaud 3), 43–56.

Schmidt, Paul (ed. and trans.), 1976. *Arthur Rimbaud: Complete Works* (New York: Harper & Row).

Schulte, Rainer, and Biguenet, John (eds), 1992. *Theories of Translation: An Anthology of Essays from Dryden to Derrida* (Chicago: University of Chicago Press).

Scott, Charles T., 1974. 'Towards a Formal Poetics: Metrical Patterning in "The Windhover"', *Language and Style*, 7, 91–107.

Scott, Clive, 1986. *A Question of Syllables: Essays in Nineteenth-Century French Verse* (Cambridge: Cambridge University Press).

— , 1990. *Vers Libre: The Emergence of Free Verse in France 1886–1914* (Oxford: Clarendon Press).

— , 1998. *The Poetics of French Verse: Studies in Reading* (Oxford: Clarendon Press).

— , 2000. *Translating Baudelaire* (Exeter: University of Exeter Press).

— , 2002a. *Channel Crossings: French and English Poetry in Dialogue 1550–2000* (Oxford: Legenda).

— , 2002b. 'Apollinaire and Madeleine Pagès: Translating the Photography of a Relationship', *Forum for Modern Language Studies*, 38/3, 302–14.

Scott, David H.T., 1977. *Sonnet Theory and Practice in Nineteenth-Century France: Sonnets on the Sonnet* (Hull: University of Hull Publications).

— , 1979. 'Rimbaud and Boucher: "Fête d'hiver"', *Journal of European Studies*, 9, 185–95.

Segalen, Victor, 1956. *Les Immémoriaux suivi d'une étude d'Henry Amer sur Victor Segalen* (Paris: 10/18).

Simmel, Georg, 1997. *Simmel on Culture: Selected Writings*, ed. by David Frisby and Mike Featherstone (London: Sage Publications).

Simon, Sherry, 1999. 'Translating and Interlingual Creation in the Contact Zone: Border Writing in Quebec', in Susan Bassnett and Harish Trivedi (eds.), *Post-Colonial Translation: Theory and Practice* (London: Routledge), 58–74.

Sloate, Daniel (trans.), 1990. *Arthur Rimbaud: 'Illuminations'* (pref. Robert Walton) (Montreal: Guernica Editions).

Solt, Mary Ellen (ed.), 1970. *Concrete Poetry: A World View* (Bloomington: Indiana University Press).

Sontag, Susan, 1994. 'Against Interpretation', in *Against Interpretation* (London: Vintage), 3–14.

Sorrell, Martin (ed. and trans.), 1995. *Elles: A Bilingual Anthology of Modern French Poetry by Women* (Exeter: University of Exeter Press).

— (ed. and trans.), 2001. *Arthur Rimbaud: Collected Poems* (Oxford: Oxford

University Press).

Soulages, François, 1998. *Esthétique de la photographie: La Perte et le reste* (Paris: Éditions Nathan).

Steiner, George, 1985. *Language and Silence: Essays 1958–1966* (2nd edn) (London: Faber and Faber).

Steinmetz, Jean-Luc, 1989. *Arthur Rimbaud: Œuvres III: 'Illuminations' suivi de Correspondance (1873–1891)* (Paris: Flammarion).

— , 1999. *Arthur Rimbaud: Une question de présence* (Paris: Éditions Tallandier).

Stephens, Sonya, 1999. *Baudelaire's Prose Poems: The Practice and Politics of Irony* (Oxford: Oxford University Press).

Stieglitz, Alfred, 1997. *'Camera Work': The Complete Illustrations 1903–1917* (Cologne: Taschen).

Stimpson, Brian, 1995. *The Writing 'I': Subject, Voice and Language in the Work of Paul Valéry* (London: Roehampton Institute).

Sypher, Wylie, 1960. *From Rococo to Cubism in Art and Literature* (New York: Vintage Books).

Terdiman, Richard, 1985. *Discourse/Counter-Discourse: The Theory and Practice of Symbolic Resistance in Nineteenth-Century France* (Ithaca, NY: Cornell University Press).

Therre, Hans, and Schmidt, Rainer (eds. and trans.), 2000. *Arthur Rimbaud: Das poetische Werk* (Munich: Matthes & Seitz Verlag).

Todorov, Tzvetan, 1978. 'Une complication de texte: Les *Illuminations*', *Poétique*, 34, 241–53.

Treharne, Mark (ed. and trans.), 1998. *Arthur Rimbaud: 'A Season in Hell' and 'Illuminations'* (London: J.M. Dent).

Underwood, V.P., 1976. *Rimbaud et l'Angleterre* (Paris: Nizet).

Untermeyer, Louis, 1964. *Robert Frost: A Backward Look* (Washington: Library of Congress).

Vadé, Yves, 1996. *Le Poème en prose et ses territoires* (Paris: Belin).

Valéry, Paul, 1957. *Œuvres I*, ed. by Jean Hytier (Paris: Gallimard).

— , 1960. *Œuvres II*, ed. by Jean Hytier (Paris: Gallimard).

Varèse, Louise (ed. and trans.), 1957. *Arthur Rimbaud: 'Illuminations' and Other Prose Poems* (New York: New Directions).

Venuti, Lawrence, 1995. *The Translator's Invisibility: A History of Translation* (London: Routledge).

Verlaine, Paul, 1962. *Œuvres poétiques complètes*, ed. by Y.-G. Le Dantec and Jacques Borel (Paris: Gallimard).

Weinberger, Eliot, 1999. 'The Role of the Author in Translation', in Sture Allén (ed.), *Translation of Poetry and Poetic Prose: Proceedings of Nobel Symposium 110* (Singapore: World Scientific), 233–48.

Williams, Emmett (ed.), 1967. *An Anthology of Concrete Poetry* (New York: Something Else Press).

Wuilmart, Françoise, 1999. 'Normalization and the Translation of Poetry', in Sture Allén, *Translation of Poetry and Poetic Prose: Proceedings of Nobel Symposium 110* (Singapore: World Scientific), 31–44.

Žižek, Slavoj, 1994. 'Introduction: The Spectre of Ideology', in Slavoj Žižek (ed.), *Mapping Ideology* (London: Verso), 1–33.

Zola, Émile, 1968. *Nana* (Paris: Garnier-Flammarion).

Index